Kevin P. Sullivan
682-9500

WINNING COURTROOM STRATEGIES

Edward T. Wright

PRENTICE HALL
Englewood Cliffs, New Jersey 07632

Prentice-Hall International (UK) Limited, *London*
Prentice-Hall of Australia Pty. Limited, *Sydney*
Prentice-Hall Canada, Inc., *Toronto*
Prentice-Hall Hispanoamericana, S.A., *Mexico*
Prentice-Hall of India Private Limited, *New Delhi*
Prentice-Hall of Japan, Inc., *Tokyo*
Simon & Schuster Asia Pte. Ltd., *Singapore*
Editora Prentice-Hall do Brasil, Ltda., *Rio de Janeiro*

10 9 8 7 6 5

Library of Congress Cataloging-in-Publication Data

Wright, Edward T.
Winning courtroom strategies / by Edward T. Wright.
p. cm.
Includes index.
ISBN 0-13-125170-8
1. Trial practice—United States. 2. Jury—United States.
3. Forensic oratory. 4. Persuasion (Psychology) I. Title.
KF8915.W753 1994
347.73'52—dc20
[347.30752] 93-49652
CIP

Printed in the United States of America

This Book Is Dedicated to
My Dear Wife
SUSAN REHR WRIGHT
Who Shares My Fervent Desire
That Our Children, Grandchildren
and Great Grandchildren
Live in a World That Is
Fair and Just

OTHER BOOKS BY EDWARD T. WRIGHT

How To Use Courtroom Drama To Win Cases
(Prentice Hall, 1987)
Evidence: How And When To Use The Rules To Win Cases
(Prentice Hall, 1990)

Practical Municipal Law
Sources Of Municipal Revenue
Your City And The Future
Ladies And Gentlemen Of The Jury
Free Enterprise Is Not Dead

ABOUT THE AUTHOR

Edward T. Wright has been a trial lawyer for forty-four years, involved in nearly every kind of criminal and civil litigation. He now practices in Clearwater, Florida; he formerly practiced in St. Louis County, Missouri; and is a member of the Illinois, Florida, and Missouri Bar Associations.

Soon after graduating from law school at Mercer University in Macon, Georgia, he was elected a municipal judge, becoming the youngest judge in Missouri. He was one of three judges appointed by the Missouri Supreme Court to draft rules of procedure for municipal courts.

He is the author of several books, and his speeches and articles have appeared in more than forty journals and reviews. His book *How To Use Courtroom Drama To Win Cases* (Prentice Hall, 1987) is used by trial lawyers throughout the world and has been praised by leading members of the trial bar. He is a popular lecturer on trial advocacy.

WHY TRIAL LAWYERS NEED THIS BOOK

Never has a book told so clearly the winning strategy of great trial lawyers. This book zeros in on the many decisions a trial lawyer must make in the courtroom, including proven techniques and new concepts that keep a trial lawyer ahead of opposing counsel.

The author calls upon his personal experience of 44 years in the courtroom, attending seminars, and reading and writing books on trial advocacy. More important, he calls upon the experience and ideas of many of the greatest trial lawyers in America.

There are exerpts and discussions of oral arguments by Gerry Spence, F. Lee Bailey, Phil Corboy, and many others. The suggestions of several past presidents of ATLA are discussed.

The book is divided into the five phases of a jury trial: VOIR DIRE, OPENING STATEMENT, PRESENTING EVIDENCE, CROSS-EXAMINATION, and FINAL ARGUMENT.

Joe Jamail won 500 consecutive trials over a period of 28 years. Then he lost. Why? This great trial lawyer, the only one to ever obtain an $11.5 billion verdict, is positive that the reason he lost is because the judge did not permit him to participate in voir dire.

If Joe Jamail thinks voir dire is that important, so should every other trial lawyer. The author gives the reader the law on voir dire, how to use and develop expertise in jury selection, the handling of special problems, and suggested questioning for nearly every courtroom situation.

Many lawyers claim that the law or practice in their jurisdictions prohibits being dramatic during opening statement. Great trial lawyers have found ways to meet this challenge.

When Mel Belli was asked to proceed with opening statement, he bowed to the jury in oriental style and said, "Hung Chow, Hung Toy." He then turned to the judge and did the same. The judge said, "Mr. Belli, what does this mean?"

"Your Honor, this is Chinese New Year, and my client wishes you and the jury a Happy New Year." The judge smiled and said, "Thank you," and the jury smiled and nodded to the Chinese client. During the first recess, the other lawyer called the insurance company and said, "We had better settle this case, this guy Belli has the judge and jury eating out of his hand."

The author gives tips as to how you can make opening statement dramatic and persuasive, yet stay within the law and purpose of opening. Examples of opening statements by leading trial lawyers are given and analyzed.

The presentation of evidence is what proves your case, and the law and strategy of this part of the trial can make the difference between winning or losing. The author tells how the best lawyers accomplish this in a routine, yet dramatic, manner.

Cross-examination is, indeed, an art, and an extremely difficult one to master. The author discusses famous approaches formed during the twentieth century, and new techniques that can "smash" the witness and save the case.

Much of the book is devoted to final argument, because the author has seen and experienced the value of this part of the trial. A discussion of leading cases with excerpts, a full discussion and anthology of quotations, the law of final argument, brief arguments for nearly every occasion, and much more waits for the lawyer who patiently builds for those final and exciting moments of the trial.

The author brings to the pages of this book an intellectual curiosity and a dedication to winning that will inspire the reader. His deep respect for his profession has prompted him to share courtroom strategies that will help win the most fascinating battles ever to challenge the human mind—those of the trial lawyer.

CONTENTS

Why Trial Lawyers Need This Book vii

PART I *SELECTING THE JURY* 1

[1.01] How To Sell Yourself To The Jury *1*

[1.02] Help Jurors Identify With Your Client *4*

[1.03] Sell Your Cause To The Panel *10*

[1.04] How To Tell Your Story Within Voir Dire Limitations *12*

[1.05] When And How You Can Obtain "Commitments" *13*

[1.06] How To Keep A Juror From "Poisoning" Another Juror *14*

[1.07] Four Pre-Trial Requirements *16*

[1.08] Explain Voir Dire To Prospective Jurors *19*

[1.09] How To Address The Entire Panel *22*

[1.10] How To Get Jurors To Participate *27*

[1.11] How To Conduct Individual Inquiry *30*

[1.12] Maintain Interest With Demonstrative Evidence *33*

[1.13] Prepare Jurors For Any Weakness In Your Case *35*

[1.14] Adapt To The Federal Court *37*

[1.15] Challenges You Should Or Must Make Before Trial *41*

[1.16] Challenges You Should Or Must Make During Voir Dire *42*

[1.17] Challenges You Should Or Must Make After Voir Dire *46*

[1.18] What You Must Know About A Juror's Educational Background *48*

[1.19] Learn About Occupational History 49

[1.20] The Importance Of Marital Status 51

[1.21] Question Juror's Familiarity With Facts of Case 52

[1.22] Does Juror Know Party, Attorney, or Others? 54

[1.23] How To Ask The Insurance Question 58

[1.24] Establish Relationship With Experts and Other Witnesses 61

[1.25] Interrogate Fully As To Experience In Similar Matters 62

[1.26] Look Carefully For Juror's Expertise On Key Issues 64

[1.27] Use Prior Jury Services To Discover Attitude Of Juror 65

[1.28] Discuss Willingness And Ability To Follow Instructions 67

[1.29] Discuss Burden Of Proof 69

[1.30] How To Explain The Time Elements Of The Trial 73

[1.31] Be Sure Juror Has No Financial Interest In The Outcome Of The Case 74

[1.32] Discuss The Presumption Of Innocence: Criminal Cases 77

[1.33] How To Lessen Impact Of Accused Not Testifying 78

[1.34] Make A List Of Basic Questions 78

[1.35] Learn Of Juror's Reading and Television Habits 79

[1.36] Discover Attitudes Toward Courts, Lawyers, And The Jury System 83

[1.37] How To Spot The "Military Mind" 84

[1.38] How To Evaluate Juror's Travel And Former Residency 85

[1.39] How To Dig Into Significance Of Home Ownership 86

[1.40] Learn From Membership In Organizations 88

[1.41] How To Get Jurors To Talk About Hobbies And Special Interests *89*

[1.42] How To Discuss Attitudes Toward People Who Sue *90*

[1.43] What You Must Do About Health Problems Of Jurors *91*

[1.44] Save Face And Fortune By Asking, "Is There Any Reason You Cannot Serve?" *92*

[1.45] How To Discuss Whether They Really Want To Serve *94*

[1.46] Learn About And Talk About Seatbelts *96*

[1.47] When To Strike Women And Men *96*

[1.48] Model Voir Dire: Personal Injury Case *97*

[1.49] Model Voir Dire: Professional Liability Case *98*

[1.50] Model Voir Dire: Civil Rights Litigation *100*

[1.51] Model Voir Dire: Products Liability Case *101*

[1.52] Model Voir Dire: Defamation And Privacy *103*

[1.53] Model Voir Dire: Wrongful Death Case *104*

[1.54] Model Voir Dire: Slip And Fall Cases *107*

[1.55] Model Voir Dire: Premises Liability *108*

[1.56] Model Voir Dire: Criminal Cases—General *110*

[1.57] Model Voir Dire: Criminal Cases—Homicide *113*

[1.58] Model Voir Dire: Criminal Cases—Other Violent Crimes *116*

[1.59] Model Voir Dire: Criminal Cases—Sex And Morality *117*

[1.60] Model Voir Dire: Criminal Cases—Narcotics *119*

[1.61] Model Voir Dire: Criminal Cases—White Collar Crime *120*

[1.62] Investigate Fully The Publicity Factor *121*

[1.63] Start With Seriousness Of Subjective Injuries *125*

[1.64] Distinguish Sympathy And Concern *127*

[1.65] Discuss Frankly The Potential Size Of Verdict *128*

[1.66] How To Get A "Punitive Damage" Jury *130*

[1.67] Be Sure Jurors Understand Comparative Negligence *132*

[1.68] Study Computers And "Computer People" *132*

[1.69] When And How To Use PreTrial Experts *133*

[1.70] How To Develop Your Own Expertise *136*

[1.71] *Batson v. Kentucky*: Prejudice And Preemptory Challenges *140*

[1.72] *Witherspoon v. Illinois*: Qualifying Death Penalty Opponents *147*

[1.73] Great Trial Lawyers: Gerry Spence—"How Do You Feel About Indians?" *154*

[1.74] Great Trial Lawyers: Melvin Belli—Be Innovative *155*

[1.75] Great Trial Lawyers: Joe Jamail—The Trial Lawyer And Voir Dire *156*

[1.76] Great Trial Lawyers: Roxanne Conlin—"Don't Call Me 'Girl'!" *158*

[1.77] Great Trial Lawyers: Rodney Romano—Prepare The Jury For The $98,000 Whiplash Verdict *159*

PART II ***THE OPENING STATEMENT*** **161**

[2.01] Avoid "Arguing The Case" *161*

[2.02] Use Exhibits And Charts *162*

[2.03] Use The "Our Evidence Will Show" Technique *163*

[2.04] Directed Verdict After Opening Statement *163*

[2.05] How To Comment On The Law *165*

[2.06] Avoid Interruption By Avoiding Objections *166*

[2.07] How To Organize Your Opening Statement *167*

[2.08] Recognize The Importance of Primacy *169*

[2.09] Provide An Orientation To The Case And The Role Of Jurors *170*

[2.10] Be Brief, Yet Complete *171*

[2.11] Talk To Each Juror *172*

[2.12] Your Opening Statement Must Be Dramatic *173*

[2.13] Establish Credibility Or Lose *174*

[2.14] How To Begin Your Final Argument During Opening Statement *176*

[2.15] Maintain Interest With Storytelling Techniques *178*

[2.16] How To Handle Weak Points Of Your Case *180*

[2.17] Appeal To Fairness *181*

[2.18] Conduct Opening Statement As Though Your Verdict Depended Upon It—It Might *182*

[2.19] Include Essences of Good Drama *183*

[2.20] Use Words That Convey Messages *185*

[2.21] Great Trial Lawyers: Peter Perlman—Million Dollar Verdicts Begin With Opening Statement *186*

[2.22] Great Trial Lawyers: Rodney Romano—The $98,000 Whiplash Verdict *192*

[2.23] Great Trial Lawyers: Gerry Spence—Defending The Defenseless *200*

PART III *PRESENTING YOUR EVIDENCE* 211

[3.01] Present Evidence In Proper Order *211*

[3.02] How To Avoid The Leading Question Problem *212*

[3.03] Have Witness Talk To The Jury *214*

[3.04] Know WHAT You Are Proving *214*

[3.05] Great Trial Lawyers: Melvin Belli—Beware of The Trend Away From Live Testimony *214*

[3.06] Make The Witness A Storyteller *215*

[3.07] Presentation of Exhibits *216*

[3.08] How To Use Depositions *217*

[3.09] Make Notes For Appeal *218*

[3.10] Video Evidence: Demonstrative Evidence *219*

[3.11] Refreshing Recollection *221*

[3.12] Introducing Business Records *221*

[3.13] Direct Examination Of Expert *222*

[3.14] Understand DNA *224*

[3.15] Use The Blackboard *225*

[3.16] How To Introduce Photographs *225*

[3.17] How To Use Before And After Witnesses *226*

[3.18] Have Witness Speak The Jury's Language *227*

[3.19] Know When To Redirect *228*

[3.20] Special Problems In Presenting Evidence *229*

PART IV *CROSS-EXAMINING WITNESSES* 231

[4.01] Divide And Limit "Areas of Questioning" *231*

[4.02] Two Questions You Must Ask Yourself *232*

[4.03] Ask The "612 Question" *232*

[4.04] Close All Doors *232*

[4.05] Wellman's "Art" of Cross-Examination *233*

[4.06] Irving Younger's "Commandments" *237*

[4.07] End Cross-Examination With A Bang! *239*

[4.08] Give An Image Of Fairness *240*

[4.09] Attack The Witness's Memory *241*

[4.10] Attack The Witness's Perception *242*

[4.11] Attack The Witness's Prejudice *242*

[4.12] Use Depositions Effectively *243*

[4.13] Ask Hardball Questions *244*

[4.14] How To Handle Difficult Witnesses *245*

[4.15] Remember The Legal Limitations of Cross-Examination *247*

[4.16] How And When To Attack The Expert Witness *248*

PART V ***WIN WITH FINAL ARGUMENT*** **251**

[5.01] Remind Court Of Purpose Of Final Argument *251*

[5.02] How To Organize "Both Halves" Of Final Argument *252*

[5.03] How To Avoid The "First Mentioned In Rebuttal" Objection *255*

[5.04] When Is Conduct of Counsel Error *255*

[5.05] Discussing The Evidence *257*

[5.06] When To Appeal To Passion *258*

[5.07] When Can A Mathematical Formula Be Used To Determine Damages? *259*

[5.08] Know The "Golden Rule" Limitations *261*
[5.09] Bind Prosecutors To Their Special Rules *262*
[5.10] Avoid Comment On Failure Of Accused To Testify *263*
[5.11] Telling Stories *264*
[5.12] How To Use Exhibits Or Demonstrations *265*
[5.13] Prevent Appeals To Prejudice *267*
[5.14] When To Comment On Failure To Present Witness Or Evidence *268*
[5.15] How To Divide Opening And Rebuttal *270*
[5.16] How Long Final Can And Should Be *270*
[5.17] When Can You "Send Out The Message"? *271*
[5.18] Know The Limits Of The Court's Discretion *271*
[5.19] When To Attack Parties And Witnesses *272*
[5.20] How To Correct An Error *274*
[5.21] Use Matters of Common Knowledge *275*
[5.22] Keep Out Defendant's Record *275*
[5.23] How To Argue Damages *276*
[5.24] Avoid Mistrial Traps *276*
[5.25] Prepare For Law And Order Appeal *277*
[5.26] Communicate During Final Argument *279*
[5.27] Argue Briefly: Slip And Fall *281*
[5.28] Argue Briefly: Pain *282*
[5.29] Argue Briefly: The Finality Of Death *283*
[5.30] Argue Briefly: Talk About Prison *284*
[5.31] Argue Briefly: The Voir Dire Commitment *285*
[5.32] Argue Briefly: The Right To Depend On Others *286*

[5.33] Argue Briefly: Burden Of Proof *287*

[5.34] Argue Briefly: Witness Credibility *287*

[5.35] Argue Briefly: Show Malice Through Conduct *289*

[5.36] Argue Briefly: Financial Status *289*

[5.37] Argue Briefly: Punitive Damages *290*

[5.38] Argue Briefly: Injury Is For The "Rest of Life" *292*

[5.39] Get Jurors "Rooting" For Your Client *293*

[5.40] How To Use Instructions *295*

[5.41] Explaining The Counterclaim *296*

[5.42] Make Your Experts Better Than Theirs *296*

[5.43] How To Use Charts, Blackboard, And Exhibits *297*

[5.44] Differentiate Between Sympathy And Concern *298*

[5.45] Emphasize That Money Is The Only Remedy *300*

[5.46] Lay Foundation For Medical Expense Argument *301*

[5.47] Quoting: How, When, And Why *301*

[5.48] Quoting The Bible *304*

[5.49] Quoting Shakespeare *310*

[5.50] Quoting Poets And Writers *313*

[5.51] Model Final Argument: Civil *318*

[5.52] Model Final Argument: Criminal *328*

[5.53] Model Final Argument: The "Final Five" *334*

[5.54] Great Trial Lawyers: Pat Maloney—Two Multi-Million Dollar Verdicts In Two Weeks *335*

[5.55] Great Trial Lawyers: Philip Corboy—Placing Dollar Signs On Human Life *345*

[5.56] Great Trial Lawyers: Murray Sams—Half Justice Is No Justice *353*

[5.57] Great Trial Lawyers: Roxanne Conlin—Asking For A Million Dollars *356*

[5.58] Great Trial Lawyers: Tom Malone—Making The Medically Negligent Pay *362*

[5.59] Great Trial Lawyers: Bob Gibbins—Suing The Manufacturer *366*

[5.60] Great Trial Lawyers: Gene Pavalon—The Loss Of Parents *367*

[5.61] Great Trial Lawyers: Clarence Darrow—A Plea For Mercy *370*

[5.62] Great Trial Lawyers: Vincent Fuller—Arguing Insanity *373*

[5.63] Great Trial Lawyers: Paul Armstrong—Arguing The Right To Die *377*

[5.64] Great Trial Lawyers: F. Lee Bailey—Defending Patty Hearst *381*

[5.65] Great Trial Lawyers: Roy Black—Arguing Reasonable Doubt *384*

[5.66] Great Trial Lawyers: Benjamin Marcus—Argue Your Case On Appeal *387*

[5.67] Great Trial Lawyers: Scott Baldwin—"Get The Hogs Out Of The Creek" *388*

[5.68] Great Trial Lawyers: Howard Nations—Why We Ask For Money *393*

[5.69] Great Trial Lawyers: Gerry Spence—Tell Your Story In One Sentence *398*

Index 399

PART ONE

SELECTING THE JURY

[1.01] How To Sell Yourself To The Jury. It is absolutely necessary to establish goals before beginning voir dire. The most experienced trial lawyers are finding that selling themselves to the jury must be a primary goal.

CAVEAT: Credibility is what a trial is all about and the trial begins with voir dire. Nothing places successful trial lawyers in a place all their own more than the ability to cause the jury to like them and believe them.

Why did Rodney Romano obtain a $98,000 verdict in what other lawyers thought to be an "ordinary whiplash case"? He explains:

> "Before leaving for the courthouse I told my client that from this moment on we think of the seriousness of this case. Everything we do in that courthouse is serious, because my client has sustained a serious injury.
>
> "Some defense lawyers like to joke about whiplash, but I don't let them. I beat them to it. I talk about whiplash right off and I tell them how serious it is and how serious it is going to be."

What Rodney Romano does is to create the atmosphere, and he does that through his own sincerity. The jury knew this was serious business because the plaintiff's lawyer said that it was. They could tell her attorney meant it, because her attorney DID mean it.

In my book on courtroom drama, I discuss being a good guy twenty-four hours a day. Good trial lawyers have echoed this sentiment, and this needs to come through with genuine sincerity. It is absolutely necessary during voir dire. It is the simplest formula to big verdicts anyone can give you.

What is the jury really thinking? Much of the time they are thinking about you because you are talking or reacting or doing something that fascinates them. Some studies tell us that while they are judging you, they are considering:

–Your Appearance: are you dressed "appropriately," do you slouch in your chair, do you just "look like" a good guy?

–Your Sincerity: do you really mean what you say, do you exaggerate, do you look them right in the eye and tell it like it is?

–Your Professionalism: are you prepared, are you a capable lawyer, do you show respect for the court and the proceedings?

–Your Concern: are you really concerned for your client, are you concerned for jurors as they begin a new experience, are you concerned about the whole world and how it will be affected by what happens here today?

–Your Attitude Toward Jurors: are you talking down to them, do you appreciate any conflict they may have, are you making it possible for them to understand what is going on, are you sincerely trying to obtain necessary information, or are you just prying into their personal affairs?

If you are not ready to consider these questions that are in the minds of prospective jurors, you are not ready for trial. That is why you should always be ready with ways to sell yourself to the jury.

EXAMPLES:

1. "Mrs. Jones, you say you have children, will serving on the jury interfere with your caring for them?"
2. "This is not a million dollar case. My client has been damaged by the breach of the contract and is entitled to the sum of $40,000. We don't ask for a dime more than that. Is there anyone who will have any problem following the law and bringing back a verdict in that amount if such a verdict is justified by the evidence?"

3. "Mrs. Smith here at the table will be taking down a transcript of the trial, and Mr. Brown over there is your bailiff . . ."
4. "His honor, Judge O'Brien, will give you the law at the end of the trial . . ."
5. "Jim is sitting next to me here at the counsel table . . ." ("Jim" not defendant, "next to me" to show closeness, just little things that make the trial lawyer a part of his client's case)
6. "I'm not going to pry into your personal life . . ."
7. "When I say lawsuits, I don't mean divorce cases or anything like that . . ."
8. "What do you do at the phone company, Mr. Smith?"
9. "We are all concerned about crime, Mrs. Jenkins . . ."

By chatting with jurors in a way to show concern, in a friendly manner, with a sincerity that comes from believing in your client and believing in your case, and with a respect that earns respect, you begin the process of selling yourself to the jury. How well you do this during voir dire, and during all of the trial, will be one of the most important factors in winning your lawsuit.

Try to perceive yourself as the jurors might perceive you.

CAVEAT: Don't forget the "one-step above" rule. It simply means that the jurors expect you, as an attorney, to be one-step above others in the courtroom, not two steps, but one.

EXAMPLES:

1. Jurors expect you to dress one-step above others in the courtroom. If you don't dress "appropriately" they will hold that against you. They simply respect a lawyer who "looks" like a lawyer and that image is a step above the dress of others. Yet if you dress too "expensively" they will resent it. (Exception: Some attorneys can develop their own "dress," like Gerry Spence with his Western dress. Some dress to fit a certain image, where jurors expect them to be flamboyant, for instance, or to fit some other image. However, DO NOT TRY TO IMITATE!
2. Jurors expect your English grammar to be one step above others. They know you have years of education and if you use improper grammar they may feel you are "talking down" to them. On the other hand, if you use too many big words they may think you are showing off. You have friends who are less educated than you and in your normal conversation with them you naturally talk with grammar in keeping

with your education. That is what voir dire is all about, talking as you would normally talk when talking with friends.

3. Jurors expect you to be well-informed as to all aspects of the trial. They will look to you to inform them and assume you know more about the facts, law, and the procedure than anyone else. You are one-step ahead of everyone else in the courtroom and they expect that. Don't disappoint them.
4. Jurors expect you to be friendly and considerate. Not two steps above the others. They will then think you are being too solicitous. You may even run afoul of the law, or at least be embarrassed by the judge or opposing counsel. There is nothing wrong with being the friendliest and most considerate person in the courtroom, as long as you don't overdo it.

CONCLUSION: During voir dire you must begin to sell yourself to the jurors, because that is one of the most effective ways to sell your client and to sell your cause. You can do this by:

–being professional at all times,
–looking and acting like a lawyer,
–being friendly and considerate,
–being prepared, and
–being interested in your client, your lawsuit, and in every member of the jury panel.

[1.02] Help Jurors Identify With Your Client. How jurors will perceive your client and what you can do about it makes the difference of winning or losing. You must appraise your client as a party to a lawsuit the first time you meet him or her.

CAVEAT: What kind of a client you have must help you decide:

1. whether you take the case,
2. whether you settle the case,
3. whether you waive a jury trial, and
4. how you conduct your jury trial.

Many police departments will not hire an officer without reviewing a psychological test to determine if the officer is "gun-happy" or has some other hidden trait that will some night embarass the department. If a trial lawyer had such information about potential clients he would avoid many cases that cause him endless stress and cause him to lose a lawsuit he thought he would win.

Many factors go into arriving at that magic figure at which the case should be settled. None is more important than: "What kind of client do I have?" Will the jurors believe my client? Will they like my client? Will they want to award my client a lot of money?

If you have a client that you want to represent and you think the jury will like, you then request a trial by jury and begin preparing for the voir dire. This means you:

1. Determine what kind of juror will like your client (this will often mean, what kind of juror will identify with your client).
2. Determine how your client can be presented to the jury in a way that will help establish this identity.

Before you reach the courthouse you must take time to let your client understand what is going to happen and how the client can help make it happen the right way. The more the client understands about the entire process, the more comfortable he or she will be in the courtroom. Even a visit to the courtroom may help the client feel at home during trial.

There are five basic techniques a trial lawyer can use to help sell his client to the jury:

1. *Tell the client's story during voir dire.* The judge will permit you to tell something of what happened, and jurors begin identifying with your client when they learn what happened to him.

EXAMPLE:

"A year ago last October Bill was coming home from the football game. He had just seen his son play his last game for Brentwood High, and since it was a beautiful night and he lived only a few blocks away, he had walked to the game and was walking home with his wife when a car swerved onto the walk and hit him. Have any of you heard about this case?"

2. *Tell about your client's background.* There are endless experiences your client has had and some of them may have been similar to experiences of jurors. That is what identity is all about, common experiences.

EXAMPLE:

"Mrs. Brown has worked with the Girl Scouts for many years. Do any of you remember her from the Scouts, maybe you have a daughter who was in her troop?"

OR

"Mr. Smith has worked at the Kroger store down the street for many years. Do any of you trade there?"

OR

"Mrs. Tabor has a physical problem that is not related to this accident and we will not be asking damages for this problem. But I think you should know about it, since it may come up in the evidence. She has had a heart condition since childhood and though the problem is under control, she does require medication and must limit her activities. Do you agree that since this has nothing to do with the accident, she should not receive any more or any less because of this unrelated physical problem?"

3. *Control your client's appearance.* People are judged by what they wear, whether they convey a pleasant disposition, how they walk (especially if claiming injury), and with whom they associate.

EXAMPLES:

A woman's clothes can be:

(a) too sexy,

(b) too expensive,

(c) too informal, or

(d) too insincere.

Jewelry can tell the jury much about a woman. Some have not forgotten the Wild West days when the price of a prostitute could be determined by the size of her jewelry. Larry Smith, a well-known trial lawyer from New Orleans writes and lectures on the subject of nonverbal communication. The only jewelry he wears to court is his wedding ring, and he feels that telling the jury he is a happily married man helps his credibility with the jury. This is one way to do it. As an athlete I endured one summer with a ring between my finger and the bat and half a basketball season with the wedding ring in the locker room where it was stolen and not replaced. However, in every trial for forty years I have let the jury know I am a happily married man with such comments as: "When my wife and I were shopping the other night . . ."

CAVEAT: Everything a client wears or does not wear in the courtroom is important.

Don't forget recess. That is when jurors really observe your client. If the woman who was just in tears on the witness stand is seen laughing with a friend during recess, she may have little to laugh about when the verdict is read.

Even if a client has suffered serious injuries, jurors do not want to see bitterness or even constant painful expressions (which may be considered an attempt to exaggerate).

CAVEAT: Your client must look like someone the jurors like and want to give money to. Being pleasant, and even a friendly smile, helps accomplish this. Jurors want someone they can root for, someone who is positive and is trying to overcome all that is wrong in the world.

4. *Control the client's attitude.* Jurors just don't like people who think they are better than others, or people who don't care, or people who just aren't very nice. Make sure your client conveys the right attitude in the courtroom.

EXAMPLES:

–When the client is sworn in as a witness, he must be cooperative.

–When the judge tells him to speak louder he must show respect.

–When the court reporter tells him that she must change paper in the stenographic machine he must be considerate.

–When he is told that the boy he ran into was seriously injured he must show genuine concern.

–When the other attorney asks pointed questions he must not become angry.

–When giving details he must not seem bored.

Preparing the client and his attitude for trial, prepares him for voir dire.

5. *Control your client's conduct.* Everything the client does from the time he reaches the courthouse will help to determine the outcome of the trial. It is the trial lawyer's duty to control this conduct.

EXAMPLES:

–Make the client understand that he or she is always on display. When a witness is testifying as to what your client did or said, jurors are often looking at your client to see his or her reaction.

–The client who pushes his way onto the elevator ahead of others may have just pushed himself out of a good verdict.

–Prepare your client to conduct himself in a manner that will win jury approval and if you can't do that, when possible, get him out of the courtroom.

–Determine amount of client exposure. It is important to determine in advance of trial how much the client should be exposed to the jury. You must consider:

(a) Does client have a physical condition the jurors will get used to and feel less sympathetic toward after "overexposure" to the jury?

(b) Is the client the kind of person the jury simply will not like?

(c) Is the client the kind of person the jury will warm up to after they get to know him or her?

(d) Does the client have a condition the jury feels will not enable him or her to sit in the courtroom for long periods of time?

(e) Is the client a nervous type that cannot sit for long periods of time without giving the jurors the feeling he is bored with his own lawsuit?

(f) Will the jury expect your client to be in the courtroom to hear testimony against him?

(g) Will the jury understand why your client is not present during the entire trial, if trial strategy dictates his or her temporary absence?

–Make your client's presence depend upon trial strategy. There is no law or rule of court that requires your client to be present in a civil trial. Whether the client is present should be based upon trial strategy, and not because he wants to be present, or because it is the practice in your jurisdiction for the client to be present.

–Prepare your client for the courtroom. Your client is the main character in your courtroom drama, and if you do not prepare him or her for trial, you have failed in your responsibility. You should determine how much help your client needs, so you help those who need it, and do not insult those who do not need it. Remind all clients:

(1) They are being watched at all times: while they are just sitting watching the trial, while taking a break in the corridor, while getting on the elevator in the morning, while having lunch in a cafe where some jurors may be present, while conferring with his or her counsel, while being examined on the witness stand.

(2) Jurors expect your client to look good and to act good. Some things jurors look for include:

   (a) Appearance. Make sure your client understands how important his or her appearance is to the lawsuit.

   (b) Attitude. Jurors wonder how serious your client is about the lawsuit, whether he or she respects the jurors as people and as members of the jury, and whether the client will appreciate the verdict.

   (c) Concern For Others. Is your client friendly? Courteous when meeting jurors on the elevator, even though unable to talk, as directed by the judge? (A friendly smile is not illegal and failure to smile may be considered rude by the juror.) While listening to testimony, does the client show compassion? (If showing compassion during any part of the trial hurts your cause, you had better get your client out of the courtroom during that part of the trial.)

EXAMPLE:

> In a medical negligence action jurors sometimes feel the client feels bad about suing the doctor, even though he was wrong, so it may be good to have the client out of the courtroom if the client may show any sympathy for the doctor during his testimony.

–Be sure your client helps his or her own lawsuit by:

(1) Preparing your client
  - (a) Let the client know the jury is watching, even when court is not in session.
  - (b) Talk "cold turkey" if you suspect your client may be rude or otherwise may not make a good impression.
  - (c) Let the client know the jury judges his or her attitude toward the lawsuit as an indication of how serious the client is and how valid the claim is.

(2) Controlling time your client is present
  - (a) Determine when the jury expects client to be present.
  - (b) Determine how much, even with preparation, your client can be an asset while in the courtroom.
  - (c) Keep him or her out of the courtroom when necessary.

(3) Letting the jury know why the client is not present
  - (a) If it is hard emotionally or physically for the client to be present, let the jury know this.
  - (b) If you don't want your client present during a time when the jury expects the client to be present, let the jury know some reason for the absence.
  - (c) If there is no need to explain the client's absence, don't make an issue of it.

[1.03] Sell Your Cause To The Panel. Your story is the "what happened," but your "cause" is why what happened entitles you to win your lawsuit. You must start selling your cause during voir dire, because people choose sides early, whether it be in a lawsuit, a ballgame, or in a political campaign.

Find the parts of your lawsuit that involve morals, philosophy, or some issue about which people have strong opinions. If the issue is a negative for you, discover those jurors who feel strongest on the subject.

EXAMPLE:

> If your client had been drinking find out which prospective jurors are most upset about this. If your client is suing a doctor, find out which prospective jurors are most partial toward doctors.
>
> If the issue is positive for you, make the most of it during voir dire.

EXAMPLE:

> If your client is crippled for life, find out which jurors are most understanding of what this means to a human being. If your client lost his business, find out which jurors really understand what it is like to build up one's own business and then to have it taken from you by the wrongdoing of another.

Even the negative issues may have a positive aspect, and it is your job to find it. Joe Jamail, whose impressive list of courtroom victories includes the $11,500,000,000 victory of Texaco, is famous for turning negatives into positives.

EXAMPLE:

> Joe Jamail represented a drunken driver as the plaintiff in a personal injury action. He began his voir dire by walking up to the jury and saying, "Folks, I have a problem. This fellow I represent is a drunk. Now is there anyone on this jury that feels just because he is a drunk that this woman had the right to run him off the road and put him in a wheelchair for the rest of his life?" There was no such person on the jury, or if so, such person was stricken, because the jury came back with a three million dollar verdict for the "drunken driver."

People like being <u>for</u> something and will look at the lawsuit to find some party or witness and some issue to root for. Choose jurors who are most likely to support your cause, or at least will let you carve out a little exception that will fit your cause into their personal philosophy. Do not expect to change a juror's basic concepts during the brief period of a trial.

Sell your cause during voir dire by:

1. Finding jurors who accept your cause

   Q. My client was in the prime of his athletic career when he was injured. You know what this means to a man who just lives to play baseball?

2. Carving out an exception if your cause does not fit a juror's basic concept

   Q. Mr. Jones, you told the prosecutor that you feel most crime is committed by blacks, and I appreciate your being candid with us, but though my client is black he is a professor at the University, a deacon at the largest white Baptist church in town, and for many years has been treasurer of the campus bowling league. Do you think he is more likely to have committed a crime than a white person who does not have this excellent background? (Explore further to see if he will make an exception, and even if he does not, the dialogue may show others the foolishness of his bigotry.)

[1.04.] How To Tell Your Story Within Voir Dire Limitations. Many appellate opinions suggest that telling your story is not a proper use of voir dire. If you follow this approach, you had better first obtain a stipulation from opposing counsel that he will also forego this splendid opportunity to begin the story-telling process.

Fortunately, there is no way to choose a jury without talking about your lawsuit. How you talk about it will depend upon your style, and your style may contribute greatly to the effectiveness of your voir dire. The great storytellers of literature are those who structure effectively, and none of them would forego an opportunity to hint as to what is to come, to introduce characters, or to create an atmosphere that prepares the "audience" for the story.

Discussed below are two options to start telling your story as easily as possible during voir dire:

1. A summary is permitted to discover if a juror knows anything about the case, or if he has formed an opinion. Last Christmas there was

an auto accident in front of the K-Mart store. My client, Bill Smith, sitting here at the counsel table, suffered a broken back in that accident. The man who caused this accident was a fellow named Tom Barker from Canada. Did any of you hear about this or do you know anything about it?"

2. Individual questions can tell the jury "bits and pieces" of the story.

Q. Bill spent five months in a hospital as a result of these injuries. Have any of you ever been confined in a hospital for such a period of time?

Q. The evidence will show that this fellow from Canada was drunk at the time he drove his car into Bill's car. What do you think of this?

Q. Bill was old enough to retire, but he just didn't want to. Now he can't work again. What's your feeling about people working beyond retirement age? Before the jury is even selected, jurors know this is a serious case with big damages and terrible conduct on the part of the defendant.

[1.05] When And How You Can Obtain "Commitments." You must prepare the theme of your final argument to the jury before you begin the trial. During the voir dire you can obtain commitments that are an important part of the final argument.

There are basic commitments you obtain during every trial, such as: "Do you know of any reason you cannot sit on this jury and give a fair verdict to both parties?" There are also commitments that apply only to the particular trial, such as: "Are you willing to vote for a million dollar verdict if the evidence shows our client is entitled to such verdict?"

Obtain commitments during voir dire through the following:

1. Ask closed-ended questions. This is an exception to the "open-ended" rule that encourages discussion. Here you want a "yes" or "no" answer that cannot later be debated by opposing counsel. "At the beginning of this trial, each of you agreed that a police officer's word is not entitled to any special treatment in an American courtroom, that you and I and every other citizen is assumed to be just as truthful as a witness who happens to be wearing a police uniform. Now that we have heard all the evidence we know that the only way you could find my client

guilty would be to disbelieve my client and to believe the officer. Now let's look at what they said. . . ."

2. Obtain the basic commitments. In every trial you want a jury that has agreed to listen to the evidence, to apply the law, and to return a fair and just verdict. You are entitled to have a jury that has agreed to do just that.

Q. "Mr. Jones, I know you are president of a big company and have important matters back at the office, but if you serve on this jury will you agree to listen to the evidence and give this case your complete attention?" "Yes, of course." "Thank you. This case is very important to my client, as I know you understand."

3. Obtain special commitments in each case. Review each case to determine if there is a special commitment needed during voir dire.

Q. "Mrs. Smith, there has been a lot of publicity about this case, and you have indicated that you had heard about the case, but really have not formed an opinion. Can we agree then, that when you go back into the jury room to decide this case your verdict will be based upon the evidence you heard in this courtroom and not upon what some newspaper reporter heard someone say?" "That is right." "Thank you."

4. Don't ask juror to prejudge. Just as a witness must "estimate" without "guessing," a prospective juror must be asked to "commit" without "prejudging." This fine distinction may make the difference between getting your commitment and not getting your commitment.

5. Do ask that jurors follow the law. "We all have talked about a law that we would change if we were in the legislature, but during this trial we must work only with the laws that are now on the books. At the end of the trial, Judge Stussey will instruct you as to the law in this case. Are you willing to follow the law as given to you by the judge?" "Yes." "Since a main issue in this case is that of comparative negligence, I expect the judge may instruct you that under the law of our state, my client may recover a certain sum for her injuries though she was partly at fault for what happened. If the judge instructs you that this is the law, will you have any problem following that instruction?" "No." "Thank you."

[1.06] How To Keep A Juror From "Poisoning" Another Juror. The "foreman" problem is only a part of deciding which jurors will have an influence on other jurors. The trial lawyer must decide who is going to dominate the jury room and how those jurors feel about his client and his lawsuit.

The age-old "who will be foreman" speculation is a good place to start.

CAVEAT: Never underestimate the importance of the foreperson! This one juror persuades other jurors by:

(1) the very fact that he or she is the chosen leader,
(2) the education, position, or other factor that obtained the juror the position,
(3) the fact that this juror is in charge of the procedure and mechanics (why don't we take a preliminary vote right now?), and
(4) the fact that he or she sits at the end of the table where others will look for leadership.

There are two ends of that table in nearly every jury room, and the other end of that table may be occupied by a second in command who may be a real "sleeper" who doesn't want to be foreman. People influence in many ways and the man who doesn't want to be foreman may still dominate the jury.

Divide The Jurors Into Leaders And Followers.

Not all leaders will become foreperson, but all leaders will influence others on the jury. When you look at the followers try to determine whom they will follow.

You can tell during voir dire who sits next to a leader, who talks with a leader, who listens to a leader, and who is seen with a leader during a recess. If that leader is against you, the person associated with the leader may also be against you.

Spotting the leaders of a jury may be easier than knowing whether they will help you or hurt you. Often you must strike a strong person from the jury because he carries too many votes in his hip pocket for you to take a chance on his being against you.

Look For The Leaders By Considering The Juror's:

(1) age and experience,
(2) occupation,
(3) position held,
(4) education, and
(5) physical appearance.

Then Closely Watch:

(6) juror's participation in the discussion, and
(7) other jurors' reactions to the juror's discussion. (The fact that a juror talks a lot does not mean he is a leader, but the fact that others listen to him usually does.)

RECOMMENDATION: The fact that all studies show that those sitting at the side of the table do not participate in discussion during jury deliberation as much as others, cries out for change. The simple solution? Round tables in jury rooms.

When I returned from taking depositions at the New York City bar headquarters, I had a cabinetmaker build a round table for our conference room. Why can't lawyers practicing west of the Hudson River enjoy the state of the art table where all around it have equal access to documents and dialogues?

The same is true of jurors of the round table. They participate more equally and share a preferred place at the table. I am not suggesting we amend the Bill of Rights to insure fairer trials with rounder tables, but encouraging participation by all jurors should be among our goals.

[1.07] Four Pre-Trial Requirements. In addition to all other pre-trial preparation for voir dire, there are four pre-trial requirements. At pre-trial conference, or immediately before trial if there is no pre-trial conference, there are a few "housekeeping" matters that should be given your attention. Once the judge says, "You may proceed with the voir dire, Mr. Wright," he assumes these matters are behind us.

Get "Insurance" Before The Jury. Every plaintiff's lawyer wants the jury to know that there is insurance, and even though the law states that juries are not to consider it, the law also provides many ways for it to reach the jury. Your pre-trial preparation requires that two steps be taken to get insurance to the jury without a mistrial and without making an enemy of the judge:

1. Obtain the company's name prior to trial. This avoids stumbling at that part of your questioning and also avoids possible mistrial

for bringing too much attention to the insurance question. Obtain it by asking or at the pre-trial, or in a few states by discovery if that is necessary.

2. Learn the judge's procedure and limits for allowing the insurance question or questions. Judges interpret the same law differently, and each judge has his own ideas as to how much attention he will let counsel give to the subject of insurance. Learn from previous experience with the judge, from previous experience other lawyers have had with the judge, and with a direct approach, especially as to how you are going to handle the question (where the question is permitted).

EXAMPLE:

"Judge, after about six other questions, I am going to ask whether or not any member of the panel, or any member of their family, is employed by or has a financial interest in All-State Insurance Company." If there is no objection, you may proceed accordingly.

Set The Stage For The Separate Settlement. Sometimes the court is concerned about discussion of the fact plaintiff has settled with one of the defendants. States vary in dealing with the problem, but it is important that you deal with the problem by informing the judge what you are going to do and by ensuring that your procedure meets with the judge's approval:

1. Know the law of your jurisdiction so you do not risk a mistrial.
2. Adopt a procedure that will satisfy your trial strategy and also will satisfy the judge.

EXAMPLE:

"Judge, I plan on telling the jury during voir dire that we have settled our part of the lawsuit with Jones and they are only to consider the case against Smith, unless you plan on covering that in your opening remarks."

Protect The "Remarried Widow." The law of the jurisdiction is clear as to the law of evidence, and maybe even the law of damages in a wrongful death case if the widow has remarried. You must prepare for this voir dire problem before trial:

1. Know the law of the jurisdiction, prepare your trial based on that law, and be able to argue it to the court and to present citations.
2. Explain to the judge how you are going to handle this problem if there is any possibility he may question your procedure.
3. Prepare the handling of this with trial strategy in mind.

EXAMPLE:

"Ladies and Gentlemen, it has been three years since the death of Mr. Jones, and there will be evidence of all that Mrs. Jones has gone through during that three year period. There will be evidence of her recent remarriage. His honor will instruct you as to any effect that remarriage should have on this lawsuit. I assume you will wait and hear the evidence and the judge's instructions and apply his instructions to that evidence. If any of you has a problem doing that, or has personal opinions as to how that should affect the lawsuit, I would appreciate it if you would raise your hand and we can talk about it."

Persuade With Demonstrative Evidence. Demonstrative evidence can add drama and interest to your voir dire and can help the beginning of your story. However, if you don't plan ahead you may be stopped before you begin.

1. Organize your demonstrative evidence and know exactly how you are going to present it. Keep in mind how it can help you most and whether the judge will allow you to use it. Be ready to explain and be ready to adjust.
2. Get opposing counsel to stipulate at pre-trial, if possible, to avoid the "not in evidence" problem and the look on opposing counsel's face as he tells the judge he has never seen it before and doesn't have any idea what it means.
3. Discuss it at pre-trial and, if all goes well, mention at that time that you may use it at voir dire or at opening.

Whatever course you take, plan ahead. You may wish to take your chance and to waive the evidence in front of the jury and to force opposing counsel to object in front of the jury after the jury has already seen it. This may be the best strategy if you feel that the judge will rule against you at pre-trial, but plan your strategy.

One reason you prepare for voir dire is that you want to avoid a mistrial before the trial even begins. Poor preparation often means improper questions are asked, or that proper questions are asked improperly. Mistrials at the early stage frustrate the client, waste money on unused expert fees, and often cause the client to settle a case that should have been tried.

When poor pre-trial preparation for voir dire causes a mistrial, you may have just lost a jury panel that was about to give you a huge verdict. Working with opposing counsel and the judge to avoid a mistrial just makes good sense.

[1.08] Explain Voir Dire To Prospective Jurors. Once you begin the voir dire, it is helpful to tell the jury about this process. This can be a part of explaining the procedure of trying a lawsuit.

Cause Them To Appreciate Your Help. Let the jury know that you understand this is a new experience for most of them. Show that you are trying to help. Discuss the fact that a trial is not really all that complicated when you understand it.

EXAMPLE:

> "I am sure that the trial of a lawsuit is not something you are involved with every day, and there are parts of it you may not understand. How many of you watch *Matlock* or *L.A. Law*? Well, it isn't exactly like that. They never show jurors sitting in the jury assembly room for hours waiting to be called, do they?"
>
> "Neither do they spend much time telling you about voir dire, though this is the best part of the trial. In fact, this is the only time you get to talk. I would like to make a few suggestions that might help, and I would like to start by suggesting that you take advantage of this opportunity to tell us how you feel about things we are going to talk about."

Help Them Understand What Is Going On. Try to determine what is going on in the juror's mind. What questions are they asking themselves? Then direct some of your remarks toward those questions.

EXAMPLE:

> "This part of the trial will only take a few hours. I will ask some questions and then the other lawyer will do the same. Neither of us will ask any question that will embarrass you. There is no right answer to any question we ask, we just want your feeling on questions we will ask.
>
> "Feel free to tell us anything you think we should know, and just wave your hand at me if you have a question. You are all qualified to sit on this jury or you wouldn't be sitting here on this panel. We just want to know if there is anything in your experience that might cause you to lean toward one party or the other."

Be Sure They Answer Your Questions Openly and Intelligently. Explaining voir dire may come early in your chatting with the jurors. This means you must establish at this time a need for the answers to be honest and accurate. They do not understand voir dire until they understand this.

EXAMPLE:

> "Sometimes a juror will feel a question is not important and fail to tell us about it, and later the case must be retried because of this. Please answer the questions to the best of your knowledge and if you think of anything you feel we should know, please raise your hand and tell us. Some of the questions we ask may seem a waste of time, but let the judge decide that. If he permits the question, then he is telling you to answer it the best you can."

Avoid Resentment Toward Your Inquiry. Some people are anxious to chat with you, and others may feel every question is an invasion of their privacy. Let them know that: (a) you are not going to pry into their personal affairs, (b) what you are asking is important, and (c) you will put all questions in a way that will not embarrass them.

EXAMPLE:

> "We are not going to pry into your personal affairs and we are only going to ask questions that past experience tells us may help us learn if you have formed an opinion. We will not ask any question that will embarrass you, and I think you will enjoy our discussion. We all have had personal experiences that have helped us form opinions and we are trying to find out if any opinion you have formed would in any way affect your verdict."

Later:

"Have any of you ever been involved in any kind of litigation, and I do not mean a divorce matter, I do not need to know about that."

Help Them Appreciate Voir Dire. The more jurors understand voir dire, the more they appreciate it, and the more they will participate. Don't let them think it is a waste of time. The best way to do this is not to waste their time. When you ask a question, (a) ask it as though you need an answer, and then (b) listen to the answer.

Nothing disturbs a juror more than a lawyer who rushes on to the next question as though he did not wait to hear the answer. If the answer suggests further inquiry, or at least requires varying the next question, the juror becomes convinced the attorney is not really interested in the answer, unless the attorney does listen and adjusts accordingly.

Act as though voir dire is important. Tell the jury it is important. Show them it is important.

EXAMPLE:

"This is the most important part of the trial, because you have a chance to tell us about yourself, and tell us about your feelings on matters that are important in this lawsuit. I know that if you have formed an opinion that would keep you from bringing back a verdict that is fair to both sides, you would rather wait and serve on another jury.

"It is my job to help you discover your feelings and to tell you about who will testify, what the evidence will be, and what kind of case this is, so that we can have a completely impartial jury. First, do any of you know of any reason right now that you should not serve on this jury?

"If your brother is one of the parties to the lawsuit we can tell you right away whether or not you will be excused. However, if one of the parties is just someone you met once at a P.T.A. meeting, we'll have to discuss that. We want you to serve, but having an impartial jury is so important we want to make sure you won't lean just a little toward one side or the other. Do all of you agree with that?"

Avoid Restlessness And Impatience. Tell the jurors early in the voir dire how long the trial will last and about how much time the voir dire will take. Knowing the time-frame will cause less looking at the watch, and more listening to your questions.

That is not enough, however, jurors must know that the time is being well spent. WATCH THE JURORS! You can tell when a juror is becoming restless and asking him a question may keep him from falling asleep.

Bring Drama To Your Voir Dire! This is your first opportunity to let the jurors know that real live courtroom drama is more dramatic than anything they have seen on television. Let them know that you will be dealing with real live human beings. Raise and lower your voice. Stop! Be perfectly quiet for a moment. Don't stand in the same spot. Don't look at the same juror. Tell them about this lawsuit.

EXAMPLE:

> "Mary was in intensive care for twenty days. How many of you have ever been in intensive care? How many of you have ever visited a person who was in intensive care? John Wilkens visited his wife in intensive care every night for twenty nights and she did not even know he was there. How many of you have had this experience of just sitting there? There will be medical testimony as to why Mary was in intensive care, but will you also listen to other witnesses such as her husband and her mother who will tell you about those twenty days?"

Be Sure They Know The Importance Of Their Role. Jurors will participate more during voir dire, and will do a better job as jurors, if they appreciate the importance of their role in the trial. Treat them as if they are important, and tell them they are important, because they are, indeed, very important.

EXAMPLE:

> "We lawyers have spent months preparing for this trial and we will try the case before Judge Hoester, who has been a judge for several years, but all we can do is bring the case to you. You must decide the future of this young man sitting here at the counsel table, and what you are called upon to do is the most important demand we make upon a citizen, short of sending him off to war. Are all of you willing to serve on this jury and give us a verdict that you think is fair and just? If any of you can think of any reason you cannot be fair to both sides, will you please raise your hand. I thank you."

[1.09] How To Address The Entire Panel. Some judges prefer that the entire voir dire be conducted by inquiring of the entire panel. Know the law of your jurisdiction, and know the practice and procedure of your judge.

Save Time And Impress Jurors And The Judge. You know the judge wants to move the trial along, but you often forget that the jurors are equally anxious to get started. They do not realize that once voir dire begins the trial has started.

Give jurors the feeling that the voir dire is proceeding by following basic rules:

1. Never repeat what you, the judge, or opposing counsel has said. If you want to pursue a matter previously covered, do so in a way that everyone knows this is not a repetition.

EXAMPLE:

"I know the judge asked about prior jury service, but I would like to know if those trials were civil or criminal. You see there is an entirely different burden of proof in a criminal case, and sometimes a juror who has served in a criminal case does not realize that."

2. Keep your questions brief and to the point. Some attorneys ask long-winded questions that make the voir dire seem long. Several short questions will cover the same territory, yet give a feeling of getting somewhere.
3. Use computer print-outs properly. The Court will probably give you a computer print-out or similar information containing basic data on each prospective juror. AVOID having the judge say, "Mr. Smith, you have the answer to that question on the questionnaire these people have spent time filling out for you." If you need to cover a matter on the print-out, or if you are not sure of the information, handle the problem in a way that does not bring a reprimand from the judge nor a frown from the jury.

EXAMPLE:

"I understand from your questionnaire, Mr. Jones, that your brother is a law enforcement officer; which department is he with"?

OR:

"This form shows me, Mrs. Jones, that you live on Broadway, in Ellington, and I didn't think Broadway went out that far, is this right"?

Skip Around The Panel With Ease. You should avoid questioning one juror after another, by going right down the row the way lawyers have always done it. By using a little imagination and skipping around the panel, you can:

1. Keep the jury alert, since they cannot assume you will not get to them for another half hour;
2. Avoid the stiffness of going down a line and saying, in effect, "I am through with you" and "You are next";
3. Encourage participation, by turning to a juror who is not next in line, and then, turning to the panel and asking, "Has anyone on the panel had a similar experience"?
4. Use some of the "individual questions" that you would otherwise have to save for individual questioning.

Skipping around the jury panel can be done with ease if counsel approaches the panel inquiry as though he were conducting a conversation with the jurors. When you talk with a group of friends, you do not inquire of one friend and then proceed to the next in line. Your friends do not wait in line to enter the discussion. The same applies to a voir dire of the panel. Make it an informal conversation in which you are chatting with friends.

EXAMPLE:

"Mr. Jones, I understand you were in an accident. Please tell me about it?"

THEN:

"Has anyone else been in an accident?" "Mrs. Smith, will you tell me about your accident?"

THEN:

"Mrs. Smith's accident involved some pretty serious injuries. Have any of you, or a person, close to you, been involved in an accident in which there were serious injuries?"

"Mr. Brown, what kind of injuries did you sustain?" "By the way, who was your doctor?" "Your doctor is on the staff at the same hospital as Dr. Jenkins who treated my client in this case; will that make any difference to you?"

THEN:

"Dr. Jenkins will be testifying in this case; does anyone know Dr. Jenkins?"

We have talked with different jurors and we have talked about different subjects. We have chatted with the jurors pretty much as we would if we were sitting in our living room with a group of friends. Study this the next time you converse with friends. See how natural it is.

Pin Down Commitments. An attorney often thinks he has obtained a commitment when he has not.

CAVEAT: It is only a commitment when the juror thinks he has committed. There are two basic ways to obtain a commitment:

1. From the panel. This requires a special effort, since silence may mean a noncommitment to the juror. There is a need to make the commitment very specific if it comes from an entire panel.

EXAMPLE:

"Is there anyone on this panel who will not follow the judge's instruction and will not bring back a conviction, even though there is a reasonable doubt in your mind as to my client's guilt?" (Not enough) "Let me put it this way, do you agree that you will vote for a guilty verdict only if you feel he is guilty beyond a reasonable doubt?" (Still not enough) "If you feel you will have any problem following this instruction, will you please raise your hand?" (You are nearly there) "Since none of you have raised your hand, I assume you have no problem with this." (There can be no question. You have a commitment.)

2. By individual inquiry. This is much easier to pin down because of the one-on-one situation. He knows you are talking to him. There is no question, as long as the commitment is specific.

EXAMPLE:

"You will follow the court's instruction on presumption of innocence, is that right, Mr. Smith? If the state fails to prove my client guilty, you will not require me to prove his innocence, or who did it, is that right? If the state fails to make a case you are now ready to hold jurors to this commitment during final argument.

Avoid Objection And Rejection By Avoiding Repetition. Repetition at one stage of inquiry is just as boring as repetition at any other stage of inquiry.

Avoid repeating (a) what you covered while questioning the panel, (b) what the judge and opposing counsel have covered, and (c) what you have covered during individual questioning.

Tell Your Story Smoothly. Tell your entire story during the questioning of the entire panel. By the time you question jurors individually, they should be familiar with the case. Though you may tell your story in bits and pieces, it must have a structuring that tells the story smoothly.

EXAMPLE:

> "Are you familiar with the intersection of Main and Broadway?" "You are familiar, then, with the fact that the traffic at that intersection is controlled by electric traffic signals, is that right?" "There was an auto collision at that intersection a year ago Christmas, are you familiar with whether or not there has been any change in that intersection or its traffic control since that time?" "There will be evidence that defendant was intoxicated when he went through that intersection and drove into my client's car. If that is the evidence, do any of you have any problem serving on the jury and bringing back a verdict that is fair to both parties?"

Avoid Embarrassing Prospective Jurors. If you feel a juror may be embarrassed if you single him out with a question, ask the question of the entire panel and ask it in a way that will generalize as much as possible.

EXAMPLE:

> "All of us are getting a little older, and it is harder for us to sit in one position for hours. Is there anyone on the jury who feels, for physical reasons, that you would rather not serve? This is much better than, "Mr. Jones you look pretty old and physically handicapped, are you sure you can serve on this jury?"

Save A Few Questions For Individual Questioning. It would be ideal if, after questioning the panel, you have chatted with each juror and there would be no need for individual questioning. That is not what happens in the real world.

You should, therefore, save at least one question you can ask each juror during the individual questioning. If you don't, you may reach a juror and stumble for a moment because you realize you have asked this juror all that you intend to ask.

EXAMPLE:

"Mrs. Jones, I notice you work for General Electric, how long have you worked there," OR "What do you do for G.E.?" People usually like to talk about their work and it is the kind of chatting you may do at a party. It is not an intellectual discussion, but it is one step above talking about the weather. It is preferable to, "I have nothing to ask you," after asking questions of the other jurors.

[1.10] How To Get Jurors To Participate. Jurors who participate in the voir dire are more likely to listen during the trial and to participate in the discussion during jury deliberation. It is important to encourage participation. There are several ways you can accomplish this:

Project Informality. You should tell jurors about the informality of voir dire, but you should also project it. Let them know by what you do and how you do it that this is a time for them to relax and take part.

Don't pin yourself behind a podium. Move about as much as local practice permits, and this will project a lack of rigidity. Talk as though you are chatting with jurors, not giving them a lecture. Even if you follow an outline, do not let your presentation appear to be overly structured.

If you are relaxed jurors are more likely to be relaxed. Let them know how you feel about the discussion and they will be more apt to tell you how they feel

EXAMPLE:

Nobody likes to pay taxes but what I really don't like is paying for something if I feel I'm not getting what I should get in return. I just don't want to spend a dime for anything unless I know what my money is being spent for. How do you people feel about spending money? Do you think you should pay for what you get and get what you pay for? If you sign a contract do you think you should have to comply with your part of the agreement and that the other party should be required to comply with his part of the agreement? What if you had to go to court to enforce the contract, do any of you see anything wrong with that if that's what it comes down to? What about you, Mrs. Smith, how do you feel about this? By now Mrs. Smith knows that you and everyone on the panel feels both sides should honor a contract and if necessary you may have to go to court to enforce it. You have not learned much about this juror's attitude, but you have softened any feeling any juror may have about a person filing a lawsuit.

Show Them Why To Participate. You should not only talk about the importance of their participating, you should also show them. Bring this home to them forcefully, but with tact.

EXAMPLE:

"Mrs. Jones, if my client happened to be your very best friend, it would only be fair that my opposing counsel knew that so he could question you about that, we all agree about that, don't we? Well, if there were something else, such as you had worked at the same place, maybe I wouldn't think to ask you about it, but it is something we should talk about. Can you see why it is important that all of us talk about these things and that you tell us all that you think we should talk about?"

Discard Outmoded Approaches To Voir Dire. Everything you do during voir dire must be aimed at your goal, which is to educate as you choose jurors. If the way it has been done for years does not accomplish this, look for new ways.

EXAMPLE:

(a) Do not conduct voir dire from one place in the courtroom. Move about, and do it with ease.

(b) Do not divide your voir dire into a questioning of the panel, then individually. It is perfectly natural to go from one to the other and to intersperse both kinds of questioning.

(c) Do not go "down the line." Jump around the panel.

(d) Do not let it appear to be a "questioning." Make it a "conversation," by asking questions the way you would in normal conversation.

Create An Atmosphere That Will Start The Winning Process. Jurors will react to whatever atmosphere you create for them. You must project the feeling you need from the very beginning of voir dire.

EXAMPLE:

(a) If you have a serious case with serious injuries, you will want to have an atmosphere in which jurors will be thinking about the seriousness of the injuries. You can keep it from getting too heavy, but still keep the jury thinking about the tragedy that has occurred.

CAVEAT: Keeping your client out of the courtroom during most or all of the voir dire enables you to lighten the atmosphere without relinquishing seriousness that will lead to a large verdict.

(b) Clarence Darrow said that jurors will not send a man to prison if they are enjoying their experience on the jury. He tried to keep the atmosphere light. Once he began a murder trial in which his client was charged with murdering his wife, by saying, "It was his own wife, wasn't it?" The jury never got serious enough to convict.

(c) Never let jurors think you are insincere or playing games about any part of the trial. During every minute of the trial, even during recess, jurors are observing you, your client, and your witnesses. If they detect the slightest sign of insincerity credibility is destroyed and the lawsuit is lost. Telling your client about a funny television show you saw the night before may bring laughter that can cost the lawsuit. Jurors will think you are talking about the trial.

Ask Questions That Will Require Their Involvement. Many questions on voir dire are general and could be asked to any member of the panel. You must ask some questions that really make the juror feel you are talking directly to him or her and to no other person in the world. This requires that juror to become involved.

EXAMPLE:

"Mrs. Jones, I see you are a school teacher. What courses do you teach?"

THEN:

"Do you have any duties at school other than teaching these courses?"

THEN:

"How do you spend the summer months?"

By now the juror is telling you about herself!

Ask Questions That Reveal Their Philosophy. The juror's philosophy is based on attitude, and the juror's attitude, will tell you how he will decide many issues in your lawsuit. Determine the juror's philosophy:

EXAMPLE:

(a) "What magazines and newspapers do you read?"

(b) "What books do you read?"

(c) "What is your employment?"

(d) "How do you feel about the so-called crisis involving lawsuits?"

Create a "Cross–Discussion." The dialogue need not be limited to questioning the jurors. It can, through counsel, become a discussion among the jurors. This can be done by getting various jurors involved in the same discussion.

EXAMPLE:

"Mrs. Jones, I see you and Mrs. Smith both work at the same place, do you know each other?"
"I don't think so, I work in accounting, (turning to other juror), where do you work?"
"I'm in sales, but I think I have seen you. Didn't you used to work in Administration?"
"Yes."

OR, THROUGH COUNSEL:

"How do you feel about your previous jury service, Mr. Jones?"
"I enjoyed it."
"Mr. Williams, how did you like your experience on the jury?"
"Well, I can't say I enjoyed it. It was a murder trial. I think I would have enjoyed a civil case like this, but a murder trial was pretty heavy."
"Mr. Jones, yours was not a criminal case, was it?"
"Oh, no, I know how Mr. Williams feels, if I had been on any kind of a criminal case I don't think I could have felt the same. I know I couldn't serve on a murder trial."

[1.11] How To Conduct Individual Inquiry. In most jurisdictions, counsel is permitted to inquire individually of prospective jurors. When this is permitted, you should take advantage of it to the fullest, for it is an opportunity you will not have during the remainder of the trial.

Know Any Limitations That Will Be Imposed. Before you begin voir dire, you must know the law of the jurisdiction and the policy and procedure of the court. This especially applies to individual questioning, since judges often place their own limitations on this part of voir dire.

Do not let this disrupt the smooth flow of your voir dire. Have an understanding in advance. If the judge is going to limit individual questioning, know what those limitions are and work around them.

EXAMPLE:

If the judge furnishes information on each juror, don't ignore this. Don't say, "Have you served on a jury before?" if that information is on the computer print-out. Say, "I understand you have served on a jury, was that a civil or criminal case?"

OR

If the judge feels most questions should be addressed to the entire panel, do as much "individual questioning" during the inquiry of the entire panel as possible.

CAVEAT: Be sure you have "individual chatting"!

Use Open-Ended Questions. You will encourage discussion with open-ended questions, and this applies during individual questioning as well as when questioning the entire panel. Open-ended questions force jurors to "open up" and talk.

EXAMPLE:

"What do you think about seat belts?" requires the juror to talk about seat belts. "Do you agree with the law requiring seat belts?" lets the juror off with a "yes" or "no" answer.

Obtain Commitments. One exception to the open–ended question rule is the use of "closed-ended" questions to obtain a commitment. When you want a commitment, you want a "yes" or "no" question.

EXAMPLE:

"If you serve on this jury will you bring back a conviction only if you feel my client is guilty beyond a reasonable doubt?" calls for a "yes" or "no" and a "yes" means you have a commitment.

Listen To The Answers! It is an insult to anyone to ask a question and then not to listen carefully to the answer. You should never insult someone who is about to decide the fate of your client.

The answer should lead to the next question. You should begin with definite questions, but they should really constitute "lines of questioning" that lead to other questions. When an answer suggests a question, it shows concern and interest, and this makes the prospective juror feel that you really care.

Control The Inquiry. You decide how you will proceed with the voir dire. The fact a certain procedure has been followed for a hundred years in your county does not mean that is the best way. Plan how your voir dire should be structured, and then be ready to adjust as the voir dire proceeds.

This means you must (a) plan the beginning with something that will catch the jury's attention, (b) structure the questioning so that you maintain interest with interjecting interesting questions where there seems to be a lull, (c) plan the order of individual and panel inquiries on the basis of what order will have most dramatic impact (panel inquiry then individual inquiry is NOT always the best procedure), and (d) keep an eye on the jury and direct your questioning toward those areas which are getting the best reception.

EXAMPLE:

> The jurors were not really getting into the spirit of voir dire until a question was asked relative to what law programs they watch on television. Jurors seemed anxious to talk about it. Stop the voir dire! Spend a little more time on this subject. You are in control. Don't make the mistake of wasting time. Find a way to stay with this subject a bit longer. "Why do you like *L.A. Law*?" "Do you expect me to find the real killer, like *Perry Mason* does?" "What do you think of *Matlock*?"

Five Important Techniques of Individual Questioning

1. How to begin individual questioning. Do not begin with, "I would now like to ask you a few questions." Go ahead and ask questions, or just begin chatting with the jurors, and not in any special order. If you are talking with a friend you never say you are going to ask a question, unless you want to raise the person's guard. Though you must end with a question, you may want to begin with just talk and lead up to the question.
2. How to structure the inquiry. Decide where you want to go with the questioning and lead toward that goal. If you have a weakness in your case, decide when would be best to discuss it and how you will lead into it. Face up to it early in the voir dire.

   Build your voir dire around those issues you want to be the central crux of your voir dire. Build around it and let all else just fall in place.

3. Be informal, friendly, and sincere. People tell friends much that they will not tell strangers. By chatting informally, as a friend would, you get answers that tell you about the juror and the juror's attitude. You will also start persuading if you are informal, friendly, and sincere.
4. Be sure "small talk" is "big talk." Jurors often think that voir dire is a waste of time, and some attorneys contribute greatly to this concept. "Chatting" is not "small talk." It is a relaxed way to accomplish a great purpose, that of learning if the person has "formed an opinion" or has "hidden feelings." Let the jurors know this and it will add stature to your voir dire.
5. Ways to include all jurors. Some people on the panel will do much of the talking during voir dire. That quiet juror sitting in the corner will follow someone on the jury, and it is your job to find out whom he or she will follow.

   SUGGESTIONS:

   –Purposely turn to a member who is not participating and ask a question.

   –Make notes and look for voids that should prompt you to ask an individual question.

   –Ask questions that require all jurors to raise a hand or to participate in some way.

   –Ask follow-up questions, so the nonparticipating juror can give a "yes" or "no" and go back to sleep.

[1.12] Maintain Interest With Demonstrative Evidence. Too often lawyers save demonstrative evidence "for the trial." This approach fails to recognize the fact that the trial begins with voir dire!

Every reason to use demonstrative evidence during your case-in-chief, during cross-examination, and during final argument, cries out for use during voir dire. Demonstrative evidence maintains interest in the trial, and during voir dire it prevents the jury from losing interest before you begin.

First impressions are extremely important, and before opening statement jurors will decide whether or not the trial is worth their time and attention. Nothing will help impress the jurors more than demonstrative evidence.

Get Court Approval. If you have had no experience with the judge, learn from others his policy on use of demonstrative evidence during voir dire. If you feel chances are he will permit it, take it up at the pre-trial conference.

If the judge's objection is based on the fact that the object to be used is not in evidence, then try to obtain a stipulation. If none can be obtained, show that there is no way it will not be in evidence.

Determine what you intend to portray with the evidence, and see if there is a substitute that will serve the same purpose if the evidence cannot be used during voir dire.

EXAMPLE:

> You would like to show several checks to the jury during voir dire, using blown-up photos of them. The judge warns you he will not permit them during voir dire or opening statement because they are not in evidence. You can then, in most courts, present a chart showing a list of these checks and ask questions about the chart.

Know The Law And Cite It. The court had permitted a mathematical formula to be written on the blackboard during final argument, it was held error to permit the formula, but not error to permit use of the blackboard to "illustrate or demonstrate." *Gladys Affett v. Milwaukee & Suburban Transport Corp.*, 106 NW2d 274, 86 AR2d 227 (Wis. 1960). The court stated, "What the ear may hear, the eye may see."

In one case it was held that writing figures as to damages plaintiff expected to prove was proper during voir dire. *Eichstadt v. Underwood*, 337 SW2d 684 (Ky 1960). Though use of demonstrative evidence depends upon the sound discretion of the trial court, *Ratner v. Arrington*, 111 So2d 82 (Fl. App 1959), the argument that the charts, blackboards, and other demonstrations cannot be used until supporting evidence is introduced is refuted in many cases in which their use during opening statement has been approved. *Kimbell v. Noel*, 228 SW2d 980 (Tex. App 1950).

The jury should be instructed that the exhibit, like oral argument, is not evidence. *Miller v. Loy*, 140 NE2d 38 (Ohio App 1956). Like oral argument, the exhibit should have a reasonable foundation. *Johnson v. Charleston & W. C. R. Co.*, 108 SE2d 777 (SC 1959). Like oral argument, failing to object to it can result in a waiver, and that the objection should be accompanied by a proposed instruction. *Hernandez v. Baucum*, 344 SW2d 498 (Tex. App 1961).

Properly Prepare! Often counsel does not obtain court approval, or does not use demonstrative evidence during voir dire effectively because he has not prepared it. Follow these three important steps:

1. Decide what you are going to use. Don't OVERUSE, and be sure that what you do use will be effective. Remember any time restraints the judge will place upon you, and be sure that the use of the demonstrative evidence will be a highlight and will be one that cannot be maintained for a long period of time.
2. Decide how you are going to use it. Relate it to a certain part of your questioning. Relate it to a certain part of your telling the story. Ask yourself what this evidence is going to say and have it say it as eloquently as possible.

   CAVEAT: Voir dire is a series of questions, so use it as a part of the question.
3. Decide when you are going to use it. Structure your voir dire with demonstrative evidence in mind. Keep your eye on the jury, and when you feel that the voir dire needs a little pep reach for something that will catch their attention. Change a question to a different part of the voir dire if it can be used at a time when the accompanying demonstrative evidence will serve you best.

Make The Presentation Dramatic. You are using demonstrative evidence to make voir dire more dramatic. Make it more dramatic! Use timing! Let the jury know that this is important! Don't let it sit in front of them until they are bored with it. Present it with all of the fanfare the moment must receive if it is to accomplish its purpose.

[1.13] Prepare Jurors For Any Weakness In Your Case. If you represent the plaintiff or the prosecution, you have first chance to "confess your sins." If you represent the defendant in a civil or criminal case, you must wait your turn, but when your turn does come you must walk right up to the jury and tell them about it.

Gain The Jury's Respect By Talking About Your Weakness.

Q. "The only eye witness is an ex-convict. Are you willing to sit and listen to this witness, and hear what he has to say without first deciding you are not going to believe him?" "Do you think a man who stole a car ten years ago could tell the truth today about what he saw at the accident?"

Q. "My client is eighty years old, and some of you may think she should not be driving, but the evidence will show she was driving and was driving carefully. Are you willing to listen to the evidence and decide the case from the facts you hear, and not just assume my client did something wrong because she is an older driver?"

Q. "Mary Smith did not suffer any broken bones, but the damage to her is much more serious than that. She is suffering from something that will not heal like a broken bone, she is suffering from something she will live with for the rest of her life, something you can see on an x-ray. It is something you can see when you talk with her and know what she is going through."

Develop Your Own Style Of Frankness.

1. Study the style of great trial lawyers. There is one thing Joe Jamail and Gerry Spence, two of the greatest lawyers in America today, have in common. They both walk right up to the jury box and say, "Folks, I have a problem." By the time they explain their problem, the jury wants to help them.
2. Develop your own style. Every lawyer has his or her own way of dealing with the case's weakness during voir dire. Knowing that great lawyers deal with this effectively does not tell you how to do it, that just tells you that you must do it. How you let the jury know must depend upon your own style.

Establish Credibility Through Frankness. There is nothing more important in a trial than credibility, and your first chance to establish credibility is during voir dire. You can do this by being perfectly frank with the jury, even about your weakest issue. Remember four basic facts of frankness:

1. Voir dire is your FIRST opportunity to talk frankly with the jury about your weakness. Use it!

2. By being CANDID you will establish credibility with the jury.
3. By making it a part of YOUR STORY you will relegate it to a less important status than if opposing counsel bursts forth with it during cross-examination or argument.
4. It is better to EXPLAIN than to have it presented at a time when you are unable to explain.

[1.14] Adapt To The Federal Court. The federal judge in most courts will conduct the voir dire. This has mislead lawyers into thinking their role in federal voir dire is a minor one. It is, in fact, extremely important because he has to work harder to get his questions asked.

Know The Federal Rule.

> Rule 47. Jurors
>
> (a) Examination of Jurors. The court may permit the parties or their attorneys to conduct the examination of prospective jurors or may itself conduct the examination. In the latter event, the court shall permit the parties or their attorneys to supplement the examination by such further inquiry as it deems proper or shall itself submit to the prospective jurors such additional questions of the parties or their attorneys as it deems proper.
>
> Rule 47, *Federal Rules of Civil Procedure.*

The federal rule in criminal cases is similar. Rule 23, *Federal Rules of Criminal Procedure.* Local practice is covered in local rules, and local custom depends upon the judge presiding at the trial. If a question is a proper one to be put to the jury, it will reach the jury in any federal court if counsel presents it properly to the court.

The Sixth Amendment to the U.S. Constitution provides:

> "In all criminal prosecutions, the accused shall enjoy the right to a speedy and public trial, by an impartial jury. . . ."

The Fifth Amendment provides:

> "No person shall . . . be deprived of life, liberty, or property, without due process of law."

The Seventh Amendment preserves the "right of trial by jury" in civil cases. These three amendments have guaranteed the trial lawyer the right to obtain an impartial jury through proper inquiry, but the manner of that inquiry has been historically left to the sound discretion of the trial judge. *Connors v. United States,* 158 US 408 (1895).

Take The Three Steps In The Federal Court.

1. Learn the procedure of the trial judge.
2. Request the right to participate in the voir dire. (Some judges are beginning to grant that request.)
3. Prepare questions for the judge to submit.

Where the judge erroneously excused a government's challenge for cause, no error, since impartial jurors tried the case. *U.S. v. Prati,* 861 F2d 82 (5th cir. 1988). State constitutions and statutes are not always followed in federal court. *Pointer v. U.S.,* 151 US 396 (1894). In federal court, there is no error in requiring that suggested question be submitted prior to voir dire. *Haslam v. U.S.,* 431 F2d 362 (9th Cir. 1970).

Know The Three Procedures Followed By Federal Judges

1. Address the entire venire at once;
2. Address the first twelve;
3. Address the number to serve plus the number of peremptories.

CAVEAT: It is not unusual for the federal judge to follow a procedure during voir dire that is similar to the practice in the state courts of his district (except, of course, for the custom in most federal courts for the judge to conduct the voir dire in spite of local state practice.)

Submit Questions In The Federal Court.

1. Prepare questions well in advance.
2. Refer to questions asked by federal judges in other cases.
3. Submit the questions far enough in advance so the judge will have time to study them.
4. Word the questions so they are fair, but ask what you want to be asked.
5. Be brief.

Where counsel gives the court a list of questions that are not asked, he has not protected his right of appeal if he has not objected to a specific question the appellate court might feel should have been asked. *U.S. v. Leftwich*, 461 F2d 586 (3rd Cir. 1972).

The federal judge need not adopt counsel's "phrasing," *U.S. v. Bamburger*, 456 F2d 1119 (3rd Cir. 1972), nor must counsel be permitted to inquire further. *Featherston v. U.S.*, 491 F2d 96 (5th Cir. 1974). Federal judges are at least as quick to excuse a prospective juror as a state judge, but they do not rely upon the appellate courts for help if he does not. *U.S. v. Wooten*, 518 F2d 943 (3rd Cir. 1975). Counsel was forced to use a peremptory on a juror who admitted bias against unions, *U.S. v. Nell*, 526 F2d 1223 (5th Cir. 1976) and it was not necessary to excuse all residents of a city which was a party. *U.S. v. Brown*, 540 F2d 364 (8th Cir. 1976).

Where two jurors expressed prejudice against IRS, it was proper for the judge to inquire of them in camera. *U.S. v. Booher*, 641 F2d 218 (5th Cir. 1981). Where counsel permitted to examine, judge could prevent "unnecessary and argumentative" examination. *U.S. v. Anderson*, 562 F2d 394 (6th Cir. 1977).

Know The Limits Of Judge's Discretion. Federal judges have been reversed where: Judge refused to ask if anyone knew government witnesses, *U.S. v. Washington*, 819 F2d 221 (9th Cir. 1987). Judge curtailed inquiry that would have shown juror had two sons in prison on drug convictions, *U.S. v. Eubanks*, 591 F2d 513 (9th Cir. 1979). Judge did not excuse jurors who would believe law enforcement officers more than prisoners, and some were related to law enforcement officers, *Darbin v. Nourse*, 664 F2d 1109 (9th Cir. 1981) and though there was no reversal, appellate court was not happy with lack of uniformity in questioning (court inquired of one juror in depth, then "skimmed over" the rest.) *U.S. v. Giese*, 569 F2d (9th Cir. 1978).

Federal Judges Must Balance Contempt Power With Voir Dire Rights.

EXAMPLE:

Trial lawyers show proper respect for the court and so it is not often we learn how far the trial judge must go in affording a party rights under voir dire. During the sixties seven young radicals were tried by a federal court in Chicago and did everything possible to disrupt the trial. Public reaction to this, and the defendant's conduct at the democratic convention, made selecting a jury difficult.

After a full day of voir dire, the judge conducting the examination received suggested questions from counsel. The judge asked the panel:

1. Acquainted with employees of FBI or Justice Department?
2. Acquainted with defendants, counsel, associates?
3. Could agree to follow law as given them?
4. Keep an open mind until time for verdict?
5. Could treat testimony of government agent same as others?
6. Would prior jury service keep you from being impartial?
7. Any reason you cannot be fair and impartial?

Fifty-eight protested and appealed trial court's failure to ask their questions, and this is what the appellate court stated:

1. "We recognize that there is no generally accepted formula for determining the appropriate breadth and depth of the voir dire, except that the court's discretion is subject to the essential demands of fairness."
2. Quoted *Swain* rule that peremptory challenges must be "exercised without a reason stated, without inquiry and without being subject to the court's control." *Swain v. Alabama,* 380 US 202 (1965). The court added, "It is essential to explore the backgrounds and attitudes of the jurors to some extent in order to discover actual bias."
3. The court noted that the Supreme Court of the United States has held, "although not required by the Constitution, is one of the most important of the rights secured to the accused." *Porter v. U.S.,* 151 US 396 (1894). The court added, "Defendants must, upon request, be permitted sufficient inquiry into the background and attitudes of the jurors to enable them to exercise intelligently their peremptory challenges."
4. The court held that the trial judge should have permitted questions that "would have elicited a prospective juror's attitude toward dissent, and public protest against the Vietnam War, toward long hair, beards, unorthodox clothing, and lifestyles differing from his own; and toward policemen and law enforce-

ment." This is exactly what separated the defendants, known as the "Chicago Seven," from the rest of the world.

5. The court questioned the form and even the purpose of the questions, but concluded, ". . . their request raised a judicial duty to do what was reasonably practicable to enable the accused to have the benefit of the right of peremptory challenge or to prevent unfairness in the trial." *U.S. v. Dellinger*, 472 F2d 340 (7th Cir. 1972).

CONCLUSION: The court held that the most disrespectful and sometimes obnoxious conduct by the defendants could not take from them their right to a fair trial, and that trial begins with voir dire. Demand no less than that for your client!

[1.15] Challenges You Should Or Must Make Before Trial. Peremptory challenges cannot be made until trial, but challenges for cause must often be made before trial. This is true of every challenge to the array. There are two basic challenges for cause:

1. Proper Defectum, which is:
   (a) Lack of legal qualification

EXAMPLE:

School teacher in state that disqualifies school teachers from jury service.

   (b) Court has no discretion and must excuse the juror

EXAMPLE:

Relative in state where that degree of relationship disqualifies the juror.

2. Proper Affectum, which is:
   (a) A bias or prejudice

EXAMPLE:

Juror shows bias but judge must decide if it would keep him from returning an impartial verdict.

(b) Court has discretion as to whether or not to excuse the juror.

EXAMPLE:

Juror knows of case, but judge must decide if he can return impartial verdict.

HISTORICAL NOTE: At common law, in addition to Proper Defectum and Proper Affectum, courts talked about Proper Honoris Respectum, out of respect of honor or rank, and Proper De Lictum, because of the crime. These terms are seldom used today, but when they are used, it is important to know their meaning.

It is necessary to keep these classifications in mind, because a trial judge, and especially an appellate judge, may be thinking in these terms. Every challenge for cause will fit into one of these categories.

The timeliness of a challenge is important when challenging the array. Before the trial even begins certain matters should be investigated and brought to the court's attention:

1. Trial publicity, including pre-trial publicity. A move for a change of venue, or a challenge to the entire panel may result from publicity about the trial. This move is based on the belief that no jury could be selected in the jurisdiction that would be fair to your client. Take this matter up as soon as possible.
2. Local Prejudice. Publicity is not the only reason your client may be denied a fair trial within the jurisdiction. Often a popular police officer has been killed; a person of a race, religion, or nationality has been discriminated against in that county; or other prejudice runs so high in that community at that particular time, that a fair trial is not possible. Seldom are such challenges granted, but when justified, they must be made and made in time.

[1.16] Challenges You Should or Must Make During Voir Dire. Once the voir dire begins, you must continue to look for challenges that can be made for cause. It is sometimes necessary to make the challenge before voir dire ends to avoid a waiver. It is more often necessary to make the challenge for strategic reasons.

The trial judge exercises much discretion and may refuse even to consider challenges for cause until the end of the voir dire. Even then, it may be best to make the challenge for the record, especially if prejudice results to your case by that juror remaining on the panel. It also starts the judge thinking about the matter, and may give you an opportunity in front of the jury to show that you want a fair jury and you want to avoid delay by ridding the panel of an obviously prejudiced prospective juror.

Much dialogue reaches the jury while the court is deciding whether or not to grant a challenge for cause. You may or may not want the jury to hear this, and if you don't, you should move swiftly, diplomatically, and probably at side-bar to avoid a poisoning of the panel. If you feel this dialogue will help you, use the prospective juror to your advantage as long as the judge will permit and the jury will appreciate.

Poisoning The Panel. This poisoning process can either help or hurt you. If you represent the defendant in a criminal case, and a law and order prospective juror is explaining to the panel that the defendant is obviously guilty or else he would not have been arrested, you must immediately sum up the entire situation, including the members of the panel, the atmosphere of the courtroom, and how much the prospective juror can be used during the next five minutes of the trial.

EXAMPLE:

If a law and order juror is not being well received by the jury and you can make his lack of appreciation for the Constitution reflect on his thinking, you may want to keep him stage center and to use him as "Exhibit A" in a lesson in American democracy.

Q. Mr. Jones, do you really believe, as they do in Russia, that just because a man is arrested he is presumed to be guilty?
OR

Q. Mr. Jones, how many times have you read about or heard of a case where a person was found guilty and later another person admitted to the crime?
OR

Q. Mr. Jones, do you mean that my client starts this trial having to convince you he is innocent, even though our Constitution guarantees him a fair trial in which he is presumed to be innocent?

However, many prospective jurors may feel exactly as does Mr. Jones and his speech on law and order may give comfort to the others. When this poisoning of the panel occurs, *get rid of the prospective juror*!

Other Challenges For Cause. The trial judge has broad discretion in deciding whether or not a prospective juror should be dismissed from the panel for cause. There are criteria, however, and it is important that the trial lawyer be familiar with them. The trial judge may sustain a challenge for cause where:

1. There is a FIXED OPINION that keeps juror from being impartial.
   Steward v. State, 405 So.2d 404 (Al. App 1981).
2. There is a DIRECT FINANCIAL INTEREST in the outcome of the case.
   DeMott V. Smith, 486 P2d 451 (Col. 1971).
3. There is a FEELING TOWARD A PARTY that would influence his verdict. *Cole v. State*, 352 So.2d (Ala. 1977).
4. The NATURE OF THE CASE makes it impossible for prospective juror to be impartial. *Hobbs v. State*, 617 SW.2d 347 (Ark. 1981).
5. The prospective juror would require STRONGER PROOF from one party than from the other.
6. INTIMATE RELATIONSHIP with a party that would INFLUENCE THE VERDICT. *Oliver v. State*, 239 So.2d 637 (Fl. App 1970).
7. PREJUDICE AGAINST PARTY'S RACE OR NATIONALITY. *Ham v. South Carolina*, 409 US 524 (1973).

EXAMPLE:

Where difficult to forget his race during deliberation. *Larence v. Scully*, 523 FSupp 1290 (SDNY 1981). However, not merely because of unfavorable opinion of people of that race. *State v. Guiidice*, 153 NW 336 (Ia. 1913).

8. STATUTORY DISQUALIFICATION. See law of particular jurisdiction.

NOTE: Exemption from service, such as age, can be waived by prospective juror. *State v. Rodgers,* 347 SO2d 610 (Fl. 1977).

9. Where there is SINCERE, SUBSTANTIAL AND PERSISTENT DOUBT. *Commonwealth v. McBee,* 405 A2d 1297 (Pa. 1978).
10. Where prospective juror CANNOT ASSURE IMPARTIALITY. *Carter v. State,* 420 So2d 292 (Ala. 1982).
11. Where PREJUDICE AGAINST CLASS keeps a prospective juror from acting with entire impartiality. *Naylor v. Metropolitan,* St. Ry. Co., 71 P. 835 (Ka. 1903).

These criteria can best be understood by studying circumstances which prompt the cause.

EXAMPLES:

1. Tenant of party. *Harrisburg Bank v. Forster,* 8 Watts 304 (Pa.).
2. Employed by law enforcement agency. *State v. Pratt,* 244 SE2d (W.Va. 1978).
3. Recently employed one of attorneys. *Marshall Durbin, Inc. v. Tew,* 381 So2d (Miss. 1980).

Striking for cause depends upon information obtained during voir dire that gives counsel the basis for cause. This requires a looking into the mind of each person on the panel. You may inquire as to the state of mind of the prospective juror on:

1. Any matter to be submitted to the jury.
2. Any collateral matter likely to the jury unduly. *Corens v. State,* 45 A.2d 340 (Md. 1946).

During the voir dire, you should keep an eye on all members of the panel at one time. Impossible? Well, do your best! How the jury reacts to what is happening is important, and courts recognize this:

EXAMPLES:

1. A mere outburst by one juror will not cause the panel to be dismissed ("I'd give him the maximum right now"). *State v. Taylor,* 324 SW2d 643, 76 ALR2d 671 (Mo. 1959).

2. "I have heard so much against the defendant that I am prejudiced" disqualifies the juror, but not the panel. *Coates v. State*, 140 SE 287 (Ga. 1927).

Courts talk about that unusual outburst that could poison the panel, but have not found one. Be prepared—yours may be the first!

[1.17] Challenges You Should Or Must Make After Voir Dire. When voir dire is completed, it is time to look at the panel and to determine whether or not you are satisfied with it. If you are, any further action must be made carefully and only to protect a point on appeal. If you are not satisfied, you should review the possibility of challenging the array.

Any technical objection as to any procedure that occurred after the voir dire began can be raised at the end of voir dire. This often depends upon state statute or local rule, and such objections should be considered. The more likely objection, however, will be raised as to the fact that your client has not received a fair and impartial jury. Prejudice will usually be found in a poisoning of the panel or discriminatory use of peremptory challenges.

Poisoning Of Panel On Matters That Must Wait Until After Voir Dire. The fact individual jurors may be prejudiced does not constitute a basis for attacking the entire panel. *U.S. v. Gordon*, 253 F.2d 177 (7th Cir. 1958). This was true even where one of the prejudiced jurors made an outburst during voir dire. *State v. Taylor*, 324 SW2d 643, 76 ALR2d 671 (Mo. 1959).

If a poisoning takes place, such as mention of insurance in an improper manner, a motion for a mistrial is the proper remedy. This can be made during voir dire or at the end of voir dire. The judge, an attorney, or a witness can make a statement that forms the basis for such a motion. The judge will be given wide discretion, but the basic question is whether or not the jurors can still return a fair and just verdict for both sides.

Discriminatory Use Of Peremptory Challenges. The courts have until recently refused to question the use of peremptory challenges. In 1880 the Supreme Court of the United States made an exception when it decided that systematically excluding prospective jurors because of race or color violates the Fourteenth Amendment. *Stauder v. West Virginia*, 100 US 303 (1880).

Even as late as 1964 the majority of the court held that questioning the prosecution's use of peremptory challenges, even though no blacks had served on the jury in recent years, would be "wholly at odds with the peremptory challenge system as we know it." *Swain v. Alabama*, 380 US 202 (1964). In 1986 the court shifted the burden by holding that "purposeful discrimination" can be shown by defendant's case without looking into the prosecutor's mind. *Batson v. Kentucky*, 476 US 79 (1986).

This began a series of cases from the circuits making "impartial" a real part of impartial jury. *Clark v. City of Bridgeport*, 645 F2d 890 (D.Conn 1986). At least one court took the position that this protection applies to civil as well as criminal cases. *King v. County of Nassau*, 581 FSupp 493 (E.D.N.Y. 1984).

The Court has held that there is no constitutional right to question about racial attitudes during voir dire. *Ristaino v. Ross*, 424 US 589 (1976). The court has granted an exception where defendant is charged with a capital offense involving interracial violence. *Turner v. Murray*, 476 US 28 (1986).

By 1989 the courts were recognizing the importance of *Batson*. Citing that case as authority, one court required defendant to give a rationally neutral explanation of why two blacks were stricken (leaving an all-white jury) in a case in which a black was suing a police officer for violation of civil rights. *Fludd v. Dykes*, 863 F2d 822 (11th Cir. 1989). The court pointed out that peremptories cannot be used to rid the panel of a particular race.

When the Supreme Court of Florida held that even a white defendant is entitled to blacks on his jury, controversy followed. Defense counsel Bill McClain said, "The court is pushing toward greater fairness in our system by eliminating racial discrimination," but prosecutor George Bateh said that it proved the court is "out of touch with reality." *St. Petersburg Times*, p. B-1, August 13, 1989.

At the end of voir dire consider:

1. Any objection that should have been made earlier—make it! (Better late than never.)
2. If you are satisfied with the jury make only an objection that can be a basis of appeal—make sure you do not lose a good jury.
3. If you feel the jurors have been poisoned for any reason—object to the panel.
4. If you feel the opposition has misused the peremptories for any reason, object to the panel.

[1.18] What You Must Know About A Juror's Educational Background. A woman once told me that she was excused from the jury because she was "too educated." The very next day I heard a jury selection expert explain why her client obtained a multi-million dollar verdict; she had advised the client to choose a jurisdiction in which the jurors would be highly educated.

Today there is a great need to understand complicated issues. There is also a more intelligent jury based on the abundance of information available outside the classroom. The education and intelligence factors must be considered carefully.

CAVEAT: In considering the ability of jurors to grasp issues:

1. Choose a jurisdiction (if there is a choice) with this in mind.
2. Consider prospective juror's educational background.
3. Consider "technical" background versus "liberal arts" background.
4. Consider experiences that may substitute for educational background.
5. Consider the type of case being tried.

You would not, of course, ask, "How educated are you?," and you would not ask, "What college did you attend?" of a person who may not have attended college. It is better to ask, "What schools have you attended?"

Plaintiffs should avoid occupations and backgrounds, such as accounting, engineering, science, and mathematics, that are technical and exact. Complex cases need intelligent jurors, and special knowledge in the area of dispute requires special consideration of whether he will help or hurt. The more educated the juror, the more likely that juror will become foreman, so the more important it will be to determine whether or not that juror will be favorable to your cause. Use your voir dire to learn how juror's education may affect his or her verdict.

EXAMPLES:

"Mrs. Jones, I understand you are a college graduate. What kind of courses did you study?" (A sociology major who is now in business may still have some of the concerns that caused the juror to study sociology.)

"Which college or university did you attend?" (Some are more liberal or conservatively-oriented than others.)

"How did you enjoy college?" (The fact that a Southerner did not like school in the North, or a Northerner did not like school in the South, may have been because of philosophical differences.)

"Was your entire college experience spent at Engineering School?" (One professor has claimed that since 80 percent of what is taught at engineering school is engineering, engineers often do not have a broad approach to problems.)

"What were you best at in school?" All studies show that in civil cases the "exact" people are not good plaintiff's jurors. Those who study accounting, engineering, mathematics, science, and computers do not usually put as much emotion into their verdict as those who studied history, art, or literature.

In criminal cases, the studies raise a question as to how "prosecution prone" exact jurors are. They "expect" the defendant to comply with the law, but they also "expect" the prosecution to do its job and to tie up all the loose ends for the jury.

[1.19] Learn About Occupational History. How a person spends, or has spent, his working hours is extremely important. The occupation listed on the computer printout is only the beginning of the inquiry.

CAVEAT: You must learn the following about the juror's occupational history:

1. What "kind of work" he does.
2. If retired, determine former occupation.
3. Determine spouse's occupation.
4. Is there conflict?
5. Does occupation make him or her foreman material?
6. Does his work experience make him friendly or unfriendly to your lawsuit?
7. Get the full history. People change jobs and careers today.

Plaintiffs generally strike and insurance company lawyers keep the "exact" people: accountants, engineers, scientists. There is a growing

feeling among courtroom psychologists that computer operators who work with exactness all day lean toward the defense in civil cases.

What do people talk about on the job? At an insurance company there may be talk about people who sue who are not entitled to recover. On the construction job there may be talk about companies that take advantage of people.

Learn to adjust! A person who deals with figures all day usually is not a good plaintiff's juror, but if figures are important to be understood, he may be helpful. A construction worker who earned good money may be more conservative once he retires and may count his money more closely.

Women listen to their husbands at the dinner table, but a woman who works may be more independent and form her own opinions. Nurses may feel like part of the medical profession being sued, but are even more likely to know that doctors make mistakes and to resent superiors.

One study showed members of certain occupations voted for plaintiff in the following percentages:

Skilled tradesmen	86%
Professional people	70%
Clerical workers	68%
Salesmen	67%
Blue collar workers	66%
Housewives	63%
Self-employed	62%
Retired	62%
Executives	61%

Personal Injury Valuation Handbook, Vol. 8, Jury Verdict Research, Inc., Special Report 104 (1989).

CAVEAT: Most people want to talk about their work, and if they don't you want to know that, too. Discussing occupational history should be a pleasant and helpful part of voir dire.

EXAMPLES:

"How long have you worked at . . ." (People are proud to have been on the same job for a long period of time, and that may also tell you something about the juror.)

"What did you do at MAC?" (The juror's job is important to that juror and you should consider it important.)

What other kind of employment have you had?" (This may tell you military history, where he lived, if he travelled with his work and something about his financial status and supervisory position he might hold or have held in the past.)

CAVEAT: Every question you ask relative to occupational history does two things:

1. It tells you much about the juror.
2. It gives the juror an opportunity to open up and talk about the one subject he may want to talk about.

[1.20] The Importance Of Marital Status. The marital status of the prospective juror must be explored, including present and past status. Counsel must consider how all of this affects the prospective juror's impartiality. During voir dire, you must:

1. Weigh the effect of marital status.
2. Find out if divorce is a factor.
3. Find out if death of a spouse is a factor.
4. Determine if any children were born to the marriage.
5. See how role of spouse or parent will enable the juror to identify with clients or witnesses.
6. Weigh the effect of a long-term marriage with question of stability.
7. Remember that single women are more apt to be in the work force.

Most courts now supply attorneys with a computer printout that includes information as to marital status. Do not rely upon this. It is often inaccurate and robs you of a chance to talk with the juror about "family," a subject that people "chat" about outside the courtroom. Discuss marriage in a way that:

1. Helps your credibility.
   "You work at Heilman's? My wife and I eat there often. Do you remember seeing me there? (A lawyer's marriage does add to his credibility.)
2. Avoids any appearance of prying.
   "I understand your son attends the same school as mine. Have our families met at a PTA meeting or something?" (This opens the door for, "I don't think so. My husband and I are divorced and I work at the restaurant at night so have been unable to attend PTA meetings.")
3. Tells you as much as possible about the juror.
   "Mrs. Jones, I understand you work for the police department. Do you talk about your job at home?" (This leads to dialogue between husband and wife, from which you learn how juror feels.)

[1.21] Question Juror's Familiarity With Facts Of Case. Knowledge of the case does not automatically disqualify the prospective juror, but it does open the door both for disqualification for cause and for inquiry that enables counsel to properly use his peremptories. Once that door is open, an in-depth inquiry is in order.

Courts have given the trial judge broad discretion in keeping a prospective juror who has knowledge of the case. *Kunk v. Howell*, 289 SW2d 874, 73 ALR2d 1304 (1956). In Kunk the court stated: "If the knowledge of the juror is of such a nature as to raise a strong inference or presumption of bias he should be excused. But a knowledge of undisputed facts or of facts merely collateral or incidental will not render incompetent a juror who disclaims any opinion on the merits of the case."

The fact that a juror walked by the site of the accident for three years did not disqualify him. *Genova v. Kansas City*, SW2d 38 (Mo. App 1953) ("would in no way affect my verdict"). Juror who knew plaintiff and several of his witnesses and had heard "something of the shooting" was qualified. *Morrow v. Flores*, 225 SW2d 621 (Tex. App 1949) ("would not influence my verdict").

HISTORICAL NOTE: At early common law, jurors were expected to base their verdict on what they knew before trial, as well as evidence they heard at trial. *Schmidt v. New York Union Mut. F. Ins. Co.*, 67 Mass 529 (Mass. 1854). This ancient doctrine has been repealed by time and decisions, but the drafters of the Federal Rules of Evidence thought it necessary to specifically provide that a juror cannot testify in a case. *Federal Rules of Evidence*, Rule 606(a).

Where a juror knew of the case before trial and was permitted to remain on the jury, he could not, during deliberation, talk about that which was not in evidence at the trial. *Merrit v. Ash Grove Lime & Portland Cement Co.*, 285 NW 97 (Neb. 1939). Excusing jurors is seldom prejudicial error, even though a juror knows about the case. *Lewis v. State*, 70 So2d 790 (Ala. 1954).

Where in second day of trial juror admits knowledge of case but parties consent to continuance of trial, any objection is waived. *Cook v. Kansas City*, 214 SW2d 430 (Mo. 1948). The court cannot let a juror restore himself to competency, *Laverty v. Gray*, 3 Masrt 617 (La. 1815), but must decide whether any opinion formed is "positive," or "of a light and transient character." *Smith v. Ames*, 4 Ill 76 (Ill. 1841).

CAVEAT: The juror's knowledge of the case may:

1. Lead to excusing for cause. If juror witnessed an accident, or for any reason formed an opinion that would prevent a fair and impartial verdict, the juror should be excused for cause. SUGGESTION: Try to get first crack at this juror. If you want the juror to go, and opposing counsel or the judge says, "You can still give both sides a fair trial, can't you"? the juror thinks he should say, "Yes." If you are able to show him how unfair it would be for him to remain on the jury he leans toward answers that would disqualify him.

EXAMPLE:

> "I am sure you have a lot of respect for your family doctor and if there is a conflict between what he and another doctor say, I am sure you would lean toward your doctor. This really wouldn't be fair to my client, would it?" ALSO, if you want the juror to say that the opposite will be true and you will be asking the "you can still give a fair trial" line of questions, then you will still want first crack at him, or will at least follow through at first opportunity.

2. Cause you to use a peremptory challenge. How to use peremptories is what voir dire is all about. Here is where you do every-

thing possible to strike for cause, but if that does not work, then you must feed all this into your computer-like mind and must decide if this is a juror who must go.

3. Require you to determine whether this knowledge will make him a favorable or unfavorable juror. If what he knows will hurt you, he must go. If what he knows will help you, he should stay. The kind of case and kind of client may help decide this. If your client is not really a nice guy, you hope no juror knows anything about him. If the other party's conduct was outrageous, you hope someone on the jury knows how outrageous.
4. Open the door for discussion of the case. Before anyone even answers, you have a right to explain the facts briefly. Once a juror raises his hand the door is open, and you have an opportunity to tell more of your story.

[1.22] Does Juror Know Party, Attorney, Or Others? Your client will assume anyone who knows the other party will automatically be dismissed. That is simply not the case and your job just begins when obtaining such information about a prospective juror.

You must obtain and use information relative to any relationship of a juror and party:

1. You must inquire as to such a relationship.
   Q. Do any of you know the defendant?
   Q. Do you know any of his family or friends?
   Q. Mr. Jones runs a ship on Fourth Street. Have any of you been in his shop?
2. You must pursue circumstances that might suggest such a relationship.
   Q. Mrs. Smith, you and the defendant are both teachers. Do you know him from teacher's meetings or any other association you may have as teachers?
   Q. Mr. Black, I notice you live in the same neighborhood as the defendant. Do you see him or hear anything about him from the neighbors?

Q. Mrs. Townsend, you said that he looked familiar. Can you remember where you have seen him? He goes to the Methodist church on Turner Avenue. Does that help? He has been a Boy Scout leader for years. Have you had any sons in the Scouts? (You can tell just about everything good about your client you can think of while pursuing this, but don't overplay it).

3. You must follow up with questions that might show bias or prejudice.

   Q. How long have you known the defendant?

   Q. How often do you see him?

   Q. Have you ever had any financial relations with him?

   Q. Do you have the same friends?

   Q. What do you talk about when you are together?

   Q. If you had to return a verdict against him, would that place you in an embarrassing or uncomfortable position?

   Q. Has he talked to you about this case?

   Q. If one of our witnesses says something unfavorable about the defendant, how would you react to this in view of your relationship with the defendant? Do you think you may be less apt to believe the witness than others on the jury?

4. Try to get unfavorable juror struck for cause, based on the relationship.

   Q. You agree, do you not, Mr. Jones, that in fairness to my client, and in view of your relationship to the defendant, you should be excused? I guess so. And, though you would do your best as a juror, you really couldn't forget this friendship and it would enter into your deliberation? I guess so. And so, you really would be unable to return a verdict that is fair and impartial? I guess that is true. "Your Honor, I ask that the juror be excused." (Don't turn him over to the judge until you have a commitment or the judge may commit him the other way.)

5. If the juror is not excused for cause, you must then decide whether to use a peremptory challenge. This juror will be high on your list and should be struck, unless you are caught in the old voir dire numbers game.

If the attorney-client relationship ever existed between a juror and opposing counsel or his firm, you must:

1. Try to get juror to admit bias.
   - Q. Have you had personal contact with the attorney?
   - Q. How many times have you met with him?
   - Q. I assume you would take his word on a matter, or you wouldn't have hired him as your attorney, is that right?
   - Q. You have never met me before today, and really know nothing about me at this time, except that I have been retained by Mrs. Smith in this lawsuit, is that right?
   - Q. I assume that under these circumstances it is only natural that if I say one thing and opposing counsel says another thing, that you might lean a little toward him, is that right?
   - Q. In fairness, do you feel you should be excused from this jury?
2. Explore the possibility of financial conflict.
   - Q. Have you had any financial dealings with this law firm? Yes, we have made investments together in some limited partnerships.
   - Q. Do those investments depend in any way upon both of you continuing to invest money in the partnership? Yes.
   - Q. Then you could profit from his success in the courtroom? That is unlikely, but . . .
3. Learn what kind of legal matters were involved.
   - Q. I don't want to pry into your personal affairs, and I certainly don't want you to discuss any communications with your attorney, but could you tell me what kind of legal matters were involved? He represented our corporation.
   - Q. And what kind of a corporation was it? Public relations.
   - Q. Now, Mr. Smith, you told us you teach at the University. Are you also part owner of a public relations firm? Yes.
   - Q. And who are some of the clients of this firm? Our biggest client is the insurance industry.
4. Try to get juror excused for cause.
   - Q. Mr. Smith, you have known opposing counsel for five years.

You have had him as your lawyer for a business which has been telling the public only one side of the tort reform story. Don't you think it would be difficult to be fair and impartial to both sides?

5. If you don't get juror excused for cause, then he is an excellent candidate for a peremptory.

Nearly every judge will let you ask questions as to a prospective juror's being related to a lawyer, judge, officer, prosecutor, or court employee, but such a relationship is not a cause for excusing that juror unless the relative is directly involved in the case being tried. Even if the relative is directly involved, it is amazing how many courts still keep the juror as long as he mutters such magical words as "I will be impartial," or "that won't affect my verdict."

When a prospective juror is related to a lawyer, judge, police officer, prosecutor, or court employee, you must:

Inquire further:

Q. WHO is the relative?

Q. HOW OFTEN do you see him?

Q. WHAT do you talk about?

Q. HAVE YOU DISCUSSED . . . ?

Q. WOULD this affect your serving on this jury?

The reason the judge should permit you to pursue such questioning is that you have a right to an impartial jury and that people who talk to certain people on a regular basis acquire preconceived ideas. A lawyer who spends all day in court suing an insurance company usually does not tell his friends and relatives about how great insurance companies are, and his opposing counsel is not talking about the unfortunate people who are injured in auto accidents. A police officer who has a list of people he arrested who were "let off" because of "technicalities" does not waste much time talking about the constitutional rights of the accused.

A judge was a lawyer before he became a judge, and his views may be based upon that experience or upon new experiences he has had from the bench. Court reporters, bailiffs, and other court employees are very much a part of what goes on at the courthouse. They tell people what they think, and often what they think is based on certain experiences they have had.

The appellate decisions are full of cases in which the bailiff had given jurors under his custody "inside information" that prejudiced them. Court officials do have interesting things to say, and they do say them to friends and relatives.

The real danger in friends and relatives of law enforcement officers is the "law and order" syndrome. During the 1960s, certain radicals called the police "pigs," and much of the nation divided themselves into those who wanted "law and order" and those who wanted rights.

Knowing those who are close to the court system often leans a juror toward what he has heard from these friends or relatives and this subject must be fully explored:

1. To find possible reason to excuse for cause.
2. To help determine which jurors should be excused with peremptories.
3. Avoid possible setting aside of a verdict, if a relationship is not disclosed that should have been disclosed.

[1.23] How To Ask The Insurance Question. Appellate decisions are full of suggestions that the purpose of voir dire is a very narrow one that would not permit a question that would merely convey a message to the jury. However, the plaintiff's counsel may want the jury to know Farmer Brown will not have to sell his farm to pay the judgment, and failure to ask "the insurance question" may constitute a breach of duty to his client. In asking the "Insurance Question," remember:

1. Most courts will permit:

   Q. Are you or any member of your family employed by or have a financial interest in Ajax Insurance Company? (Some states permit "an insurance company" but not the name of the company unless further questioning becomes necessary.)
   Kiernan v. Van Schaik, 347 F.2d 775 (3rd Cir. 1965). See Appendix E for Opinion and Comment.

2. One federal court held:
   (a) The Court MUST permit, when requested:
      Q. Are any of you employed by or stockholders in an insurance company which is engaged in the casualty insurance business?
      Q. Are any of you engaged in the general insurance business or are you an agent for a casualty insurance company?
      Q. Have any of you ever worked as a claims investigator or insurance adjuster?
   (b) The court MAY, in the court's discretion, permit when requested:
      Q. Have any of you read any article or advertising in periodical publications which tend to indicate a relationship between the amount of personal injury verdicts and increases in insurance premiums?
      Q. (If any of the jurors answer the preceding question in the affirmative) Notwithstanding an opinion which you might have formed regarding the subject of the advertising or articles just mentioned, would you be able to decide the question of liability and damages in this case solely on the evidence and the law without being influenced by such an opinion?
      Kiernan v. Van Schaik, 3437 F.2d 775 (3rd Cir. 1965). See Appendix E of this book for Opinion and Comment.

There is language in *Kiernan* that every plaintiff's attorney should memorize and that every attorney who defends insurance companies should be ready to meet:

> "A wide discretion necessarily resides in the trial court, which is familiar with the nature of the case, the demeanor of prospective jurors and the general circumstances which surround the opening of the trial."
> BUT:
> "This broad discretion as to questions to be asked on voir dire is subject to the essential demands of fairness."
> LOCAL PRACTICE MUST GIVE WAY WHEN IT:
> ". . . drastically curtails . . . the right of challenge for cause. The rejection

of appropriate questions on voir dire for such erroneous reasons amounts to an abuse of discretion."
AND:
"A jury's impartiality cannot be assumed without inquiry, as in the case of a judge."
AND:
"Litigants therefore have the right, at the least, to some surface information regarding the prospective jurors. Such information may uncover ground for challenge for cause. If it does not, it will be available in the intelligent use of the peremptory challenge."
THE COURT STATED THAT KEEPING INSURANCE FROM THE JURY:
". . . is based on the desire to assure a fair trial to a defendant, and it may not be permitted to destroy the plaintiff's equal right to a fair trial."
AND THEN ADDED:
"If the question of racial bias may be opened up for reasoned judgment regardless of fears of unleashing an ugly, smouldering racial bigotry, there is even less cause to stifle inquiry regarding bias against personal injury claims because of fear that it may let loose the realization of the existence of casualty insurance."
THEN NOTED:
"A juror's identification with the business of investigating and paying claims affects his impartiality as significantly as does a juror's employment by a lawyer who is a specialist in prosecuting such claims."
AND CONCLUDED:
"The word 'insurance' is not outlawed from the courtroom as a word of magical evil. Jurors are not unaware that insurance is at large in the world and its mention will not open to them a previously unknown realm. If it is in fact more realistic for the judge to dissolve the phantom by open talk in the courtroom than to have it run loose in the unconfined speculation of the jury room." Circuit Judge Waterman.
HOWEVER, another court held:
"Knowledge of defendant's insurance has traditionally been treated as fruit of the forbidden tree. Courts have consequently guarded juror's ears from statements tending to show that the defendant in a negligence action carried liability insurance." *Stehura v. Short, 315 NE2d 492* (Ohio App 1974).

Some states have codified the question. Minnesota provides that the defendant must disclose the name of the company, plaintiff may inquire (collectively but not to individual jurors) as to whether "any of them have any interest as policyholders, stockholders, officers, agents or otherwise in the insurance company or companies interested." If an affirmative answer, counsel may inquire "as to his or their interest in such company, including any relationship or connection with the local agent of such interested company, to determine whether such interest or relationship disqualifies such juror." Rule 31, *Minnesota Code of Rules*.

Local practice can be extremely important, and counsel should be sure he knows that practice. In Missouri, judges would often say, "I'll let you ask the question, but don't make it your first or last question, and don't call attention to it." Failure to follow such a practice can result in a mistrial.

Mistrials and new trials have also been granted because of conduct of a juror. Telling other jurors of insurance, or basing a vote on the fact the insurance company will pay have been such a basis. *Littrell v. Smith*, 311 SW2d 204 (Tenn. 1958).

[1.24] Establish Relationship With Experts And Other Witnesses. Discovery has told you who the witnesses will be. Voir dire should tell you how the jurors will react to those witnesses.

In one case plaintiff's counsel learned during voir dire that a juror was related to his expert witness, but did nothing. That night he told his expert not to talk with the juror, but was told that he had already told him he was going to testify. The following day defense counsel learned of the relationship, but did not move for mistrial. HELD: defendant was not entitled to new trial. *Southern Railway Company v. Miler*, 285 F.2d 202 (6th Cir. 1960). The court felt that disclosing the relationship would have been "better conduct" for plaintiff's counsel. It seems the appellate court would have done better had it based its decision upon waiver, rather than upon the sound discretion of the trial judge.

It has been held that even a relative of a witness can serve on the jury. *Tidmore v. Mills*, 21 So2d 782 (Ala. App 1947). In another case, a judge was commended by the appellate bench for, on his own, dismissing a juror whose brother was going to testify. *Core v. Core's Admrs.*, 124 SE 453 (Va. 1924).

Discover if juror knows the witnesses.

1. Ask the question if the judge or opposing witness has not

   In Florida the judge usually reads the list of witnesses from the pre-trial order and asks if any jurors know any of the witnesses. If the judge does not do your job for you, be sure it is done!

2. Be sure the simple question is enough

   Q. Judge Allbritton read a list of witnesses to you and you indicated you do not know any of them. I think I should point out that Dr. Jennings is the doctor whose name was in the paper a few months ago. Did any of you read that article? Does my mentioning this cause any of you to remember the name?

3. Where juror does know a witness, learn how important this will be

   Q. Mr. Smith, you say that you know Dr. Jones. Has he treated you? He will be giving an opinion and another doctor will be giving a somewhat different opinion in this case. Do you think your having been treated by Dr. Jones will cause you to lean a little in his favor?

4. If you think the juror will hurt you, pursue an argument to excuse for cause

   In *Core*, more than fifty years ago, the Court took the enlightened position that jurors must be "absolutely impartial," and that the court must avoid "any suspicion of unfairness." PURSUE THIS APPROACH, BUT LAY THE FOUNDATION FOR IT!

   Q. It is only natural that you will lean toward the testimony of this witness, isn't that true?

   Q. So, this will make it difficult for you to return a verdict that is fair to both sides, isn't that true?

The nature of the witness's testimony has been considered an important factor in deciding whether or not to excuse the juror. In most instances, however, the judge lets the prospective juror tell him whether or not that juror can bring back a fair and impartial verdict.

[1.25] Interrogate Fully As To Experience In Similar Matters. The courts have wrestled with the problem of how similar the matter must be that a juror was involved in to disqualify that juror for the case to be tried. Counsel must explore this area carefully, because he does not want a juror who has already decided against him.

Where a juror said during voir dire that she did not have relatives with arm defects, but during deliberations did remember she had a niece and nephew with such defects, and mentioned it to the other jurors who were discussing the possibility of people with such defects leading normal lives, this was basis for a new trial. *Strickland v. Tegler and Northland Obstetrics & Gynecology*, No. 40,248 2-28-89 (Ma. WD 1989).

It is the defense counsel in a civil case who is more concerned about "similar matters" because of previous claims. In one leading case, the court refused to grant a new trial on the basis of two jurors who did not disclose prior suits in which they were parties, where:

1. One juror had not told of a suit in which his wife had not paid for, and the wife testified she had, in fact, kept her husband from knowing about the suit.
2. Another juror had not told of a suit in which she was named as a party, where the suit was ten years ago, she did not know she was a party and had never talked to a lawyer about it. *Schiles v. Schaefer*, 710 SW2d 254, 66 ALR4th 465 (Mo. App 1986).

The court held that regarding concealments of information by jurors, "the factual issues, including the question of intent, are for the trial court to resolve." The court added, ". . . a juror might withhold information for purely personal reasons unrelated to the action being tried, and while such conduct cannot be condoned, neither should it result in a new trial."

The previous lawsuit problem must be met or a good verdict may ultimately be set aside. Notice how Jim Hulverson, one of the nation's leading trial lawyers, handled this in the above-cited *Schiles* case:

> "Let me ask, folks, there's a thing called a lawsuit. That usually means somebody goes down and files a paper in court. Then there's a claim. That means someone says he has an action or claim against you. Those are two different kinds of situations. But I want to address both of them because they're both important to both sides of the lawsuit.
>
> "We really want to know if any of you folks—I don't care about domestic relations, I don't care about divorces and things like that. I don't care about collection where Famous Barr might have dunned me or you or any of us for a bill or things like that. What I do care about is any kind of claim or lawsuit where anybody got hurt or claimed to have been hurt."
>
> LATER:
>
> "I hate to dwell on this, folks, but I can't impress on you the significance

of it. There's nothing in the world worse than getting a verdict and having them run downstairs, check the records, and say, Hey, juror Jones forgot to tell you about this broken thumb he had in Oregon 12 years ago."

Reasons jurors give for not telling of prior litigation:

1. Didn't understand the question.
2. Forgot about it.
3. Didn't think you meant this kind of lawsuit.
4. Thought you meant what was pending.
5. Didn't hear the question.
6. Thought he meant me, not my family.

Avoid misunderstanding by being perfectly clear!

[1.26] Look Carefully For Juror's Expertise On Key Issues. Expert witnesses are playing an increasing important role in lawsuits, and whether or not the jury decides in your favor may well depend upon its faith in your expert. You must face up to a special problem when another expert is sitting as a juror. When a prospective juror is an expert on a key issue of the case, decide how good your expert testimony will be and how much expertise this "expert" juror actually has.

EXAMPLE:

During voir dire I found that a prospective juror had been an electrician for nearly twenty years. An important issue of the lawsuit was what caused a fire. Opposing counsel would surely argue that my client was negligent in making an electrical installation.

I called my client aside and talked cold turkey. "How good is our expert?" He convinced me that they could not shake him and at trial they did not. They dismissed the case just before it went to the jury and if they had not, the electrician we left on the jury would have become either foreman, our in-house expert, or both.

There are degrees of expertise, and there are jurors who talk a good game and those who know what they are doing. Beware of both! The true expert can murder you if you do not have a very sound basis for any theory you submit to them. The juror who imagines he is an expert may convince other jurors that he is and may subject them to some rather unusual expertise.

If a prospective juror claims expertise on an issue of your lawsuit:

1. Learn exactly how much of an expert he is.
2. Determine how persuasive he will be, other than through use of his expertise.
3. Learn for sure, how good your expert evidence is going to be.
4. If you decide he must go, let him go gently without other jurors deciding you were the one who did not want a juror who knows too much about the main issue to be decided.

[1.27] Use Prior Jury Service To Discover Attitude Of Juror. It is difficult to think of a case in which a trial lawyer would not want to know of a prospective juror's previous experience. Often some information on this matter is given to the attorneys on the jury printout or on other pretrial communication.

It has been held that failure to answer the question properly can be a basis for a new trial. *Nuchols v. Commonwealth of Kentucky*, 226 SW2d 796, 12 ALR2d 1478 (Ky App 1950). Though this case involved a juror who had served within the past 12 years and who could have been removed for cause, the court talked about peremptory challenges and the "intelligent exercise" of challenges.

Prior courts had applied the old rule that regardless of how much a prospective juror failed to answer correctly, the accused had no right to a new trial because the juror was a "fair juror," the accused was "manifestly guilty," and the defendant had a "fair trial." *Harris v. People*, 160 P2d 372 (Colo. 1945). A strong dissent in *Harris* pointed out that the question is not whether or not the juror was impartial, but whether or not "a proper tribunal was established."

Even if a state or federal law or rule provides that the juror not serve because of recent service, failure to disclose the fact of prior service is not a basis for a new trial. *Bell v. State*, 46 SE 533 (Ga. App 1915); *Brickey v. U.S.*, 123 F2d 341 (8th Cir. 1941). One court points out that the juror merely "failed to respond" and did not actually make a false statement. *Wilder v. State*, 25 Ohio St 555 (Ohio 1874).

There is an overlapping of the "prior jury" problem and the problem of "similar litigation" and even that of "similar experience." See *Durham v. State*, 188 SW2d 555; 160 LR 746 (Tenn. 1945). The bottom line is, however, that prior knowledge of the pending case is insufficient to challenge for cause, so what one knows of similar cases is hardly enough to excuse a juror without using a peremptory challenge. *State v. Walton*, 796 P2d 1017 (Ariz. 1989).

Prior jury service is important.

1. Explain the difference between burden of proof in a civil case and in a criminal case (beyond a reasonable doubt).

   Q. Mr. Jones, was the case you served on a civil or criminal one?

   Q. I am sure the judge instructed you in that case that before you can return a verdict of guilty, you must find the defendant guilty beyond a reasonable doubt?

   Q. This is a civil case and Judge Richardson will instruct you at the end of trial that my client must only prove his case with a preponderance of evidence. Do you understand that?

   Q. Would you have any problem following this instruction?

2. Learn what you can from juror's prior jury service

   Q. During the jury deliberation, did you participate in the discussion?

   Q. Were you satisfied with the outcome of the case?

   Q. Would you have rather served on another kind of case? Why?

3. Consider the kind of case

   Q. Mrs. Jones, you indicate it was a criminal case. What kind of crime was involved?

   Q. Mrs. Smith, you indicate it was an auto accident case. Was there any question as to who was at fault?

   Q. Mr. Brown, you indicate that it was a products liability case. Do you understand there are different laws that apply to this case?

4. Learn how this has affected juror's attitude toward the justice system

   Q. Were you satisfied with the verdict?

   Q. Was the overall experience a satisfactory one?

Q. Do you really want to serve again?

Q. Would you be able to base your verdict in this case on the evidence and law of this case, and not refer to what happened in the other case?

Q. Do you think the jury system works?

[1.28] Discuss Willingness And Ability To Follow Instructions. There is no problem asking the jury if it will "follow the law," even if it disagrees with it. The difference in decisions comes with asking the jurors if they would follow the law under certain circumstances.

Usually there is no problem with the burden of proof and reasonable doubt inquiries when tied into the instruction question or when "the range of penalty" inquiry occurs in death penalty cases. Courts become concerned, however, when counsel comes even close to getting a commitment as to how the jury will decide the case to be decided.

Be sure jurors can and will follow instructions.

1. Give proper respect to the role of the judge

   Q. His Honor, Judge Weber will instruct you as to the law . .

2. Avoid discussions of legal theories

   Q. Under Florida law I need only prove this case with the greater weight of evidence. (Permitted in most states.)

   Q. Under Florida law the degree of care in which a doctor's performance of his duties is such as to subject him to liability (Permitted in most states.)

3. Cover law on basic areas (which most courts permit), such as:

   (a) burden of proof

   (b) reasonable doubt

   (c) failure to testify

   (d) credibility of witnesses

   (e) lawyer comments are not evidence

4. Don't seek commitment on specific issues.

EXAMPLE:

Q. Would you agree that this doctor should be liable in damages if he. . . .

5. Don't compound the hypothetical problem.

EXAMPLE OF WHAT NOT TO DO:

Q. Will you decide for my client if I show. . . .

6. If you find a law is not in your favor:
   (a) Cover it diplomatically under the "discuss with jury your weakness" part of the voir dire
   (b) But don't make a big deal of it as a rule of law.

EXAMPLE:

Prosecutor will usually not spend much time discussing the law of reasonable doubt.

7. Recognize the changing law under which we practice.

EXAMPLE:

A judge permitted prosecutor to read both potential instructions to jury and state law as to first degree murder in the second voir dire of capital case. *State v. Holt*, 758 SW2d 182 (Mo. App 1988). (New situations bring new laws that might apply in old situations.)

8. Inform jurors they may not agree with the law.

Q. We have all read about a law we didn't agree with and if we were senators we may try to change a few of them. In this trial we are not allowed to change any law, in fact each of you will be asked to swear under oath that you will follow the law. If you serve on this jury, will you have any problem following all of the law his Honor gives you, even if you don't agree with a particular part of the law?

Q. You may remember that following the Oliver North trial, one juror said that Colonel North was his hero; yet he voted to convict him of three felonies because he was following the law. How would you feel about that? Do you think it takes an honest and sincere juror to vote that way? Do you think

> you could take your job as a juror that seriously and could keep your oath and follow the law, even if it meant finding your hero guilty?

[1.29] Discuss Burden of Proof. The trial lawyer has the right to know whether or not the prospective juror has formed any opinions, and that forms the basis for questioning about burden of proof. Judges who are strict in avoiding questions of law or instructions nevertheless do let counsel inquire as to an understanding of burden of proof.

Counsel usually approaches the question as a follow-up on the question relating to prior jury service.

> Q. When you were a juror in the criminal case, you were working under the principle that the prosecution had to prove its case beyond a reasonable doubt. Do you understand that in this case we need only prove our case with preponderance of the evidence?

The burden of proof question is not, however, limited to that use. Often the defendant in a civil case will state:

> "Under the law of our state, I don't need to prove anything. It is up to the other side to prove its case. Do you see anything unfair about this? Will you have any problem operating under that principle?"

Talk about burden of proof with prospective jurors:

1. Some jurors think about reasonable doubt because of:
   (a) Prior jury experience and
   (b) Watching too much television.
   So, this means you must:
   (a) Educate jurors to proper proof requirement and
   (b) Get rid of those who will not be educated to this difference.

EXAMPLES:

> Q. You understand, Mr. Smith, that I need only prove my client's case with a preponderance of evidence?

Q. It is like a baseball player running to first base. If the ball gets there just a fraction of a second before the runner, he is out; he doesn't have to be out by several feet, or if one person has a million dollars and another person has a million dollars and a penny, the second one is wealthier than the first, because it doesn't matter by how much. Do you see what I mean?

Q. Would you have any problem bringing back a verdict for my client, even though the proof was not more than just the greater weight?

2. When representing the defendant, be sure jury will hold plaintiff to proper proof.

   Q. You understand that I don't have to prove anything. If plaintiff does not prove his case with a preponderance of evidence, we win and we go home. Does everyone understand?

   Q. Do you have any problem with this?

   Q. Do you see the problem I would have if I had to prove that something did not exist, compared to the requirement plaintiff prove what he claims does exist?

3. In criminal case talk about reasonable doubt and presumption of innocence.

Selecting jurors who understand and really believe in the American constitution is the trial lawyer's challenge during the voir dire of a criminal case. Keying in on reasonable doubt is the most important part of that inquiry.

Leading off with that question may cause jurors to wonder if that is your only defense. Working this into the voir dire after you are well into the questioning may be more effective. However, let prospective jurors know that it is important and obtain a commitment from them.

I prefer working into the subject through a story or other introduction that gets the jury's attention and explains the concept.

EXAMPLE:

"Back in St. Louis we had a judge who enjoyed giving speeches to the jury about constitutional rights and one day he dropped by the prosecutor's office and said that his favorite niece had been assaulted on a bus and he would appreciate being kept informed. Later that day when the prosecutor dropped by and told the judge the man had been caught, the judge became excited and with great hope shouted: 'Did the police beat the hell out of him?' What is your reaction to this judge?"

In most courtrooms, if you are going to tell such a story during voir dire be sure that you can do it in two sentences, as I have just done. This introduction led to an interesting discussion of constitutional rights. I soon stated: "I'm sure we all know how the judge felt, but I am sure none of us feels the judge should sit as the judge in the trial of this defendant he had hoped the police would beat up on."

One juror raised her hand and volunteered an interesting point of view that was helpful with all jurors. She said that she saw no reason a judge could not sit as the judge in such a case. She explained that she is a nurse and takes her duties very seriously and if a judge took his duties that seriously he would preside with complete impartiality.

What a beautiful moment to talk about reasonable doubt. "I assume that if Judge Parker instructs you that you cannot bring back a verdict of guilty unless you believe my client to be guilty beyond a reasonable doubt, that you will take your duty as a juror seriously, will take our American constitution seriously, and will follow his honor's instruction? Is that right? How do you others feel about that?" (Note I talk about the American constitution and not the federal constitution, since people are more pro-America than pro-federal government).

Talk to prospective jurors about reasonable doubt.

1. Stress the importance of this concept.

   Q. Nothing makes America different from dictatorial countries more than the fact that in America you are innocent until proven guilty beyond a reasonable doubt. Is there anyone here who does not agree with that? (You may learn little from the juror the way this is put to him, but you deliver a message, and if he doesn't agree with this message you certainly want to know it.)

2. Use stories or examples to explain this concept.

   Q. Have you heard about men being in prison, even on death row, and then they find that someone else committed the crime?

   Q. What do you think about that?

   Q. Do you think that is why the men who drafted our Bill of

Rights wanted to prevent this by requiring that the jury find a person guilty beyond a reasonable doubt before it can convict him?

Q. Do you really believe in this Bill of Rights?

Q. Are you willing to send my client home to his family if you do not find beyond a reasonable doubt that he is guilty of the crime with which he has been charged?

3. Obtain a commitment. Many appellate decisions hold that you cannot obtain a commitment and many trial judges seem to be waiting to stomp on you if you ask a question that even sounds like a commitment. However, if you do not obtain basic commitments you are not doing your job, especially as to reasonable doubt. See the *Hearst* transcript at the end of this section and you will learn that the federal judge in the *Hearst* trial did an excellent job of obtaining a commitment.

4. Ask the question in a few different ways, but above all, be sure you do ask the question.

Q. Do you feel that if there is any reasonable doubt as to my client's guilt, that you should vote to find him not guilty?

Q. Do you understand, in fact, that if the State fails to prove its case beyond a reasonable doubt that you have no choice, that you must vote for acquittal?

Q. Does that bother you?

Q. Will you be able to abide by your oath and to follow the law and acquit the defendant, even though you have a strong feeling he is guilty?

Q. How strong? Let's talk about that, Mr. Jones. If you have a reasonable doubt, you must find him not guilty. Do you agree with that?

Q. Would you vote for acquittal if you decided any feeling you had about his guilt was not strong enough to remove any reasonable doubt?

The trial judge acted properly in excusing a prospective juror who would not vote for a guilty verdict, unless there was "absolutely no doubt" in her mind. *Bennett v. Commonwealth*, 374 SE2d 303 (Va. 1988). Anytime a juror requires more than reasonable doubt, he is disqualified. *Little v. State*, 758 SW2d 551 (Tex. Cr 1988).

In the *Hearst* trial, the judge conducted the following voir dire on the subject of reasonable doubt.

Q. Are you willing to give Miss Hearst the benefit of the presumption that she is innocent until proven guilty?

A. I certainly am.

Q. On the other hand, you know the very purpose of the United States is here—is to attempt to prove her guilty beyond a reasonable doubt. And, that's what they'll be offering testimony to attempt to do in this case. Do you understand that's what they're here . . .

A. Yes, sir.

Q. Their very purpose for being here. Now, if that evidence does establish proof beyond a reasonable doubt, will you have any hesitation in returning a verdict of guilty?

A. No, sir.

Q. If it fails to establish proof of guilt beyond a reasonable doubt, then what will you do under those circumstances?

A. I'll say she is not guilty.

Q. All right. You feel you could be fair to both sides in that kind of decision-making process?

A. Yes, sir."

Voir dire of Mrs. Buckert, *U.S. v. Patty Hearst*, supra.

[1.30] How To Explain The Time Elements Of The Trial. Plaintiff and prosecutor miss a good opportunity if they fail to let the jury know they are concerned about its time. If they fail to, the defense can do so, even though they did not go first.

Discuss frankly the time needed for the trial.

1. This lets the jury know you value their time and other commitments.
2. This excuses (usually by peremptory but possibly for cause)

jurors who would be thinking of picking up the children by five when they should be listening to you.

3. It helps to organize the trail in the minds of the jurors. (They do not get restless during the second day of what they thought was a one-day trial if they know it is a three-day trial.)
4. It gives you an opportunity to let them know the role of the judge.

EXAMPLE:

"Mrs. Jones, his Honor, Judge Edwards, was a trial lawyer for many years and has been a judge for many years and he is not going to let us lawyers waste a lot of time, and you will be out of here in plenty of time to leave Friday on your vacation."

5. This gives counsel an opportunity to talk about the prospective juror, to the prospective juror. It gives the juror a chance to talk on a noncontroversial issue and may give interesting information about the juror:

EXAMPLE:

Is the juror anxious to leave to pick up children, to return to a big business deal, to attend a tea, or just because he or she is bored with the entire matter? The answer may tell you a lot about the juror.

The judge often mentions the time element, and if he does, it will not hurt to add a few words to assure the jury you will not waste its time. If the judge does not mention time, grab the ball and run with it!

[1.31] Be Sure Juror Has No Financial Interest In The Outcome Of The Case. There is no disqualification more certain than if the juror has a financial interest in the outcome of the lawsuit. What constitutes a "financial interest," however, is not so simple.

Consider possible economic interests.

1. Disclose any possible economic interest or conflict. "Your Honor, I see my client's wife among the prospective jurors and suggest she be dismissed."

2. Discuss with client any possible economic interest or conflict. "Do you see anyone on the panel you know? Yes, Mr. Smith is a shareholder in our little company that is being sued."
3. Inquire of prospective jurors as to any direct conflict. "Do any of you have any interest in the company my client is suing? Yes, my husband is on the board of directors."
4. Inquire of prospective jurors as to any indirect conflict. "Mrs. Jones, I notice you are a taxpayer in the city we are suing. Do you think you can be fair to my client, even though taxes could pay for a part or all of any judgment this jury returns?"

CAVEAT: Approach cautiously the thought that a taxpayer may have to pay a part of the judgment where the prospective juror is a taxpayer. You may lose the objection for cause, run out of peremptories, and then have a juror who is not about to render a large verdict that his tax dollars will help pay.

One of the most troubling "economic interest" problems during voir dire is that of prospective jurors and their relationships with one of the attorneys or his law firm. In one leading case, counsel did all that he should have done:

1. Showed that partner of defendant's attorney was general attorney for the prospective juror
2. Argued that juror's statement that this "would not influence him" did not satisfy his objection
3. When judge refused to remove for cause, counsel used a peremptory to remove him
4. Counsel used all of his peremptories
5. Counsel told the court he needed another peremptory challenge in order to have a fair and impartial trial
7. Counsel appealed an adverse ruling claiming an abuse of discretion. *Redwine v. Fitzhugh*, 329 P2d 257, 72 ALR2d 664 (Wyo. 1958).

In reversing, the appellate court stated something not stated often enough by appellate courts: "The term 'abuse of discretion' does not mean any reflection upon the presiding judge, and does not carry with it an implication of conduct deserving censure, but is strictly a legal term indicating that the appellate court is of the opinion that under the circumstances the trial judge committed error of law in the exercise of its discretion."

The court agreed with appellant that the state and federal constitutions require that a juror be excused who has a disqualifying relationship, and stated, "It is fundamental that every litigant is entitled to have his rights fairly and impartially determined, and it is the duty of a trial court to see that a jury of competent, fair and impartial persons is impanelled."

In most cases, wide discretion is given the trial judge, but a review of the following cases can be very helpful:

1. The attorney-client factor must be left to the trial judge and can be reviewed only if the judge clearly abused his discretion. *Border v. Carrabine*, 120 P 1087 (Okla. 1912).
2. Judge sustained where he refused to excuse for cause those prospective jurors who were employed by a company that defendant's attorney represented even though jurors did not know the attorney and claimed they would be impartial. *Harrison v. Missouri, K.&T.R.Co.*, 89 SW 455 (Tex. Crim 1936).
3. Where prosecutor was executor of estate in which prospective juror was beneficiary, refusing to excuse for cause was within sound discretion of trial judge. *Klink v. State*, 179 NE 549 (Ind. 1932).
4. Some cases hold that if statute sets out relationships that disqualify, court is limited to those disqualifications. *People v. Conte*, 122 P 457 (Cal. App 1912).
5. Other cases hold that the statute does not limit which relationships are disqualifying. *State v. McGraw*, 59 P 178 (Idaho 1899). However, where the statute provides for certain disqualifying relationships, and "no others," the court upheld such a limitation. *Sorseleipo v. Red Lake Falls Mill Co.*, 126 NW 903 (Minn. 1910).
6. A few states have held that it is none of the legislature's business and that "the courts were charged with the imperative duty of affording every person accused of crime an opportunity of being tried by an impartial jury." *Block v. State*, 100 Ind. 357 (Ind. 1885).
7. Even where it is shown that attorney is presently acting as attorney for prospective juror, judge must feel the juror would be influenced by the relationship. *Bailey v. McCleod*, 56 P2d, 460 (Kan. 1936).

Be sure there is no economic conflict:

1. Try to strike for cause.
2. Use peremptory, if necessary.
3. Diligent inquiry may avoid concealing of conflict.

[1.32] Discuss The Presumption Of Innocence: Criminal Cases. The presumption of innocence is closely akin to proof beyond a reasonable doubt, but they are two separate doctrines and should be treated separately. They should be discussed in the same part of the voir dire, but covering one is no excuse for not covering the other.

Note the way the court handled this in the voir dire in the *Hearst* trial. See §1.31, supra. The judge began with the presumption of innocence rule and then immediately proceeded with the reasonable doubt question. Often you can summarize the whole discussion with, "Then you agree that you presume my client to be innocent and will not find him guilty unless you feel he is guilty beyond a reasonable doubt."

Ask about presumption of innocence.

1. Tell them how important this is to the entire system of American justice. It is frightening to think that in some countries you are presumed guilty just because someone alleges you are.
2. Explain exactly how this works. "You jurors must decide this case, and there is no way anyone could receive a fair trial if a trial started with one side having an advantage."
3. CAVEAT: Most Americans really don't agree with that part of the American Constitution. It is naive for a trial lawyer to think a juror attaches no significance to the fact a police officer arrested his client and a prosecutor is prosecuting him.
4. Appeal to the best in a prospective juror. A juror must be sincere about: (a) the oath he takes, (b) his belief in the American constitution, (c) his honesty in answering questions during this part of the voir dire, and (d) his position that there is no reason he cannot sit on this jury and render a verdict that is fair and impartial to both sides. How sincere he is, or how much you know about his sincerity or lack of sincerity, may well depend upon the effectiveness of your voir dire.

[1.33] How To Lessen Impact Of Accused Not Testifying. One of the most crucial questions defense counsel must answer in a criminal trial is whether or not his client should testify. He often will not know for certain until the prosecution has presented its case.

During voir dire, a trial lawyer must prepare the jury for the fact the accused may not testify. It is only when counsel is absolutely certain that the client will not be called to the witness stand, that he or she can fail to cover the subject during voir dire.

First, learn from answers to other questions the juror's attitude toward the Constitution. If a juror smirks at the concept of reasonable doubt and presumption of innocence, that juror will not likely be impressed by your argument on failure to testify.

Next, explain the importance of this concept. Make jurors proud to follow the Constitutional provision that forbids forcing a person to testify against himself. Jurors have pictured people being tortured for not giving evidence. Capture that as a part of the concept, not a "law and order" theme that looks upon Constitutional provisions as technicalities that permit the guilty to go free.

If you are not sure whether your client will testify, don't hesitate to let the jury know. You might simply say that you do not know what the state's evidence will be, but if there is nothing your client need explain, there will be no need for him to testify.

Look toward final argument. If you expect to discuss the fact your client did not testify, then you must condition the jury for this during voir dire. The fact the prosecutor cannot refer to it does not mean jurors may not be thinking about it.

CAVEAT: Be posititive about this part of your case. You are on the side of the Constitution and on the side of all that America stands for. You are on the side of common sense that stands for the proposition that a witness need not testify if his testimony is not needed.

[1.34] Make A List Of Basic Questions. Every lawyer has his basic list of questions that he might use in every voir dire. I have added to my own list the lists of other trial lawyers. The following list should be considered in every case and, once considered, should be edited and then used with other questions based on "special factors," "kinds of litigation," or relating to "identity" or "prejudice." Ask the following while inquiring of the entire panel:

1. Do any of you know anything about this lawsuit?
2. Do any of you know any of the attorneys? (You have, of course, scratched any questions the judge or opposing counsel has already asked.)
3. What about the parties to the lawsuit?
4. Do you know any of the witnesses? I want to especially call your attention to the expert witnesses. Have any of you been treated by Dr. Alexander Smith?
5. Are any of you, or a member of your family, employed by or have a financial interest in State Farm Insurance Company (where applicable)?
6. Have any of you had any experience relative to any matter that is an issue in this lawsuit? For example, we will be talking about highway engineering. Do any of you have any expertise in this field?

[1.35] Learn Of Juror's Reading And Television Habits. What a juror reads may tell you much about the prospective juror. You can obtain this important information from the juror by: (1) observing the juror, (2) asking directly, or (3) asking indirectly.

Jurors come to the courthouse ready to read something. They have, through their own experience or that of others, learned that jurors sit for hours. Observe what they bring. When you reach that part of your inquiry, do it with diplomacy. You don't ask a juror, "Can you read?" and, under certain circumstances, you may not want to ask, "What do you read?"

What the juror reads is important:

1. Consider what you learn if the prospective juror reads:
   - (a) *The Wall Street Journal*
   - (b) trashy books

(c) a liberal magazine (compared with liberal newspaper which may be the only good newspaper in town)

(d) *the National Enquirer*

(e) *Penthouse* (not even the good literature that is found in *Playboy*).

2. Observe what they bring to court.
3. Ask indirectly.

EXAMPLE:

"Mrs. Jones, do you subscribe to any magazines? Which ones? Have you read any articles in those magazines about lawsuits against doctors?"

CAVEAT: What a juror reads may be what a juror thinks, and may tell us how a juror thinks. Irving Younger liked jurors who read mysteries because they have imagination. He also was cautious of jurors who laboriously read technical information, especially if not required by their occupation. These people just indulge too much in detail to get caught up in the facts you are trying to make fascinating.

Today, the fact that a juror reads at all may tell you something. What may be equally important is how a juror reacts to what he reads. During World War II many people read Hitler's *Mein Kampf*, and how they reacted to what they read told much of their philosophy and often reflected in the reader a complete lack of human concern.

How to learn from the juror's reading habits:

Q. We are going to be talking about death in this trial. Have any of you read any books on this subject?

Possible Answers:

1. A person dying of AIDS. This subject has been a special challenge for many people. An interest in such a story may show that the juror is a person with human compassion.
2. A macho man who beat people. You may be trying a lawsuit, such as a police brutality case, in which attitudes toward people being beaten is important.
3. A young person suffering from pain. This may mean the reader is becoming accustomed to pain, or this may mean

the reader is very sympathetic toward a person suffering from pain.

How to evaluate what you learn about juror's reading habits:

Q. What did you think about the book:

1. A person may tell you, first, how understanding he may be about another person's lifestyle, and second, how he feels about a person with AIDS.
2. You may find the reader is outraged at the conduct of the macho man beating people, or you may find feelings ranging from silent approval to hero worship.
3. You may find which jurors accept pain and are not likely to place large dollar signs on pain and suffering. You may also find a person has genuine sympathy, and when a plaintiff finds such a person he wants that juror to stay, and opposing counsel will be equally emphatic that the juror must go.

CAVEAT: I often think of the story of the British lady who wept in the theatre for two hours for a poor character on stage, while her servant froze to death waiting for her in the carriage. Some people who relate to characters in fiction do not relate to people in the real world. Find out how genuine a juror's concern really is.

Discover what television shows a juror watches: During the 1950s and 1960s, we asked jurors if they watched Perry Mason on television, and whether they expected us to produce the real villain during the course of the trial. Television changes with each decade, but the need to know how television is affecting jurors remains with us.

The latest "need to know" was discussed by Tony Cunningham, a leading trial lawyer, in his address to the 1989 Academy of Florida Trial Lawyers' Workhorse Seminar (as later reported in the Academy's *Journal*):

> . . . it's pretty hard not to mention the propaganda of the large insurance companies and other giant corporations on the subject of lawsuits, plaintiff's lawyers, plaintiffs, etc. He said an approach he has used to advantage is to start off on this point by mentioning a subject not directly related—the many fiction TV programs over the past quarter of a century, such as *Perry Mason, Matlock, Miami Vice, L.A. Law,* etc. . . . Ask the jurors if they

believe those programs necessarily represent law as it is practiced in real life . . . then ease into the insurance industry propaganda business.

Some of the insurance company propaganda has been so offensive to the concept of a fair trial that it has been withdrawn, but there is still much of it out there and neither side of the counsel table should ignore this factor during voir dire. Talking about it reminds jurors of it, and not talking about it subjects counsel to another of those "hidden feelings" voir dire is supposed to expose.

What television the juror watches is important:

1. Law-oriented programs:
   (a) Form attitudes toward lawyers, clients, and courts
   (b) Form false opinions as to law and courtroom procedure
   (c) Cause jurors to adopt attitudes toward issues and classes of litigants
2. Insurance and medical profession propaganda:
   (a) Reaches jurors through commercials
   (b) Reaches jurors through news programs
   (c) Reaches jurors through editorials
3. Nonlaw-oriented programs:
   (a) News and Views: People who watch the news may be better informed; people who watch nothing but situation comedy may not take matters seriously; however, anyone who watched the classic episode on capital punishment on "In The Heat Of The Night" and was at all impressed with it, would have to be a defendant's juror in a capital case. Viewers saw an old law-and-order police chief, played by the former Archie Bunker character, watch a person being executed. Viewers shared the Chief's feelings as he began to question whether putting a person to death was really a proper punishment.
   (b) Inner feelings of people: There are many television movies today that center on social issues. If a juror thinks any such program is a waste of time he may think your case is a waste of time. Much television glorifies wealth, and its audience may tell you something about its viewers. Those

who can't wait to watch the latest from Wall Street may be better off financially than other jurors. You may, or MAY NOT, learn about racial attitudes from what jurors watch. Many whites still prefer black actors to be Amos and Andy characters. Their racial attitudes may be more accurately analyzed by whether they appreciate black actors in more serious roles.

[1.36] Discover Attitudes Toward Courts, Lawyers, And The Jury System. People operate better in a positive environment. This is why jurors who respect the judicial process bring an attitude to the courtroom that makes them better jurors.

Discover the juror's attitude toward courts, lawyers, and the jury system:

1. Prior jury service.
2. What jury reads and watches on television.
3. Occupations of friends and relatives. (Today a doctor's wife may not hear good things about lawyers at the dinner table.)
4. Income of juror. (Low-income juror may not relate to attorney who he imagines to be wealthy.)
5. Personal views. (Just come right out and ask him how he feels about courts, lawyers and the jury system.)
6. Political views. (Radicals to the right approved of Colonel North's ignoring the Constitution, and radicals to the left during the Vietnam War did not look to the courts as a proper forum. Toward the middle of the political philosophies conservatives may preach law-and-order, but liberals show greater appreciation for constitutional rights.)

   CAVEAT: Trial lawyers must forget their own philosophy and at least try to listen to what experts tell us about the juror's political philosophy. In a murder trial where the jury would be called upon to lean toward a young man who claimed complete innocence, defense counsel paid much money to an expert who said, "Strike all Republicans." It is not that simple, but political attitudes are important.

Once you know the prospective juror's attitude, you must know how to use what you have learned. Those who think jury duty is a waste of time will not listen closely to your presentation. Those who think jury verdicts are "crazy" have often formed that opinion on the basis of talk about "runaway juries" who bring back larger verdicts than the juror would favor. Those who resent lawyers may not want a lawyer to obtain a large verdict, realizing the lawyer may receive a part of that verdict. A juror who thinks a judge can do no wrong may put too much importance on a judge's ruling against you. Those who have no negative attitudes toward courts, lawyers, and the jury system will enjoy the juror experience and be more effective jurors.

Questions that help you discover attitudes:

Q. What did you think of your experience serving on the jury? Tell me about it.

Q. What relations have you had with lawyers? Were they satisfactory?

Q. Do you know any lawyers or judges, personally?

Q. Do you belong to any organizations that take a position on any issues that relate to lawyers or the legal system?

Q. We know that the penny post card no longer costs a penny and the nickel candy bar no longer costs a nickel, and we know that legal fees are much higher than they were when I started practicing law. What do you think of legal fees?

Q. Do you know of anyone personally who you feel was not treated fairly by a lawyer or by the court?

[1.37] How To Spot The "Military Mind." Military background of a prospective juror can be very important. Many cases require this information, and in every case the "military mind" has already decided certain issues.

The military background factor:

1. What "military traits" are important? Courtroom consultants talk about "perfectionists" and "authoritarians," two profiles

that don't usually give people a break. Such attitudes are often a part of military philosophy.

2. How do you "spot" this attitude? Why was he in the military? A wartime volunteer or draftee may not have been as fully indoctrinated as a "regular army man." A private may not have been as enthusiastic about authority as a captain.
3. When is the attitude important? In criminal cases it is always a factor, but in different ways. Though a military attitude may not take excuses from a defendant, it may require more of the prosecution. In a case where plaintiff did not wear a seatbelt the military mind may not excuse the client as much as another juror would.

All jury stereotypes are suspect, and none is more suspect than keeping or excusing a juror because of a military background. There is a "military mind" attitude, however, that must be understood, and trial intuition will help recognize it.

Questions that may help discover the "military mind":

Q. I notice you served in the Navy. When was that?

Q. How long did you serve? Did you like it?

Q. What rank or grade were you? For how long? How did that advancement occur?

Q. Do you have a special interest in the military? Do you read any books on the subject?

Q. Have you ever been exposed, as a witness or observer or any other way, in a court martial? Have your friends told you about these proceedings? Did you think those cases you heard about were conducted fairly?

Q. What do you think is the most important requirement of a military person? Discuss!

[1.38] How To Evaluate Juror's Travel And Former Residency. Where a person has lived or travelled can be important during voir dire. Knowing where a person lives now tells us much, but that tells us only about a narrow part of the life of a prospective juror.

During voir dire you are trying to discover what experiences a person has had. Where a person lives or has lived tells you the kind of economic neighborhood, possible cultural experiences, and a broad exposure to ideas. Where a person has travelled tells you more of the same.

Learn about a prospective juror's former homes and travels:

1. Indirectly: "By the way, have you always lived in this county?" or "Where have you practiced your profession?"
2. Directly: where it fits into the dialogue of voir dire. "This accident took place on one of those highways out in Kansas. Have you ever driven on those wide stretches of highway," or, "This lawsuit involves a cruise on which Mrs. Smith was injured. Have you ever been on one of those cruises?"

Questions that help discover travel and residency:

Q. Why did you move to Clearwater, Mrs. Smith?

Q. Mr. Jones, you say you served on a jury. Was that here in Pinellas County?

Q. Is your job one in which they may send you from one state to another?

Q. This company is from New York. Any of you have any special loyalty to New York? Any of you root for the Mets, or root against the Mets?

Q. My client is from Eastern Europe. Have any of you travelled to that part of the world?

[1.39] How To Dig Into Significance Of Home Ownership. How important home ownership is depends upon the type of lawsuit and upon other factors about the prospective juror. People who own a home have definite feelings about protecting that property interest and about the stability that comes from home ownership.

Remember, however, that in many areas, most people own their homes, unless circumstances have prevented it or have made it economically unwise. Large corporations often pay for personnel to lease while at a location for a few years, and those who have moved to a community may be looking for a few years before buying. Many factors make the usual home-owner profile a renter.

A generation ago an average family lived in the same home for 25 years, but today the average family lives in the same home about four years. A generation ago few families lived in a condominium, but today we have a completely new "home owner," with new experiences.

Whether a prospective juror is a home owner is important:

1. In certain cases. If damage were done to a home or if a home were burglarized, in eminent domain cases, and in other cases where home ownership could be an issue, whether the juror is a home owner is important. Here the inquiry should be made directly.
2. To a degree in all cases. Even where ownership may not be a factor, it may tell us about the juror. It may tell us something about stability, economics, even religion (where people live in "parish" neighborhoods). Younger people who are on the way up may afford a conservative philosophy sooner than they can afford the home that goes with it. Consider a less direct approach. "When your company moved you here last year, what arrangements did they make for housing?" may be softer than what may sound like, "You mean you don't own your own home?"

Questions that explore home ownership:

Q. Some courts have stated that a man's home is his castle. What do you think about that?

Q. In this case we will be talking about a condominium. Do you think the same thing applies?

Q. What if a man rents an apartment for three months and that lease treats him as though he owned the apartment for those three months. If the law treats him like an owner would you treat him like an owner?

Q. It costs a lot of money to own a home today. Do you think the real estate taxes are too high? Do you think owning a home is worth it, even though it does cost a lot?

Q. In this case my client was injured on this man's property, and the judge will instruct you as to the legal effect of his being on someone else's property. Will you follow that law as Judge Weinstein gives it, and not on some preconceived idea? Do you agree that a person has to follow the law, even on his own property?

[1.40] Learn From Membership In Organizations. America is a nation of joiners, and what a prospective juror joins may tell you much about him or her. In certain cases, knowledge of organization involvement is absolutely essential.

Counsel who challenges for cause has the burden of showing how membership in an organization would be prejudicial. *State v. White,* 535 So2d 929 (La. App 1988). However, it was held that asking about membership in the Ku Klux Klan was a "legitimate inquiry," especially where defendant was a member of the Klan. *Mize v. State,* 378 SE2d 392 (Ga. App 1989).

Membership in organizations is important during voir dire:

1. Certain cases. If use of firearms is in issue, then membership in the National Rifle Association would be helpful. If civil rights is involved, then membership in the Klan or in ACLU would be important. In a products liability case, the president of the National Association of Manufacturers would probably not be a good plaintiff's juror.
2. In all cases. Membership might be an important part of a juror's profile. Religious and political organizations tell much about a juror's philosophy. Social organizations may tell about a juror's economic position or about his or her concern for people. Professional organizations take a stand on issues that often reach the courtroom.

Questions that help explore organization membership:

Q. Mr. Jones, we will be talking about the use of firearms in this case. Do you belong to the NRA or to any other organization that has taken a position on firearms?

Q. You mentioned, Mrs. Smith, that you are active in the PTA. Are there any other organizations you are active in?

Q. My client is a doctor and belongs to certain medical associations. Do any of you belong to any kind of organization that relates to your employment?

Q. During the trial we will have to follow certain laws that are now on the books, even though we don't agree with them. Do any of you belong to any organization that works toward changing a law or court decision or keeping a law or court decision?

CAVEAT: You have just asked who actively favors or opposes abortion, who actively favors or opposes tort reform, who actively favors or opposes gun control, and who actively favors or opposes many issues that might tell you much about the prospective juror.

[1.41] How To Get Jurors To Talk About Hobbies And Special Interests. What a prospective juror is really interested in may tell you much about how he will feel regarding your lawsuit. What they discuss on the golf course may be different than what volunteers at an abuse center discuss. Hobbies that leave no room for error are often enjoyed by those who leave no room for error.

Hobbies and interests are areas of voir dire that can be dealt with directly. Asking direct questions about this causes no problem, since people want to talk about their interests and do not feel you are prying. "Mr. Jones, I see you retired last year. How do you like retirement? Does this mean you spend time playing golf or bowling?" Follow up.

If hunting is a juror's hobby, he may be less sensitive to pain than other jurors. Any juror who enjoys his hobby usually has a positive feeling toward people and may be more likely to bring back a plaintiff's verdict. This is only one factor, however, and a person who loves golf may also love the economic status that enables him to enjoy this hobby, and that may not make him a good plaintiff's juror.

Questions that get jurors talking about hobbies and other interests:

Q. I notice you live on the beach, Mr. Jones. Does that mean you spend time walking the beach or swimming, or do you just like the beautiful sunsets? What other hobbies do you have?

Q. Officer Jones, do you spend much time at the range? Is this because you are required to spend that many hours, or is this also sort of a hobby of yours?

Q. This case involves a boating accident. Do any of you spend time boating? Do any of you ride a motorcycle? (Follow through with jurors who may be involved in risk-taking activities.)

Q. I understand you are retired, Mr. Smith. Do you enjoy retirement? How do you spend your time?

[1.42] How To Discuss Attitudes Toward People Who Sue. In the Wisconsin Study, a million dollars was spent to determine exactly how litigious America is today. The result was that only one out of ten people who have a lawsuit file a claim. Don't try to convince a jury of this during the short time of a lawsuit.

Be prepared for the fact that most jurors feel we live in a litigious society in which people are constantly filing frivolous lawsuits. Learn how they feel about lawsuits in general, and then learn how they feel about the kind of lawsuit they will hear in this trial.

Learn about attitudes toward people who sue:

1. What have they read in the newspapers? "Have any of you read anything in the newspapers about a 'lawsuit crisis' or a need for 'tort reform' or a 'doctor shortage' because of medical negligence suits? What have you read? How do you feel about this? Does any of this make you feel Mrs. Smith should not receive the damages she would otherwise be entitled to for her injuries sustained in this accident?"
2. Have you discussed this? "Have you ever talked about this with anyone? With whom?"
3. Formed an opinion? "Have you formed an opinion on this subject? What is that opinion? Don't you feel this would make it difficult for you to be completely impartial and give my client a fair trial? Don't you think, in complete fairness, it would be better for you to serve on another jury where you could start without any preconceived thoughts about the case?"
4. Have you or those close to you been involved in lawsuits? "Who was involved? What kind of a case was it? Were you

satisfied with the outcome? During this experience, did you talk with a lawyer or other person about who can and should file a lawsuit?"

5. Believe in our court system? "In some countries people do not have a right to go to court and recover their damages. What do you think of that right we have in America? In Russia a person can sue for property damages, but not for personal injuries. Do you think that is right? Do you think whether you sue or not is a personal choice? Let me put it this way, if someone owed me a hundred dollars I would just forget it, I wouldn't sue. But I have a friend who would be sure this guy didn't get by with it and he would take it to court. Do you think less of me because I wouldn't file a suit, or less of my friend because he would?"

[1.43] What You Must Do About Health Problems Of Jurors. The health of a prospective juror can affect his role as a juror in many ways. You must observe and inquire and make sure this factor does not work against your client and your cause.

Consider carefully the health of a prospective juror.

1. Observe carefully. You may notice it would be difficult for the juror to sit and concentrate for long periods of time. You may notice an emotional problem that would affect the juror's ability to reason properly. You may notice a limp that suggests a person has become accustomed to pain and may not place great importance on the pain of others.
2. Inquire diplomatically. You simply do not ask a person whether he or she is mentally and emotionally capable of serving on a jury. Even questions as to physical capability must be asked with diplomacy. "Do you know of any physical problem that might keep you from sitting for long periods of time and concentrating on evidence," is much better than, "Is there anything wrong with you, physically?" "Have any of you sustained an injury at all similar to the one I described?" is a proper question.

Where prospective juror was tardy, slept during voir dire, was under medication, and gave incoherent and contradictory answers, the juror should have been excused for cause. *Woodward v. State*, 533 So.2d 739 (La. App 1989).

The court should use the alternate juror, when a juror suffers from illness during trial. *People v. Bettistea*, 434 NW2d 138 (Mich. App 1988). Where juror refuses to cooperate, the judge can, in his discretion, dismiss the juror, whether the illness is real or imagined. *People v. Dry Land Marina, Inc.*, 437 NW2d 391 (Mich. App 1989).

One appellate court held that it was prejudicial error to accept a juror who "acknowledged a longstanding fear of closed places," and to deny counsel the right to interrogate her. *People v. Kurth*, 216 NE2d 154, 20 ALR3rd 1409 (Ill. 1966). Where a juror's son died during trial, it was not error to excuse him due to his being upset. *State v. Davis* 7 SE 24 (W.Va. 1888). However, where a juror's wife was injured during trial the trial judge decided the injuries were not serious enough to keep juror from performing his duties. *U.S. v. Ross*, 203 FSupp 100 (DC Pa. 1962).

Though a juror had an application for nervous and mental disability with the U.S. Government, the trial judge found that he was mentally capable of serving as a juror. *McKenzie v. State*, 11 SW2d 172 (Tex. Crim 1928).

One court held that the fact a woman was upset because her son was ill at home was not a "physical or mental incapacity" that justified the judge excusing the juror and proceeding with only eleven jurors. *Houston & T. C. R. Co. v. Waller*, 56 Tex. 331 (Tex. 1882). Where a trial judge learned that the prospective juror had a hearing disability and placed him nearest the witness stand, ensured witnesses spoke loudly, and did not have a complaint from the juror about not hearing during the trial, it was held on appeal that the trial judge did not violate the wide discretion that must be given trial judges. *Lindsey v. Tennessee*, 225 SW2d 533, 15 ALR2d 527 (Tenn. 1949).

Courts have generally held that a lack of hearing is a "proper defectum" class disqualification, not a "proper affectum" based on bias or prejudice, so it is waived if not objected to. *Tollackson v. Eagle Grove*, 213 NW 222 (Iowa 1927). Even where counsel claimed he did not suspect a hearing problem until the juror was sworn, the court held it was too late to object. *State v. Parsons*, 285 SW 412 (Mo. 1926).

[1.44] Save Face And Fortune By Asking, "Is There Any Reason You Cannot Serve?" You will feel much more comfortable during voir dire if you know you are not going to make a fatal mistake that may cause you to lose the trial. The most experienced trial lawyer can make such a mistake and the most inexperienced lawyer can avoid the problem, or at least lessen the effect of failure, by asking what should have been asked.

PROBLEM: You simply cannot ask every question you would like to ask because:

1. The judge will not give you that much time.
2. You cannot tie yourself to a long list of questions because this is not how people normally talk to people and because it is not how a voir dire should be conducted.
3. During voir dire you hope to become involved in a series of chatty questions that takes you far from your set questions, and this may cause you not to return to a question you intended to ask.
4. You may just simply forget.

SOLUTION: Some time during the voir dire you simply ask, "Do any of you know of any reason you cannot serve on this jury and help bring back a verdict that is fair to both sides?"

There, you have done it. You have saved yourself the embarrassment of being told you forgot to ask a certain question. You can now reply, "Of course, I asked that question, didn't you hear me? I asked if there were ANY REASON, and courts have held that any reason covers a lot of territory."

EXAMPLES:

1. Juror related to a party. Of course, that is a reason, and juror must tell you.
2. Juror knows a witness. Of course! Even if you don't ask the specific question.
3. Knows something about the case. Sure, the juror must tell you.
4. Doesn't like the looks of your client. Probably not, but if the prejudice runs deep you must dig deep.

CAVEAT: Making a mistake on voir dire can embarrass you, cost you a verdict, subject you to professional criticism, cost you money, and add to the stress that plagues the trial lawyer today. Much of this can be avoided by asking the "any reason" question. However, don't use it as a crutch. Ask the specific questions and don't feel you entirely pass the burden to the juror to tell you what you would have learned with a specific question.

[1.45] How To Discuss Whether They Really Want To Serve. My favorite of all questions, and one I ask in every trial of any kind, is one relating to whether or not the prospective juror really wants to serve on the jury. I just feel that a person does much better at anything he really wants to do.

Select jurors who really want to serve:

1. They pay better attention.
2. They will be more sincere.
3. They will vote more conscientiously.
4. They will appreciate your concern about their serving.

However, learn WHY he or she wants to serve. If a prospective juror just wants to send someone to prison, defense counsel in a criminal trial will not want that person on the jury.

This is where counsel can "chat" with a prospective juror on a pleasant subject. Those who really don't want to serve may give you reason to want to excuse them. You may accomplish with a cause strike what would have cost you a peremptory challenge.

EXAMPLE:

Where prospective juror indicates he does not want to serve:

Q. Why don't you want to serve, Mr. Smith?

A. I just can't be away from the office at this time. My partner just died and we are involved in a lawsuit of our own. I am just so upset about all of this I could not possibly concentrate on this case.

Q. Are you telling us there is no way you can sit on this jury and help bring back a verdict that is fair to both parties?

A. I honestly could not. Some other time I would enjoy serving on a jury, but not now.

The judge exercised his sound discretion and excused the juror.

Follow up with those who really want to serve and learn which ones have a positive reason. It is here you will enjoy and benefit from chatting with jurors.

EXAMPLE:

Let the entire courtroom know this is going to be a positive dialogue. Make the person being questioned feel good about her attitude.

Q. I'm glad you want to spend the week with us, Mrs. Smith. I think you are going to enjoy this experience.

A. I hope so.

Q. Do you think it is your duty to serve?

A. Yes, I do.

Q. Do you belong to any civic organizations?

A. I'm secretary of the League of Women Voters.

Q. So, if you are getting others to be a good citizen, you have to be a good citizen yourself, is that right?

A. Yes, it sure is (smiling).

OR

Q. Mrs. Brown, do you think it would be interesting to be on this jury?

A. Yes, I do.

Q. Do you watch "Matlock" on television?

A. Every Tuesday night.

Q. I hope you won't be disappointed, but real trials aren't as exciting as trials on television.

A. I'm sure.

Q. But, what makes the courtroom even more exciting is that we are dealing with real people with real problems. Don't you think that makes up for the fact we won't have Mr. Matlock with us this week?

A. Yes, I sure do.

Q. Mrs. Brown, I have been around courtrooms for forty years and I think it is a fascinating place, but (becoming serious) we deal with serious problems that greatly affect the lives of people. I am sure you understand that. Are you willing to accept this responsibility?

A. Yes, I am.

Q. Thank you, Mrs. Brown. I know you are.

[1.46] Learn About And Talk About Seatbelts. Seatbelts are required by law, but that does not mean everyone wears a seatbelt at all times, and it does not mean people are happy about wearing them. Many states have permitted evidence of nonuse of seatbelts as a means of lessening damages.

During voir dire consider the seatbelt problem:

1. Know the law of the jurisdiction of the trial.
   The law on this subject is changing and many states have clearly held such evidence is not admissible. Do not begin voir dire until you are certain of the latest law in your jurisdiction.
2. Learn about the prospective juror's habits and attitude.
   - Q. What role do you think seatbelts play in auto accidents and any resulting injuries?
   - Q. Do you always use your seatbelt? Explain.
   - Q. Some people claim that in some accidents you are better off without a seatbelt; what do you think?
   - Q. Do you think it is possible to determine how much less the injuries, if any, would be if the injured person had used a seatbelt?
   - Q. Are you willing to base your verdict upon the evidence in this case, and not upon some notion someone might come up with as to what might have happened?

[1.47] When To Strike Women And Men. The experiences and attitudes of men, compared with women, are usually quite different and the sex of the prospective juror cannot be ignored. When we think of minorities or other groups we are going to analyze, we are usually thinking about someone with whom we do not have a close association. Being close to a wife, mother, or sister is no guarantee that you fully understand the attitudes of the two sexes.

It has been held that underrepresentation of women on a jury violates the Sixth Amendment. *Berryhill v. Zant*, 585 F2d 633 (11th Cir. 1988). In this case 52 percent of the adult population were women, and only 39 percent of those on the master jury list were women.

Consider the attitudes of men and women on the jury panel:

1. Is your client male or female?
   Some women are jealous of other women and some women identify with other women. The sex of your client is important, but a factor that will depend upon other factors.
2. Is your client a young person? A woman will identify as the mother of a young person (especially in a criminal case) more than a man will identify as a father.
3. What kind of case are you trying? A scar on the face of a woman will impress some women and not others.

Neither men nor women want to be ignored, nor discriminated against. You should keep in mind the sex of the juror as a factor, without announcing that to the jury.

Questions you might ask women:

Q. What organizations do you belong to?

Q. If you had a choice, would you prefer working in the home or on a job away from home?

Q. Which television programs do you prefer?

Q. Do you think women are treated fairly as far as job opportunities?

Q. What do you think about men and women who live together but are not married? (One woman said that she would not believe either of them under oath, since both are immoral people.)

Questions you might ask a man:

Q. What organizations do you belong to?

Q. Do you like your work?

Q. How do you spend your time away from work?

Q. What do you feel about men and women living together who are not married?

[1.48] Model Voir Dire: Personal Injury Case. Personal injury litigation is still the most important in the American legal system. Jurors decide the economic future of those injured, and some jurors are willing to award much more than others. Throughout this book are sections that deal with various parts of personal injury litigation. A study of each section will give the reader questions to ask and strategy to apply.

In every personal injury case damages are extremely important. Talk about money in the voir dire. Talk about money, even though it is not a big money case.

EXAMPLE:

The following can be used in nearly every personal injury case:

"How many of you have gone to Albertsons or some other grocery store, and when you got to the cash register some young person handed you a little bag of groceries and said, "Fifty dollars." How many of you said to her or to yourself, "That's a lot of money?" I have, I do it every week when I go shopping with my wife.

How many of you have said, "Fifty dollars? That is a lot of money. Would you take forty dollars?" The young lady would probably think you were crazy. But when you are back in that jury room, and you have heard all the evidence and all the law and based on that evidence and based on that law you feel that the verdict should be a quarter of a million dollars, will any of you say, "That's a lot of money, how about making it $200,000?"

Will any of you hesitate to vote for a verdict just because it is a lot of money? Will you base your verdict on the evidence and the law?

[1.49] Model Voir Dire: Professional Liability Case. The atmosphere during a medical negligence voir dire is different than that of any other voir dire. The trial lawyer must adjust to this and must be ready for jurors who think the plaintiff is trying to punish a person who may some day save his or her life.

Other professionals enjoy this atmosphere to a lesser degree. There are some on the jury, however, who are simply waiting to decide the fate of a doctor, accountant, or lawyer. Lawyers "enjoy" a very special anticipation with some jurors.

If defendant is being sued for professional negligence:

1. Determine juror's attitude toward professional people, in general. Some people respect professional people while others are

jealous of them. There are psychological and economic reasons for these feelings.

2. Determine juror's attitude toward the particular kind of profession. People may love doctors, yet hate lawyers or accountants. They may love family doctors, yet hate "high-priced specialists."
3. Determine juror's attitude toward the defendant. The doctor you are suing or defending may not look like the juror's favorite doctor on television.
4. Determine the juror's feelings about the kind of negligence involved in this lawsuit. Is it the kind of conduct the jury will get excited about? If not, is this prospective juror one who will think you are wasting his time, or one who will respect your client's right to sue, even if conduct were not outrageous?
5. Has juror had happy or unhappy experience with a doctor?
   - Q. Have you had an experience with a doctor that was so good or so bad that it could affect your ability to return a verdict that is fair to both sides?
6. Do you have friends or relatives who are doctors? Do you talk with them about their practice? Ever talk with them about lawsuits that are filed against doctors?
7. Apply the same approach to other professions.
8. Inquire as to "crisis."
   - Q. Have you read anything about a "Lawsuit Crisis"? What do you think about it? *Babcock v. Northwest Memorial Hospital,* 767 SW2d 705 (Tex. 1989).
9. Familiarity with professional's expertise? Know medical terms? Had similar operation? Any legal training? How much known about accounting?

   Section 1.49 includes a medical negligence voir dire.

Since there may be a "pro-doctor" feeling among jurors, there is a need to fight for equality from the beginning:

- Q. Would you agree that it would be unfair to have someone on the jury who is against doctors?
- Q. Would you also agree that it would be unfair to have someone on the jury who would lean in favor of doctors?

Q. Have you formed any opinion at this time as to how you feel about doctors?

Q. Have you formed an opinion as to lawsuits against doctors? You have no thoughts on this subject?

Q. Have you formed an opinion as to what effect lawsuits against doctors have on medical services? You have no thoughts on this subject?

Q. What do you think about a patient's right to make his own decision as to whether or not he should be operated on? (In informed consent cases.) Do you think the doctor has a duty to give the patient all possible information so that he can make an intelligent and informed decision?

[1.50] Model Voir Dire: Civil Rights Litigation. If there were no prejudice then there would be no need for civil rights actions. Don't expect that prejudice to disappear when you arrive in the courtroom.

Civil rights is an issue that is voted on from time to time in Congress and other legislatures. Such issues have even been submitted to the people by initiative or referendum. People have had an opportunity to stand up and be counted on such issues, and the juror's "voting record" of voting directly or indirectly should be studied. Membership in certain organizations may tell much of the juror's philosophy.

In civil rights cases:

1. Consider the type of case. Some jurors are concerned about racial prejudice but not about sex discrimination. Some are concerned about religious discrimination but not discrimination against the handicapped.
2. Is action based on statute or common law? People may or may not agree with what Congress adopted. You may want to talk about a state. You may want to talk about "basic" rights that were there without an act of Congress.
3. Can juror relate to your client's situation? What is juror's employment history, experiences, politics, association with organizations, religion, neighborhood, and attitude?

4. "Good" or "bad" experience. Most jurors have no day-to-day experience that really creates an attitude on discrimination. He or she usually adopts attitudes created by others. There may be an experience in the life of a juror that left a lasting impression. Look for that experience, for it may be all the juror thinks of during the trial.
5. Warm or cold person. Many people feel for a person who comes up with the short end of a situation, and many others feel there must be some reason for what happened, based on some master plan that doesn't allow for excuses. In a civil rights action the plaintiff must look for people who accept the Biblical suggestion, "understand with your heart."
6. Choose jurors strong enough to resist social pressure. The need to protect the rights of a minority is based on the fact the majority does not voluntarily respect the rights of a minority. There is pressure in the jury room and there is pressure at home, at work, and in the community to follow the attitude of the majority. Avoid those seeking social approval and search for those seeking self-approval, where "self" would not approve of bigotry or a lack of love and respect for fellow man.
7. How dedicated is juror to outworn ideas. Some people do not change with the times, and some are quite willing to accept new ideas. There have been exciting things happening relative to rights of blacks, the handicapped, women, and others. Just how excited has the juror been about all of this? A trial lawyer may be interested in knowing what the juror thinks about how much progress has been made. Some claim absolutely no progress has been made, though America today does not in many ways even resemble the America of not too many years ago. Others pretend the battle for equality is over, completely ignoring the still present discrimination against blacks, women, the handicapped, and especially those from the gay community.

[1.51] Model Voir Dire: Products Liability Case. There are issues involved with products liability that are not involved with other tort actions. These issues must be considered during voir dire. Some of the issues date back to the beginning of the industrial revolution, and some began with the strict liability concept.

In product liability cases:

1. Acquaint jurors with law of your jurisdiction. Jurors have had some familiarity with the tort system. An attorney may have told a juror he cannot recover for lack of fault, and such may not apply in this case.
2. Find jurors who will understand the technical testimony. You cannot tell your story without explaining very technical information, so you will want a jury that can appreciate the expert testimony.
3. Find jurors who fit the "plaintiff profile." The plaintiff's attorney must remember that all the requirements of any personal injury case must be met, and that he should not get lost in the special needs of products liability litigation.
4. Beware the pro-establishment juror. In many personal injury cases one driver is suing another driver and there is not necessarily an anti-establishment conflict. Not so with the products liability case. It is extremely unlikely that the defendant will be any other than a deep-pocket defendant that typifies the establishment.
5. Learn of juror's personal experience as a consumer. Whatever other background a prospective juror has, there may be a special experience as a consumer with this kind of product or any kind of product that will influence him or her. Look for it!
6. Who is the shopper in the family? The housewife is the shopper for most items and is often a plaintiff's juror in such cases. Now that husbands are doing more shopping, their chances of being a plaintiff's juror is increased.
7. Look for special requirements of special cases. There are many kinds of products liability and each has its special requirements.

EXAMPLE:

In suit against a drug company plaintiff's jurors would include women, older people, people who have used drugs a lot, and people who have complained about drugs.

Questions you might ask in a products liability case:

Q. Do you buy a product because of the brand name?

Q. When you buy a new car, do you automatically buy the same kind, or do you consider a new company each time? Please explain.

Q. Who does the shopping in your family?

Q. Do you prefer Coke or Pepsi? Why? Does your wife agree with you? When one of the chain restaurants cuts out your favorite soft drink and uses the competitor, do you tell them about it?

Q. Do you think most manufacturers make mistakes, like the rest of us?

Q. Do you think they should pay for those mistakes?

Q. Have you ever belonged to a labor union? Have you served as an officer of the union or had any special responsibility for the union?

Q. Do you think unions are good for workers? For people as a whole?

Q. What is the longest you have ever worked for the same company? Do you think you were treated fairly by that company?

Q. Do you think a company should do more than the minimum required of it by the federal government?

Q. Do you have any training or experience that might help you decide why my client was injured?

Q. Do you think experts can help us establish that?

Q. Will you base your verdict upon the evidence presented at this trial and upon the law the judge will give you in his instructions?

[1.52] Model Voir Dire: Defamation And Privacy. Every prospective juror has been defamed and has had his or her privacy invaded. Plaintiff's attorney must select jurors who are sensitive to this breach of conduct, and defendant's attorney must select those who think it is insignificant.

In a lawsuit for defamation or invasion of privacy.

1. Determine prospective juror's personal experience in such a matter.
   - Q. Have you ever felt that you were subjected to a defamation or an invasion of privacy that you could have filed a suit over if you had decided to?
   - Q. Did you ever take any action relative to such an experience? What did you do?
   - Q. How did you feel when you learned someone lied about you?
2. Determine prospective juror's attitude toward such conduct.
   - Q. What do you think about people who lie about other people?
   - Q. What do you think should be done about them?
3. Ask about punitive damages.
   - Q. Do you think people who lie about others and damage another's reputation should be punished?
   - Q. If his Honor instructs you that in this case you may consider punitive damages and may award such damages in addition to the actual damages my client sustained, would you be willing to consider punitive damages?
     See Section 1.65.
4. Attitude toward substantial damages. Some jurors just don't get excited about awarding large verdicts. See Section 9.12. Other jurors want to see broken bones. See Section 9.10. In this kind of litigation, the plaintiff needs jurors who have an imagination, jurors who can place themselves in the shoes of the defamed and who can feel an injury that does not appear on an x-ray.

[1.53] Model Voir Dire: Wrongful Death Case. Everything you have ever learned about voir dire in a personal injury case must be used in a wrongful death case—and more. People think about death and talk about death. Placing a dollar value on the death of a human being involves endless questions of logic and emotion.

When you are retained to try a wrongful death case, the insurance adjuster has already asked your client in disbelief, "You don't really want to benefit financially from the loss of a loved one, do you?" You must convince the jury, as you have assured your client, that there is a certain amount your client is entitled to under the law and that it is your job to ensure that your client receives that amount. Justice demands that of you as a trial lawyer, and justice demands that of every person sitting on the jury.

In a wrongful death case:

1. Take the burden from your client, and tell the jury of your role. Don't allow a lawyer to do what the insurance adjuster tried to do. Your client has not prepared and filed a petition, you have. Your client has a right to seek legal advice, and your advice is that he or she receive that award provided for by law. No one has decided yet, and the jury is to decide this case—not the lawyer who filed the suit, not the driver who ran over and killed your client's husband, and not the corporation that employs him.
2. Consider the kind of client. How far you go and what kind of voir dire you conduct will have much to do with your client. Is the client the widow of a man who earned big money or a child whose future will never be known? Has your client remarried? Is the plaintiff a personal representative representing distant relatives?
3. What kind of defendant do you have? At pre-trial the judge said, "You mean your client is suing her own parents?" His disapproving manner told me jurors would be thinking the same question. When the man who caused my client's injury was a drunken driver, I made the driver the focus of discussion during voir dire. The defense counsel tried to convince the jury that the role of the driver was not what the lawsuit was all about.
4. The kind of accident is important. Swimming pool accidents require jurors whose education, experience, and attitude give them the best chance of fitting into how the accident occurred and of appreciating your client's side of the case. Every wrongful death case is different from personal injury cases in that placing a money value on life is affected by the juror's religious, philosophical, and economic views.

5. Any special beliefs about death or damages for death?

   Q. Do you have any religious beliefs, or any other beliefs, that would make it difficult for you to sit as a juror and to decide how much in dollars should be awarded for the death of a fellow human being? The judge will instruct you as to the law and that under certain circumstances you are to consider various damages and to bring back a dollar award for my client. Do any of you feel you would have a problem following such an instruction if given by Judge Smith?

6. Personal experiences of prospective jurors.

   Q. This case involves the death of a little girl. Do any of you feel you cannot really sit on this jury due to any personal experience you have had?

   Q. Mrs. Smith, I believe you told the judge one of your children had died, how long ago was that? How did that death occur? Do you think that would make it hard for you to sit on this jury?

7. Sympathy will be a factor. Both lawyers will tell the jurors that they are not to base their verdict on sympathy. Then the jury will retire and will bring back a verdict based on reason and emotion. To ask jurors to live in the abstract and to ignore the fact that a human being is dead because of the negligence of a person who is being sued, is quite an asking. If you represent the plaintiff the jury will want to decide in your favor, but you must give them reason, and not sympathy, as the basis of their verdict. See Section 9.11 relative to sympathy as a factor.

8. Remember the law of damages of your jurisdiction on voir dire. If the law allows damages for pain and suffering, talk about it and be sure the jurors will follow that part of the law. If estate enhancement, suffering from accident to death, and other factors are a part of your lawsuit, make them a part of your voir dire.

9. Plaintiff's lawyer has a duty to make this a "large verdict" case from the start. The old concept "it's cheaper to kill someone than to injure someone" is so inhumane it is immoral. Plaintiff's lawyer has a great responsibility to be sure that this simply does not happen. Life IS important and it is his job to find

jurors who agree with him. See Section 9.12 relative to huge verdicts.

10. Remember your client's economic loss. Too often counsel will think of the importance of compensating for death without receiving every dollar due for economic loss. In most wrongful death cases there is a loss of income or a loss of services or some other economic loss that will run for the entire life expectancy. Plaintiff needs jurors who not only are concerned about loss of life, but also understand economics and dollars.

[1.54] Model Voir Dire: Slip And Fall Cases. The danger for the plaintiff in every slip and fall case is that he can just out-and-out lose it. During voir dire counsel must find jurors who can increase his chance of winning.

In slip and fall cases:

1. Remember, the defendant is a property owner and most jurors will probably be property owners. Jurors can identify with the defendant. Even though they may carry an owner's policy, they do not like the idea of a person being sued "just because he owns property." You will be required to prove fault, and more fault with some jurors than with others.
2. Consider the substantive law of your jurisdiction. Learn how much fault you must prove and be sure that the jurors agree not to hold you to a greater burden than required.
3. Don't ignore the fact that others have not fallen under similar circumstances. Jurors tend to ask themselves why plaintiff fell and why thousands of others who walked over the same place did not fall. Attack this problem during voir dire. Be sure you don't need to prove anything but negligence of defendant and the causal relationship.
4. Talk about the injuries. You cannot recover damages unless you show liability, but nothing keeps you from talking about damages during voir dire. If the jury thinks your client has serious injuries, it might lean toward your client on the question of liability. Also, jurors are always asking themselves, "Why are

you suing"? Liability is a problem in these cases. If you don't have substantial damages, then don't sue. If you do have substantial damages, let the jury know about it immediately.

5. Talk about fault. This is especially true if the defendant is a business. One of the costs of doing business is providing a safe place, so talk to the jury about it.
6. If necessary, talk about comparative negligence. Sometimes your client's negligence is apparent. If so, you must talk about comparative negligence and start dividing fault into percentages, or at least inform the jury that your client is entitled to recovery, even though negligent.
   - Q. If his Honor instructs you that under the law of our state my client is entitled to recover damages even if she were also negligent, would you have any problem following such an instruction?
   - Q. Do any of you feel that a collision had to be caused by one of the parties and could not have been caused by the negligence of both parties?
   - Q. If his Honor tells you in his instructions that you should award a sum based on the percentage of fault, in other words, if you find my client was 10 percent at fault and the other driver 90 percent at fault, then you should award my client only 90 percent of his damages, would you have a problem following that instruction?

[1.55] Model Voir Dire: Premises Liability. Premises liability now goes far beyond slip and fall cases (See Section 1.54), and requires everything from security in motels to being injured by equipment used by a customer. Though most of these cases are filed against a business, a homeowner or other private owner of property may be the defendant.

In premises liability cases:

1. The elements and problems of the slip and fall case may be present. (See Section 8.09).
2. The age of the juror may be important, especially if age of the plaintiff is a factor.

EXAMPLE:

A young person may not be as tolerant of the physical shortcomings of an older person. Younger jurors may sympathize with a young person who may have taken a risk that contributed to the injury.

3. The sex of the juror may be important. In the leading motel-rape case, it was an all-male jury that awarded Connie Francis 2.5 million dollars. *Garzilli v. Howard Johnson's Motor Lodges, Inc.*, 417 F.Supp 1210 (ED N.Y. 1976).
4. Neighborhood of juror may be important. Many premises liability issues revolve around neighborhood factors. Keeping premises in good repair may be more the custom in one neighborhood than in another. Being secure from criminal conduct may be more presumed in one neighborhood than in another. The prospective juror's address is given counsel at the outset; it is simple to translate to neighborhood.
5. Real estate ownership is always a factor in this kind of case. Inquire further, however, to see how juror really feels about a property owner being sued.
6. The insurance question is extremely important, especially if defendant is a homeowner. Many jurors have homeowner policies and know that defendant may have one also. If your jurisdiction permits the insurance question and you don't ask it, you may contribute to the theory that insurance has nothing to do with the lawsuit, but you may also contribute to your client's receiving a smaller verdict or none at all.
7. The political philosophy of the juror is important. Property rights are very important to all American people, but often there is a balancing of property rights and human rights. Learn how the juror feels about that balancing.

EXAMPLE:

If juror feels the government "wastes money" on social programs, learn if the juror is concerned about how a program is being administered, or if the program should be administered at all. All jurors are concerned about taxes, but is the juror also concerned that one out of every eight children is hungry, or that people are homeless?

[1.56] Model Voir Dire: Criminal Cases—General. The first thing a trial lawyer must do in every criminal case is:

1. Prepare the jury for any weakness in your case, including the very fact you are representing the defendant. Jurors have formed opinions about people charged with a crime and about the criminal justice system. By asking about "presumption of innocence," you will learn which jurors respond negatively to the defendant in a criminal case.
2. Use voir dire to do something about any negative responses. Explain presumption of innocence, but don't expect jurors to ignore the fact that your client has been arrested by a police officer and prosecuted by a prosecutor.

Though jurors may think a defendant must have done something wrong to get himself into the courtroom, they seem to embrace the reasonable doubt concept more easily, and a large percentage of all acquittals are based on the jury not feeling beyond a reasonable doubt that the defendant is guilty. The defense lawyer knows this as he begins voir dire, and he uses voir dire to create a climate in which his client will be given a fair trial as guaranteed by the constitution.

The prosecutor will have the advantage of going first in voir dire. Defense counsel must offset this with any advantage there is in observing the jury during the prosecution's part of voir dire.

In all criminal cases:

1. Obtain commitment and educate as to value of our constitution:
   (a) Presumption of Innocence—See Section 1.34
   (b) Reasonable Doubt—See Section 1.29
   (c) Whether Accused Testifies—See Section 1.33 (if applicable)
2. Learn of any criminal experiences:
   Q. Have you, your family, or close friends ever been a victim of a crime?
   Q. Have you discussed or expressed an opinion about the problem of crime?
   Q. Do you have any opinion as to what could be done to reduce crime?

Q. Have you discussed this case with anyone or expressed an opinion to anyone about it?

Q. Have you formed an opinion about this case, an opinion you have not expressed to anyone?

Q. Are you willing to decide this case entirely upon the basis of the evidence and the law? This means you will not decide the case upon the basis of what some other juror thinks, is that right? This means you will not base your opinion upon what the prosecutor or I say, but rather upon the evidence and the law. Is that our understanding? And, of course, you will, under your oath to follow our American constitution, place no importance on the fact some police officer arrested him, is that right?

3. Inform jurors of their importance. The prosecutor has excellent opportunity to inform them that they CAN do something about crime, and defense counsel has a duty to inform them that their role is not that of a prosecutor, but rather that of a real guardian of liberty.

PROSECUTOR: Will Rogers said, "Everyone talks about the weather, but no one does anything about it." Well, today you are a part of the greatest justice system in the world, and I know you will take that duty seriously. It is my job to prosecute this man, and it is your job to listen to the evidence and to listen to the law, and then to do your duty. And if that means finding him guilty, would you have any problem doing that?

DEFENSE COUNSEL: Serving your country is a great thing, and how well you serve our justice system today depends upon how seriously you take the oath you give to follow our constitution. It will be easier for you to do this if you really believe in our Constitution. For example, if you really don't presume this man to be innocent, if you feel he may be guilty just because he has been brought into this courtroom, I would like to know that now, so we can talk about it. Does anyone feel that way?

4. Observe jurors from moment they enter courtroom. Observation is important in every voir dire, but especially in a criminal case, e.g., how the jurors dress, how they look at your client, how friendly they appear, what they are reading, how they respond to certain words or sentences. Don't trade this for all the expertise in the world.

5. Ask the questions that tell you which jurors fit the "defense" or "prosecution profile."

   Q. What is your occupation?

   Prosecutors look for "authority" people, such as those who enforce laws, rules or regulations. They also look for the "exact" people, such as accountants or engineers. Social workers and people in the arts respond better to defendant's argument for leniency.

   Q. Have you ever been a victim of a crime? Please explain.

   Those who have been victimized will identify with the victim. Those who are in a business where others in a similar business have been victimized will identify with the victim. Those who are in a business where others in a similar business have been victimized can identify with the victim.

   Q. Do you have any religious or philosophical beliefs on the subject of punishment? By including the word "philosophical" you give the juror the opportunity to tell you what he thinks without its being labeled a religious view. Some religions have strict views on punishment and these views affect the juror's attitude in deliberating.

   Q. If his Honor instructs you that you cannot vote to convict my client unless you find him guilty beyond a reasonable doubt, will you have any problem following that instruction? This gives you a chance to talk about the basic question in every criminal case. If you represent a defendant in a criminal case and jurors seem to really believe in this part of our Constitution, you have found jurors with a "defense" profile.

6. Fit the voir dire to the crime. In certain criminal cases women are good jurors, but in others they are not. A juror with strong beliefs about alcohol may be a prosecutor's juror in a Driving While Intoxicated case, but a defense counsel's juror where the victim was the user of alcohol.

7. Choose jurors who can identify with the defendant. Learn

   –where juror lives,

   –where juror works,

   –what organizations juror belongs to,

   –what are juror's hobbies and interests, and

   –what constitutes juror's family.

These are five of the most basic questions that can be asked, yet the answers will find some common area of identity. Try it the next time you first meet someone. You will be surprised how much you can identify with another, even if it is just living in the same area, both being Rotarians, or the fact you both have grandchildren.

8. Defense counsel should avoid jurors with friends or family connected with law enforcement or similar activities.

The courts have held that a defendant simply cannot receive a fair trial if jurors have preconceived ideas and that merely assuring the court they will be fair is not enough. *Irvin v. Dowd,* 366 US 717 (1961). Even one juror can prejudice a panel. *Petteway v. State,* 758 SW2d 861 (Tex. 1988). The judge must consider the demeanor and all factors to determine if juror will be fair. *Commonwealth v. Lane,* 555 A2d 1246 (Pa. 1989).

Trial judges have been permitted to keep a juror who had a fixed opinion that would require proving him innocent, if juror later assured court he would base verdict on the evidence. *Thomas v. State,* 539 SO2d 375 (Ala. Cr App 1988). Refusal to excuse where there is valid challenge for cause can, however, be abuse of discretion. *State v. Schwer,* 757 SW2d 258 (Mo. App 1988).

Where juror vacillates on questions, he should be excused. *Perillo v. State,* 758 SW2d 567 (Tex. Cr App 1988). The defendant is entitled to an impartial jury, and that means impartial in every respect. *State v. Sacoman,* 762 P2d 250 (N.M. 1988). Counsel must, however, object to protect his client's rights. *Felder v. State,* 758 SW2d 760 (Tex. Cr App 1988).

Questioning voir dire as to credibility of witnesses who plea bargained testimony was improper. *Underwood v. State,* 535 NE2d 507 (Ind. 1989). Improper to ask questions about facts to be introduced to illicit juror's interpretation of the law. *Commonwealth v. Smith,* 555 A2d 185 (Pa. Super 1989).

[1.57] Model Voir Dire: Criminal Cases—Homicide. In a homicide case, counsel has a double responsibility: (1) he must find jurors who will listen on the question of innocence or guilt and (2) he must know how jurors feel about punishment.

In a capital case, attitudes toward punishment are especially important, not only because the jury in most cases will make a recommendation on the death penalty, but also because those who are willing to put a person to death may be more likely to find a person guilty.

Every lawyer who tries capital cases should be familiar with an excellent guide for voir dire during capital cases, *Speak the Truth,* published by the Southern Poverty Law Center, but distributed by Alabama Capital Representation Resource Center, 444 Clay Street, Montgomery, Alabama, 36104.

In *Witherspoon,* the Supreme Court rendered an opinion that has been interpreted and reinterpreted, but remains the basis or guidepost of all death penalty cases. *Witherspoon v. Illinois,* 391 US 510 (1968). The Court invalidated an Illinois statute that excluded from the jury anyone with "conscientious scruples" against capital punishment or with objections to capital punishment, per se.

The Court rejected *Witherspoon's* "cross-section of the community" argument, but held that jurors must be excluded who would "automatically" vote against capital punishment, because this would interfere with the juror making an impartial decision on guilt.

Remember, in *Witherspoon,* Judge Douglas agreed with the majority in knocking down the Illinois statute. This liberal member of the Court did not fully agree, however, with the court's reasoning, adding:

> The Court permits a State to eliminate from juries some of those who have conscientious scruples against the death penalty; but it allows those who, having such scruples, nevertheless are deemed able to determine after a finding of guilt whether the death penalty or a lesser penalty should be imposed. I fail to see or understand the constitutional dimensions of those distinctions.

The trial lawyer must know the attitude of the public in order to know the chances of a prospective juror's being in favor of the death penalty. In an ABA poll, 68 percent of lawyers polled favored the death penalty. *American Bar Journal,* Vol. 71 p. 44 (1985). In a California referendum at the time of controversy over the "Rose Bird" Court, 80 percent of the voters favored the death penalty. *Time Magazine,* November, 1986, p. 53. A Florida study conducted by Cambridge Survey Research for Amnesty International (#0369) 1985, showed that 85 percent of the people surveyed favored the death penalty.

The voir dire procedure has become important in capital cases. A California case pointed out the need to sequester during individual inquiry. *Hovey v. Superior Court of Alameda County*, 616 P2d 1301 (Cal. 1980). Florida was among the first to adopt a bifurcated voir dire in capital cases. *Florida Statutes, 1985, Sec. 775.082(1)*. Former State Attorney Mark Ferraro estimated that in Florida it takes one day in 75 percent of the capital cases, and two days in the other 25 percent to select a jury. "Capital Jury Selection in Florida and Texas—A Quantitative Distinction Without A Legally Qualitative Difference?" Judge Hugh D. Hayes, *Nova Law Review*, V. 12, p. 743 (1988).

A few law review articles should be studied by those who try capital cases: "The Empirical Challenge to Death-Qualified Juries: On Further Examination," *Nebraska Law Review*, V. 65, p. 21 (1986); "Death-Qualified Juries: The 'Prosecution-Proneness' Argument Re-examined," *University of Pittsburgh Law Review*, V. 41, p. 353 (1980).

In capital murder cases:

1. Remember the *Witherspoon* Rule: Excludes prospective jurors in capital cases if "they could never vote to impose the death penalty."
2. Remember cases that have followed *Witherspoon*.

EXAMPLE:

Juror who "might be able to consider death penalty" properly excused. *State v. Williams*, 550 A2d 1172 (N.J. 1988); juror who would "always impose death sentence where state proved aggravating circumstances permitted on jury where he said he could put aside that opinion. *State v. Jones*, 378 SE2d 594 (S.C. 1989); "unequivocal opposition" to death penalty would prevent following instructions, juror properly excused. *State v. Thompson*, 768 SW2d 594 (Tenn. 1989); where juror said that she was "irrevocably committed not to vote for death penalty," she was properly excused, though defendant claimed it was unclear that she would never vote for death penalty. *State v. Allen*, 372 SE2d 855 (N.C. 1988); where juror made unequivocal statements but later said could "consider full range of punishment," properly permitted to remain on jury. *State v. Holt*, 758 SW2d 182 (Mo. App 1988); judge properly excused juror who replied in the negative to: "Is your conviction so strong that you cannot take an oath, knowing that a possibility exists in regard to capital punishment?" *Lockett v. Ohio*, 438 US 586 (1980); it is improper to exclude those who may be "affected" by the death in that the "lethal consequences of their decision would invest their deliberations with greater seriousness and gravity or would involve them emotionally." *Adams v. Texas*, 448 US 38 (1980); juror must be given opportunity to demonstrate (1) an "unequivocal" commitment to vote against death penalty, or (2) a "willingness to consider all penalties prescribed by law." *McCorquodale v. Balkcom*, 705 F2d 1553 (11th Cir. 1983); *Witherspoon* simply means you must exclude those who "automatically" vote against capital punishment. *State v. Blair*, 638 SW2d 739 (Mo. 1982).

3. Know the law, practice, and procedure of your jurisdiction.
4. Be sure any batson objection is raised.
5. Insist upon all inquiry and all excuses for cause you would raise in other criminal cases, but more so, because a human life is in issue.
   - Q. How do you feel about capital punishment?
   - Q. Under what circumstances do you think the State should take the life of a human being?
   - Q. Have you ever had a personal experience, to you or anyone you know, in which you feel the death penalty would have been an appropriate penalty?
   - Q. How do your religious or philosophical beliefs affect your feelings on this subject?
   - Q. Regardless of your views on this subject, would you still be able to follow the court's instruction and to consider all penalties that would be available under the law?

CAVEAT: In all homicide cases (1) You may aim your case at one juror who at least can give you a hung jury and (2) you may need to use insanity as a defense. We would all like to think a normal person would not take the life of another human being. Jurors involved with hospital work and social work and who for other reasons make good criminal defense jurors will be most likely to agree with you on this important issue.

[1.58] Model Voir Dire: Criminal Cases—Other Violent Crimes. There is something very unique about a violent crime that gets a juror's attention. Fear is an important force and violent crime elicits the kind of fear not experienced in other cases.

Where the crime with which your client is charged is a violent crime:

1. Use all the voir dire techniques required in other criminal cases.
2. Ask those questions that must be asked in this case.

   Q. Have you, or anyone close to you, ever had an experience similar to the one we are talking about?

   Q. What is your reaction to the amount of violence we see on television and in the world today?

   Q. Is there anything about your home, your workplace, or anywhere else you spend time that causes you to be concerned for your safety?

   Q. Will you be able to judge this case on its evidence, and not on something you saw on television or experienced yourself?

   Q. How do you feel about gun control?

   Q. Do you know any police officers? Have you talked with them about crime?

   Q. How would you describe the neighborhood you live in?

   Q. Have you ever kept or used a firearm?

   Q. Do you belong to any organizations that take a stand on the use of firearms?

[1.59] Model Voir Dire: Criminal Cases—Sex And Morality. Attitudes toward most crimes are based on a fear of such conduct being aimed at us personally, the need for order in our society, and a resistance toward people getting away with something. Though such behavior as rape is closely associated with violence, many sex and moral crimes are the subject of religious and philosophical attitudes.

It is especially important in this kind of case to distinguish between what is cause for excusing a juror and what is proper inquiry in use of peremptory. Where a prospective juror's niece had been raped, the court held everyone is opposed to rape and, since the juror agreed to be impartial, there was no cause for excusing her. *State v. Gray*, 533 SO2d 1242 (La. App 1988). The same result was reached where juror expressed concern about sitting on a child abuse case. *State v. Weatherbee*, 762 P2d 590 (Ariz. App 1988).

Where juror said that defendant would have to prove his innocence and that she would have a problem sitting on a child abuse case and being open-minded, juror need not be excused since this was the type of concern every mother would have and court corrected her original misconception. *State v. Wilson*, 771 P2d 1077 (Utah App 1989). Juror who as a doctor worked with rape patients and whose wife was a rape counsellor need not be excused for cause since he said that he could be impartial and that any bias was against the crime, not against the defendant. *Burley v. State*, 378 SE2d 329 (Ga. App 1989). Prosecutor was permitted to ask if any juror would tend to disbelieve a child because she delayed in reporting a sexual abuse. *State v. Lottmann*, 762 SW2d 539 (Mo. App 1988).

The courts have recognized, however, the explosive nature of certain cases. Where a prospective juror in case of child molestation said that she had "seen the change in the children" the judge should have excused the panel, or at least inquired of the jurors to assure impartiality. *State v. James*, 557 A2d 471 (R.I. 1989). Where prospective juror was so disturbed about rape that she could not follow the law, she was properly excused. *McCoy v. Lynaugh*, 874 F2d 954 (5th Cir. 1989).

In a case involving sending obscene material through the mail, the federal judge's questioning included the following:

Q. Do any of you believe as a matter of principle that material should never under any circumstances be barred from the mails on the ground that it is obscene?

Q. Do any of you believe that the freedom of the press is absolute and that nothing can properly be banned from the mails?

Q. Have any of you read any news stories about what the Supreme Court or other courts have held to be obscene matter, which articles would affect your deliberations in this case?

Q. Are any of you unable to ignore any such articles entirely in acting as fair and impartial jurors in this matter?

Q. Would any of you for any reason prefer not to act as a juror in this type of case?

Q. Are any of you members of the Legion for Decency or any other organization that seeks to raise the general standard of reading material, motion pictures, or TV shows now available?

Q. If you find the material personally distasteful could you set aside your personal feelings and follow the instructions of the court as to how the material should be judged?

Q. Would you be willing to consider the testimony of experts as to community standards in accordance with instructions of the court?

Q. Have you, in your discussions or readings on the issue of obscenity and morality, become influenced in such a way that you couldn't give these defendants a fair trial? *U.S. v. Klaw,* 63 CR 580 (SDNY 1964) (from brief of Appellee No. 288876, 2d Cir.).

A few special questions in criminal cases involving sex and morals:

Q. Do you think many women who are raped encouraged it by the way they dressed or acted? Do you think a woman consents to having intercourse when she quits fighting because she is afraid for her life?

Q. Do you think a woman should do anything in bed that her husband insists upon?

Q. How far should we go in letting two consenting adults do what they want to do in the privacy of their own bedroom? What if they are of the same sex? Do you think homosexuals are discriminated against?

Q. Do you think mere nudity is obscene? What if the people portrayed are involved in sexual conduct?

Q. Do you think it is all right for someone else to have a different standard relative to sex and morals than you do?

Q. What films do you see? Is there any program on television that offends you?

Q. Would you rather not serve on a jury in which you may have to view photos or films that show explicit sex scenes?

[1.60] Model Voir Dire: Criminal Cases—Narcotics. Drug abuse trials are crowding court dockets throughout the world. Feelings are strong about such cases and the trial lawyer must learn what feelings prospective jurors have toward drugs and about the particular kind of case they must decide.

Drug cases require special considerations:

1. Attitude toward use of illegal drugs.
   - Q. What do you think would happen if the use of all drugs were made legal?
   - Q. Do you use alcohol? Have you heard the claim that alcohol is our worst drug problem? What do you think about that?
   - Q. Do you think the use of illegal drugs occurs more often among people of certain races or certain economic levels? Please explain.
2. Personally affected by drug problem?
   - Q. Has anyone close to you been affected by the illegal use of drugs?
   - Q. Have you been the victim of circumstances where you felt the problem was caused by drug abuse?
   - Q. Have you or anyone close to you been involved in any program of education or law enforcement relating to drug abuse?
3. Attitude toward the particular kind of drug case being tried. Marijuana versus cocaine, possession versus selling, selling to adult addicts versus selling to children, all play an important role in the voir dire of a drug trial.
4. Your client and his image. Your client's image is important in every criminal trial, but especially important in a drug abuse trial. Who would do this and why? Was a young person pressured into it? Will the problem go away without harsh punishment? Is this the sort of thing my child could innocently become involved in? The prospective jurors are asking themselves many questions before the voir dire even begins.

[1.61] Model Voir Dire: Criminal Cases—White Collar Crime. In a white-collar criminal case you don't throw away your entire "book" on criminal voir dire, but you must certainly reexamine it. Your client is likely to be a defendant who does not fit the criminal image and may, in fact, be the very person you would strike from the jury when defending a criminal case or when representing a plaintiff in a civil case.

In white-collar crime cases, special questions should be asked:

Q. In this case we will be talking about a nonviolent crime in which no physical harm could have resulted to anyone. Yet the charge is one that my client takes very seriously and one that we will defend very seriously. If you serve on this jury will you give our evidence the same attention you would if my client had been charged with a violent crime?

Q. My client has been charged with forgery. Have you, or anyone close to you, ever been a victim of such conduct? (Inquire as to employment that might show experience with crime charged.)

Q. My client is presumed to be innocent until proven guilty. Do you have any problem with that concept guaranteed by our Constitution? (In this kind of case push the presumption of innocence especially hard, since this is one kind of criminal case in which jurors are most likely to believe in this concept.)

Q. This may seem similar to a civil case in that my client is charged with having money that the prosecution claims belongs to someone else, but a guilty verdict would give my client a criminal record and could send him to prison. So you cannot, under our American Constitution, find him guilty unless you are sure beyond a reasonable doubt. Do you have any problem with that?

[1.62] Investigate Fully The Publicity Factor. When the judge denies your motion for a change of venue based on pretrial publicity, your job has just begun. You must now look into the minds of prospective jurors and learn what they know and how that would affect their verdict.

The layman is likely to ask, "How can anyone who lives in California not know all about the Patty Hearst case?" Let's look at this case and see how the pretrial publicity problem was handled.

Example of "publicity" voir dire: The *Hearst* Case:

Q. Mr. McGregor, it's the time in the case where it's my duty to interrogate you in more detail concerning what you've read and heard about this case. In discussing what you've read and heard, we'll go into areas of your television, radio, and newspaper experiences, and, secondly, your contact with other people. . . . I should ask you, however, before we begin, that if you now feel presently disqualified, you will not have to go through this intensive and extensive investigation. Do you presently feel there is anything from what you've seen or read from any other source which would make it difficult or impossible for you to sit as a fair and impartial juror in this case?

A. No, there is nothing.

Q. All right. You feel you could be fair and impartial under these circumstances?

A. Yes.

Q. . . . Would you tell us what newspapers you read, what television you listen to, and what radio stations you listen to?

A. I live in Santa Rosa. So it's the *Press-Democrat*. Sometimes I read the morning *Chronicle* at work, and usually Channel 5 news on television.

Q. . . . Any radio stations?

A. KABL

Q. . . . Would you start from the beginning. . . . February of 1974 . . . tell us what you remember about that and whence you heard it?

A. I remember seeing her—listening to it on television. When it happened I might have heard it on the radio, I am not sure.

Q. . . . What was it you remember hearing?

A. I believe I remember hearing them interviewing Steven Weed about what happened.

Q. Would you tell us who you believed Steven Weed was from the report.

A. I believe it was her boyfriend at the time.

Q. What pictures do you recollect having seen on television or in the newspapers?

A. It was pointed . . . she was standing.

Q. You say she. You mean Miss Hearst?

A. The commentator was telling it, where she was at. She was standing there while this robbery was taking place.

Q. What about the details of the pictures? What was in the picture? What did she have, if anything?

A. She was supposed to have had—looked like a machine gun.

The only voir dire question raised in the district court in *Hearst* was the propriety of the trial judge's *in camera* questioning of a sequestered panel. The presiding judge ruled: "It is an unquestioned principle in the federal criminal justice system that the conduct of the jury voir dire is best left to the sound discretion of the trial judge. *U.S. v. Hearst*, 412 F.2d 877 (N.D. Cal. 1976). No voir dire was even mentioned in the appeal to the Ninth District.

What are the guidelines? In *Silverthorne*, the court established interesting guidelines for handling pretrial publicity that have been cited with approval by trial and appellate courts:

1. It was within sound discretion of the trial court to deny continuance where request was to permit adverse publicity to abate.
2. Trial judge has wide discretion but with persuasiveness of modern communications, trial court must take strong measures to ensure that the balance is never weighed against accused.
3. "When pretrial publicity is great, the trial judge must exercise respondingly great care."
4. Trial judge must decide if "nature and strength of opinion formed" raised "the presumption of partiality."
5. Appellate courts will not interfere with trial courts' voir dire decisions unless there was a "clear abuse of discretion."
6. Trial judge can insist upon conducting the voir dire, but must exercise a "sound 'judicial' discretion in acceptance or rejection of supplemental questions proposed by counsel, to be propounded by the judge."
7. The trial court's voir dire did not "adequately dispel the probability of prejudice accruing from pretrial publicity," where (a) court's questions were calculated to evoke "subjective responses" in which prospective jurors "were called upon to assess their own impartiality," and (b) the voir dire was "too general to adequately probe the prejudice issue."
8. "Merely going through the form of obtaining juror's assurances

of impartiality is insufficient"—where all 65 prospective jurors know something about the case. The trial court must ascertain what information the jurors had accumulated to determine the "impact caused by this pretrial knowledge on the juror's impartiality."

9. It is not required that jurors be "totally ignorant of the facts and issues involved," and the "mere existence of any preconceived notion as to the guilt or innocence of an accused" does not disqualify a prospective juror if the juror can set aside his impression or opinion.
10. Where 30 percent of prospective jurors expressed opinion of appellant's guilt and where there was voluminous pretrial publicity, court should have granted accused's request that court inquire "what information they had obtained relative to the case and their source of knowledge."
11. "Because of the voluminous publicity . . . the court's voir dire examination should have been directed to the individual jurors."
12. The fact that a prospective juror does not respond to questionings does not mean he is free from prejudice.
13. The "right to explore for impartiality" may include permitting counsel "to interrogate the prospective jurors."
14. ". . . an order prohibiting the reading of newspapers in the jury room would have been proper, and, indeed necessary."
15. Where publicity during trial prejudices jury, an offer by court to interrogate the jurors individually will not suffice.
16. Where jurors read newspaper articles about the case during trial, accused is entitled to have jury questioned by judge.

    Silverthorne v. U.S., 400 F.2d 627 (9th Cir. 1968).

Questions where publicity is a factor:

Q. Have you read or heard about this case?

Q. What newspapers do you read?

Q. Which television programs do you watch?

Q. Which radio stations do you listen to?

Q. Did you learn anything about the case from any of these sources?

Q. What did you read or hear about this case?

Q. Have you discussed this case with anyone?

Q. Please tell me about those discussions.

Q. Have you expressed an opinion to anyone about this case?

Q. Have you formed an opinion that you have not discussed with anyone?

Q. Please explain why you feel that way. Would you be able to serve on a jury and to return a verdict that is fair and impartial to both sides?

Q. Is there anything you can think of that would keep you from starting in a completely neutral position?

[1.63] Start With Seriousness Of Subjective Injuries. Jurors are impressed by X-rays and photographs. When they must use their imaginations to picture an injury, they must be capable of understanding the nature of the injury. The trial lawyer not only must look for jurors who will understand, but also he or she must prepare the jurors for this kind of lawsuit.

The ability to imagine and the ability to feel for people who suffer are important in all personal injury cases, but they are especially important if the injuries are subjective. You and your client must begin the task of selling the jury on this kind of injury before the voir dire even begins.

If injuries are subjective, remember:

1. The important credibility factor is even more important. Before voir dire begins the jury is evaluating the claim. If plaintiff appears to be exaggerating, or if he is too lively or too restricted, then the jurors are looking for something upon which to base an opinion. When the jury learns the injuries are subjective they will know your whole lawsuit will depend upon credibility.
2. Explain the nature of the injury and learn their attitude toward such injury.

   Q. Some of the doctors who will testify in this case may call this kind of injury a "whiplash injury." Have any of you heard that term? What does it mean to you? Are you willing to listen to all of the testimony from the doctors who will testify for each side, and then to form your opinion about this kind of injury?

Q. Much of the damage to my client has been in the form of emotional distress, for which she is entitled to recovery under our state law. We cannot bring in X-rays of broken bones to show this because the mind and nervous system are much more sensitive, sophisticated, and fragile than that. We will bring in the best doctors we have been able to find who are experts in this field. Will you wait to base your opinion upon what these doctors and the other lawyer's doctors testify on this subject, and not upon any preconceived idea you might have had about this kind of injury?

3. Use whatever scientific help that is available. If thermography will help win your case, be sure to use it. If you are going to use such help during the trial, talk about it during voir dire.

   Q. Have any of you heard of a relatively new concept for determining pain called "thermography"? His Honor has indicated that he will permit such evidence to be presented to the jury. Are you willing to listen to this scientific evidence, and any evidence the other side may introduce, and then to base your verdict upon all of the evidence you hear? Do any of you feel uncomfortable listening to scientific evidence? (If so, talk about it, don't lose a good juror but let him know how simple it is so that he will feel comfortable. Use this opportunity to help the jury understand the scientific evidence you will introduce.)

4. Use lay evidence that will help. Some of your best evidence as to a subjective injury will come from nonexpert witnesses, so prepare the jury for this during voir dire.

   Q. We will introduce the best medical evidence available in this case, but by the end of the trial I think you will agree with me that the people who really know about this injury are the people who live with it every day. My client's wife and people who worked alongside my client on the job before and after the accident are going to testify. Will you consider their testimony, even though they are not doctors?

[1.64] Distinguish Sympathy And Concern. Plaintiff's lawyer knows that opposing counsel is going to mention sympathy, so why shouldn't he be the nice guy and let the jury know he does not want sympathy. If your client deserves sympathy then he or she will get it, and all the talk about it by either counsel will not shake that from the juror's mind.

Think "final argument" during voir dire and you may find what you want to chat about with the jurors. Example of how you might handle sympathy during final argument:

> "I stopped at the ice cream stand over on Gulf-to-Bay last week and there are a couple of picnic benches outside and at the bench was an eight year old boy and a fourteen year old boy. I could hear the older boy say,
>
> *Now, when your mother gets married, the man will be your stepfather. Do you have any problem with that?*
> *No.*
> *And I guess I will be a half-brother or something. Do you have any problem with that?*
> *No.*
> *I just want for you to be happy.*
> *I'm happy.*
>
> "I felt that the young boy did not want sympathy during this challenging time in his life, but I could tell that this boy did appreciate the fact the older boy was concerned enough to take him down and buy him an ice cream cone and to talk to him. My client is a lot like that little boy—he doesn't want your sympathy, but he sure appreciates concern for what happened to him."

Direct your voir dire toward how sympathetic a juror would be regarding your client. Why not? Isn't that what you want, a sympathetic jury? Remember what the judge did in the MCI/AT&T case: he asked each juror to spend about two minutes telling about himself or herself. All attorneys agreed that it was an extremely effective voir dire.

Deal with the sympathy factor during voir dire:

1. Plaintiff's counsel should discuss it first, but if he fails to, defense counsel will have a real advantage and should use it effectively.

   Q. Under the law of our state you cannot base your verdict upon sympathy, but must base it upon evidence and the law. Do you have any problem doing this? (This question can be asked by plaintiff or defendant. Plaintiff, however, will want to add: "My client does not want sympathy, but he does want a jury that will listen to all of the evidence and will be concerned about what happened, and will bring back a verdict that is fair to both sides.")

2. Encourage jurors to "root for" your client. Jurors want "winners," someone they can "root for." This means any sympathy that they have for your client cannot originate with your client. Your client must project a picture of "in spite of this, I am going to make it." A client who asks for sympathy will not get it. The juror must perceive the circumstances that warrant sympathy, and the plaintiff's lawyer must select the jurors with the best perception of that kind.

[1.65] Discuss Frankly The Potential Size Of Verdict. Prior to 1962 there was no such thing as a million dollar verdict. Million dollar settlements and verdicts are common, and billion dollar verdicts have arrived. This means that the smaller verdicts of yesterday are larger today and talk of huge verdicts may help the plaintiff in nearly all personal injury cases.

Where plaintiff talked of potential amount of award during voir dire, jurors could be reminded that any award must be supported by evidence. *Stewart v. Alvarez*, 583 NE2d 646 (Ill. App 1989). Where jury had been questioned on attitudes toward damage awards, it was not improper to exclude questions about "liability crisis" or "lawsuit crisis." *Russo v. Birrenkott*, 770 P2d 1335 (Colo. App 1988).

Another case held that where court had asked general questions about whether jurors had read or experienced anything that would affect the amount of compensation they would be willing to award, it was proper to deny questions about whether they had read articles which blamed high cost of insurance and loss of medical personnel on large jury award. *Doe v. Hafen*, 772 P2d 456 (Utah App 1989).

Discuss huge awards during voir dire, where applicable.

1. Does a juror have a "reluctance" to award a huge verdict? Most jurors are willing to apply the court's instructions to the evi-

dence, so there must be a problem a juror has in being reluctant to award adequate damages to a person who has been injured.

Q. How do you feel about a case in which a person files a lawsuit for a huge amount of money? Without having heard anything of the case, do you have any opinion as to the largest amount that should be awarded to a person?

Q. There will be a considerable loss of income and loss of capacity to earn a living in this case. This figure will come to many thousands of dollars. Do you have any problem awarding my client a huge sum of money in payment of these damages, just because it will come to a lot of money? Are you willing to listen to the evidence and to base your verdict upon that evidence under the law as his Honor will instruct you?

Q. The past and future medicals in this case are just enormous. His Honor will instruct you as to what my client is entitled to under the law. Will you have any problem following these instructions, even though this may mean you must return a huge verdict for damages?

Q. Under the law of our state, you are not only to make my client whole as to the economic losses he sustained as a result of this accident, but also you are to award damages he sustained for pain and suffering, emotional distress, being unable to live the way he lived before the accident. In this case I will suggest to you that these damages are substantial and from the evidence you may find them to be substantial and if, under the evidence you feel my client is entitled to a huge verdict, would you for any reason have a problem voting for such a verdict, simply because it would be for such a large amount?

2. Can the juror comprehend large sums of money? Some people deal in large sums of money daily and have no problem with huge figures, including large verdicts. Others are simply unable to deal with this and would have a hard time bringing back a million dollar verdict. Unfortunately for the plaintiff, some of the most sympathetic jurors of the past are simply unable to comprehend huge verdicts. Unfortunately for defendant, some of his "ideal," those "exact" kind of people, understand the economic basis for a huge verdict.

3. Will a juror understand and agree with your experts?
   (a) Medical experts. Causal relationship, reasonableness of expenses, kind of expenses (often defense argues for cheapest custodial care), and speculative nature of future medicals depend upon medical experts the jurors must believe.
   (b) Economic experts. The economic damages in this kind of case are complicated and should not be left in the hands of jurors who cannot comprehend them. A basic ability to comprehend and a willingness to listen to and evaluate expert testimony are required.

[1.66] How To Get A "Punitive Damage" Jury. Most people favor some kind of punitive damages when the concept is explained to them, but a growing number of jurors are associating this form of damages with huge verdicts they oppose. Plaintiff's lawyers have the special problem of jurors not being willing to punish others unless the conduct really warrants it.

Jurors simply will not award punitive damages unless they understand the purpose of it and see some social significance to its application. Few jurors on criminal cases really enjoy sending someone to prison, but nevertheless reach that kind of verdict after they see the need for it.

During voir dire counsel for plaintiff must begin orientation, but not by asking for punitive damages or even by spending much time directly on the subject. The jury must know the unacceptable conduct and that someone sustained actual damages BEFORE there is even mention of punitive damages. If the jury is not going to get excited about your lawsuit and the need to do something about the defendant, then you may do well not even to pursue punitive damages.

The greatest purpose of punitive damages is to keep this defendant, and others, from behaving so in the future. People like to be a part of keeping awful things from happening. During voir dire you must find jurors who are receptive to satisfying this need, and then you must let them know what must be corrected.

If you are seeking punitive damages:

1. Tell jury about the conduct.
   Q. This is a case in which the defendant newspaper published a story about my client even though some of the staff knew

it was false. Do any of you have any problem serving on a jury where you may be called upon to bring back a verdict against the newspaper?

2. Tell about the damages.

   Q. If our evidence shows that my client lost his job as a result of the article published by this newspaper, would you have any problem following the judge's instructions if he told you this was one of the elements of actual damages you are to consider?

3. Tell them about punitive damages.

   Q. Since this article was published with full knowledge that it was false, and since we feel this was intentional, wrongful, and malicious, we are asking that you return a judgment for punitive damages, in addition to any actual damages you may find appropriate. The purpose of punitive damages is to punish such conduct, so that this company and others will not do such a thing in the future. How do you feel about this concept of law?

   Q. Do you feel that there is certain conduct that will continue and get worse if we don't do something about it? How do you feel about people telling lies about other people? What if those lies are read by a million people; do you think the need to stop such conduct is even greater?

   Q. Under the law, the punitive damages go to the person injured and not to the state or some other government, as in the case of a fine; do you have a problem with that?

   Q. Whether or not you decide to return a verdict for punitive damages is entirely up to you, after hearing all the evidence. Are you willing to listen to all of the evidence and then, if you feel there is a need to discourage such conduct, to consider whatever amount you feel it will take to keep this defendant, and others, from doing this in the future, even if that amount is a substantial sum?

If plaintiff does not discuss this, defendant should.

The jury should know it is entirely in its discretion, but if plaintiff covers it as he should, he can follow up with as close to a commitment as the court will permit.

[1.67] Be Sure Jurors Understand Comparative Negligence. Comparative negligence is here to stay, but some jurors remember outmoded concepts that are no longer the law. During voir dire you must explain what the law is under comparative negligence, and what the law is not.

In law school my wife was intrigued as I explained the "last clear chance doctrine." When I returned to Missouri, I found lawyers intrigued with the "humanitarian doctrine," and in other states contributory negligence was keeping seriously injured people from receiving a dime for their injuries.

Juries must understand that under pure comparative negligence, a client can be 90 percent at fault and still receive 10 percent of his or her damages. They must also know that if a person is not at fault, he or she should be fully compensated.

Where the comparative negligence doctrine is applicable:

1. Explain the law.

   Q. The law in our state is. . . . How do you feel about this?

2. Explain how the law is applied.

   Q. This means that if you find that my client was 50 percent at fault, he is still entitled to recover 50 percent of his damages. Do you have a problem with that?

   Q. This means if my client were not at fault, and if the other party were entirely at fault, then you should return a verdict for all of the damages sustained by my client. Do you have any problem with that?

CAVEAT: Not only the law on comparative negligence, but also the procedure followed differs from state to state. It is important to be familiar with the law and procedures, and local rules and practices.

[1.68] Study Computers And "Computer People." Computers have become a way of life in the legal profession, but they have made one contribution that has gone nearly unnoticed. The computer industry has created a new class of worker in America, one that must be understood by the trial lawyer during voir dire.

People who work with computers are very "special" people.

1. They form a large part of our population. On every panel it is likely you will talk with someone who is employed in the computer industry.
2. Determine the nature of their involvement. A salesman who sells computers may have all the "plaintiff profile" features of other salesmen, and yet he may be a different kind of salesman. Further inquiry is definitely required. If the juror works all day with computers, then he or she will probably have some of the "computer profile" characteristics.
3. Look for the "computer profile." Lawyers who pride themselves on spotting the exactness trait of an engineer or accountant fail to recognize this same trait in the computer specialist. It is a brand new ballgame with some brand new players about to decide the economic future of your client.

Questions you might ask "computer people":

Q. What do you do relative to computers?

Q. How long have you done this?

Q. What did you do before you got this job?

Q. What training have you had with computers?

Q. How do you like this kind of work?

Q. Do you consider yourself good at math?

Q. Do you think computers ever make mistakes, or is it the people who make mistakes?

Q. I guess we all make mistakes, don't we?

Q. If you serve on this jury, will you listen to all of the evidence and to the law as it is given to you by the court, and decide the case based upon that law and evidence?

[1.69] When And How To Use PreTrial Experts. Many experts can help you even before you reach the courtroom. In preparing for the voir dire, you are preparing for trial and preparing for settlement. Some of the pretrial expertise avenues available include:

1. Surveys to obtain jury profiles. Having a survey of the area from which the jurors will be drawn to determine which "profile" of jurors will lean toward your side is one of the most expensive, yet most effective, methods of preparing for voir dire in advance. Phil Corboy spent $22,000 for such a survey but felt it was well worth the price when he settled the case for more than 5 million dollars before trial. This approach is definitely reserved for the high-figure case.

How can you benefit from this approach in the case that does not warrant the expense? Know what is available. Use part of the expertise, or find a less expensive way to acquire some of the knowledge you would pay big money for in a big case.

EXAMPLE:

There is often a single question you want answered. You may have it answered without paying for the entire survey. Explain your problem, including lack of money, and see what the expert has to offer.

2. Profiles without survey. Many consultants will prepare a profile in advance of trial that is based upon their own expertise and not upon a survey. This is less expensive, but may not have the "tailor-made" advantage of a profile based on a survey. Since trial lawyers usually have their own profile that is based upon experience and intuition, any professional help in preparing the profile will be extremely helpful.

Explain your problem to the expert. See what the expert has to offer and decide if the expert can help you. This will help you find out what you will need to know.

3. Mock juries. Some professionals will actually find people from a cross section of the community who will agree to sit as "jurors" and give their reaction to a condensed version of the trial. Such jurors give their impression of witnesses, concepts, and other factors that will be judged by the real jury. This

method is not very expensive; and though not justified in small cases, is not reserved for cases where counsel expects a million dollar verdict.

There are many ways this can be accomplished. Some experts offer this service and some law firms have their own personnel ready to perform it. Some firms use it on a case-by-case basis, while others use it in every jury trial. Some use the pretrial mock jury during trial, and others do not.

4. Pretrial investigation of prospective jurors. Lawyers should have much information that can readily be applied to the information gathered about prospective jurors. Neighborhoods, schools, places of employment, and many other factors tell you much about how people of this group feel regarding certain issues. Once you learn the relevant facts about the prospective juror, it is a simple matter of applying it.
5. Use of amateurs. Many firms use people around the office (friends and others) to form mock juries or to show evidence to, or to play a video statement to, or otherwise to obtain an impression of how a jury will react. This is an inexpensive and effective way to prepare for voir dire.

Talk about your cases. Ask people what they think of a certain fact or a certain witness. Have your clients review their video statements and tell you what they think. Discuss your weakness and see how you can overcome it.

6. Other uses of pretrial expertise. There are many ways experts can help counsel before trial.
   (a) Selecting a jurisdiction. Often you can choose between two or more jurisdictions. You can make this decision more intelligently if you know what kind of juror will help you, and which jurisdiction has such jurors. An expert can help you accomplish this.
   (b) Obtaining a settlement. You cannot arrive at that magic figure at which a case should be settled until you know what kind of jurors will decide your case. Experts can help you do this.

(c) Preparation of proof. Some jurors will require more proof than others. Experts can tell you how much proof you will need on certain issues. This will save time and money by allowing you to establish realistic priorities of proof.

(d) Evaluation of witnesses. You often have a choice of which witnesses you will use. This is particularly true with experts. The courtroom consultant can help you decide which witnesses to use and how to prepare the jury for witnesses you must use.

All of this must be done before voir dire, and all of it will help prepare for voir dire!

[1.70] How To Develop Your Own Expertise. Whatever expert help you obtain before or during voir dire, you are on your own once the judge instructs you to proceed. That is why it is imperative that you develop your own expertise, using what you have learned both from others and in the courtroom.

There are a few suggestions in this chapter that can get you started, using the newest techniques. Read everything you can find, attend seminars, but most of all, develop your own talent. In addition to the methods you will learn from experts, practice those techniques that all lawyers use and make them a part of your voir dire talent.

Observing the methods of good lawyers is the best way to develop your talent. Never imitate the style of another lawyer, but learn from every lawyer you see in court. Often you will learn what not to do, but nearly every lawyer has some method that can be adopted with your own style.

Watch the judge during voir dire. He has been there before and if he thinks a lawyer is just wasting time there is a good possibility that the jury feels the same way. Learn what kind of question causes a judge to interfere. It is important to know the thinking of judges in general, and extremely important to know the thinking of the judge who will try your case.

1. Learn to ask follow-up questions. Are you a practical nurse or a registered nurse? Do you work at a hospital, or from a registry,

or what? The Nurse's Report is, of course, a very important part of the hospital record; have you ever been responsible for keeping such a record?

2. Maintain a genuine interest in the dialogue you engaged in with the prospective juror:
   (a) If you are not really interested, it will show through and you will appear to be artificial and just going through the motions.
   (b) You may not hear the answers and you will not be part of the dialogue.
   (c) Once you are just going through the motions you will not follow up with questions that will give you the answers you need.
3. Ask open-ended questions that will encourage discussion.
   (a) Questions that call for a "yes" or "no" answer discourage dialogue and should only be used when obtaining a commitment.
   (b) "Tell me about it" shows an interest in what the juror is about to say and gives the juror a chance to talk.
4. Practice the interview method daily. The interview method of communicating, whether through the news media or in the courtroom, is nothing more than being an effective and considerate conversationalist. Use it every day!

EXAMPLE:

Next time a friend mentions that her son is attending Missouri University, don't just say, "That's nice" or "Is he that old?" Why not reply with any one of the numerous questions that say, "Tell me about it"? Why not let her know you know something about the school? "Mizzou has a great school of journalism;" "I hear the basketball team is going to do well this year;" "Columbia is a neat little city." Why not ask, "What is he studying?" or "How does he like it?" or "Why did he choose Missouri University?"

5. Look like a lawyer. Men should usually wear dark blue or dark gray suits. A woman should not "look like a man," but rather like a lawyer. The "hard" look may be one of authority, but a softer look may be more appreciated once the circumstances

give the lawyer as much authority as he needs. (Often a red tie with a blue suit; some criminal lawyers wear less authoritative suits.)

Men should wear little, if any, jewelry. Women should wear jewelry, but not ostentatiously. Glasses are an advantage, but should be conservative and removed at times. Dress a notch above others in the courtroom, but not two notches above anyone. Jurors assume you own more than one suit!

Throughout this book I have suggested ways to develop your technique as a trial lawyer and this has included suggestions that have been made by leading courtroom experts. In this chapter I have discussed experts who are available before and during trial. In this chapter you will find some of what the experts are telling us. All of this and all of the seminars you can attend and books on courtroom psychology will give you an expertise that will help you during voir dire. None of this, however, will take the place of your own observation and talent for sizing up jurors, but it will certainly help tremendously.

Since Clarence Darrow first suggested that criminal defense lawyers should strike Germans and keep Italians, lawyers have been trying to put jurors into pigeon holes. Experts have found that certain traits are found in people of all nationalities, religions, and economic levels. These experts have looked for groupings based upon psychological factors.

There are four groupings I would like to discuss because experts write and talk about them. These experts, especially Dr. Thomas Sannito in his writings and lectures, divide personality types as follows: (1) authoritarians, (2) perfectionists, (3) egomaniacs, and (4) sympathetic indulgers.

1. AUTHORITARIANS. Criminal Defense: strike; Civil Plaintiff: it depends. The authoritarians insist that everyone else be like them. They are cold, hard to convince, and seek power through conformity. They try to dominate those below them and seek approval of those above them. They are severe with those who don't conform.

   They obviously must be stricken by a criminal defense lawyer, and it appears they would be a poor choice for plaintiff's lawyer, but he must consider the type of case, the parties, witnesses, and other factors. If your client is a police officer who was run into by a "hippie" who violated the law, the authoritarian may not be a bad juror.

Identify them by a "Yes Sir" that they give subserviently, hoping for the same respect from someone under them; by the way they act with authority; and by their response to questions. (Love is not as important as discipline, being embarrassed gives them more concern than hurting someone's feelings.)

2. PERFECTIONISTS. Criminal Defense: it depends. (Female perfectionists make good criminal defense jurors). Civil Plaintiff: strike. They set extremely high standards for themselves and others. They may think an injured person should have been more careful and is not entitled to any money he or she did not earn.

   In a criminal case they may hold the prosecution to a high standard of proof. This conflicts, however, with their demand for proper conduct and may make them a great risk to criminal defense counsel. NOTE: Female perfectionists usually make good criminal defense jurors because they demand more of the prosecution before they will send someone to prison, but this is not always true of male perfectionists. Identify them by looking for those who are fussy about their appearance; by their employment in jobs that require exactness, like accounting and computers; and by their responses to questioning (since he controls his destiny he would not buy a lottery ticket, he hates surprises, and is concise in his budgeting).

3. EGOMANIACS. Criminal Defense: strike. Civil Plaintiff: strike. Criminal Prosecution: strike. Civil Defense: strike. Who needs him? No one! In the other groupings, I have assumed opposing counsel would use the converse, but not here. The egomaniacs are entirely undependable and could ruin either side's lawsuit.

   Jury trials should not be a form of Russian Roulette, and if you don't have enough confidence in your lawsuit to try it before a proper jury, you should settle it or dismiss it. Egomaniacs are so much in love with themselves that they will not listen to either side of the lawsuit.

   WARNING: They often have education, wealth, or position that gives them influence over other jurors and even a shot at becoming foreperson. Their arrogance is a poor substitute tor reason.

Identify them by counting the number of times they say "I"; by observing their dress and appearance, which is aimed at impressing you with their importance; by asking a few questions that give them a chance to talk about their importance.

4. SYMPATHETIC INDULGERS. Criminal Defense: keep on jury. Civil Plaintiff: keep on jury. Generous and softhearted! Not strict with themselves or others. They are warm and loving.

    Identify them by their appearance—they dress for comfort; by asking questions that tell you of their compassion, warmth, and concern for others.

This is just a peek into what we can learn from courtroom psychologists and other experts who can help us during voir dire. This is just an invitation to explore what they are telling us, and a challenge to become an even better trial lawyer by using every technique your opposing counsel may be using.

[1.71] ***Batson v. Kentucky*****: Prejudice And Preemptory Challenges.** Preemptory challenges are the most important part of voir dire, and *Batson v. Kentucky* is what peremptory challenges are all about. It is imperative that the trial lawyer study this case and master its meaning.

In 1965 the Supreme Court told the trial bar that even though prosecutors cannot discriminate, the peremptory challenge was a trial lawyer's tool that should not be easily disturbed. *Swain v. Alabama,* 380 U.S. 202 (1964). Though the Court in *Swain* recognized a "purposeful or deliberate" discrimination to be unconstitutional, it found no "systematic striking" where of eight black jurors, two were exempt and six were struck by the prosecutor.

In *Swain,* the Court reminded the bar that "The peremptory challenge has very old credentials." So old, that the Court hung onto it in spite of the fact that even though about seven Blacks were on every jury panel, not a single one had served on the jury in fourteen years.

It is the reverence for the peremptory challenge that made *Swain* so important, and that now makes *Batson* even more important. In Justice White's concurring opinion he said: "The Court overturns the principal holding in *Swain v. Alabama,* 380 U.S. 202 (1965), that the Constitution does not require in any given case an inquiry into the prosecutor's reasons for using his peremptory challenges. . . ."

Writing for the majority, Justice Powell wrote: "While we recognize, of course, that the peremptory challenge occupies an important position in our trial procedures, we do not agree that our decision today will undermine the contribution the challenge generally makes to the administration of justice."

In a concurring opinion, Justice Marshall reminded the Court that more than a century had passed since the Court had found laws prohibiting blacks on a jury to be unconstitutional. *Strauder v. West Virginia*, 100 U.S. 303 (1880). He offered many statistics to show that *Strauder* did not keep prosecutors from discriminating.

Justice Marshall said that even under *Batson*, prosecutors are only required to hold their discrimination to an "acceptable" level. He concluded: "The inherent potential of peremptory challenges to distort the jury process by permitting the exclusion of jurors on racial grounds should ideally lead the Court to ban them entirely from the criminal justice system."

Radical as this may sound, he points out that in *Swain*, Justice Goldberg wrote that if we must decide between peremptory challenges and a fair trial, peremptory challenges must go. He also pointed out that some judges and authors have felt prosecutors should be denied peremptories, but defense counsel must have the right to exercise them as a part of a "fair trial."

Chief Justice Burger was joined by Justice Rehnquist in a dissent. "Today the Court sets aside the peremptory challenge, a procedure which has been part of the common law for many centuries and part of our jury system for nearly 200 years."

Though the dissent questioned the Court's considering equal protection and overruling *Swain*, since Petitioner did not raise either issue, it did discuss the role of peremptories, stating: "The peremptory challenge has been in use without scrutiny into its basis for nearly as long as juries have existed."

In *Batson* the prosecutor struck all four black prospective jurors, and the trial judge said that attorneys can "strike anybody they want to." The Supreme Court held that a *prima facie* case of discrimination is made where juror was member of "cognizable racial group" and that prosecutor used peremptory challenge to remove him; that there was a "selection practice" that permits "those to discriminate who are of a mind to discriminate"; and there is inference that prosecutor used peremptories to "exclude" prospective jurors "on account of their races."

Much has been written about voir dire, and much has been written about peremptory challenges. In *Batson*, the reader finds an excellent discussion by those who serve on the Supreme Court. It is required reading for every trial lawyer! By mastering *Batson*, you master the use of peremptories, the tool of your trade.

It is only with this knowledge that we can save the right to peremptory challenges. The civil trial lawyer cannot assume this is only a matter for criminal trials. What is lost in the criminal trial will be lost in the civil trial, where "tort reformers" are already tinkering with the system. Being unable to excuse certain jurors without showing cause could result in a great injustice.

BATSON v. KENTUCKY, 476 U.S. 79 (1986).

FACTS:

During the criminal trial in a Kentucky state court of petitioner, a black man, the judge conducted *voir dire* examination of the jury venire and excused certain jurors for cause. The prosecutor then used his peremptory challenges to strike all four black persons on the venire, and a jury composed only of white persons was selected. Defense counsel moved to discharge the jury on the ground that the prosecutor's removal of the black veniremen violated petitioner's rights under the Sixth and Fourteenth Amendments to a jury drawn from a cross section of the community, and under the Fourteenth Amendment to equal protection of the laws. Without expressly ruling on petitioner's request for a hearing, the trial judge denied the motion, and the jury ultimately convicted petitioner. Affirming the conviction, the Kentucky Supreme Court observed that recently, in another case, it had relied on *Swain v. Alabama*, 380 U.S. 202, and had held that a defendant alleging lack of a fair cross section must demonstrate systematic exclusion of a group of jurors from the venire.

HELD:

1. The principle announced in *Strauder v. West Virginia*, 100 U.S. 303, that a State denies a black defendant equal protection when it puts him on trial before a jury from which members of his race have been purposefully excluded, is reaffirmed. Pp. 84–89.

(a) A defendant has no right to a petit jury composed in whole or in part of persons of his own race. *Strauder v. West Virginia*, 100 U.S. 303, 305. However, the Equal Protection Clause guarantees the defendant that the State will not exclude members of his race from the jury venire on account of race, or on the false assumption that members of his race as a group are not qualified to serve as jurors. By denying a person participation in jury service on account of his race, the State also unconstitutionally discriminates against the excluded juror. Moreover, selection procedures that purposefully exclude black persons from juries undermine public confidence in the fairness of our system of justice. Pp. 85–88.

(b) The same equal protection principles as are applied to determine whether there is discrimination in selecting the venire also govern the State's use of peremptory challenges to strike individual jurors from the petit jury. Although a prosecutor ordinarily is entitled to exercise peremptory challenges for any reason, as long as that reason is related to his view concerning the outcome of the case to be tried, the Equal Protection Clause forbids the prosecutor to challenge potential jurors solely on account of their race or on the assumption that black jurors as a group will be unable impartially to consider the State's case against a black defendant. Pp. 88–89.

2. The portion of *Swain v. Alabama, supra,* concerning the evidentiary burden placed on a defendant who claims that he has been denied equal protection through the State's discriminatory use of peremptory challenges is rejected. In *Swain,* it was held that a black defendant could make out a prima facie case of purposeful discrimination on proof that the peremptory challenge system as a whole was being perverted. Evidence offered by the defendant in *Swain* did not meet that standard because it did not demonstrate the circumstances under which prosecutors in the jurisdiction were responsible for striking black jurors beyond the facts of the defendant's case. This evidentiary formulation is inconsistent with equal protection standards subsequently developed in decisions relating to selection of the jury venire. A defendant may make a prima facie showing of purposeful racial discrimination in selection of the venire by relying solely on the facts concerning its selection in his case. Pp. 89–96.

3. A defendant may establish a prima facie case of purposeful discrimination solely on evidence concerning the prosecutor's exercise of peremptory challenges at the defendant's trial. The defendant first must show that he is a member of a cognizable racial group, and that the prosecutor has exercised peremptory challenges to remove from the venire members of the defendant's race. The defendant may also rely on the fact that peremptory challenges constitute a jury selection practice that permits those to discriminate who are of a mind to discriminate. Finally, the defendant must show that such facts and any other relevant circumstances raise an inference that the prosecutor used peremptory challenges to exclude the veniremen from the petit jury on account of their race. Once the defendant makes a prima facie showing, the burden shifts to the State to come forward with a neutral explanation for challenging black jurors. The prosecutor may not rebut a prima facie showing by stating that he challenged the jurors on the assumption that they would be partial to the defendant because of their shared race or by affirming his good faith in individual selections. Pp. 96–98.

4. While the peremptory challenge occupies an important position in trial procedures, the above-stated principles will not undermine the contribution that the challenge generally makes to the administration of justice. Nor will application of such principles create serious administrative difficulties. Pp. 98–99.

There is no case since *Miranda* that has caught the imagination of the appellate courts the way *Batson* has. In civil as well as criminal cases, the trial lawyer must constantly ask himself or herself whether or not a *Batson* situation exists.

Listed below are a few of the cases that have been decided during the past few years. There are many more to come, so be prepared for them.

BATSON v. KENTUCKY ANNOTATIONS

FEDERAL

1ST CIR: Court must consider prosecutor's systematic excuse of black jurors "over period of time." *U.S. v. Campbell,* 766 F2d 26 (1985).

2ND CIR: Prosecutor explained his reasons and they seemed reasonable to the court. *U.S. v. Ruiz,* 894 F2d 501 (1990).

3RD CIR: Where prosecutor struck because he thought juror was Asia-Indian and he was concerned about religious beliefs, no discrimination. *U. S. v. Clemmons,* 892 F2d 1153 (1989).

4TH CIR: No per se rule exists to show discrimination, nor prosecutorial checklist to avoid it. *U.S. v. Grandison,* 885 F2d 143 (1989).

4TH CIR: Fact residents of popular black congressman's district were struck, no discrimination. *U.S. v. Mitchell,* 877 F2d 294 (1989).

5TH CIR: Civil litigant need not show reason for strike. *Edmonson v. Leesville Concrete Co., Inc.,* 895 F2d 218 (1990).

6TH CIR: All prosecutor's strikes were against blacks; that alone was not discrimination where seven blacks remained on panel. *U.S. v. Sangineto-Miranda,* 859 F2d 101 (1988).

7TH CIR: Where defendant tried in court in white area instead of court in black area in same district was not found to be discriminatory. *Humphrey v. U.S.,* 896 F2d 1066 (1990).

8TH CIR: Excluding two of six blacks does not make prima facie case. *U.S. v. Young-Bey,* 893 F2d 178 (1990).

8TH CIR: Though two blacks remained on jury, discrimination shown by striking blacks and history of excluding blacks in the district and no acceptable explanation. *U.S. v. Hughes,* 864 F2d 78 (1988).

9TH CIR: Making prima facie case does not require showing "cause." *U.S. v. Power,* 881 F2d 733 (1989).

10TH CIR: Prosecutor can strike for "legitimate reasons tangentially connected with his race." *U.S. v. Brown,* 817 F2d 674 (1987).

11TH CIR: To show intentional discrimination you must raise inference. *U.S. v. Alston,* 895 F2d 1362 (1990).

DIST. CT. Court should consider remarks and questions of prosecutor. *Pottinger v. Warden, Northpoint Training Center* (716 F. Supp. 1989).

DIST. CT.: Prosecutor's failure to remember and give specific reason for striking does not reubut prima facie case. *U.S. v. Cunningham,* 713 F.Supp. 165 (MDNC 1988).

U.S. Supreme Court: Batson applies to civil cases, *Edmonson v. Leesville Concrete Co.,* 114 L. ED2d 660 (1991), and to defendant *Georgia v. McCollum,* 112 S.Ct. 2348 (1992).

STATE

ALA: *Batson* applies to civil as well as to criminal cases. *Thomas v. Diversified Contractors, Inc.,* 551 So2d 343 (1989).

AK: Excluding reservation residents was not discriminatory without showing their view necessary to constitute cross section. *Wyatt v. State,* 778 P2d 1169 (1989).

ARK: No prima facie case where prosecutor used four of six challenges to exclude blacks and two blacks were on jury. *Everett v. State,* 769 SW2d 421 (1989).

ARIZ: Trial judge must consider all circumstances. *State v. Holder,* 745 P2d 138 (1987).

CONN: No discrimination shown where juror not "straightforward and unequivocal" in answers. Prosecutor was not required to "articulate nondiscriminatory reason." *State v. Tappin,* 566 A2d 709 (1989).

DEL: Fact black defendant's jury had eight whites and four blacks not determinative of discrimination. *Feddman v. State,* 558 A2d 278 (1989).

FL: Once prima facie showing of discrimination, prosecutor has "imposing obligation" to give "reasonably specific race neutral" reason. *Woods v. State,* 556 So2d 752 (1989).

GA: Prosecutor must show "legitimate, racially netural reasons." *Martin v. State,* 388 SE2d 420 (1989).

IL: Showing 4.3 percent Hispanic population where five Hispanics on panel, not showing of discrimination. *People v. Flores,* 549 NE2d 1342 (1990).

IND: Striking five of six blacks made prima facie case. *Minnefelt v. State*, 539 NE2d 464 (1989).

KY: Defendant must show a "pattern" of strikes. *Commonwealth v. Hardy*, 775 SW2d 919 (1989).

LA: Complaining party must show membership in "cognizable racial group." *State v. Young*, 551 So2d 695 (1989).

MD: Where prosecutor used three of seven strikes and all-white jury resulted, prima facie case shown. *Chew v. State*, 562 A2d 1270 (1989).

MICH: Where prosecutor had eleven challenges left and allowed a black to remain on jury, no prima facie case and no requirement to explain. *People v. Williams*, 435 NW2d 469 (1989).

MINN: Striking one of two black members of 25 member panel did not make prima facie case. *State v. Lynch*, 443 NW2d 848 (1989).

MISS: Striking five of six blacks made prima facie case. *Conerly v. State*, 544 So2d 1379 (1989).

MO: Prosecutor could be shown to discriminate, though he had reason for the strikes. *State v. Boyd*, 784 SW2d 226 (1989).

NEB: Prosecutor's striking because one juror was single and another would have difficulty understanding was taken as sufficient reason. *State v. Pratt*, 452 NW2d 54 (1990).

NJ: Where all blacks struck by prosecutor, prima facie case. *State v. Watkins*, 553 A2d 1344 (1989).

NM: Once prima facie case is made, burden is on prosecution. *State v. Moore*, 782 P2D 91 (1989).

NY: Striking five of 18 Hispanics did not show discrimination. *People v. Munoz*, 550 NE2d 691 (1990).

NC: Where case was tried before *Batson*, defendant could not have known of his right and could not have waived it. *State v. Davis*, 386 SE2d 418 (1989).

OH: Must be member of cognizable group. *State v. Podborny*, 534 NE2d 926 (1987).

OK: Where white defendant complained of black jurors being excused, no discrimination. *Liteer v. State*, 783 P2d 971 (1989).

PA: Must show (a) cognizable racial group, (b) struck member of group, and (c) "inference arising from totality of circumstances." *Commonwealth v. Jackson*, 561 A2d 335 (1989).

RI: Juror struck must be member of defendant's race or other circumstances. *State v. Kelly*, 544 A2d 632 (1989).

SC: "Vacillating responses" relative to death penalty were enough to offset charge of discrimination. *State v. Elmore*, 386 SE2d 769 (1989).

SD: American Indian failed to show prejudice where panel was selected from voter registration. *State v. Lohnes,* 432 NW2d 77 (1988).

TX: Showing juror was friend of defendant's family offset showing of discrimination. *Tims v. State,* 779 SW2d 527 (1989).

WASH: Prosecutor gave "satisfactory netural explanation." *State v. Powell,* 781 P2d 101 (1989).

WISC: Peremptory can remove "discreet segment of community." *State v. Horton,* 445 NW2d 46 (1989).

WYO: Prosecutor cannot use reason juror would side with defendant of same race. *Bueno-Hernandez v. State,* 724 P2d 1132 (1986).

IMPORTANT DECISION

Since *Batson,* courts have wrestled with the question: "In a criminal case, does a white defendant have a right to a trial by a jury in which black jurors are not struck discriminatorily?" The Supreme Court of the United States has now answered that question in the affirmative. *Powers v. Ohio,* 111 SCt. 1364, 113 LEd 411 (1991). Only Justices Scalia and Rehnquist dissented, so it is now clear: *Batson* is here to stay! *Batson* will not be diluted with a narrow intepretation.

[1.72] ***Witherspoon v. Illinois:* Qualifying Death Penalty Opponents.** The Supreme Court has held that in a death penalty case, jurors cannot be excluded "simply because they voiced general objection to capital punishment or expressed conscientious or religious scruples against its infliction." *Witherspoon v. Illinois,* 391 U.S. 510 (1968). This case deals with much more than the death penalty; it is a rare case in which the highest court in the land discusses circumstances under which jurors can be stricken for cause.

Peremptory strikes under *Batson,* or strikes for cause under *Witherspoon,* raise questions in civil as well as in criminal litigation. The Supreme Court is involved in these two cases because of constitutional questions, but those questions must be answered in every trial, because in the answer we find whether or not our client received a fair trial.

In his concurring opinion, Justice Douglas said: "Challenges for cause and peremptory challenges do not conflict with the constitutional right of the accused to have a trial by an 'impartial jury.' No one is guaranteed a partial jury."

Sound familiar? In civil cases would we not have a more impartial jury if we could properly inquire of prospective jurors as to their feelings on all subjects that would affect their verdict, even their feeling toward laws that might be in issue?

Justice Douglas further speaks of the "right to a jury representing a cross section of the community." He added: "We can easily assume that the absence of those opposed to capital punishment would rob the jury of certain peculiar qualities of human nature as would the exclusion of women from juries."

Justice Black, joined by Justices Harlan and White in his dissent, said that the Court was, in effect, forcing states to try their murder cases before "biased juries." He took the position that the statute permitting the prosecution to challenge those with "conscientious scruples against capital puishment" actually guarantees an impartial jury.

In a civil case if a prospective juror said, "I do not like the comparative negligence doctrine, but I will follow it," do we have a more impartial jury if we just get rid of him? Is it possible to learn whether jurors will actually follow the law without counsel having much leeway in questioning as to the jurors' attitude toward the law?

The majority had pointed out that the Court had previously made sure the accused was not tried before a tribunal "organized to convict." Does *Witherspoon* go that step further and hold that in a death case the accused will not be tried before a jury "organized to put to death"?

One important issue discussed, but not decided, in *Witherspoon* was whether or not a person favoring or opposing the death penalty was more "prosecution prone." By striking any segment of the cross section, you also may be striking attitudes on various issues that need to be represented on the jury.

Justice Black questions the majority view that those who have "conscientious scruples" can be compared with the impartiality of those who have no opinion on the subject. What if the Illinois statute had really tried to obtain an impartial jury by adding that those who had strong feelings "in favor" of capital punishment were also disqualified?

In *Witherspoon*, the Court discusses a juror making the "discretionary choice of punishment entrusted to him by the state" and obeying the "oath he takes as a juror." The divided Court came face to face with the problem of jurors who don't fully agree with the law they are to consider, a problem that must be met in many ways during voir dire. **Every trial lawyer must know *Witherspoon*:**

THE FACTS
[Footnotes Omitted]

The petitioner was brought to trial in 1960 in Cook County, Illinois, upon a charge of murder. The jury found him guilty and fixed his penalty at death. At the time of his trial an Illinois statute provided:

> "In trials for murder it shall be a cause for challenge of any juror who shall, on being examined, state that he has conscientious scruples against capital punishment, or that he is opposed to the same."

Through this provision the State of Illinois armed the prosecution with unlimited challenges for cause in order to exclude those jurors who, in the words of the State's highest court, "might hesitate to return a verdict inflicting [death]." At the petitioner's trial, the prosecution eliminated nearly half the venire of prospective jurors by challenging, under the authority of this statute, any venireman who expressed qualms about capital punishment. From those who remained were chosen the jurors who ultimately found the petitioner guilty and sentenced him to death. The Supreme Court of Illinois denied post-conviction relief, and we granted certiorari to decide whether the Constitution permits a State to execute a man pursuant to the verdict of a jury so composed.

I.

The issue before us is a narrow one. It does not involve the right of the prosecution to challenge for cause those prospective jurors who state that their reservations about capital punishment would prevent them from making an impartial decision as to the defendant's guilt. Nor does it involve the State's assertion of a right to exclude from the jury in a capital case those who say that they could never vote to impose the death penalty or that they would refuse even to consider its imposition in the case before them. For the State of Illinois did not stop there, but authorized the prosecution to exclude as well all who said that they were opposed to capital punishment and all who indicated that they had conscientious scruples against inflicting it.

In the present case the tone was set when the trial judge said early in the *voir dire*, "Let's get these conscientious objectors out of the way, without wasting any time on them." In rapid succession, 47 veniremen were successfully challenged for cause on the basis of their attitudes toward the death penalty. Only five of the 47 explicitly stated that under no circumstances would they vote to impose capital punishment. Six said that they did not "believe in the death penalty" and were excused without any attempt to determine whether they could nonetheless return a verdict of death. Thirty-nine veniremen, including four of the six who indicated that they did not believe in capital punishment, acknowledged having "conscientious or religious scruples against the infliction of the death penalty" or against its infliction "in a proper case" and were excluded without any effort to find out whether their scruples would invariably compel them to vote against capital punishment.

Only one venireman who admitted to "a religious or conscientious scruple against the infliction of the death penalty in a proper case" was examined at any length. She was asked: "You don't believe in the death penalty?" She replied: "No. It's just I wouldn't want to be responsible." The judge admonished her not to forget her "duty as a citizen" and again asked her whether she had "a religious or conscientious scruple" against capital punishment. This time, she replied in the negative. Moments later, however, she repeated that she would not "like to be responsible for . . . deciding somebody should be put to death." Evidently satisfied that this elaboration of the prospective juror's views disqualified her under the Illinois statute, the judge told her to "step aside."

II.

The petitioner contends that a State cannot confer upon a jury selected in this manner the power to determine guilt. He maintains that such a jury, unlike one chosen at random from a cross section of the community, must necessarily be biased in favor of conviction, for the kind of juror who would be unperturbed by the prospect of sending a man to his death, he contends, is the kind of juror who would too readily ignore the presumption of the defendant's innocence, accept the prosecution's version of the facts, and return a verdict of guilt. To support this view, the petitioner refers to what he describes as "competent scientific evidence that death-qualified jurors are partial to the prosecution on the issue of guilt or innocence."

The data adduced by the petitioner, however, are too tentative and fragmentary to establish that jurors not opposed to the death penalty tend to favor the prosecution in the determination of guilt. We simply cannot conclude, either on the basis of the record now before us or as a matter of judicial notice, that the exclusion of jurors opposed to capital punishment results in an unrepresentative jury on the issue of guilt or substantially increases the risk of conviction. In light of the presently available information, we are not prepared to announce a *per se* constitutional rule requiring the reversal of every conviction returned by a jury selected as this one was.

III.

It does not follow, however, that the petitioner is entitled to no relief. For in this case the jury was entrusted with two distinct responsibilities: first, to determine whether the petitioner was innocent or guilty; and second, if guilty, to determine whether his sentence should be imprisonment or death. It has not been shown that this jury was biased with respect to the petitioner's guilt. But it is self-evident that, in its role as arbiter of the punishment to be imposed, this jury fell woefully short of that impartiality to which the petitioner was entitled under the Sixth and Fourteenth Amendments. See *Glasser v. United States,* 315 U.S. 60, 84–86; *Irvin v. Dowd,* 366 U.S. 717, 722–723; *Turner v. Louisiana,* 379 U.S. 466, 471–473.

The only justification the State has offered for the jury-selection technique it employed here is that individuals who express serious reservations about capital punishment cannot be relied upon to vote for it even when the laws of the State and the instructions of the trial judge would make death the proper penalty. But in Illinois, as in other States, the jury is given broad discretion to decide whether or not death *is* "the proper penalty" in a given case, and a juror's general views about capital punishment play an inevitable role in any such decision.

A man who opposes the death penalty, no less than one who favors it, can make the discretionary judgment entrusted to him by the State and can thus obey the oath he takes as a juror. But a jury from which all such men have been excluded cannot perform the task demanded of it. Guided by neither rule nor standard, "free to select or reject as it [sees] fit," a jury that must choose between life imprisonment and capital punishment can do little more—and must do nothing less—than express the conscience of the community on the ultimate question of life or death. Yet, in a nation less than half of whose people believe in the death penalty, a jury composed exclusively of such people cannot speak for the community. Culled of all who harbor doubts about the wisdom of capital punishment—of all who would be reluctant to pronounce the extreme penalty—such a jury can speak only for a distinct and dwindling minority.

If the State had excluded only those prospective jurors who stated in advance of trial that they would not even consider returning a verdict of death, it could argue that the resulting jury was simply "neutral" with respect to penalty. But when it swept from the jury all who expressed conscientious or religious scruples against capital punishment and all who opposed it in principle, the State crossed the line of neutrality. In its quest for a jury capable of imposing the death penalty, the State produced a jury uncommonly willing to condemn a man to die.

It is, of course, settled that a State may not entrust the determination of whether a man is innocent or guilty to a tribunal "organized to convict." *Fay v. New York,* 332 U.S. 261, 294. See *Tumey v. Ohio,* 273 U.S. 510. It requires but a short step from that principle to hold, as we do today, that a State may not entrust the determination of whether a man should live or die to a tribunal organized to return a verdict of death. Specifically, we hold that a sentence of death cannot be carried out if the jury that imposed or recommended it was chosen by excluding veniremen for cause simply because they voiced general objections to the death penalty or expressed conscientious or religious scruples against its infliction. No defendant can constitutionally be put to death at the hands of a tribunal so selected.

Whatever else might be said of capital punishment, it is at least clear that its imposition by a hanging jury cannot be squared with the Constitution. The State of Illinois has stacked the deck against the petitioner. To execute this death sentence would deprive him of his life without due process of law.

ANNOTATIONS OF *WITHERSPOON v. ILLINOIS*

FEDERAL

U.S.: Where defendant's co-defendant was charged with murder in bifurcated trial, death-qualifying did not prejudice defendant though he was not charged with capital crime. *Buchanan v. Kentucky*, 107 SCt 2906 (1987).

U.S.: Sentencing jury in capital case must be of those capable of expressing conscience of the community on the ultimate question of life or death. *McClesky v. Kemp*, 107 SCt 1756 (1987).

5TH CIR: Excluding one juror improperly is enough to set aside conviction. *Porter v. Estelle*, 709 F2d 944 (1983).

9TH CIR: Excluding juror who could not "under any circumstances vote for imposition of the death penalty" did not violate defendant's rights. *Harris v. Pulley*, 852 F2d 1546 (1988).

10TH CIR: The trial judge's questioning must be determined fairly if juror's views on death penalty would impair his performance of duties as juror. *Davis v. Maynard*, 869 F2d 1401 (1989).

11TH CIR: Death-qualifying is not unconstitutional, even though jury's recommendation is not binding. *In Re Shriner*, 735 F2d 1236 (1984).

11TH CIR: "I don't think I could do it, I really don't," was enough to excuse juror. *McCorquodale v. Balkcom*, 721 F2d 1493 (1983).

DIST. CT.: Even though death-qualified jury may be more "conviction prone," no rights were denied. *Byrd v. Armontrout*, 686 F. Supp. 743 (EDMO 1988).

DIST. CT: Where jurors' feelings on death penalty disqualified them, no constitutional issue. *Kordenbrock v. Scroggy*, 680 F. Supp. 867 (EDKY 1988).

STATE

AL: Where juror would not consider death penalty under any circumstances, properly excused. *Jackson v. State*, 516 So2d (1985).

AR: Where juror would find it more difficult to convict because of the death penalty, juror should be excused. *State v. Wiley*, 698 P2d 1244 (1985).

CA: Juror who can be fair on guilt issue cannot serve on that part of trial if cannot qualify under death penalty. *People v. Keenan*, 758 P2d 1081 (1988).

DE: Death-qualifying jurors in guilt-innocnce part of trial does not violate state or federal constitution. *Lovett v. State*, 516 A2d 455 (1986).

FL: Jurors who cannot or possibly would not impose the death penalty should be excused. *Masterson v. State*, 516 So2d 256 (1987).

GA: In bifurcated proceeding same jury can decide both issues and be death-qualified. *Frazier v. State*, 362 SE2d 351 (1987).

ID: Death-qualifying jury proper, though this jury would not participate in sentencing process. *State v. Johns*, 736 P2d 1327 (1987).

IL: Judge properly questioned at length as to feeling of jurors on death penalty and how this would affect their determination of defendant's guilt or innocence. *People v. Freeman*, 516 NE2d 440 (1987).

IN: Jurors who cannot conscientiously vote for death penalty should be excused. *Fleenor v. State*, 514 NE2d 80 (1987).

LA: Even though several jurors may be excused beause of death-qualifying process, no constitutional problem. *State v. Faulkner*, 447 So2d 1139 (1984); *State v. Miller*, 489 So2d 268 (1986).

MO: Death-qualifying does not violate constitution or state statute. *State v. Jones*, 726 SW2d 400 (1987).

MISS: Those with scruples against death penalty properly excluded. *Stringer v. State*, 500 So2d 928 (1986).

NE: Those who oppose capital punishment are not cognizable group and excluding them does not result in conviction-prone jury. *State v. Burchett*, 399 NW2d 258 (1986).

NEV: Defendant has burden of showing non-neutrality of jury in death case. *McKenna v. State*, 705 P2d 614 (1985).

NJ: Death-qualifying does not condition jurors to assume defendant to be guilty. *State v. Rose*, 548 A2d 1058 (1988).

NM: Jurors who would automatically vote against death penalty would violate their oath, so should be excused. *State v. Simonson*, 669 P2d 1092 (1983).

NM: Jurors who would automatically vote against death penalty should be excused. *State v. Trivitt*, 548 P2d 442 (1976).

NC: Those who are unequivocally opposed to death penalty should be excused. *State v. Vereen*, 324 SE2d 250 (1985).

NC: Where juror said she was opposed to death penalty, but would follow court's instruction, she was properly seated on jury. *State v. McLaughlin*, 369 SE2d 57 (1988).

OH: Those opposing death penalty do not constitute "identifiable group" for fair cross section purposes. *State v. Esparaza*, 529 NE2d 192 (1988).

OK: Death-qualifying does not cause more conviction-prone jury. *Johns v. State*, 742 P2d 1142 (1987).

OK: Excluding those who have doubts as to death penalty does not cause conviction-prone jury. *Smith v. State*: 737 P.2d 1206 (1987).

PA: Excluding jurors who cannot impose death penalty does not result in conviction-prone jury. 526 A2d 749 (1987).

TENN: Death-qualifying is not only constitutional, but results in jury that applies the law and finds facts according to their oath. *State v. Bobo*, 727 SW2d 945 (1987).

TX: *Batson* not in issue if the blacks peremptorily struck were unable to impose the death penalty. *Modden v. State*, 721 SW2d 859 (1986).

VA: Death-qualification applies to guilt or innocence process. *Pruett v. Commonwealth*, 351 SE2d 1 (1986).

[1.73] "How Do You Feel About Indians?" We who are trial lawyers spend much of our career trying to discover which jurors are prejudiced against our client, especially when we represent a member of a minority group. In forty years of pursuing this technique, I was most impressed by one used by Gerry Spence:

> "Folks, I have a problem. You see, I represent this Indian in this murder trial, and the problem is, I am prejudiced against Indians. It isn't some big thing that eats away at me, but it's something I'm not real proud of. You see, when I think of an Indian, I think of the one that broke into our ranch house, or I think of going to town on a Saturday night and seeing some Indian lying on the street drunk.
>
> "During this trial I have to set aside that prejudice, because I represent this Indian and I can't do my job unless I am able to do that.
>
> "How do you feel about Indians? If you serve on this jury can you set aside any prejudice and do your job as a juror and give this Indian a fair trial?"

COMMENT:

Sharing your problem with the jury is being used more today, but no one does it better than Gerry Spence and Joe Jamail. Getting the jury to suddenly put themselves in your shoes is an added feature of this dramatic technique.

Gerry Spence has told his fellow trial lawyers to quit taking so many depositions. He did not want the president of McDonald's hamburgers to even see him until the day of trial. When the president did see him, he saw all he wanted to, as the gruelling cross-examination helped bring in a $52 million verdict.

This has caused some trial lawyers to speculate that Gerry Spence does not prepare for trial. Quite the contrary! This great trial lawyer claims that he may spend months preparing his voir dire questions.

Some of this time may be spent sitting in his ranch house gazing across at the Grand Teton, but however he does it, he is effective. Trial lawyers have come to respect his ability to go into any courtroom.

Most trial lawyers have some reservations as they enter a Manhattan courtroom when they have travelled any distance at all. Lawyers who watched the voir dire in the Imelda Marcos trial told the *National Law Journal* that "Spence was very effective."

Knowing what questions to ask and asking them the right way is the art known as voir dire. Whatever courtroom you enter, you will be prepared for trial only if you are prepared for voir dire. This is an art Gerry Spence has mastered, yet he keeps working on it. Shouldn't we all?

[1.74] Great Trial Lawyers: Melvin Belli—Be Innovative. Melvin Belli has conducted seminars, in which trial lawyers exchange ideas, for fifty years. The purpose of these "think tanks" is to find new strategies that will work in the courtroom.

At one seminar, the King of Torts suggested, "Why not use the 'golden rule' idea during voir dire?" Great trial lawyers responded with assurance that no judge would let that happen. "It's against the law."

Mel agreed that there were hundreds of cases which hold that you cannot use the "golden rule" argument during final argument. He added, however, that he had never seen a single case holding that you cannot use it during voir dire. Lawyers argued the same conclusion would be reached and the judge just would not permit it.

Then it was revealed to all present, that Mel HAD tried it, and the judge DID permit it. Why? During summation you are arguing your case and trying to persuade the jury. The courts are very cautious about letting counsel argue on a basis that is not well-founded in the law.

Voir dire is, however, quite another cup of tea. Counsel is asking questions that will help him decide which jurors he will strike from the panel. Prior to *Batson, Swaine* was the accepted rule and in that case the Supreme Court made it clear that a lawyer could use his peremptory challenge as he deemed best for his cause.

Today, that part of *Swaine* is still the law, as long as the objections found in *Batson* are not present. If a lawyer can use his peremptory as he wants, then he should be permitted to ask questions that help him decide how to use that challenge.

The lesson learned here is that it is important to understand the law, the history and reasoning of the law, and whether or not the law is applied differently under different circumstances.

Melvin Belli has tried lawsuits in every part of the United States and this seems, to some trial lawyers, an impossible task. Not if you are innovative!

One problem you have in a jurisdiction away from home is that you don't understand the people of that community and their problems. What does an innovative trial lawyer like Melvin Belli do? In one case, he subscribed to the newspaper of the city where the case was to be tried.

During voir dire he made references to matters that had been in the news and had been of concern to those on the jury panel. This helped erase the perception that he was an outsider, and jurors appreciated his concern for their problems.

There is no formula for being innovative. That is the beauty of this quality. It is always there. Use it!

[1.75] Great Trial Lawyers: Joe Jamail—The Trial Lawyer And Voir Dire. When Joe Jamail obtained the $11.5 billion verdict in *Penzoil v. Texaco*, and the estimated $450 million fee that went with it, the whole world knew what Texas lawyers had known for a long time. Joe Jamail is one great lawyer!

What does a great lawyer think of voir dire?

"The selection of a jury is probably the most significant procedure in the entire trial process. It involves a use of the social sciences blended with the rules of law, and cumulates in the art of advocacy in its truest sense."

What should a trial lawyer try to accomplish during voir dire?

"(1) Eliminate those prospective jurors who cannot or will not relate favorably to your client or his case.
(2) Individualize the feelings and emotions of prospective jurors, and
(3) Involve them in the drama that will unfold before them."

Joe Jamail warns, however, that you cannot select one jury that would be good for every case. You must select a jury that will be receptive to this particular client and to this particular set of facts. You must let the jury know you are concerned for THIS client and his cause.

Get your jury involved from the start. Let them know you have an exciting case and introduce your client to them right away. Tell them as much about your client as you can. Appellate judges may tell you that is not a purpose of voir dire, but Joe Jamail knows what trying a lawsuit is all about and he says it is extremely important.

Joe Jamail warns against relying on stereotype analysis that oversimplifies the process. He said, "I would rather have a warm curious banker than a pragmatic, prejudiced, frightened plumber."

How does this great lawyer handle the age-old problem of sympathy that the insurance company's lawyer likes to talk about?

First, he gets the first lick in during voir dire, and then follows the same theme when discussing damages:

> "You may not find a verdict on the basis of sympathy. The responsibility of this defendant may not be determined because of your sympathetic attitude toward my client. This is the law and this is proper law. I say that sympathy is a form of charity; charity is demeaning to a person of pride. My client was and is and has a right to be a person of pride. I want you to promise that whenever you hear about sympathy—and you will not hear about it from me again—you will resist it and not let your verdict be tainted by it. Because like charity, sympathy is not only demeaning, it is usually inadequate."

How do you establish rapport with jurors? You do this with questions that make them understand they will be: "(1) righting a wrong, (2) meeting full justice, not partial justice, (3) setting standards of conduct for their community, and (4) compensating for damages done to the 'whole person,' not just to part of him."

What is the most important thing you can do during voir dire? "APPEAL TO A SENSE OF FAIRNESS." Joe Jamail points out that all prejudice is really just an absence of fairness, and you must do all possible to obtain a commitment from each juror that he or she will be fair.

[1.76] Great Trial Lawyers: Roxanne Conlin—"Don't Call Me 'Girl'!" Roxanne Conlin was the Democratic candidate for Governor of Iowa, is a great trial lawyer, and was the 1990–91 Vice-President of the American Trial Lawyers Association. She told an audience of plaintiffs' lawyers: "I am your kind of juror, I would be very sympathetic to your client and your lawsuit."

"However," she added, "if you call me 'Girl' I will be annoyed." Fifty-three percent of women surveyed seriously resented such treatment, and most of the others probably do not appreciate it. Yet, lawyers make the same mistake of referring to adult females as "girls," with the same insensitivity as they refer to adult black males as "boys."

She admits to the same stereotyping we all do in the courtroom, her target being "white-haired ladies," who she felt were wondering, "Why isn't this woman home raising her children"? Then one day the "numbers game" caught up with her and she didn't have enough peremptories to remove all of the "white-haired ladies."

After the jury returned an extremely good verdict for her, she was approached by the woman she would have removed, if she had not run out of peremptory challenges. "I was sure glad to see you in the courtroom; I have a granddaughter in law school, and I think it is about time they treat women fairly."

Roxanne Conlin believes voir dire is one of the most important parts of the trial. She tells trial lawyers to prepare for voir dire by finding out what is going on in the world. "Read 'Dear Abby,' and you will find out what problems people in the real world are thinking about."

She feels two of the most important questions are:

1. Have you ever written a Letter to the Editor? If so, follow up. Learn what the prospective juror is thinking.
2. What part of the editorial page do you read? Most people read

a column that agrees with their political philosophy. If there is any question, follow up with more questions.

"People who love animals make good plaintiffs' jurors." She used to ask the "pet" question directly, but found it confused jurors and caused them to wait for some evidence about a dog or a cat. She now asks: "What hobbies do you have, how do you spend your spare time, what pets do you have"?

In one case she was about to excuse a juror because his wife worked for the hospital her client was suing. She asked a question, however, that prompted a response that told her the man had two toy poodles. She followed up and chatted with the prospective juror, liked him, and kept him on a jury that brought back a very good verdict.

During the twelve years I served as a municipal judge in St. Louis County, Missouri, at least 500 lawyers tried cases before me, and all but one were male. Today, women are not only trying lawsuits in increasing numbers, they are winning cases that other lawyers may lose. Roxanne Conlin wins big cases, and she does it by starting with voir dire.

[1.77] Great Trial Lawyers: Rodney Romano—Prepare The Jury For The $98,000 Whiplash Verdict. What some lawyers thought was just "an ordinary whiplash" case became a $98,000 verdict for Rodney Romano, because he does not think there is anything ordinary about a whiplash injury. His serious approach to this "subjective" injury began during voir dire.

Rodney Romano began his voir dire with the usual questions he would ask in any other civil action. He then turned to a few "medical" questions.

Q. Have you, your family, or close friends ever been treated by an orthopedic surgeon?

Q. Does that experience create any strong feelings one way or the other about orthopedic surgeons?

Q. Have you, your family, or close friends ever been treated by a chiropractic physician?

Q. Has that experience left you with strong feelings one way or the other about chiropractic physicians?

Then Rodney Romano turned to the "whiplash" part of his voir dire. He maintained a dedicated approach that maintained his credibility:

Q. Does anyone here have any negative feelings about a whiplash type of injury?

Q. Does anyone feel that I am starting out this case with one strike against me because of the type of injury involved?

Q. There are no broken bones, cuts, or lacerations. Does anyone feel that it is wrong or a waste of taxpayers' money to bring a case before a jury unless there is paralysis or other catastrophic injury?

Q. Is there anyone who feels that if there really is an injury, it should show up on an x-ray or some type of lab test and if those tests are normal, then there can be no injury, despite what the doctors find in their clinical exams?

The following comments were made by Rodney Romano relative to the whiplash voir dire:

> If the judge will let you, give some information on your client's injuries. Plaintiff's injuries consist of damaged muscles and ligaments in her neck and mid-back, which cause frequent severe headaches and neck pain. This type of injury is commonly referred to as a "whiplash" because of the way it happens.
>
> One of the things that I am concerned with is that a prospective juror might have a preconceived notion that such an injury is very minor or even a fraud because of what they may read in the newspapers or see on television. There is nothing wrong with having your own set of honest feelings and no one here will judge you on your feelings. In fairness to all parties, we ask that each of you be completely candid.

This voir dire carried out the twofold purpose of voir dire: (1) deciding which jurors shall serve, and (2) educating the jury. It took the "best six" of those on the panel, and it took some educating of those six as to the serious nature of the injury. This is how you set the stage for the $98,000 whiplash verdict.

PART TWO

THE OPENING STATEMENT

[2.01] Avoid "Arguing The Case." Nothing slows and interrupts a good opening statement more than an objection that counsel is "arguing the case." Often the objection is not warranted, but often it is sustained nevertheless.

At a NITA conference a judge, law professor, and a few of us trial lawyers discussed this problem and concluded that MANY LAWYERS AND JUDGES SIMPLY DO NOT KNOW THE LAW RELATIVE TO OPENING STATEMENTS.

EXAMPLES:

1. Counsel says in a monotone, "Our evidence will show, Mary Smith is dead."
   No objection.
2. Counsel says in a monotone, "Mary Smith is dead."
   Probably no objection, though a few attorneys and a few judges feel better if everything begins with, "Our evidence will show. . . ."
3. Counsel shouts dramatically, "Mary Smith is dead."
   Probably an objection. Raising one's voice suggests drama to some, and drama suggests "arguing" to those same some, and this means you just can't do it during opening statement.

4. Counsel lowers his voice and softly says, "Mary Smith is dead." Probably no objection. Though lowering your voice and speaking softly, especially after a moment of complete silence, may be much more dramatic than shouting, it is not usually so perceived, and doesn't flash red lights to opposing counsel.

Is there a law that requires you to put the jury to sleep? Is there a law that says you cannot raise or lower your voice? Is there a law that says you must begin every sentence with "Our evidence will show," or "Our evidence will prove"?

I think not. In fact, after the exhaustive research required in the writing of this book, I know not. It is only in the minds of a few lawyers and judges who have misinterpeted appellate decisions that such laws exist.

Let's look at the law. Most courts grant counsel an opening statement, as a matter of right, *Weghman v. Hadley*, 292 P2d 909 (Cal. 1956). Other courts, however, consider opening statement a privilege, *Graham v. Cloar*, 205 SW2d 764 (Tenn. App 1947).

The courts give counsel wide latitude during opening statement, *Hilyard v. State*, 214 P2d 953, 28 ALR2d 961 (Okla. 1950). The judge will remind counsel, however, that the purpose of opening statement is to tell the jury what he intends to prove, and counsel can tell the court he has a right to do just that, *Anderson v. Universal Delta*, 234 NE2d 21 (Ill. 1967).

The manner of conducting opening statement is generally left to the discretion of the trial judge, *Tyler v. Kansas City Public Service Co.*, 256 SW2d 563 (Mo. 1953). Courts usually use this discretion to keep counsel from arguing the theory of the case, or the merits of the case, *State v. Fleming*, 523 SW2d 849 (Mo. App 1975). It is from this general approach that counsel is not permitted to "argue," but no law tells the judge or the lawyer how dramatically he can tell the jury what he intends to prove.

[2.02] Use Exhibits And Charts. If you are to tell your story during opening statement, you must tell it with full force and with everything at your command. If the story can be told more effectively with exhibits and charts, they should be used, and used properly.

CAVEAT: Have all exhibits and charts marked before they are used in opening statement. The judge and opposing counsel have a right to know what you are using, and the court reporter will need to know in preparing the transcript.

If there is any question as to whether opposing counsel will object or whether the judge will refuse permission without objection, take the matter up with the judge before trial. "I'm going to use this during opening statement, I assume there is no problem" is all that need be done, but if objection is still raised, be ready to meet it.

Be sure that what you are about to do will actually HELP the jury. If the exhibit is too complicated you don't want to use it and they won't let you use it. Under modern procedure, opposing counsel has seen your exhibits, and if he has a reasonable objection he should raise it. If he has none, the court should have no reason not permitting its use during opening statement.

In addition to what is going to be introduced into evidence, there are helpful forms of visual explanation. If you have five issues or five figures you will be offering evidence relative to, it may help to write them on a blackboard.

Don't just tell the jury. Show the jury!

[2.03] Use The "Our Evidence Will Show" Technique. It should never be necessary to say, "our evidence will show," but sometimes it is. Trial judges and trial lawyers sometimes find perfectly good opening statement to be objectionable.

If you are telling the jury what you are going to prove, you are NOT arguing your case, you are performing the very purpose of opening statement. Sometimes an argumentative manner suggests argument and invites objection. This should be avoided.

Try a few paragraphs of your opening statement beginning with "our evidence will show," and if you are properly presenting your case, the preface will sound appropriate. Then strike this unnecessary phrase and the story will flow better without the interruption.

Then, when counsel starts to object, tell counsel and the court: "This is what our evidence will show." When necessary, go back to a sprinkling of the phrase throughout parts of the opening statement to avoid objection.

[2.04] Directed Verdict After Opening Statement. One of the most frightening things that can happen to a young lawyer is to finish what he thought was a great opening statement, only to have opposing counsel rise and say, "I move for a directed verdict, your Honor. Counsel has failed to state a case." The judge is not likely to take such drastic action, but the mere possibility should cause us to make sure it never happens. This means we must know the law, and follow the law.

Most courts let a lawyer try his case the way he wants to try it and do not require him to cover all essential elements in his opening statement. (*Hessler v. Nellpowitz*, 55 NYS2d 692 (N.Y. 1945)). Suggesting anything that requires opposing counsel to present evidence will usually suffice. (*K. & S. Realty Co. v. Rosen*, 72 NE2d 116 (Ohio App 1946)).

The court will not hold counsel to details of his opening statement, but expect his evidence to accomplish this. (*Taylor v. Blake*, 191 A. 923 (Vt. 1937)). Courts are warned to exercise great caution in rendering judgment after opening statement. (*Ellis v. Victor Elec. Products*, 88 NE2d 275 (Ohio App 1949)). The trial judge must assume the truthfulness of all statements made and must give a reasonable and liberal interpretation to them. (*Basiak v. Board of Ed. of City of Cleveland*, 88 NE2d 808 (Ohio App 1949)).

The danger lies in the fact that statements made in opening statement may be admissions against your client. (*Gilbert v. Rothschild*, 19 NE2d 785 (N.Y. 1939)). There must be, however, an admission of every fact necessary to defeat counsel's case. (*Wainscott v. Young*, 59 NE2d 609 (Ohio App 1944)).

One court held such drastic action should be taken only where counsel deliberately conceded facts and had been given an opportunity to qualify, explain, and amplify. (*Johnson v. Larson*, 49 NW2d 8 (Minn. 1951)). One court held that remarks in an opening statement do not bind counsel unless they are clear as they relate to the facts. (*Liberty Mutual Ins. Co. v. Mercantile Home Bank & Trust*, 241 SW2d 493 (Mo. App 1951)).

Trial strategy: Avoid directed verdict after opening:

1. Cover all essential elements.
2. If objection is made, argue:
   (a) Any shortcoming of the opening statement must "ABSOLUTELY PREVENT RECOVERY."
   (b) Any motion must be based on statements KNOWINGLY and COMPLETELY made. (*Caylor v. Casto*, 22 P2d 417 (Kan. 1933)) See 5 ALR3rd 1405.

It must be shown either that plaintiff has no cause of action or that defendant has no defense. (*Scarborough v. Arizona Light & Power*, 117 P2d 487 (Ariz. 1941)). If there is any doubt, it must be presumed that counsel did not make a statement that would be fatal to his cause. (*Rodgers v. Crum*, 215 P2d 190 (Kan. 1950)).

[2.05] How To Comment On The Law. Only the judge can give instructions on law during the trial. This too often causes lawyers, trial judges, and appellate judges to take a narrow view on counsel's commenting on the law. It is important for the jury to understand the issues as the law is applied to them. Opening statement is an excellent time for counsel to help the jurors, and there is no law that keeps counsel from doing so.

CAVEAT: Much trouble arises because counsel does not make it clear to the jury that it is the judge who will instruct as to the law. Trial judges are quick to correct any impression that what counsel says is the law.

Howard A. Spector, a leading trial lawyer, approached the problem as follows:

> What we'll be talking about is negligence, medical negligence, and the death of a baby who was deprived of a chance to live because of that negligence. Later, Judge Smith will also explain the legal meaning of negligence to you. In a medical case, negligence is nothing more than the failure to exercise the reasonable care that would be expected of a physician under the circumstances. You take into account all of the advances and available information in medicine at the time.
>
> The defense may, from time to time, refer to it as 'medical negligence' for whatever reason, but understand that we'll be talking about negligence, simple negligence. 'Malpractice' has a kind of evil sound to it and may even have some emotional suggestions.
>
> I have to tell you what we are seeking to prove and what we are not. We're not claiming or trying to prove that any doctor is evil, which is where the word 'mal' comes from, or that his license or practice is affected in any way.
>
> It is simply a case where the evidence will show that the doctors did certain things wrong with respect to one family and one baby and caused one death.

Notice how Howard Specter made it clear to the jury that its instructions on the law would come from the judge. Notice also, how effectively he explained the law and its effect upon this lawsuit. He knew juries were thinking all sorts of bad things and he cleared up the law as applied to those issues promptly and effectively.

[2.06] Avoid Interruption By Avoiding Objections. The opening statement should go smoothly, with as few interruptions as possible. This means you should avoid what is properly objectionable, and even that which prompts an objection which is not well-founded.

You can never be sure of avoiding ill-founded objections, but you can avoid waving a red flag in front of opposing counsel. Certain words and acts prompt objections from the inexperienced attorney and from the experienced attorney who wants to interfere with your presentation and feels that the judge may overrule the objection yet not criticize him for making it.

Powerful words should be used throughout the trial, but they should be used during opening only when they appear to be safe.

EXAMPLE:

"This totally irresponsible driver was drunk" may cause an objection, and in some states the objection would be sustained. "This man drove his car while drunk" may be just as powerful during opening, because the conduct itself will suffice. Characterizing the driver as being "totally irresponsible" doesn't add that much and may cause an unnecessary interruption.

There is absolutely no reason a trial lawyer cannot be dramatic during opening statement. There is no rule requiring you to talk in a monotone or to otherwise put the jury to sleep. The first sign of emotion, however, prompts some opposing counsel, through ignorance of the law or a knowing abuse of the right to object, to automatically jump up and object. Prepare for this attempt to disrupt your opening statement.

EXAMPLE:

There is no way you can say, "Little Johnny Brown is dead," without its sounding dramatic. Try saying that as softly as you can and it sounds dramatic. Say it as loudly as you can and it will still sound dramatic. For some reason, opposing counsel does not object when you speak those words as softly as you can, though this may be the most dramatic way the words can be spoken. If you raise your voice to create an emotional atmosphere, it may be wise to begin with: "Our evidence will show that little Johnny Brown is dead."

Consider the judge, the local law, and your opposing counsel before you decide to interrupt the flow of your opening statement with an interspersing of "our evidence will show." Never use it if you can avoid it. THE BASIC RULE: Tell the jury what you are going to prove, don't tell them what you are going to tell them. Though this rule is based on the best of communication skills, you must depart from it if you feel an "our evidence will show" will avoid an objection, even if the objection is overruled.

A simple rule to avoid objections during opening statement is to stick to the facts! Once you start arguing your case you have left the purpose of opening. At this stage of the trial the jury wants to know the facts. They are really not ready for argument. Telling the story, and telling it in a dramatic way, is the furnishing of facts. The jury wants to hear the story and they want it to be interesting.

The objection issue often arises when the facts are dramatic in and of themselves. Be prepared for it. Try to avoid it. If you still get an objection, clear the air immediately. Let the court, opposing counsel, and the jury know that you ARE telling what you are going to prove and THAT is the purpose of opening statement.

Make opposing counsel sorry he objected. Every objection during every part of the trial is an attempt to keep the jury from learning something, and the jury knows this. Make it clear that what you are talking about IS evidence, it IS important, and opposing counsel's attempt to keep it from the jury simply will NOT work.

[2.07] How To Organize Your Opening Statement. If jurors place importance on opening statements, the trial lawyer must give it special attention. You can do this by deciding what you want to accomplish and then by setting forth in specific form how this can be accomplished.

Though it is unusual for a motion to dismiss to be sustained at the end of opening statement, that is a good place to start. Make a list of what MUST be proven and tell the jury. CONVERSELY, avoid saying anything that could possibly cause the judge to sustain such a motion.

EXAMPLE:

> "We will introduce no evidence on notice since no one in the world really knows if there was notice. You are just going to have to decide that issue from all the evidence." Some courts will hold that since you must prove notice to make a case and since you have admitted you have no evidence of notice, then your case must be dismissed.

If you were hoping to luck out during trial with someone admitting notice, you could have merely begun with, "Our evidence will show three things, that the defendant had a duty, that he had notice, and that my client was damaged." In most courts saying nothing about notice would have avoided a dismissal.

In opening statement be sure to cover:

1. The essential elements of the case.
2. The STRONG points of your case.
3. The WEAK points of your case.

You cover the essentials of your case not only to satisfy any local requirement imposed, but also to satisfy the jury. The first question jurors ask themselves is, "Why are we here?" You should let them know they are here because you have a good lawsuit and you will prove to them what is necessary for them to return a verdict in your favor.

You then go to the strength of your lawsuit. Start with what is going to get them excited about your case. You don't have to do it in detail, just be sure they hear enough to put them in your corner at the very beginning.

EXAMPLE:

> "Dr. William Jenkins, the best known orthopedic surgeon in our state, is going to testify that Billy Smith will never walk again because this man's car came up on the sidewalk and carried Billy 200 feet on the hood of his car." Strong stuff? If you have it, use it.

You talk about the weakness of your case for two reasons: first, because if you don't opposing counsel will, and secondly, if neither counsel mentions it, the jury may still be wondering about it.

EXAMPLE:

> "I will not introduce any evidence as to why my client did not immediately call the police. He will tell you he does not know why, he was excited and did not realize it was necessary to call immediately. He thought calling when he got home was soon enough. Frankly, I have told him you should always call immediately and he knows that now. What our evidence WILL show is that the other driver came on the wrong side of the road and. . . ."

It is not good trial practice to read an opening statement, and it may not be natural to give a verbatim prepared opening, though this can be done effectively. What IS necessary is that the organization of the opening be put in writing. The outline should have as little detail as possible and should be studied thoroughly enough to avoid needing to refer to it during the opening statement.

If you are going to use demonstrative evidence during opening make the moment you are going to use it an important part of your outline. Use it at a time when the opening needs a little help, but use it when it will be most effective. Create interest with it before you begin, but do not let it detract from your opening while you are getting to it.

CAVEAT: Remember, you are telling a story. Tell it as though you are having lunch with a friend or telling your family at the dinner table. This book includes many forms of story-telling, so choose your form, and then work it into your outline.

Your beginning must create interest and start persuading right away. Your middle cannot sag and must be pumped with all that's necessary to maintain interest. Your ending must tell the jury dramatically so that they will want to listen to every word, because this trial is IMPORTANT!

[2.08] Recognize The Importance Of Primacy. First impressions are important in life, and in the courtroom. The rule of primacy tells us that what we learn first we remember longest.

Primacy means that the opening statement is important, and it means that the first part of the opening statement is important. Those first words you say during opening statement should "grab" the jurors and impress them. It should tell your "theme," if possible, and it should be favorable to your position.

EXAMPLES:

> "Last New Year's Eve, Mary was all dressed up and having a wonderful time when this drunk came up to her and sexually assaulted her. Mary has never been the same since then, and never will be." "Bill put up all of the money, but he let Fred be an equal partner just to help him out. Then one night Bill went through the books and found Fred had taken about ten thousand dollars from the business he had no title to." "Billy ran out into the street, but he didn't run out from behind a car. In fact, there was nothing to block the view of this man as he came down this residential street at thirty miles an hour." "When John Jones gets up every morning he has to have someone dress him, he has to have someone feed him his breakfast, and has to have someone take him out on the porch where he can sit and wait for someone to fix him his lunch. Before the accident John Jones was the best tennis player in town."

Some of the above examples dealt with liability and some with damages. You usually talk about liability first, but if damages is the only issue, or the big issue, it is good trial strategy to talk about damages immediately and to use the primacy advantage.

The jurors want to know what the case is all about and you must tell them. If a drunk goes through a red light and puts a man in a wheel chair for the rest of his life, the main issue in that case is NOT whether or not the drunk is liable. The issue is HOW MUCH the plaintiff should receive in damages, and that is what you should talk about, immediately.

[2.09] Provide An Orientation To The Case And The Role Of Jurors. Ask any friend who has served on a jury and you will find his or her first concern was trying to determine exactly what was happening. Jurors feel more comfortable when they understand the surroundings and proceedings, and they are usually grateful to the person who explains it all.

Most bailiffs take pride in their job and do it well, so by the time you meet the jurors they have already found a friend in the courthouse. You should acknowledge this help and add to it. They may expect help from an employee whose job it is to help them, but they will be pleasantly surprised to find that as an advocate you, too, are going to help them in their orientation.

EXAMPLE:

> "Bill Smith has been around the courthouse for many years and I am sure by now he has told you where the washroom is and the best place to have lunch. There are a few other things I think you may want to know. When we finish the opening statements I will put on our evidence and I expect that to take about two days. Then Mr. Gardner will put on his witnesses and that usually doesn't take quite as long as mine. After the evidence there will be final arguments and the judge's instructions. So, you can see we expect to finish this trial by the end of the week. The judge will give us a break every two hours and if you have any special problems just let Bill know. In our state the jury decides only the innocence or guilt so you won't have to be concerned about what penalty, if any, should be assessed."

Anything you can tell jurors that will help them feel comfortable in the courtroom will help make them your friend. If you make friends with the jury they will be more likely to listen to your argument. There is nothing wrong with being considerate and helpful. In fact, by showing concern for the jurors in this respect, your overall concern for your client and justice may become more apparent to the jury.

Explain their role as jurors. Let them know how important it is. Let them know how important you think it is. Then tie your cause into their concern.

[2.10] Be Brief, Yet Complete. Most judges do not set a time limit on opening, but they do "move you along" if you take more time than they think is necessary. For this reason, it is preferable to inform the judge in advance how much time you will need and to work out any problems. If you really think you need more time than the judge wants to give you, be ready to set forth your reasons.

The purpose of opening statement is to explain what you intend to prove, and the jury knows this. It follows that if you use an hour for opening statement, then the jury will conclude that you have an awful lot to prove. They may require you to prove every little thing you talked about during opening statement.

Tell the jury exactly what you must prove and do it with as small a "list" as possible. Add to that list of "must prove" only that which will add drama to your opening statement and that which will be obvious to the jury that you do not have to prove.

EXAMPLE:

"All we have to prove is that my client did the work and he hasn't been paid. This we will do with the defendant's own testimony. We will also show that he admitted to my client that he did a good job and that all his friends commented on what a beautiful job my client did. It has been six months since the job was completed and the defendant has not paid one dime of what he owes."

[2.11] Talk To Each Juror. There are as many votes on a jury as there are jurors. That makes it necessary to *communicate* with all jurors if you are to *persuade* all jurors.

There are three ways to communicate directly to an individual juror during opening statement and final argument:

1. Move across the jury panel, looking at each juror as you talk.
2. Stop and talk to an individual juror.
3. Aim your argument, in what you say, toward individual jurors.

EXAMPLE:

Counsel stops in front of a juror who indicated during voir dire that she is concerned about crime. "We are all concerned about crime. We can see what it is doing to our country and to our lives."

CAVEAT: Remember, in most jurisdictions you cannot address jurors by their names or otherwise appear to be currying favor with a juror. Even if the judge permits such conduct, jurors usually see through it, and it has an adverse effect upon your credibility.

Eye contact is the best way to communicate with and persuade an individual juror. Looking between jurors is such a waste, when it is just as easy to look at one juror right in the eye and then to do the same with the next juror. You cannot look at all six or twelve jurors at the same time, but you can look at all the jurors by going from one to another.

This can best be done by walking along the jury box, where you are not tied to a podium. Do it with ease and comfort. Pause to get attention and to break up too methodical a walk or presentation. Move to one side of the podium and then the other, giving as much movement to your argument as possible.

When you talk to a group of friends, you try to include everyone in the conversation. When you stand before a jury, it will be easy to do the same. Each juror will appreciate your interest.

[2.12] Your Opening Statement Must Be Dramatic. An opening statement is too important to ignore any effective means of communicating with the jury. Drama is one factor that should always be used. It brings a new dimension that persuades. Good drama appeals to emotion and reason. Since it appeals to emotion, it permits argument to enter the minds of the jurors without first qualifying with proof.

EXAMPLE:

> "Defendant's car hit and injured the plaintiff" tells the jurors nothing. They want some proof as to what happened. The same jurors will begin the process of being persuaded if they are told: "Little Billy was coming home from school and was standing talking with another boy when this man drove his car up on the walk and hit Billy and carried Billy on the hood of his car for two hundred yards. Billy's mother was coming to get him and saw the car heading at Billy. She screamed but it did no good. She had to stand there and watch this happen."

Add drama to your opening statement with:

1. Words. Pictures of a mother "screaming" or a little boy being "carried on the hood of a car" appeal to emotion as well as to reason. You not only KNOW the driver did something wrong, you FEEL it, and this prompts you to want to do something about it.
2. Emotional part of story. Talking about liability often is a boring part of the story. Find what part of the liability issue contains

drama and use it. Is the victim a little boy, the defendant a drunken driver, the eye witness a mother, the speed at which defendant was driving twenty miles over the speed limit, the road conditions hazardous, the defamation one made maliciously, or the violation of the law made knowingly? If so, talk about it during opening statement. It will add drama.

3. Use demonstrative evidence. "He drove up on the sidewalk" is only one way to communicate that fact to the jury. A chart showing how far he came off the road onto the sidewalk may be more effective. A photo of the little boy standing on the exact spot where he was hit may be even more effective. It is usually wise to let the judge know you are going to do this.
4. Use your voice effectively. Study the use of voice in dramatic presentations. A change in volume avoids boredom. Raising or lowering the voice adds emphasis. Complete silence for a brief period demands attention. A natural voice will convey sincerity. A friendly voice will cause jurors to be more receptive.
5. Structure with drama in mind. Structuring your story will make it sound more reasonable, but structuring it for dramatic reasons is equally important. Create interest! Build toward the important part of the story.

EXAMPLE:

> "Billy was only six years old. He was standing there on the sidewalk, six feet back from the roadway. This man sitting over there came out of a tavern and got into his car, and drove toward that very spot where Billy was standing. At that very moment Billy's mother was coming to get him. She walked around the corner of the building just as the car came off the road and onto the sidewalk. . . ."

[2.13] Establish Credibility Or Lose. Winning a lawsuit depends upon credibility, and the opening statement is a good place to begin establishing credibility with the jury. You establish credibility by causing the jury to believe in you, your client, and your cause.

There are important ways to establish credibility:

1. Appearance. Before the jurors hear you, they will see you. Be-

fore going to court look into a mirror and ask yourself, "Would I buy a used car from this lawyer?" If there is any question, ask, "Why not?" Imagine for one moment that the jurors will decide the case entirely on the basis of your appearance. They won't, but why start with even the slightest handicap?

2. Nonverbal communication. It is not just what you say, but how you say it. It is your facial expression and what you do with your arms and body. It is the manner in which you speak and the feeling you give off as you perform in the courtroom. All of this is a part of nonverbal communication and all of this helps persuade.

   Jurors can tell how you feel. If you really don't like a juror he can probably tell that. If he survives voir dire and you must live with him for the rest of the trial, recognize this problem and deal with it. You know such people in the real world and you know you must make a special effort to be natural, but nice.

   Being a good guy and being sincere are two qualities that jurors seems to "sense." These are also two qualities that are extremely important in establishing credibility. Jurors just "want" to believe good guys who are sincere. Establish this trust and NEVER violate it.

3. Verbal communication. The words you use can help establish credibility. Jurors can relate to words they understand and they do not want someone to talk down to them. Choose words with credibility in mind.

4. Don't exaggerate. Tell what you can prove, but don't tell what you cannot prove. Nothing hurts your credibility more than saying something the jury learns to be untrue. Be careful about: (a) telling the jury a certain witness will appear in person if there is a chance the witness will not testify in person, and (b) telling the jury certain proof will be in the form of specific testimony if you are not sure of that testimony.

EXAMPLE:

"I hope Dr. Smith will be able to testify in person, and if his surgery schedule permits he will. If not, I will read his deposition to you." "Our evidence will show that the defendant had notice and we can do this either with an admission of the defendant or through the testimony of another witness."

5. Be reasonable. Jurors use common sense and are not impressed by technical arguments. They expect you to be reasonable. They do not like objections, but if the judge sustains an objection they may feel the judge had good reason for interfering with what the attorney was doing.
6. Be fair. Jurors demand fairness of you. They judge you by your fairness. If they suspect you are being unfair they will penalize you for it. Your remarks about parties, attorneys, and witnesses may tip them off as to how fair you are going to be.

[2.14] How To Begin Your Final Argument During Opening Statement. The final five minutes of the final argument begins soon after counsel is retained to try the lawsuit. Opening statement must be based on the theme of that final five minutes. In fact, opening statement must be planned with final argument in mind.

In preparing opening statement:

1. Identify the theme of your case and put it in as few words as possible. This should be covered in the first paragraph of the opening statement and in the final five minutes of your final argument.

EXAMPLE:

"William Smith made a horrible mistake. He got involved with drugs. But that was several years ago. He paid for that mistake and he learned from that mistake. He has been one hundred percent clean ever since. When he went to interview for a job last May, a drug bust occurred and the police arrested everyone within a thousand yards, including William Smith. Now, society may make a mistake. Don't let that happen."

2. Cover what you need to prove. Make a list of those elements of the lawsuit that "make your case." Be sure you cover them in opening statement.

EXAMPLE:

"The State must prove, first, that the defendant was driving, and second, that he was intoxicated at the time. That is ALL we have to prove in this case and we will prove that beyond a reasonable doubt."

3. Talk about anything else that will prepare the jury for final argument. There is much in final argument that although need not be proven, still adds to the strength of your lawsuit. If you are going to argue it in final, you should consider whether or not you want to mention it in opening.

EXAMPLE:

(a) You do not have to prove the defendant was drunk while driving, since his negligent acts will prove your case. You will want to talk about that during final, however, and it is necessary to talk about it during opening, when jurors are trying to decide which side to be on.

(b) You know one of their key witnesses is going to lie under oath and you will spend much time during final talking about it. To talk about it during opening would merely enable opposing counsel to prepare for it.

4. Establish priorities of opening and final, before giving the opening statement. Two different approaches are presented to the trial lawyer as he or she plans opening and closing. In opening he or she must anticipate what will be proven and the extent of persuasiveness the jury will attach to each issue. In closing, counsel can look back and know how much priority to give an issue because he or she can now see how the jury perceives that issue.

EXAMPLE:

(a) "I expect the evidence to show that alcohol was a factor in this case. You will determine from the evidence how much effect it had on the driver, but I want you to look at ALL the evidence, not only the condition of the driver, but what the driver did."

(b) "In opening statement I mentioned that alcohol may be a factor in this case and we now know it was a very important factor. One

> of the defendant's own witnesses testified this man was so drunk he couldn't stand up."

Jurors will not remember every word you say in opening, just as they will not remember every word you say in final. That is why it is necessary during opening to (a) emphasize that which is favorable, and (b) emphasize that which you are sure you can prove. If it is favorable, but you are unsure about your proof, hint at it, but do not close any doors behind you.

[2.15] Maintain Interest With Storytelling Techniques. Storytelling is an art which should be mastered by the trial lawyer. Mastering means learning the proper techniques discussed below and using them.

Parallel story approach. One of the most effective techniques is the telling of two stories at the same time. The jury can then compare what is happening and reach conclusions as to conduct.

EXAMPLES:

> "At eight o'clock that morning Mary was on the way to school where she would meet her friends. At that very moment, John Smith was having a glass of vodka with his breakfast."
>
> "Bill was trying to get one more job for his boss, working late, but hoping to help his employer. At the same time, his boss was telling lies about him, lies that would give him reason to fire Bill, and reason for other companies not to hire him."
>
> "At 11:00 A.M., John was planning how they could rob the drugstore. At that very minute, Ralph was buying a gun to use in the robbery. Down the street, Bill was stealing a car they would use in the robbery."

The parallel can be used throughout the opening statement. Go back and forth and hold interest by showing what is happening in different places at the same time. Look for this device in movies, and see how effectively it is used. The movie "Patton" is an excellent example, where the director took you into Patton's tent and then Rommell's tent.

Flashbacks. Movies are also an excellent place to study the use of flashbacks. When an audience, or jury, is listening to a story, it knows the whole story cannot be told in chronological order. In fact, it should not be confined to set sequences.

EXAMPLES:

"The ambulance was carrying Betty to the hospital, and the wrecker was hauling the auto to the garage. But that is not where this story begins. It begins about four hours earlier when this man Brown and two of his buddies enter the local saloon."

"Bobby is now dead. In fact, he was pronounced dead before he reached the hospital. Let's look back a few days, a few months, and see what Bobby was like, what he did and what he hoped to do. We will now show you a day in the life of Bobby through actual videos his parents took during the past year."

Jurors watch television and movies and they are familiar with flashbacks. They feel comfortable with this approach to storytelling.

First person. Good writers like to tell a story in the first person. It is a familiar way of telling a story. It is a personal way. It can be very effective in front of a jury.

EXAMPLES:

"John Brown was killed in the accident so he cannot testify today. Others will tell his story, but if he were here I think he would tell you this: My name is John Brown. I was in the fifth grade at Watson School the day of the accident. I played baseball in the summer and basketball in the winter."

"John Smith will testify in this lawsuit by deposition, and this is what he is going to tell you: It was about seven-thirty in the evening when I was standing at the bus stop at Grand and Main. I saw this big black car come from nowhere and run up on the curb and strike this little boy and carry him a hundred feet on the front of his car."

Third person. Telling the story in the third person is still the most popular way to communicate. Remember, the jury is hearing it come from you, so establishing your credibility during voir dire is extremely important.

EXAMPLES:

"John left for work early that day and he drove over the usual route and made the usual stops. When he came to the intersection of Fourth and

Chestnut he stopped his car and waited for the light to change. About ten seconds after his car had come to a stop, the car driven by the taxi driver plowed into the back of his car."

"Mary worked at the plant for ten years before the accident. She had hoped to continue working there until she got her two boys through college. Because of this accident, she will never work there again.

CAVEAT: Some of the story should not come from the lawyer or his client. It should come from an independent witness, and counsel should make that clear during opening statement.

EXAMPLES:

"Mary is in pain. She does not like to talk about this but several witnesses will tell you how clear it is to them that Mary is in constant pain."

"Jack is a great person. Three of the most respected citizens of our community will take the witness stand to tell you all about Jack."

Dramatizing certain details. Your story should not be told in a monotone. It should have ups and downs, and the most favorable part of your story should be dramatized so the jury will remember it.

EXAMPLES:

"If you remember nothing else from the evidence presented in this case, please remember the testimony of Jim Stark. He was there! He saw what happened! He heard this man over there say that he had ten beers within four hours before the accident."

"You will see and hear much evidence during this trial, but I want you to look at this photo of the clamp that was left in Mrs. Johnson's body. And during this whole trial, I want you to listen carefully and try to find out WHY it was left there."

[2.16] How To Handle Weak Points Of Your Case. It is not entirely by accident that two of the best trial lawyers in the world, Gerry Spence and Joe Jamail, begin their lawsuits by discussing the weakest part of their cases. This (a) puts the jury on their side and (b) takes the wind out of opposing counsel's use of the weakness.

"I have a problem, folks. . . ." What an invitation to the jury to listen and sympathize. Everyone has problems. Some people don't like to talk about them. Most people like to listen, as long as they are someone else's problem.

People who serve on juries want to accomplish something during their short stay at the courthouse. If someone has a problem, they would like to feel they played some role in solving it. These two great lawyers invite them to solve the problem, or at least to tell them their views on it.

Joe Jamail lets the jury know at the outset that if the problem is insurmountable to them, he might as well pack his papers into the old briefcase and return to the office and work on another case. No one on the jury would let Joe do that.

Gerry Spence uses the weakness of his case to let the jury know he is one of them. That he is concerned for his client, and that it is very important that his client win. He then shows how insignificant that weakness is when put alongside the real issues of this lawsuit.

Every trial lawyer knows it is better for bad news to come out on your client's direct, or on your witness's direct, than to come out on cross. It gives the jury the feeling you have nothing to hide. It gives the client or witness a chance to explain, or to otherwise soften the blow.

Carry that theory to its logical conclusion and you find it is better to talk about a weakness during opening statement than during your case-in-chief. Jurors consider opening statement as the beginning of the trial, so begin by overcoming your weakness with frankness that builds credibility.

Remember, opposing counsel may cover the weakness during his or her opening. Beat him to it!

[2.17] Appeal To Fairness. Most jurors want to do a good job and they cannot do a good job unless they are fair to both parties. Impress that upon the jury every opportunity you get.

During voir dire, talk about it directly. During opening statement your message is more indirect, but it must be loud and clear. You are telling a story and that story must be one that requires justice for your client.

You cannot argue the case. You must let the facts argue the case.

EXAMPLES:

> "John worked for this company for ten years. He worked hard and he was loyal to this company. He had a chance to better himself so he took another job. When he took that job he knew that his success depended upon his reputation in the industry. This company John had worked for told lies about him to other companies, and those other companies stopped doing business with John's new company. John was fired!"

Through these few words you have told of an injustice and the jury already wants to be fair with your client. They cannot wait to hear more!

[2.18] Conduct Opening Statement As Though Your Verdict Depended Upon It—It Might. For many years the Chicago Study was misquoted. It did NOT conclude that 80 percent of all cases were decided by jurors at the end of opening statement. However, losing early is such a real possibility that the misquoting may have served a worthy purpose.

Only once during 44 years, has opposing counsel argued for dismissal for failure to state a cause of action during opening statement. Though the motion was summarily denied, it struck a fear in me that makes me sure each time that I have covered all that must be covered.

What about the other thousands of times in which opposing does NOT make such a motion? Are you home free? Does this mean the jury has not already decided the case? Don't bet on it.

We don't need a Chicago Study, or any other study, to tell us how important first impressions are. We begin winning or losing our case during voir dire. Remember, however, that the jury doesn't really know what the case is all about until opening.

The jury subconsciously begins deciding during voir dire. It forms impressions of people and issues. It knows, however, that it should not decide until it learns more. Once opening is over, that restraint is lifted.

Once opening is concluded, the jurors know that they have been told what the case is all about. They know both lawyers have had a chance to give them their best shot. Why shouldn't they begin deciding the case?

They have been told that what lawyers say is not evidence. They are happy to wait and hear the evidence, but they accept what the lawyers say as being very important. What the lawyer says IS the case until they hear more.

It is easier to learn than to unlearn. Once a juror forms an opinion it is difficult to change that opinion. The jurors WILL be forming opinions during opening statement, so it is your job to help them form those opinions in your favor.

[2.19] Include Essences Of Good Drama. Good trial lawyers must be good storytellers, and good storytellers must understand good drama and develop a talent for using it. Every writer of fiction knows the importance of creating atmosphere, introducing characters, and advancing the plot.

Create atmosphere! The outcome of your trial may depend upon the atmosphere in which the case is tried. If you are defending in a criminal case, you may want the jury to believe the whole matter to be a joke. If you are arguing a personal injury claim you will want a serious environment that lends itself to a large verdict.

Being flippant about a serious matter will not get the job done. You may, instead, do irreparable harm. You create the atmosphere within limits established by the kind of case, the kind of jury, and often the kind of judge.

Let's look at the classic case where Darrow started his opening statement in a murder trial with, "Well, it was his own wife, wasn't it?" The jury laughed and the prosecutor whispered to his assistant that if we don't get the jury more serious, we'll never get a conviction.

One reason the approach worked was that it was Clarence Darrow doing it! Don't ever try something just because a famous lawyer succeeded in doing it. I have seen judges knock themselves out to hear cases argued by famous lawyers. Once that lawyer is before them, they give them more latitude than they would most lawyers.

What if it were John Smith, one year out of law school, who made that statement during opening? You can imagine the trial judge saying, "Save your humor for the next bar party, Mr. Smith. Your client is charged with murder and the court considers that to be a serious subject." This would, indeed, create an atmosphere, one which the young lawyer would want to disappear as soon as possible.

EXAMPLES OF CREATING ATMOSPHERE:

"Mary Smith is dead."
"This client admitted on deposition she didn't know she was hurt until her lawyer told her she was."

"Our evidence will show there were a thousand fish found dead in that stream. Our experts will tell you what that means to children who swim in that same water."

"The prosecutor laughed about what Johnny told the police. He didn't tell you Johnny has a learning disability. Did you look at Johnny and his mother as they sat in the courtroom and had to listen to this man with a college degree and a law degree, a man who teaches public speaking at the community college, talk to you about how poorly Johnny communicated with the police?"

Introduce characters! You should introduce yourself and your client during voir dire, but really get down to the business of introducing all your characters during opening statement. Even your weakest characters must be introduced, so that they will be introduced in the best possible light. Also, so their whole person can be introduced.

Imagine Joe Jamail walking up to the jury and his first words are: "This man sitting next to me at the counsel table is a drunk." Or, Gerry Spence walking up to the jury and saying, "The man I represent in this trial is an Indian."

You may say, "The jury can see he is an Indian," or "The jury is soon going to learn the man is a drunk." That does not matter! The ATTORNEY said what they are going to be thinking, and that is important.

Joe Jamail will follow up with: "How many of you folks think that woman over there had the right to come across onto his side of the highway and put him in a wheelchair for the rest of his life, just because he is a drunk?"

Gerry Spence will follow with a story, or his own feelings, or whatever gets the jury feeling a real duty to give the man a fair trial, even if he is an Indian.

EXAMPLES OF INTRODUCING CHARACTERS:

"Dr. Brown, the famous surgeon down at Barnes Hospital, will explain to you how this injury will affect David's ability to earn a living."

"John Brown is an eye witness. He is a good athlete who has good eyesight. Some people don't like John since he wrote a controversial article in the school paper, but he can still see just as good as he did before he wrote the article."

"I represent Bill Jenkins. Many people will tell you about Bill during the trial. He was awarded the highest award ever granted any employee at

Watkins. He works with children at the Center, and he has a wonderful wife and three children."

Tell your story! Telling your story is the real purpose of opening statement. Jurors want to know what comes next! They are accustomed to having a story told in logical order. They are accustomed to having a story told in an interesting manner.

You must state the problem, and you must give the solution to the problem. That is storytelling! You do not have to argue the case in order to tell your story or to give the solution.

Who shot Duncan? My client was in New York at the time. My client did not shoot Duncan! This is a perfectly good opening statement, though you are certainly arguing your case during opening.

Judges sometimes object to an opening statement that is too dramatic, but if given properly, you can not only survive objection, but also avoid it. Remember, the jury wants you to present your case in an interesting manner, and the jury will decide the fate of your client.

[2.20] Use Words That Convey Messages. Opening statement is the telling of a story and a story is told best with powerful words. Remember, however, they should be words that tell facts, because conclusions and characterizations require jurors to pass judgment sooner than they may wish to.

EXAMPLE:

(a) "This man drove his car at 90 miles per hour and smashed into my client's car" merely tells what happened, and the jury is prepared for such a statement. The word "smashed" is more powerful than "ran into." Using "drunken driver" instead of "man" would be more powerful, but may be better used later in the trial when you have prepared the jury for this judgment of a fellow human being.

(b) "This man maliciously ruined my client's reputation" may be premature during opening until you have prepared the jury. "Maliciously" is a powerful word, but the jury would be better prepared to give it the impact it deserves, if you first said, "The defendant KNEW it was a lie, he KNEW it would have a devastating effect on Jill, and he sent the letter anyway. From the evidence you will know that he did this maliciously."

Make a list of words that apply to your lawsuit that have power. Write them down. Study the list and see if there is a more powerful word. When you finish a paragraph of your opening statement study it for increased word power. You will find many words that just don't tell the story with drama.

EXAMPLE:

> "My client was standing on the curb when the car hit her," cannot compare with, "Mary Smith is a beautiful eighteen-year-old girl who was waiting in front of the drugstore for her mother when the defendant put his hand on the thigh of the woman sitting next to him in the car, causing his car to jump the curb and smash into Mary and crush several bones in her legs."

Notice in the above example that the word "client" has become "Mary Smith, a beautiful eighteen-year-old girl." "Waiting" suggests that she was not moving into the street. "Mother" is one of the most powerful words of all. "Thigh" suggests sexual behavior more than placing his hand on her leg. "Jump" is an active word which creates a picture of the car flying across the curb. "Smash" is stronger than "hit" or "ran into." "Crush" is a word that can be heard by the jurors a year after the accident.

[2.21] Great Trial Lawyers: Peter Perlman—Million Dollar Verdicts Begin With Opening Statement. The trial lawyer must be a great storyteller, and opening statement is his time to tell his story. In most cases, this story will be told in the third person, but it must be told convincingly.

Peter Perlman of Lexington, Kentucky, is Past President of American Trial Lawyers Association, and among his writings is *Opening Statement* (ATLA PRESS). He has agreed to share with his fellow trial lawyers a perfect example of explaining the case in the third person.

OPENING STATEMENT IN *KING v. KAYAK MANUFACTURING COMPANY*

"May it please the court, counsel, ladies and gentlemen of the jury. The case, which you have already heard discussed, involves a catastrophic injury. It involves the quadriplegia of Clifford King on August 10, 1985, just two days after his thirty-third birthday.

COMMENT:

He does not begin with an explanation of voir dire. He begins by telling the jury why we are here and that this is serious business. He creates atmosphere with powerful words like "catastrophic injury" and "quadriplegia." In two sentences he has not only created atmosphere, but also has introduced the leading character of his courtroom drama, a 33-year-old man who is a quadriplegic.

"This case will have two basic themes. The first will be the dangerous and unsafe design, production, sale, promotion, and distribution of a swimming pool. The second theme will be the effect that the injury has had upon this man's life and the quality of living he will experience for the rest of his life.

COMMENT:

By the third sentence counsel is telling us the story. He has already started the three basic purposes of dialogue in drama: (1) creating atmosphere, (2) building character, and (3) advancing the plot. Some lawyers put the jury to sleep before they reach this point in their opening statement.

"I'd like to tell you about Clifford's background. He is one of six children. He has a sister, Anne, who is married to Jack, his brother-in-law. He has an eighth-grade education. He was honorably discharged from the military after serving in Vietnam. There will be no claim that he was rich. In fact, he was a self-employed carpenter and was not making a lot of money at the time he was hurt. The injury occurred August 10, 1985, a Saturday afternoon.

COMMENT:

Counsel tells more detail about his leading character. The jury will return a large verdict only if it likes this character.

"You will have the evidence about that day. Clifford was at his mother's home and planned to work in a truck. His brother, Robert, came by and asked him to go swimming at Jack's pool. Clifford agreed to go and on the way they stopped to get some beer. They got either a twelve-pack or two six-packs; it was not uncommon to drink beer at Jack's pool. They arrived between 1:00 and 1:30 in the afternoon. Clifford was like all of us. He took his health and the simple pleasures of life for granted. He didn't realize that day at 1:30 P.M. that he was going to spend the rest of his life in a wheelchair.

COMMENT:

Now comes the telling of the story. The jury is ready for this and counsel tells the story well.

"Let me tell you a little about Kayak, the manufacturer of this pool. The company was founded by several businesspeople in the mid-1960s. While the pool you will see today carries the Kayak name, and the brochure carries the Kayak message, the pool wasn't designed by Kayak. In fact, Kayak doesn't employ any design engineers. You will learn that Kayak is not even a manufacturer. It is an assembler. It takes parts made by other manufacturers and puts them together. The company is a fabricator.

"You will learn that the original design did not come from a patent or a blueprint. One of the Kayak officials said in a deposition, 'How do you patent a box?' You will hear from the evidence that when designed and installed properly, the pool is much more sophisticated than a box.

"We will prove to you that Kayak's own promotion and marketing encouraged unsafe practices in the pool. A large adult man diving into this pool was not only allowed, it was encouraged. Kayak's sales pitch, and they advertised in malls and in *TV Guide,* was that you could have a recreational center right outside your door. Kayak designed a pool to fit every yard and every wallet. The concept is, you don't need a country club, you don't need a local pool, you can have an above-ground pool right in your own backyard. Once they sold it, they walked away from it.

COMMENT:

Now it is time to tell about the antagonist of the drama. The jury cannot give the plaintiff a dime unless it finds he (or it) did something wrong.

"They left it up to the buyer, Mr. Marks in this case, and the salesperson to pick the location. 'Where on your lot is the best place to put this pool? You tell us.' And that's where they put it. It was left to the buyer to approve the construction and the installation. You will see where the pool is located today. Daniel Flesher, a local engineer, will tell you that Kayak used principles, procedures, and practices unacceptable in the construction industry for excavation and compaction. They did no compaction test. They only dug through one level of soil. They paid a person a flat fee to install it, $625 I think. They didn't come back after it was installed to check it for proper installation.

"The result is that this pool didn't have a solid foundation. It didn't have an even bottom, and that is going to be critical when you hear what happened to Clifford King on August 10. There were variations between one depth and another depth, particularly around the center of the pool where there is a drain that sticks up about an inch and a half.

COMMENT:

Now the jury knows what the antagonist did that was wrong.

"The expert who will talk about this and about the dangers of this pool will be Dr. Milton Gabrielsen from Plantation, Florida. He has been associated with swimming pool safety for fifty years. He has written many of the standard texts on swimming pools and safety and he will testify to you why this pool is dangerous, why it is unsafe, and why somebody like Clifford King would have no way of knowing that. When you dive, which Kayak promotes, you suffer a real and serious risk of becoming a quadriplegic, which is what Clifford King is.

COMMENT:

Counsel has prepared the jury for expert testimony. He has introduced to the jury an important character in today's courtroom dramas—the expert.

"You will hear about a vinyl liner which lines both the bottom and sides of the pool. You also will see that it is a blue and white pebbly-type liner, and we will introduce evidence that this type of liner hinders rather than helps a swimmer's or diver's depth perception.

"You will hear and see that there are no depth markers on the sides, the deck, the bottom, or anywhere else in the pool to tell people how much water is in the pool, or how deep it is. These markers were available and feasible at the time the pool was designed, yet Kayak simply didn't offer them as an option. Kayak didn't include them in the package and they are not there.

"You will find that there are no bottom markers or lines, nothing for the swimmer or diver to judge the depth. In this case, while the pool is advertised as being a four-foot, above-ground pool, you will hear that it is actually not that at all. It is actually only three-and-a-half-feet deep.

"You will hear a lot about warnings, and you will find that there are no manufacturer's warnings on this pool about diving, about quadriplegia, or about the risk of injury from diving. You will hear that Kayak furnished the owner with two 'No Diving' stickers, like bumper stickers, and then left it up to him to decide where to put the stickers.

COMMENT:

> Counsel has prepared the jury for complicated issues. He has explained to them in a way that will persuade as he tells.

"This case is also about the risk of very severe injuries. As we present the evidence in this case, you are going to hear a contrast. You will hear what Kayak and the pool industry knew, contrasted with what Clifford King and the public did not know. Most people who suffer a severe injury, quadriplegia or paralysis, in a diving accident have no head injury at all, or only a bump or a minor bruise. Yet their neck breaks, their spinal cord is severed, and they suffer the most permanent injury of all, quadriplegia, with only a bruise to show. Kayak knew this. The public and Clifford King did not know this. For the average person, and specifically for Clifford King, diving into an empty four-foot pool would be risking serious injury. The untrained or recreational diver doesn't know that diving at a clean angle into a pool with four feet of water is hardly safer than diving into an empty pool. The untrained or recreational diver doesn't know, but Kayak does know, that the better the dive, the greater the risk of serious injury.

COMMENT:

> Conflict is the essence of drama! The jury expects there to be another side to the story. Trial lawyers learn to live with conflict and even use this moment during opening to lessen the impact of any weakness in the case. Counsel uses the opportunity to begin the telling of injuries.

"I will tell you about Clifford's injury, but we won't go into it in any great length because you will hear the evidence. Let me tell you first that Clifford won't sit here throughout the trial, not because he is not interested, but because we have advised him that he shouldn't be here during the entire trial. So when he is not here, that will be the reason. We believe it would not serve any useful purpose for him to be here throughout the entire trial.

"Clifford was a recreational diver. He had no formal training. He had no experience with above-ground pools. He had been to this pool only once before, and that was the previous summer in 1984. He said he jumped in the pool that time, but others were diving in the pool, too. That was the previous summer. Then, on August 10, 1985, his brother picked him up, they got some beer, and went over to his brother-in-law's pool. He was there for thirty minutes or so. He saw his nephew, Bobby, trying to dive and belly flopping instead, so he offered to teach him. So Clifford demonstrated a couple of dives from the end of the pool long-ways, and then Bobby would follow. Then Clifford moved over to the side of the pool about four feet from the edge so that he was ready to dive in and swim across to the ladder at the other side, and he will tell you that all three dives were about the same: they were shallow. They were done with arms and hands extended.

"The third dive coming from the side going toward the ladder was the critical one. That is when he hit the drain because afterwards there was some scalp and hair stuck on the drain. He hit a solid object protruding from the bottom and that caused his head to stick. The body would keep moving forward but the neck is only designed to support a head weighing twelve to fourteen pounds, not a body that weighs 170 pounds. The neck becomes the point of least resistance. That is what makes somebody a quadriplegic.

COMMENT:

Now counsel tells about the injuries and ties them into the cause.

"We know basically what the position of the other parties in this case will be and I will comment on that very briefly. They will say that Clifford did a sailor's dive, and a sailor's dive, from what I understand, is when you keep your hands at your side and dive in head first. Ladies and gentlemen, you will hear the evidence, and Clifford will tell you that he didn't do a sailor's dive. And his brother, Robert, who came in for the trial, saw the two previous dives, although he didn't see the last one, and he will tell you that the first two were shallow dives. Clifford will tell you that he doesn't even know how to do a sailor's dive and has never done one.

"You will also hear the defense tell you that he did a one-and-a-half revolution flip from the side of the pool into a body of water four-feet deep or less. Clifford will tell you that he didn't do a one-and-a-half flip. Our experts tell you that unless you are a world-class gymnast, it is impossible to do a one-and-a-half flip in that body of water. The people Clifford talked to after the accident asked about his history and what happened; there is no mention of a sailor's dive, or a flip, but you will be able to hear the evidence and make your own judgment.

COMMENT:

Now counsel goes into detail as to opposing counsel's case. This takes steam out of opposing counsel's opening.

"The damages in this case are substantial. Clifford was at the West Virginia Medical Center for about two weeks—that was his initial care—and was treated for compression injuries, a fracture of the sixth cervical level of the neck. He was at the VA Medical Center in Richmond for about six months for active and extensive treatment and rehabilitation. Presently, he needs rehabilitative care, physical therapy, and continuous monitoring. He will need nursing care for the rest of his life, and his earning capacity has been destroyed.

"Ladies and gentlemen, this is a serious and catastrophic case. As you all agreed when you were chosen, your decision is to be based on the evidence and the evidence only, and we expect that the evidence will overwhelmingly support a verdict for a very substantial amount. Thank you."

COMMENT:

Before counsel sits down he opens the door and lets the jury peek into the damages of the case, just enough to let it know this is serious business and we are talking about a lot of money. The jury is now ready for trial!

[2.22] Great Trial Lawyers: Rodney Romano—The $98,000 Whiplash Verdict. Many lawyers would have looked upon it as just another "whiplash" case, but Rodney Romano approached this case with serious thoroughness. His pursuit of an adequate verdict began with an effective voir dire, and then with an opening statement that began persuading the jury.

After a few introductory remarks, Rodney Romano went right to the issue of the case and laid the groundwork for his verdict. Since it is an example of a brief opening, I will give the entire text, beginning at this point, with comments.

OPENING STATEMENT IN *SCALA v. ACOSTA*

"Now in this case, it will be your responsibility basically to judge four issues. And there will be many other side issues, but the four big issues you will be asked to judge are: Number one, the negligence of Laura Acosta; number two, the negligence of David Hardy; number three, whether the negligence of either one of them or both of them caused permanent impairment to Karen Scala; and number four, the losses arising out of that damage.

"Now unfortunately, it is not within your power to restore Karen Scala to her health before this injury was inflicted on her, and so the American jury system requires that you make a judgment or . . .

COMMENT:

An objection at this point was overruled.

". . . that you make a decision with regard to how much money will it take to compensate Karen and Frank Scala for the injuries that they suffered.

"No doubt this part of the case, the losses part of the case, will be the most difficult aspect of the case for you to decide because you are going to find that the Defendants are, on the whole, likeable people.

"But the Plaintiffs will ask you to say: 'Hey, we are sorry. We know you are likeable people and we know you didn't hurt Karen and Frank on purpose, but nevertheless, through your negligence you did hurt them and it is our job to require you to make them whole by compensating them.' And so that is a tough thing to do.

COMMENT:

Counsel knows damages is the big question and he immediately tells the jury of its task.

"The other issues are fairly easy issues in comparison. Now the evidence will show that all three drivers were westbound on Forest Hill Boulevard and that David Hardy first slowed down, then stopped in the westbound lane of Forest Hill Boulevard obstructing traffic. Karen Scala slowed down and stopped appropriately to avoid hitting Mr. Hardy, but Laura Acosta did not slow down and she plowed into the back of Karen Scala. That is it in a nutshell.

"Now let me give you a few more details. David Hardy had just come from the K-Mart on Forest Hill Boulevard and Military Trail where he had gone to look at souvenir T-shirts so his dad could take them back to England.

"Finding none there, he knew of a fruit stand on Forest Hill Boulevard on the way home. So he figured he would stop there on his way home. So David Hardy was westbound on Forest Hill Boulevard.

"He drives by the fruit/T-shirt stand that he had . . . he knew where it was, goes by it one hundred to one hundred fifty feet before he stops, slows down, stops. Karen stops and then Laura Acosta, who is going to readily and openly admit to you that she saw the T-shirt stand on the side of the road, it caught her eye and she took her eyes off the road for a moment.

"She states that she was traveling about six to nine car lengths behind Karen Scala at the time she took her eyes off the road. When she looked back, she had closed in on Karen Scala, slammed her brakes and her brakes screeched, but it was too late and she plowed right into Karen Scala.

"Now Mr. Hardy does have a different story. He admits and agrees he had been to the K-Mart and couldn't find any T-shirts. He admits he knows where the fruit/T-shirt stand was. And it was his intention to go there. But he says when he got near the T-shirt stand or went slightly by it, he put on his right-turn signal, then made a hand signal in addition to the electrical signal, then gradually slowed down, gradually put his brake on and eased off the road.

"That is one conflict you will have to resolve based on the testimony that you hear and who you believe.

"The investigating officer in this case was Trooper Robert Borman, whose name I mentioned to you earlier. Officer Borman has been a Florida Highway Patrol trooper for more than fifteen years. Of those fifteen years, he has been in the last nine years a certified traffic homicide investigator. That is the highest traffic accident investigator certification that a law enforcement officer can receive.

"And he did a complete investigation and his investigation revealed that both David Hardy's act of obstructing the westbound lane and Laura Acosta's act of following too closely and taking her eyes off the road, both contributed to the collision that caused Karen Scala's injuries.

"By the way, Laura Acosta admits that prior to taking her eyes off the road, she was traveling about forty-five miles per hour. Damage to her 1980 Mustang was over three thousand dollars and Karen Scala was driving an old 1976 heavy Cadillac and that car was totaled.

"The impact was the center of Laura Acosta's car to the rear center of Karen Scala's car, right in the westbound lane of Forest Hill Boulevard.

COMMENT:

Counsel then covers the liability question effectively, pointing out what may be in conflict.

"On impact, the impact was so violent that Karen's head went backward with such force that her sunglasses flew off of her face and landed in the back of the car. And that is why this type of injury is called a whiplash, because the head whips back with such violence and force, the same way the tip of the whip makes a loud sound by having two pieces of leather snap together.

"Now, Dr. Sandall, who is an orthopedic surgeon, will teach you how whiplash works. He will show you what happens on impact is the car and the main part of a person's body is pushed forward. But the head, being a heavier object, tends to remain stationary.

"So actually, the head doesn't flip back. What happens is, the body goes forward and the head, relative to the body, goes back, injuring muscles and ligaments in the front of the neck and damaging them. Then the body, trying to compensate, tenses these muscles to pull the head back and tenses them with such force that it over-compensates and pulls the head forward, damaging ligaments and muscles in the back. That is what whiplash is.

"Trooper Borman, who is trained to evaluate people's injuries on the spot and he is not a doctor, but they have to evaluate the level of a person's injuries, he evaluated Karen Scala's injuries as being incapacitating at the scene of the collision.

"Now SAVES Ambulance came to the scene and took Karen Scala, put her in a neck brace, and on a back board to keep her body immobilized, and took her and Laura to Palms West Hospital for treatment where they were both treated, examined, and released.

"Karen was released with instructions. Karen's symptoms did not improve, so six days later, on March 11, 1986, Karen went to see Dr. Edward Sandall, who is an old family doctor. I don't mean he has treated . . . he is a family doctor who they have known for a long time. Treated Karen's husband and sons.

"He is a Board Certified orthopedic surgeon and he first examined her and he found that Karen had mild muscle spasm and he prescribed Flexeril, Naprosyn, and Tylenol 3. All of these are prescription muscle relaxers as he would testify in his videotape deposition.

"Now these drugs did help relieve Karen's pain which included neck pain and head pain, just the pain goes up the back of the skull and winds up here and becomes very debilitating. The problem with the drugs, though, is it made Karen so drowsy she couldn't even function normally. So she had a choice, she could be pain-free and dopey or alert and saddled with chronic pain.

"Karen sincerely wanted to get better and resume her normal life. And so she sought out the services of John D'Amico, a chiropractic physician.

"Why John D'Amico? In 1983 she had an onset of neck pain, not related to any accident. She had gone to Dr. D'Amico and he treated her for eleven visits over a period of two months and she got better. She had no more problems from that time in 1983 until this rear-end collision.

"So she went to Dr. D'Amico and he treated her first in August of 1986. The history he took revealed complaints of neck pain, head pain, and fatigue which is a common symptom with this type of injury.

"His clinical exam, meaning his hands-on office exam that he did, revealed neck pain, problems in flexion and extension, pain in those areas. An abnormal Kemps test, which is a clinical exam designed to reveal damage, and he will explain that to you.

"An abnormal compression test which is pushing down on the head to determine whether there is any muscle or nerve damage, which he will also explain to you. He also noted spasm in Karen's neck and shoulders.

"Now spasms, one of the things you will be listening to is the difference between objective testing and subjective testing. Subjective testing is when you move a person in a certain way and they say ouch, that hurts; or, I can't do it any further, that hurts.

"A doctor has no way to prove whether a person's pain is real or whether they are faking it.

"However, the doctor will tell you that part of their training is to observe people and that to make a judgment as to whether they're malingerers or whether their symptoms are credible or believable.

"Dr. D'Amico also found abnormal X-ray findings. Now he had taken X-rays in 1983, then in August of 1986 when Karen first came to see him. And then, oh, about a year or two years later a third set of X-rays, which he felt showed significant improvement in the spine.

"Now Dr. Sandall and Dr. Penner both looked at those X-rays and read them as normal and there is a degree of interpretive license that I suppose doctors can take. One doctor can reasonably look at something and say it is normal, and another can say there is abnormal changes there, and you will have to discern that for yourself.

"Dr. D'Amico will take you through his medical records. Take you through his findings. Take you through a number, I believe in excess of eighty visits over a period of three years and show you that Karen has had persistent problems with pain, persistent problems with spasms, I think I started to talk to you about spasm and the difference between objective and subjective testing.

"Spasms are something you don't have to rely, as a doctor, on the patient to tell you about. Spasms are those knots a person can get and it is a tight type of feeling in a muscle that a doctor can feel, as opposed to a soft muscle, that softness.

"Dr. D'Amico found spasm in Karen on some visits and not on some visits. That is a very common finding with a whiplash or cervical sprain/strain type injury. People will have good days and bad days and a person can come to a doctor's office for a checkup one day and the doctor may find spasms and another day, the doctor will not find spasms.

"Yet, that person has a permanent physical impairment. Even Dr. Penner, the doctor the lawyers hired over there, will agree with that statement.

"Now Dr. D'Amico at one point stated that he felt Karen had suffered a twenty-five percent permanent physical impairment as a result of this injury. Later, after September of 1988, which he says she reached a turning point, he revised that opinion to six percent.

"The reason that he revised that opinion to six percent is two-fold: Number one, he felt she had improved with regard to the spine, and you will be able to look at the X-rays on the videotape and see how the spine has loosened up a little bit between the August 1986 X-rays and the, I believe it is December 1987 X-rays. That is one reason he downgraded the impairment.

"And the other reason is, now the new guide, the Permanent Impairment Guides had come out with a third edition and under that edition the impairment was to be considered differently.

"So he felt that Karen and feels that Karen has sustained a six percent permanent physical impairment as a result of this rear-end collision.

"Dr. Sandall says it is between five and seven percent.

"Now we asked Dr. John Russell, who is a vocational rehabilitation psychologist to evaluate Karen and determine whether he felt she had suffered any damage to her future employability or future capacity to earn money as a result of this injury. He will explain to you, he did a battery of tests on Karen as well as reviewed the records from the doctors and hospitals, and he has determined that there is a loss of earning capacity.

"There is also damage or loss to Karen's ability to function as a wife and mother in the things she does around the house and also a loss in the quality of her life, which Dr. Russell is not concerned with. He is concerned only with the tangible items, the things you can put a number on. And he will explain to you everything that he reviews. You can all have the tests he does and all of the research he does.

"So you will know his findings are reliable. He will explain to you exactly how he reached his conclusions. He doesn't pull his numbers out of a hat.

COMMENT:

Notice how counsel now turns to the subject of damages in detail and immediately talks about "whiplash." Rodney Romano feels this is where you win or lose a soft tissue case. If you for one minute think "whiplash" is a dirty word, or let anyone else in the courtroom think that, then you are in big trouble. He tells the jury what whiplash is and tells the jury what the experts will testify. He tells about his experts and he tells about his client. He gives them credibility before they testify. He hits the subject of "subjective testing" head on. He talks of "permanent physical impairment," a threshold in Florida, and he talks about "future employability or future capacity to earn money," an important factor in damages.

"One of the things you will be required to do is reduce tangible future losses to present value. In other words, as Dr. Pettingill, who is an economist, will explain to you, if you are owed a dollar in a year from now, the person who owes that to you can put something less than a dollar in the bank today, say ninety-five cents and earn interest on that ninety-five cents so within a year, the dollar will be there to pay you. And so you will be required to reduce future loss capacity to earnings, future medical damages, and other tangible future damages to present value.

"And it is kind of a complicated mathematical process and that is why we ask Dr. Pettingill to do those calculations. And he will testify, as will Dr. Russell, will explain where he gets his figures from, the United States Vital Statistic figures he relies on. And he will show you how he arrives at his conclusions so you will know his results are reliable.

COMMENT:

Counsel tells the jury as much as it needs to know about reducing future losses to present value and tells it why an economist is needed to present this part of the case.

"This past December the defense lawyers exercised their right to have Mrs. Scala examined by a doctor of their choosing. They chose Dr. Jeffrey Penner who saw Karen once on December 6, 1989. His deposition has been taken so we know some of the things he is going to say. He has already testified that he finds Karen to be credible, meaning believable and cooperative. He has already testified that he did not examine Karen over a period of months or even weeks, but for one visit for a period of twenty to thirty minutes.

"Now during that exam he found abnormal findings in all neck ranges of motion. That is like this (indicating).

"He found pain between her shoulder blades on what he calls the reaching for the bra test. In other words, when you go back like this to snap your bra, I guess you could call it the same thing for men, but pain between the shoulder blades and that is an abnormal finding.

"He admits he did not review all of the records he was provided with, but the records he did receive from Dr. Sandall and Dr. D'Amico he admits do document persistent pain continuing from the date of the injury.

"Now he testified that Karen Scala's symptoms are permanent. He testified that he diagnosed Karen as having myofascial syndrome, which he defined as being an inflammation of the muscle lining in the neck. He also agreed that pain is a major factor in the limitation of day-to-day activities and very importantly, Dr. Penner agrees that the AMA Guide to the Evaluation of Permanent Impairment, which is this book (indicating), and you will be seeing more of it, he says that is the authority in the evaluation of the permanent impairment.

"Now that will be important because after he admitted that is the authority, we will show and the evidence will show, that he doesn't follow it.

"The evidence will show that his opinion, even though he finds all of these positive findings, his review of the medical records indicate abnormal findings and persistent pain, why does he not find a permanent impairment under the guide that he says is authoritative?

"The evidence will show that his opinion is tainted by his reliance on defense lawyers for a great deal of his income. Dr. Penner earns over two hundred thousand . . .

MR. CUNNINGHAM: Objection, he is arguing.
THE COURT: Overruled.

"The evidence will show Dr. Penner is paid over two hundred thousand dollars a year by defense lawyers and their clients simply to do these types of examinations and render opinions.

"Now you will hear from Mr. Brooks and Mr. Cunningham and then you will begin to hear all of the evidence from both sides. After both sides have presented their evidence, we the Plaintiffs, Karen and Frank Scala, will ask you to render your verdict in their favor in the full amount of their damages and losses.

"Thank you very much."

COMMENT:

Notice that following the objection, counsel does not let this interrupt his sentence. He repeats the first part of the sentence, so there is no question about it. The jury knows the "hired gun" of the defendant receives over two hundred thousand dollars a year from "defense lawyers." This is a perfect example of "winning early," and doing it with a good opening statement. Jurors have formed an opinion about "whiplash" cases before they reach the courtroom. By the end of opening statement they must recognize the seriousness of this injury or they will never return a large verdict.

[2.23] Great Trial Lawyers: Gerry Spence—Defending The Defenseless. Whether it is defending Mrs. Marcos in New York, an Indian in South Dakota, or the Jones family in Oregon, often the call goes out to a little town in Wyoming called Jackson Hole. There is found one of the great lawyers of our time, Gerry Spence.

The Jones family represented to this great lawyer the essence of frustration derived from trying to work within a system that sometimes does not work. Let us examine Gerry Spence's illustrative opening statement in this case, reprinted below.

OPENING STATEMENT IN *OREGON v. JONES*

"An opening statement has a function. An opening statement is where a lawyer is given a chance to tell the jury what he honestly believes his evidence will be. It is a time when people are supposed to come forward. It is a time when people should, if they have a case, present it.

"Now I think that you noticed during Mr. Brown's case, his opening statement, that we didn't interrupt him, we didn't get up and object, we didn't cause to use a word that he feels comfortable with, we didn't cause any distractions.

"The reason we didn't do that was because we wanted him, on the behalf of the State of Oregon, to have a fair opportunity to present everything that he knows about in this case. Every bit of evidence that he is going to present, we wanted him to have a chance to tell you about it so that you would know it too.

COMMENT:

> There is much talk today about not telling what an opening statement is all about. There is an advantage to getting right to your story, but notice how counsel uses a few opening remarks to his advantage. Those who have heard Gerry Spence know that he will use every word to his advantage.

"We've already learned that a defendant isn't required to say anything, to do anything, or to present any case of any kind. I don't know how this case will unfold as the prosecution brings on his so-called 23 witnesses because they haven't told us. As if this is some kind of a secret. But the defendant in every criminal case has the right to reserve his opening until the end of the State's case.

"Now that's kind of an interesting thing if you will contemplate it. Lots of defense attorneys, many, maybe even most that represent persons charged with crimes will wait, hold back, they won't get up like we're doing here. They'll hold back and wait to see what those 23 witnesses are going to say.

"They'll wait to see what kind of a case the prosecution makes. Then they'll look for the holes in the case and get up at the close of the case and make their opening statement and we have that right to do that if we wanted to. We could hold back. We could wait to see what the 23 witnesses would say. We maybe should because certainly Mr. Brown hasn't told us what his witnesses are going to say or even very much about the theory of the case. We are coming forward with our case today. I want to stand here on behalf of my client and I am going to tell you the things that I think have anything to do with this trial and it is going to take me a little while to do that.

COMMENT:

Notice how counsel argues presumption of innocence before the trial even begins. Notice how he uses his giving up the right to reserve. Also, he lets the jury know it will take a while to tell this story, and it did, more than a hundred pages of typed transcript. Gerry Spence then talked about the prosecution's opening, pointing out that it dealt with "things" and not people. Then he proceeded to talk about people.

"The case isn't as much about landscapes, and Oregon fences, and East Oregon fences, and oceans and rivers as it is about people. A case about people. This case is about two families. This case is about the Gertulla family and the Jones family. And I think that you would first of all like to know something about who they are, what the evidence will be about who they are.

"Sandy Jones and her husband saved up their money to get enough of a down payment. They worked in Alaska. To get a down payment to buy a little kind of swamp-bottom farm on this alleged river; about 20 acres. They, uh, bought it on time. They saved their money for the down payment and this was their home. It was a place where they could be self-sufficient. They were poor but they were proud. And they weren't the kind that sought Welfare. They were the kind that took care of themselves.

"Mr. Jones had hurt himself in the lumber business, he was a lumb, he was a lumberman, lumber-jack, had hurt himself. And for a time he was paralyzed, and from time-to-time he had sporadic paralysis, that would recover, he later had a heart attack, was a man who was not able to do much work or to do long work at a time. But he worked occasionally, he would work, pick out a few days work someplace and work until as long as he could work and then he would stop.

"Mrs. Jones and the family depended very greatly upon the 20 acres to live. They, they had a garden, they had a milk cow, they raised their own beef, salmon were in the river, are in the river, kids had ponies. Sandra Jones worked as a, as a security personnel, at a trailer park and supplemented the family income in that fashion.

"Mr. Jones has very little education. Mrs. Jones is a talented woman with a high school education, uh and a woman upon whom the family depended for guidance and advice and she did that to the family. They were however a family that, that marched as I suggested to you in voir dire with a different drummer, to a different drummer, they weren't out to make a big place for themselves in the world.

"They didn't want fame, they didn't want power, they weren't looking for money. They had two children, Mike, Jr. who at the time was just 15, a little red-headed boy who grew up in this kind of rural place. A boy who has never had a problem of any kind, never been in any difficulty, never been in the juvenile courts, uh, never been the subject of the law.

"And little Shawn who was three years younger, little tyke of a girl who is now 16. What they wanted to do was raise their family, to educate their family, to isolate them if they could from the problems of today, the world today. To isolate them from drugs and crime, and the influence that kids get in the big cities.

"Their entire life was directed around these children. This was a family that had one function and one purpose and that was to raise their children. It was also a spiritual family and I got into trouble in using that word on the day before yesterday but I want to make clear what I mean by that.

"It was a family that prayed together. It was a religious family. It was a family that was spiritual in other ways as well. The Indians at Medicine Rock where this tragedy occurred, worshipped this spot, it was a spiritual place to the Indians. And Mrs. Jones was open to them. Felt kindly toward the spirituality of the Indians who worshipped their ancestors and who worshipped particular sacred places. There were burial grounds in the area that she respected.

"And these were the kinds of ideas that is concern for her Indian friends, concern for the poor, concern for her family is what the energies were that directed these people. They weren't perfect, they, I don't want you to believe that they were without fault, I don't want you to think that they, their judgments were unimpeachable, but by damned, they were solid citizens.

"She was also concerned about the environment. She had engaged herself in protesting some of the landfills around the area. One of the landfills around the area was an illegal landfill, it was across the river. And they were dumping illegally, putting dirt in the area which was causing the river's course to change. And she spent a good deal of time involved in that.

"In those kinds of work, she had, she maintained a booth at the fair, Columbia County, on behalf of the State Conservation District and it was that kind of activity that these people loved and were involved in. Among other things, Mrs. Jones taught Boy Scouts gun safety. She knew something about guns, was not an expert with a gun but she had a troop of young boys that she dealt with in that regard.

COMMENT:

I have not deleted one word of this part of the opening that tells about the "good guys" of this courtroom drama. It shows how a great lawyer sells his client to the jury. Gerry Spence does not compromise thoroughness in doing this. He then turned to the "bad guys" and told much about the Gertullas, including the father who was killed. He introduces other "characters" opposing counsel will present at trial. "You are going to hear a lot about a lawyer named Ronnau." He talked about a judge, a sheriff, and others concluding: "Mrs. Gertulla, herself, was connected to one of the wealthiest and most influential people in the country."

"So now here we are talking not about oceans and Oregon fences, we are talking about people and the conflicts that are about to arise between the people. With respect to the road, let me talk to you a little bit about that.

"You will hear a good deal about it and there may be a little bit of conflict about it. Mr. Ronnau to begin with admitted there was no public road through the Joneses, out past the Joneses, through lot 10, and on through lot 9, then up past the place where this tragedy occurred and onto his property. Ronnau admitted that was not a public road.

COMMENT:

Having introduced the characters, counsel then began his "telling of the story."

"How do we defend ourselves against multinational corporations, how do we defend ourselves against great governments when we are small and weak and our resources are limited and he knows that, and he knew that, and he knew that the Gertullas had all the money that they needed and all the power, and all the connections that were necessary for him to do whatever he damn pleased and the evidence will be that the Joneses on the other hand are very poor and don't have monies to hire fancy lawyers and don't have monies to fight that kind of battle and so his approach in this case was to break the Joneses, to frighten them, to harass them, to exhaust them and to use the power that he had with the connections that he had on behalf of his clients, Gertulla, and Gertulla became a part of that process.

COMMENT:

Counsel continues the story

"On February 3, 1984 the children are pinned down with gunfire and Mike, Sr., too. They are down in the pasture, neighbors heard it, one neighbor saw the bullets splat, the children are close to the house in the pasture when the shooting begins and they run to the house.

"Mike Jones flattens, he's further down in the pasture, he flattens himself on the ground. He's laying there, as he's laying there he sees the pickup, strike that, a Jeep Wagoneer station wagon of the kind owned by the Gertulla's, not the color but the description, the kind that Gertulla's drive, drive past.

"In April of 1984 the trial on the road is had. Mrs. Jones is handwriting each one of the pleadings and the papers and the motions, trying as best she can to defend herself. And people laughed at her, lawyers laughed at her, judges laughed at her, the people, Ronnau laughs, and Gertullas thought it was funny as this woman did what she could do under the circumstances within her cell.

"Mike Jones comes plodding up his road towards the house and Gertulla is backing his pickup up and Mrs. Gertulla is sitting in the front seat and they are both looking back and they both see Mike Jones plodding along, on the road. Mrs. Gertulla yells out, "Will, he's not going to get off the road." Mr. Gertulla answered, this is all in the public record, answered, "Neither are we" and he hit him, ran into him and knocked him down.

"Mike Jones is a big man, but he is fragile, he goes into paralysis, he's very easy, he's got a very serious back problem, he's lying on the ground. Mr. Gertulla thinks this is very funny. The woman in the house heard all this, came out of his car laughing and pointing at Mike Jones laying on the ground.

COMMENT:

Counsel then points out "the Sheriff did nothing." Mrs. Jones and children "knew he was crippled from it." The children were riding their "two little ponies" and Gertulla "comes along and shoots at them." They came home "breathless and petrified." "Why would a man shoot at little children?"

"Now here's where we are. We've got a woman who can't get any help from the Sheriff when they run over her husband, can't get any help from the Sheriff when Mr. Gertulla poisons their well, can't get any help from the Sheriff when Mr. Gertulla shoots at their children, and she's getting pretty desperate.

"And by this time the prosecutor has advised them that they're not going to prosecute and little Shawn is beginning to have nightmares. And she wakes up in the middle of the night screaming. And Mrs. Jones, Mr. Jones is gone.

"They are by themselves and she sends little Shawn from their farm to the mother in Portland, where her mother lives. She sends the little Shawn to grandma to take her away from this battlefield, this is a war scene, it's a battleground, and the family is broken up. And by this time Mrs. Jones and the family are simply utterly unequivocably plainly terrorized.

COMMENT:

Counsel details the wrongs and frustration, then prepares the jury for what "maybe wasn't the right thing to do."

"And so she does something. You'll follow her logic but it wasn't the right thing to do. You'll follow her logic—maybe you would have done it, probably not.

"Here's what she says to herself. She says—you know, I can't get justice here and the people that are in charge of justice is the judge, and the prosecutor, and Mr. Ronnau who is an officer of the court, and they are doing things in this process against us. And she felt helpless.

"And these people are obviously depriving us of justice so in a very naive way she believed that the courts are to give justice. I don't know of anybody anymore who really believes that but that's what she thought.

COMMENT:

She did not put a gun to someone's head. She sued a judge, a prosecutor, and a private attorney.

"Now I am going to tell you what happened, what the evidence will show. Mike, Sr. is out of, out working. Away from the family home. Mrs. Jones is down at the trailer house, trailer park where she is working. And she gets a call from Mike Jr. He is hysterical. He is crying. Mr. Gertulla and Mrs. Gertulla have come through the property, with another car, and they are shooting.

"They left the gate open. The pony, which is, one of the ponies is a stud, a little stallion, the pony stallion is out and, you know they had been charged with livestock running at large and had been dragged into court and had been threatened and frightened to death about that. The pony is out.

"What shall he do? The mother said, 'They are shooting again?' And he said, 'Yes.' All right, so what happens is that Mrs. Jones tells her boss, 'My god, they've shot at my kids already. She says, 'They are there again shooting, I've got to go home.' Mikey is by himself.

"She tells Mike, go to the house, get into the house, lock the door, stay in the house. There is this, a shortcut home, there is a shortcut that brings her across from the, here's the river, there is a shortcut that, this is the river, the road that comes in here and the Jones's had a little boat down here and sometimes they'd take the shortcut and whoever was at the house would come across and get them in the boat.

"It saved a lot of driving, 10 miles or so all the way around. And she is taking the shortcut home, going like a bat out of hell to get there and when she gets at the bank she gets, runs out of the pickup, parks the pickup, the family car there, and screams across the river for Mike to come and get her.

"He doesn't come. Her heart is beating in her throat—where's Mike—I told him to be in the house, he should hear me. She screams, screaming 'Mike come and get me. Mike, Mike where are you?'

"Finally he shows up, he has been way off someplace trying to chase the horse, trying to get the horse back in. I don't know if you ever tried to chase a Shetland pony, stud on foot, but I got a hunch if you had you'd know what Mike was going through.

"So Mike finally comes and gets her and as she gets the story then finally from him face-to-face 'Mikey what's happened?' 'The Gertullas are out there shooting, they left the gates open, the horse got out' and Mike takes off again to get the horse, the stud.

"Her instructions to him are when you get the horse in go into the house and shut the door. But here's the situation, she's there, her boy is out in the open unprotected chasing that pony. He's got to get it in or they are going to be charged with livestock running at large again, so she figures she had better find out what the shooting is about and to make sure that he is protected.

"She had, when she left her work she grabbed her .38 and she put it on and she went to the house and got a .22 rifle and she started up the road to find out what the shooting is all about. And she is scared to death. She is a courageous woman but she is scared to death. She doesn't know how many people are up there. She doesn't know how many, who the men are, there's a car in the rear that's got two men in it, that Mike told her about.

"There was a car, the Gertullas are there, she doesn't know what, and she is a brave woman, I just have to say this and I think the evidence will bear that out. She went there by herself, Mikie, little Mikie is down there chasing the horse, and she had told him to go to the house. She has a rupture and has never had the opportunity medically to get it repaired even to this day.

"You'll see that this hill is a quite steep hill when you're out there. She ran up that hill, she went through the second gate, she got on up through the third gate, and she sat down at the gate, panting, holding her side, almost exhausted, and while she's sitting there up comes little Mike. She's trying to get her breath back, up comes little Mike and he's got the 30-30.

"And she said, 'I thought I told you to go back to the house.' And he's a 15-year-old boy and he is crying, he isn't going to leave his mother there by herself. And no sooner had they had this conversation than down the road comes the first car.

COMMENT:

Gerry Spence tells the story the way he would if sitting and talking with you. He does not interrupt with "Our evidence will show," though a few times you will find, "I think the evidence will bear that out." He tells the story in detail and then gets to the shooting.

"Mrs. Jones begins to crawl through the fence, through the gate, and she is stooped down about like so to try and get through the gate but she has, it's hard to open. One of those things where she was tired and hurt and out of wind all the rest of it, and with her rupture she probably can't open the damn gate anyway.

"And so she is crawling through. When she is halfway through Mr. Gertulla has his fun. He slams at her with the pickup. Guns it, vherumm, vherumm, vherumm, that sort of thing and she is caught there with the pickup and she is absolutely terrorized.

"And she doesn't know how many shots she fired, but she fired one shot then and she is trying to get the, to protect herself and so the only thing she can think of to do is to shoot the tire. And he's going vherumm, vherumm, and the pickup is going like this, not moving but kicking up dirt behind and he's clutching it.

"Mikie unbeknownst to her has come up here and he shoots the rear tire when Gertulla is attacking his mother with the car, he shoots the rear tire out. Now Gertulla has had enough of this stuff. Counsel tells you that Mr. Gertulla got out of the pickup but he never bothers to tell you why.

"Gertulla had enough from this woman. He opens the door of the pickup on his side. Mrs. Jones has gotten through the fence by now. Mr. Gertulla comes over there and engages her. Now, note—he walks, he is so afraid of her with this woman that he knows, whose children he has embraced, he is so afraid of her that he walks unarmed excepting apparently with a recorder in his hand, up to her, apparently he drops the recorder, and she could have shot Mr. Gertulla if that was her intent a hundred times.

"At least she could have emptied her gun into him. She never shot at him once, not once. And when he came up to take the gun from her she didn't even shoot him then."

COMMENT:

Gerry Spence then explained how Mrs. Jones tried bravely to save the victim's life. He then concluded with "the evidence is going to show," and his great faith in the American jury. It took the jury three minutes to find his client not guilty.

PART THREE

PRESENTING YOUR EVIDENCE

[3.01] Present Evidence In Proper Order. Writers are taught that structuring is the foundation of telling your story. The reader wants to know what is coming next, and you must tell your story so it will be understood. Good trial lawyers follow the same practice. This is what Scotty Ballwin has to say:

> The direct examination must have a purpose and objective. The objective should be accomplished by telling a story. The story must be interesting, it must have a beginning, it must have substance, it must have an end.
>
> The story must unfold in a logical sequence and it must be told in an interesting fashion. The jury's interest must be pricked, cultivated, and maintained.
>
> Maintaining the jury's interest is the most difficult, yet the most important of all objectives to achieve. This can best be done by provoking curiosity, creating suspense, and arousing anticipation.

One writer suggested it is the writer's job to tell of a problem and then to give the solution. He added that the solution must be odd enough to have a few surprises, but predictable enough to give the reader comfort.

That is exactly what we have to do in the courtroom. We DO have to make it interesting. So there can be many conflicts, as long as the battles are won by your side. However, you should tell them at the outside what you are going to do and then do it. People DO feel secure when they can rely upon the predictable, so make your winning the case the natural and predictable end to the story.

Writers structure the story by planning ahead. The lawyer must do the same. He or she must know where the story is going and then lead the jury right down the path to a proper conclusion.

Once you organize your entire trial, you must then organize each individual part of it. Notice the simple, yet planned, questioning of a widow by Scotty Ballwin during a trial:

Q. Mrs. Smith, were you able to see your husband?

Q. Was he making any sound?

Q. Did he appear to be breathing?

Q. Were you aware that he was dying?

Q. When did you learn that he was dead?

Q. Now, was he a good husband?

Q. Did you and he have good times?

Q. Did he like to play with the children?

With questions like those, you don't need answers. They tell a story, and in proper sequence.

[3.02] How To Avoid The Leading Question Problem. The worst direct examination problem for a beginning lawyer is the objection to a leading question. Even for experienced lawyers, this can be a problem if opposing counsel is more interested in objecting than in trying a lawsuit, and if the judge simply fails to understand what the rule is all about.

Always look to the purpose! The purpose of the leading question objection is to prevent the lawyer asking the questions from testifying. If the lawyer asking the questions tries to avoid this situation and the judge is at all reasonable, there should be no problem.

Lawyers and lecturers have tried to comprise simple guidelines, but none are perfect. Professor James Jeans has recommended the best approach, because it makes the lawyer "sound" as though he is not testifying.

Professor Jeans, who was a trial lawyer before joining the faculty, likes to ask "whether or not" questions. This certainly tells the judge he is not testifying. By saying "Please tell me whether or not such and such happened" does not suggest an answer. However, if you were to ask, "Tell the jury whether or not this man came onto the wrong side of the road at seventy miles an hour and smashed into your car which was parked at least seven feet off the pavement," then you will be in trouble.

By asking too much, you set off a signal to the judge that you are trying to enter your own words into evidence. Asking questions that call for "yes" or "no" answers is a step in the right direction, but it is still not the answer.

One court held that if the question suggests that the right answer is "yes," or that the right answer is "no," then it is leading. But if the question does not suggest which is correct, it is not leading. *Porter v. State,* 386 So.2d 1209 (Fla. App 1980). So, the only real guideline is whether or not the question suggests an answer.

I tried one case before a judge who felt every question that is asked on direct examination HAS to be leading. "Did you see anything unusual?" may suggest he did see something unusual, but it is much better than, "Did you see blood all over his body and a six-inch cut under his left eye?"

The appellate courts, and some legislatures, have come a long way in making the leading question rule more realistic. You can lead on preliminary matters, or if a witness is having a hard time testifying, or if the jury a hard time understanding.

Good trial judges want to move the case along and appreciate your asking whatever questions will accomplish this, without attorney-testimony. Good trial lawyers do not object for the mere futility of objecting, since nothing is really accomplished by it.

We have all learned that "The car was green, wasn't it," becomes after an objection is sustained, "What color was the car?" "Green." Just appreciate the fact you are not trying the case before a judge who feels the second question is leading because it suggests the car had a color.

If the leading question rule has taught us nothing else, it has taught us to be good trial lawyers and to avoid "Mickey Mouse" tactics of trying to tell the story the client should be telling. The purpose of the rule is to prevent lawyers from testifying through the witness, and good trial judges and good trial lawyers can accomplish that without slowing the trial.

[3.03] Have Witness Talk To The Jury. One good trial lawyer had properly prepared his client for court. When opposing counsel told her to look at him and talk to him, she replied, "No. I am going to look at these people," looking at the jury.

The witness has a story to tell and the jury is to whom it must be told. Be sure every witness looks directly at the jury while testifying. Eye contact is extremely important. It keeps attention and compliments the jury.

One method of being sure the witness does this is to ask a question, and then to look at the jury. The witness will automatically look at the jury. Once the witness is in the habit of looking at the jury, it will seem natural and the witness will want to tell the story in this personal manner.

[3.04] Know WHAT You Are Proving. When preparing your witness list, know WHAT you are proving. In every case you will need a different kind of proof.

David S. Shrager, a leading trial lawyer and past president of the ATLA, suggests that if you represent an elderly person, your proof should consider the following:

1. A 50% reduction of a two-year life expectancy is half of "the whole rest of his life."
2. Loss of independence is extremely important to elderly people.
3. Elderly people want to live in their "own place," their "home."
4. Elderly partners help each other and when one is injured or dies, it has a significant impact upon the other.
5. The help elderly people receive after injury is often the "lowest level of care," a typical "nursing home environment."
6. The slightest injury can affect their "daily living."

What David Shrager has suggested as to an "elderly case," you can adopt to any other kind of case. Know what factors affect your case and then build your case-in-chief around them. Prove it!

[3.05] Beware Of The Trend Away From Live Testimony. "The trend away from the use of live testimony is the darkest cloud on the horizon," according to Melvin Belli, the "King of Torts." He was specifically referring to the practice of a few federal courts of having the expert submit an affidavit of his direct testimony, having the affidavit read by a clerk, then having the expert testify from the stand that it is his affidavit, then subjecting the expert to cross-examination.

The practice completely destroys the use of demonstrative evidence and the effect of the expert giving his own testimony. The few judges who have adopted this practice to date have based their authority on Rule 611(a) of the Federal Rules of Evidence, which reads:

> 611(a) Control By Court. The court shall exercise reasonable control over the mode and order of interrogating witnesses and presentation of evidence so as to (1) make the interrogation and presentation effective as ascertainment of the truth, (2) avoid unnecessary consumption of time, and (3) protect witnesses from harassment or undue embarrassment.

The next step, which is already used by a few judges, is submission of a summary of the deposition, instead of the deposition itself. This may save time, but it may also curb justice. The Supreme Court found such practices violate due process in criminal cases.

Though it is too early to determine how the Court will react to civil cases where such practices have been adopted, there is a real threat that trial judges will begin using the practice to clear dockets. Once again, courts must decide between justice and expediency, and it is the trial lawyers' duty to fight for justice.

[3.06] Make The Witness A Storyteller. Storytelling is an art the trial lawyer masters, but it is equally important to make each witness, particularly your client, a good storyteller. Much will be accomplished by the manner of questioning, the structuring of the testimony, and in preparation for the witness's appearance. Much more, however, must be done by the witness.

The trial lawyer must explain to the witness the manner in which direct will be conducted. Short questions with short answers can be very effective. Be sure the witness does not get ahead of the story with long answers.

There are times, however, when a narrative description can be very effective. The jury wants to hear the story in the witness's own words, and this approach can give the jury a feeling that the witness is credible and the story is real.

The danger, of course, is that the witness will run away with the story and not tell it in proper order, or will make it too long or exaggerated. Let the witness know that you may interrupt with questions, and don't hesitate to come in with a question that gets the train back on its track.

Regardless of how many times you have talked with a witness, the last minute conference is important. Telling a story in front of a jury is a new experience. Be sure the witness is ready and that the game plan, as well as the story, is fresh in his/her mind.

[3.07] Presentation Of Exhibits. The presentation of exhibits must begin long before you arrive in the courtroom. You must know what exhibits you will use, obtain them, make them known to opposing counsel during discovery, list them for pretrial, show them to opposing counsel if required by pretrial order, and have them marked before trial by the clerk or other authority.

If the exhibit is self-authenticated, it can then be introduced without oral testimony. Present it in open court, ask that it be accepted into evidence, and publish it to the jury.

If it is not self-authenticated, as in most cases, you must then decide which witness will lay the foundation for its introduction into evidence. Trial strategy may require that one witness be used, as opposed to another witness who is also perfectly qualified to perform this function.

EXAMPLES:

> Your client can identify the scene of an accident, but an eye witness may be perceived by the jury as a more independent witness. A client may be able to testify as to a garment that was worn at the time of the accident, but a nurse may more dramatically explain how she had to cut the sleeve from the bleeding arm. A partner may identify a business record, but an accountant may add weight to the evidence.

Know the local practice as to where exhibits are kept during the trial. It may be customary for each counsel to keep his own exhibits, or it may be customary for the clerk to keep them all. If the clerk keeps exhibits, decide whether it is more effective to obtain an exhibit from the clerk before the witness takes the stand, or to walk up to the clerk and obtain it after the witness is actually on the stand.

Saving time is always appreciated by the judge and jury, but sometimes that extra minute it takes to let the jury know you are obtaining an exhibit from the court and not from your counsel table is worth the effort. It affords movement that breaks up the monotony of counsel standing at a lectern and the witness sitting in the witness box.

In nearly every jurisdiction it is customary to show the exhibit to opposing counsel and, even if not required, it is a courtesy that gives the jury a favorable impression. The "may I approach the witness" may be required in some jurisdictions, but it is often overworked, especially if the court has granted permission before for counsel to approach the witness when asking the witness to identify an exhibit.

I watched another attorney approach a witness one day and ask, "I show you what has been marked exhibit 'A,' do you recognize it?" "Yes." "What does it purport to be?" The witness replied, "I don't know." This stunned the lawyer, since it was a simple document the witness had just signed. Finally, the witness said, "Oh, you mean what IS it?"

I realized the procedure used was the one I learned from older lawyers my first month as a lawyer. I also realized I had never used the word "purport" outside the courtroom. I now handle the same situation, as follows;

"I show you what has been marked Plaintiff's exhibit number one, do you recognize it?"

"Yes."

"What is it?"

"It is the contract I signed this morning."

It is so easy when lawyers talk like normal people!

[3.08] How To Use Depositions. Depositions are used during your case-in-chief when a witness is unavailable either for physical or financial reasons, or for reasons of trial strategy.

If a witness cannot be present you must show he or she is unavailable. Study the rules of evidence of your jurisdiction and be ready to comply with those rules if you are unable to obtain a stipulation or an advance ruling by the court. Being unavailable means he CANNOT be made to be present, or that for some legal reason his testimony cannot be required.

EXAMPLES:

> You have tried to subpoena a witness and he could not be served within the jurisdiction. (This is why getting the subpoenas out early is important). The witness cannot be forced to testify because he would be offering evidence that might incriminate him. The witness does not have the mental capacity to testify. It has been established that the witness cannot remember now what he testified to at deposition.

Who should read the part of the witness? Often an associate or secretary is used, because of availability, but having a male testify for a female may not be effective. The great Gerry Spence called upon a well-known news media personality in one case and felt it was very effective. He believed in using an adverse character to obtain an unfavorable response.

Where should the witness sit? In the witness box, of course. But what if you read both questions and answers, as I often like to do? Standing in front of the jury at that time is the usual procedure, but I have tried sitting in the witness chair if the judge has no objection, and I prefer it. I think oral evidence should come from the witness stand, even if it comes by deposition.

When you read the questions and answers, you can put emphasis where it is most effective. If you are going to read many depositions, don't do them consecutively. Your voice grows thin and jurors grow sleepy. I prefer letting opposing counsel read his cross, and then I come back with a reading of the redirect.

Prepare in advance which parts of the deposition will be read, so you can delete unnecessary testimony and highlight objections. I send opposing counsel and the court a copy of those parts of the transcript which will require a ruling on objections. Often, opposing counsel will withdraw an objection or the judge will indicate how he is going to rule.

Depositions, written or video, can add to your case. They are a part of the transcript you can highlight for final argument before the trial even begins. But, you must get the evidence in, and do it as effectively as possible. Never make this part of your case-in-chief a mere making of the record. Make it convincing evidence!

[3.09] Make Notes For Appeal. It is so simple, yet so important! If you don't make good notes for a possible appeal, you may not find those points for appeal when you need them.

Many good lawyers have a separate divider in their trial notebook labeled "APPEAL." Whether you use this method or write on the file, you must have all points of appeal in one place where they can be easily found.

In most states you have little time to prepare a motion for new trial or otherwise to preserve your right to appeal. It is not unusual for a client to come in on the last day and plunk down a retainer for appeal. Prepare for this during trial!

[3.10] Video Evidence: Demonstrative Evidence. The jury will learn not only from what it hears and what it sees, but also from what it hears and sees at the same time.

What percent of the evidences does a juror retain?

Oral evidence 10%
Visual evidence 20%
Combination of oral and visual evidence 65%

This means an increase of 100% is retained after 72 hours if it is visual rather than oral, and an increase of 650% if it is a combination of visual and oral. The frightening part of the many studies that reach such conclusions is that without any visual aid, jurors only remember one-tenth of the evidence we present to them.

Presenting evidence by video is not the answer to this problem. The jury can forget what a witness says on video as easily, and sometimes much more easily, than if the witness were live.

That is why video evidence should be presented only after considering the following:

1. Would the witness be more effective if testifying live?
2. Would any shortcomings of the witness be less apparent if a written deposition were read to the jury?
3. What percentage of the trial is going to be presented by video deposition?
   (a) Too much video tends to put jurors to sleep.
   (b) Highlighting a witness with a video presentation reaches a point of diminishing returns quickly.

4. What is the length and quality of testimony in the particular deposition you are presenting?
5. Is your jury one that may be prone to appreciate video testimony? Older jurors may watch television more and accept such testimony quicker than younger jurors.

Whether a witness testifies in person, by video deposition, or, within limits, even by written deposition, demonstrative evidence can be used effectively.

EXAMPLES:

1. Enlargements. Photos, charts, and exhibits can be enlarged so the jury can see them. I have often taken a letter or small document to a blueprint company and had it run off a copy the size of a blueprint. It is effective and inexpensive.
2. Photographs and videos. A Polaroid—size photo can be equally impressive if it tells a story. A video can tell that same story with action, and with THE VOICE OF A PERSON.
3. X-Rays: Negative and positive. Some lawyers prefer the negative X-ray, because it looks "official" and the doctor can dramatize it all by showing it in the lighted box. But a positive X-ray can sit in the courtroom during trial and can be taken to the jury room during deliberation. I like them because they SHOW what they are supposed to show and make it clearer to a juror.
4. Models. There is much evidence that is too large to bring into the courtroom. You can bring it by model or photograph, or by bringing the jury to the evidence.
5. Computer simulations. Accidents can be reconstructed and magic brought before the jury's eyes, if the expense is justified and if the circumstances make such a presentation appropriate.
6. Drawings. Sketch artists can prepare drawings of medical records, scenes of an accident, or other part of the evidence you want to help the jury visualize.
7. Slides and overhead projections. Some lawyers have purchased such equipment and believe it to be extremely effective. It is inconvenient, but can be a great "teacher."
8. Personal objects. The family Bible, the girl's diary, the boy's scrapbook, or an old man's pipe may add a personal touch to evidence.
9. Day in the life. If permitted, day-in-the-life videos can be very effective.

[3.11] Refreshing Recollection. Witnesses do not always remember. Even the best preparation does not always prepare the witness for a question, often on re-direct, that just draws a blank. The courts have dealt with that problem and have made a remedy available to counsel.

When a witness remembers, he cannot use a hearsay document to refresh his memory, since there is no need for refreshment. But, if the witness CANNOT recall certain facts that he or she once knew, nearly anything can be used to help that witness remember.

That which is used to refresh memory cannot, however, be admitted into evidence. It is only the refreshed memory that is admitted into evidence.

EXAMPLE:

"Do you remember the date of the accident?"
"No, I don't remember?"
"Did you ever know the date?"
"Yes, I wrote it in my diary."
"Here is your diary, will you look at it and tell me whether or not you remember the date?"
(Witness looks at the diary.)
"Yes, it was on August 10th."

[3.12] Introducing Business Records. Introducing business records, and much that doesn't even look like business records but is so labelled, can help prove your case. This evidence is introduced as an exception to the hearsay rule.

The law of evidence requires:

1. Witness is custodian or some other person familiar with the keeping of the records.
2. The record was kept in the ordinary course of business.
3. Record was made at or near time of event recorded.
4. As a part of the regular course of business, a person having knowledge of the event, or who was furnished the information, made the record.
5. It was the regular practice to make such a record.

Once the evidence qualifies as a business record, hearsay evidence in the record is admitted. Counsel objecting to a business record must show that it is not trustworthy or that there is a prejudicial part of the record that can be deleted without defeating the purpose of the evidence.

[3.13] Direct Examination of Expert. The courtroom has become a battleground of experts, and the outcome of your lawsuit may well depend upon which expert the jury believes. That is why it is important to present your expert's testimony in its most favorable light.

The rules of evidence require that you consider:

1. Will the testimony be helpful to the jury?
2. Is the testimony based on data a reasonable expert in the field would use in rendering an opinion? (If so, admissible, even though based on hearsay.)
3. Is this witness qualified to give the opinion?
4. Is the opinion one that ANY expert could properly give?
5. Is it in that limited area of opinion evidence that can be given by a person not an expert?

Once you have decided the opinion evidence is proper and your witness is a proper person to give it, you must then be sure to present the evidence properly.

You must KNOW the law of your jurisdiction in order to know HOW to ask the proper question. First, is a hypothetical question still required? Even if it isn't, is it permitted, and would good trial strategy suggest its use?

In asking THE question, the exact wording will depend upon the law and practice in the court where the case is being tried.

EXAMPLES:

1. "Doctor, can you tell the jury, with a reasonable degree of medical certainty, what effect, if any, this injury will have on my client's ability to continue work as a truck driver?"
2. "Mr. Smith, can you tell the jury, with a reasonable degree of probability, based on your experience and expertise as an engineer, how fast the defendant's car was travelling at the time of the accident?"

In every jurisdiction, there are basic questions that must be asked in introducing medical testimony:

1. Doctor, will you give us your educational background and experience, as a doctor?
2. Do you specialize in any area of medicine?
3. Do you belong to any medical associations? Are you on the staff at any hospitals? Have you attended any seminars or written any articles on your area of expertise?
4. Have you examined Mary Smith, my client? When? The circumstances?
5. What did your examation consist of? How long? Obtain history? Take x-rays? Any tests given?
6. What did you find?
7. Are you able to tell the jury, with a reasonable degree of medical certainty (probability or whatever), whether or not the conditions you found were caused by the auto accident that has been described to the jury here in your presence?
8. What is that opinion?
9. Are you able to tell the jury, with a reasonable degree of medical certainty (etc.), what effect, if any, the conditions you describe have upon Mary's ability to enjoy life, perform her daily duties, and work at her job, as described to the jury? (Can be broken into several questions.)
10. What is that opinion?
11. Are you able to tell the jury, with a reasonable degree of medical certainty (etc.), what effect this condition will have on her ability to do all of these things in the future? (Can be broken into several sentences.)
12. What is that opinion?
13. What medical costs has Mary incurred with you relative to this condition?
14. Were all of those charges reasonable?
15. Were they reasonably necessary as a part of the treatment for the condition you described?
16. Doctor, do you use some kind of rating system to determine the degree of disability a patient may suffer?

17. Please explain that system to the jury and tell the jury where you obtained that system.
18. Did you use that system in evaluating Mary's condition?
19. What was your finding?

[3.14] Understand DNA. Judge Bruce E. Kaufman told the Criminal Section of ATLA that DNA has cast a "seductive effect" upon jury trials. He said that once DNA is brought into a case, "there is concern that all other evidence is diminished to the point that the DNA becomes the sole focus of the action."

This means the trial lawyer must know as much as possible about this scientific development. Comparisons are made by extraction of hairs, semen, or blood.

The procedure is basically, as follows:

1. The DNA is removed from the speciman and "washed" with an organic solvent.
2. The extracted DNA chain is then cut into fragments at specific sites by mixing it with a restriction enzyme.
3. The DNA is then placed on a gel to which an electrical current is applied, causing separation of the fragments into bands according to their length.
4. The DNA bands are then transferred to a nylon membrane while retaining the same positions they previously occupied on the gel. The double-stranded bands are then treated with a chemical that causes them to separate into single strands.
5. Radioactive genetic probes (DNA clones) are applied; they each bind to a specific complementary DNA sequence on membrane. The excess probe is then washed off.
6. The membrane is exposed to an X-ray film and developed so that the DNA banding patterns and their lengths can be visualized. Finally, the autoradiograph is interpreted by comparing the DNA print to one from another DNA sample to determine if there is a match, based on band length.

If this does not make it perfectly clear, read the technical evidence discussed in *U.S. v. Lee,* 134 FRD 161 (ND Ohio 1991) and *U.S. v. Two*

Bulls, 918 F2d 1127 (8th Cir. 1990). When the expert shows the similarity in the prints, the jury can grab that conclusion and disregard all the scientific evidence that led to it, as well as all other evidence at the trial.

Such evidence may be used in civil, as well as criminal, proceedings, e.g., paternity cases and proving who was the driver. Judge Kaufman suggests that during voir dire, counsel must:

1. Obtain promise from juror not to give greater weight to scientific evidence than to other evidence, and
2. Obtain promise to hold experts to "meaningful and intelligent opinions to which the juror can relate."

[3.15] Use The Blackboard. The blackboard is still the simplest aid for the jury to understand and the easiest for the trial lawyer to use of all communication devices. Jurors tend to believe what they see on the blackboard, and they may see it long enough during a trial to reaffirm their acceptance of the evidence.

Though use of the blackboard depends upon the discretion of the court, its use is generally permitted to add meaning to testimony. It can be used as well during final argument. *Mid-Texas Development Co. v. McJunkin*, SW2d 788 (Tex. Civ App 1963).

Suggestions:

1. Take a photograph of the blackboard for use on appeal.
2. Be sure the probative value outweighs any prejudice.
3. Be sure the diagrams, etc., are accurate and if possible, based on evidence.
4. Have the witness make the drawing or write the figures, if possible.
5. DON'T CLUTTER! You want the jury to be able to see it and understand it.
6. Know local law, and practice and prepare for it.

[3.16] How To Introduce Photographs. One of the easiest, yet one of the most important, tasks of a trial lawyer is getting photographs into evidence. You must have it marked, show it to opposing counsel, and then follow these important steps:

1. Mr. Jones, are you familiar with the scene of the accident as it appeared on the day of the accident? *Yes.*
2. I show you what has been marked exhibit "A." Do you recognize it? *Yes, it is a photograph.*
3. What is described in this photo? *The scene of the accident.*
4. Does this photo fairly and accurately show the scene of the accident as it appeared on the date of the accident? *Yes, with one exception.*
5. What is that exception? *There was a tree about where the building is in the background.*
6. Other than that, does it fairly and accurately show the scene of the accident as it appeared at the time of the accident? *Yes.*

HOWEVER:

1. If any prejudice caused by the photo outweighs its probative value, it will not be admitted.
2. If any confusion caused by the photo outweighs its probative value, it will not be admitted.
3. If its effect is so cumulative that it adds nothing to the proof, it will not be admitted.
4. If the photo is so substantially different from what it purports to show, it will not be admitted.
5. If what is shown has been "manipulated" to give a certain effect, it will not be admitted.

CAVEAT: Remember, photos should be marked in advance, as are other exhibits. This is especially true when you are going to show the witness several photos.

[3.17] How To Use Before And After Witnesses. An important part of every lawsuit is the issue of damages, and an important method of proving damages is through the use of before and after witnesses. These witnesses must be chosen wisely and used effectively.

EXAMPLES:

"Mr. Jones, did you know Bill before the accident?"

"Yes."

"How did you know him?"

"We worked together at the plant."

"What did you notice about him prior to the accident, as to his work on the job?"

"He was one of the hardest workers at the plant. He was there early and stayed late. He did more than his share of the work."

"What have you noticed since the accident?"

"He just can't do the work anymore. He tries, but he gets down on himself because he just can't do it. I have seen him finish about two cartons an hour lately, working real hard at it. He used to do three times that much. He also seems depressed. He used to joke all the time, but he just isn't the same." (Conclusion? If so, help him.)

A spouse or other member of the family makes an excellent before and after witness, and even the client can testify on this issue. However, independent witnesses who observed the plaintiff on the job and in other parts of life before and after the accident are important to your lawsuit.

Some courts limit the number of before and after witnesses, and good trial strategy keeps you from running a good thing into the ground. However, argue the need to cover all aspects of this part of the case with as many witnesses as seem necessary.

Assure the court that each witness will be brief. Be sure their testimony actually IS brief. The jury will appreciate your making your point and proceeding to the next proof in your case.

[3.18] Have Witness Speak The Jury's Language. The most important witness you put on the stand will not help you unless he or she communicates with the jury. To communicate is to cause the jury to understand.

If the witness speaks the jury's language, he or she will not only communicate, but also will enable the jury to identify with the witness.

During voir dire, counsel can learn each juror's "language," and then help witnesses use that language.

EXAMPLES:

> Big words do not impress jurors who have a limited education. Words that show prejudice will certainly not be well received by most jurors. Words that offend a person's religious views are especially harmful. (Seemingly innocent phrases such as "my God" are considered irreverent by many.) Technical words or foreign words do not communicate with many jurors and might cause a juror to think the witness is talking down to the jury. Poor grammar hurts the ears of many jurors.

Counsel should not put words into the mouth of a witness, but should notice, before trial, the "language" used by a witness and should make suggestions. During trial counsel should listen to how it is being said, as well as what is being said.

If a doctor is using terms the jury will not understand, counsel should say, "Would you explain that in words the jury and I will understand." The jury will appreciate your consideration and will understand the doctor.

[3.19] Know When To Redirect. The right to conduct a redirect is a precious one that should be used with caution. It is NOT to be used automatically!

Redirect should be limited to situations in which:

1. There is a need to "clear up" evidence;
2. There is a need to "expand" on the direct, AND you have a right to do so; or
3. The cross-examination has discredited the witness.

The judge and jury want to proceed with the trial and there is a feeling that if possible, you should have brought it out on direct. Cumulative evidence should never be gotten into on redirect. Federal and most states' rules of evidence discourage evidence that is a "waste of time."

[3.20] Special Problems In Presenting Evidence. No two lawsuits are alike and no two proof situations are similar. Some proof presents a particular problem and must be considered in advance.

1. Reconstructing an event through an expert. If you think you do not need a reconstruction expert, notice what Murray Ogborn lists as areas such an expert can cover: (a) speed, (b) which side of the road the vehicles were on, (c) point of impact, (d) evasive tactics taken, (e) who was driving, (f) delay in perceptions and reactions, (g) mechanical condition of the vehicles, (h) vehicular malfunction, (i) seatbelt questions, including whether they were being worn, injury enhancement, or reduction of effectiveness, (j) avoidance measures that could have been taken, (k) roadway design deficiencies, (l) whether traffic control devices were operational or sufficient, and (m) whether damage to vehicle parts, such as tires, was the cause of the crash or were caused by the crash.

That is what can be done in a motor vehicle case. I have watched such experts testify as to why a ceiling fell and why a piece of machinery did not work. Such experts turn back the clock and let the jury sit there and see what happened, or what the expert thinks happened. Such experts can discuss: (a) the physical factors that relate to the collision; (b) the cause of the collision; and (c) the cause of injuries.

2. Proving discrimination. Sheldon Stark has listed ways of proving discrimination. You can establish lack of just cause to terminate employment through: (a) participants in decision, (b) witnesses to decision, (c) memoranda or recordings of decision, (d) reasons for decision, (e) perfunctory warning, or lack thereof, (f) prior oral or written criticism, or lack thereof, (g) prior favorable performance reviews, (h) other documents favorable to plaintiff, such as letters of commendation, letters of recommendation, or mortgage letters, (i) inadequate investigation of incident leading to termination, (j) inconsistent action regarding plaintiff, and (k) less severe treatment of other employees in similar circumstances.

3. Toxic tort cases. Linda Miller Atkinson has found three basic tools for proving a toxic tort: (a) discovery, (b) industry reports, and (c) government reports. Four good government sources are EPA, Food & Drug Administration, OSHA, and National Institute of Health. Once a report is made about your particular case, you can request a copy under the Freedom of Information Act.

She lists as toxic properties you must understand: (a) chemical or biochemical reaction, (b) physiological responses, (c) carcinogenicity and mutagenicity, and (d) susceptible populations.

Proving such a case requires experts in the toxic arena as to cause and injuries. It also requires expertise as to this area of the law. Medical and legal issues get extremely complicated.

4. Medical negligence. Standard of care is extremely important in medical negligence cases. Mary Beth Ramey has put together an excellent list of sources for establishing the standard of care:

(a) *Standards for Obstetric-Gynecologic Hospital Services*, published by American College of Obstetricians and Gynecologists.

(b) *Accreditation Manual for Hospitals*, published by Joint Commission on Accreditation of Hospitals.

(c) *Judicial Counsel Opinions and Reports*, including the principles of Medical Ethics and Rules of Judicial Counsel, published by American Medical Association.

(d) *Toward Improving The Outcome of Pregnancy*, Committee on Perinatal Health, published by National Foundation—March of Dimes.

(e) *Hospital Care of Newborn Infants*, published by the Academy of Pediatrics.

(f) *Code for Nurses*, published by the American Nurses Association.

(g) *Standards for Obstetric-Gynecologic* and *Neonatal Nursing Functions and Standards*, published by the American College of Obstetricians and Gynecologists.

(h) *Obstetric, Gynecologic, and Neonatal Nursing Functions and Standards*, published by the Nurses Association of Obstetricians and Gynecologists.

PART FOUR

CROSS-EXAMINING WITNESSES

[4.01] Divide And Limit "Areas Of Questioning." It is imperative that counsel cross-examine on as few issues as possible and that those issues be divided into areas of questioning. You will ask several questions in each "area of questioning," but the "areas" should be limited to three or fewer, if possible.

Start by recognizing the purposes of cross-examination. Dean John Henry Wigmore said: "Cross-examination is the greatest legal engine ever invented for the discovery of truth."

The great Max Steuer said: "If the witness is a decent, unprejudiced citizen who has told the substantial truth or has said little to hurt you, leave him alone; smile at him but don't cross-examine him.

"And, if you do decide to cross-examine him, you should definitely have in mind what you hope to gain by your cross-examination. You will find it more elaborately in the books, but in my book, cross-examination should be pointed to two objectives: either to destroy the story told by the witness or to destroy the witness himself."

During cross-examination, you must help your cause, hurt their cause, AND PREPARE FOR FINAL ARGUMENT!

[4.02] Two Questions You Must Ask Yourself. If an author learns but one thing in 44 years of cross-examining witnesses, he must share that discovery with the reader. It was only after many years that I learned to pause before cross-examination and ask myself: (1) How do the jurors perceive this witness? and (2) How far will the jurors let me go in changing that perception?

There is simply no way you can cross-examine a witness without knowing how to attack. If the jury believes the witness, you can prove him a liar only with overwhelming evidence. If jurors suspect he is lying, then they expect you to show that through your cross-examination.

If the jurors really like a witness, they will resent your attacking the witness, unless you have some heavy artillery. Evaluate your problem with accuracy, determine what ammunition you have at your disposal, and then attack to the degree you feel necessary to accomplish your purpose.

[4.03] Ask The "612 Question." Judge Frederick Lacy, a well-known federal jurist and lecturer, has warned lawyers always to ask the "612 question," which is: "Prior to testifying here today, did you use any papers or documents to refresh your memory?" This question is based on Federal Rule of Evidence 612 which provides that a "yes" answer to that question enables counsel to see the document and to use it during cross-examination.

It may not be practical to begin every cross-examination with this question. Knowing the nature of the testimony, and having the benefit of discovery, you may suspect when documents may have been used to refresh the witness' memory. It is also possible to direct discovery at this very issue.

[4.04] Close All Doors. There is no greater joy during cross-examination than to catch a witness in a colossal lie. This can be a hollow victory, however, if you have not closed all doors through which the witness might escape.

EXAMPLE:

"Were you at the scene at the time this happened?"
"Yes."
"Did you observe what happened?"
"Yes."
"Did you file a report as to what happened?"
"Yes."
"You filed that report within an hour after it happened, is that right?"
"Yes."
"Was that report based on what you saw or what people told you?"
"On what I saw."
"Was that personally prepared by you?"
"Yes."
"Did it fairly and accurately reflect what happened?"
"Yes."
"Have you since learned that this report is not an accurate reporting of what happened?"
"No."

NOW, THE WITNESS IS TRAPPED! When it is shown that the report states that the defendant went through a red light and the witness wants to change his testimony, he cannot explain it away with such excuses as, "I made that report at a much later date," or "The report was made by an inexperienced assistant of mine," or "It really didn't reflect what happened out there," or "The report was based on what people told me," or "I have since found that the report is not accurate."

[4.05] Wellman's "Art" Of Cross-Examination. For nearly a century, law students have learned about the real world of trial advocacy through Francis Wellman's *The Art of Cross-Examination*. Trial lawyers who have taken the time to return to this classic have found how well it has stood the test of time.

Wellman set the tone for his book with a quote from a famous English barrister: "There is never a cause contested, the result of which is not mainly dependent upon the skill with which the advocate conducts his cross-examination."

The four questions Wellman asked must still be asked today: "Has the witness testified to anything that is material against us? Has his testimony injured our side of the case? Has he made an impression with the jury against us? Is it necessary for us to cross-examine him at all?"

The "ART" is divided into the following:

1. The "MANNER" of cross-examination. Though each lawyer may have his own manner, each manner must reach the goals of "separating truth from falsehood" and of "reducing exaggerated statements to their true dimensions."

Wellman warned that we must discredit the testimony, not the witness. If you attack the witness he will straighten up and defy you. However, a courteous manner invites the witness to loosen up, and he is more likely to say what you want him to say.

2. The MATTER of cross-examination. Cross-examine on matters that really count with the jury. Wellman warned against "endless and pointless cross-examinations." This is as important today as it was early in the century when Francis Wellman was trying lawsuits in New York City.

Find the weak spot in the direct testimony and go right to it! It is only after establishing the subject of cross-examination that you plan "how" you are going to cross-examine.

3. Cross-examining the perjured witness. Wellman maintained "the greatest ingenuity of the trial lawyer is called into play" when cross-examining the perjured witness. He pointed out that you need only to look for a part of the testimony to be perjured.

He suggested that if the testimony appears to be a fabrication, then ask the witness to repeat the answer. This is NOT in violation of the modern theory of not letting the witness repeat a story unfavorable to your cause.

This repetition is with good reason. The witness will repeat the story in identical form. Then you inquire as to the middle of the story, then the beginning. By skipping around, the witness is unable to tell the story as rehearsed, and the jury recognizes the fabrication.

Wellman wrote of witnesses with a low grade of intelligence, suggesting you watch the voice, study the vacant expression of the eyes, a nervous twisting about in the witness chair, and especially in the use of language not suited to their station in life. Obviously, this does not always apply to uneducated witnesses experienced in testifying.

4. Cross-examining experts. The modern trial lawyer did not invent the expert witness, nor did the Federal Rules of Evidence create the need to cross-examine that witness. More than seventy years ago, Wellman wrote: "The expert is more and more called upon as a witness in both civil and criminal cases."

Wellman scoffed at Lord Campbell's conclusion that "skilled witnesses come with such a bias on their minds to support the cause in which they are embarked, that hardly any weight should be given to their evidence." What should be has had little to do with the great weight a jury may give the most "bought" of all experts.

Wellman warned against the perils of fighting the expert "on his own ground," especially against "lengthy cross-examinations along the lines of the expert's theory." He preferred "putting the expert to some unexpected and offhand test at the trial, as to his experience, his ability and discrimination as an expert."

5. The sequence of cross-examination. A playwright structures his story and the trial lawyer must do the same. Wellman said, "You should never hazard the important question until you have laid the foundation for it in such a way that, when confronted with the fact, the witness can neither deny nor explain it."

Remember, Wellman said, "deny," NOT EXPLAIN. He was aghast at the inexperienced trial lawyer who showed a witness a letter and asked, "What have you to say to that?" He suggested leading the witness through his direct testimony, saying after each crucial point, "I have you down as saying so and so; will you please repeat it?"

Only after all doors are closed do you show the witness the letter and ask him the question or questions that will destroy him. Wellman suggested that you change your attitude toward the witness once it is shown he is lying. This will signal the jury to be equally disgusted with the witness.

As the plot thickens, the trial lawyer should not stop until he or she has crossed the finish line. It was said of Sir Charles Russell that he never let a nail hang loosely, that he never stopped until he drove it home, and no man could ever pull it out again.

Sometimes it is best to sting the witness during the first few minutes of cross-examination, but Wellman recalled a case in which he saved a bundle of documents until four o'clock and asked only that the witness identify his signature, that he would have all the following day to examine the documents. He did spend all day on the documents, but it was too late for the witness to question their authenticity.

The sequence of the trial, as well as the sequence of the cross-examination, must be considered. Today's trial lawyers would be amused to learn that even in earlier times, clients were disappointed when counsel did not immediately destroy the witness with a precious "pearl," but rather saved it for final argument when the client can join everyone in the courtroom as the saved pearl destroys the witness at a time when he cannot explain away his answer.

6. Silent cross-examination. The hardest words for a beginning lawyer to say are, "No questions, your Honor." Wellman said: "Nothing could be more absurd or a greater waste of time than to cross-examine a witness who has testified to no material fact against you."
7. Cross-examination to the "fallacies of testimony." Wellman examined the "elements of human nature and human understanding" that cause even the honest and unbiased witness to conceal the truth. This tells us courtroom psychology had its day in court long before there were courtroom psychologists.

Wellman said that we must go to the SOURCE of false testimony, if we are to deal with it effectively. He said that our physical senses record data accurately, but once we think about it consciously, the facts are colored by experience, motive, and character. Once facts are interpreted, they become the perception of the interpreter.

Wellman talked of the "intensity of attention" one person gives compared to another. When one witness has paid less attention, has colored what he has seen or heard, and has a desire to help one side, his testimony needs close scrutiny on cross-examination. Add to this the fact that one believes what one wants to believe and that one only remembers what one is capable of remembering, and you begin to understand the source of false testimony.

8. Other factors. Wellman said that we don't seek truth, but "probable truth." He agreed with Lord Mansfield's conclusion that in deciding facts, we "should be regulated by the superior number of probabilities on the one side or the other."

You can cut off "half" of a witness's story by asking what attracted the witness's attention. If a "loud noise" attracted the attention, then all that happened before that was not within the witness's personal knowledge.

Sir James Scarlett allowed judges and juries to discover for themselves the best parts of a case. He said that it "flattered their vanity." Wellman suggested that to do this, the trial lawyer must know human nature, know the questions and interests involved, and have a keen imagination that sees all possibilities of the case. He added, however, that "self-restraint" must also be a quality of the cross-examiner, because it is simply too tempting an invitation to destroy a witness who might destroy the questioner.

Just one more tip for the trial lawyer, reread *The Art of Cross-Examination* by Francis L. Wellman. It is overflowing with masterful cross-examinations.

[4.06] Irving Younger's "Commandments." Irving Younger was America's most popular law lecturer, a former trial lawyer, judge, and author. He was a master showman who made law more entertaining than television, and who made all of us trial lawyers proud of our profession and determined to improve upon whatever talent God gave us.

While the jury was deliberating in a trial in the Missouri Ozarks, opposing counsel and I waited with the judge in his chambers. A few terms the judge had used during the trial prompted me to ask him if he had ever heard of Irving Younger. He replied, "I listen to his tapes on evidence as I drive from courthouse to courthouse." I later told Irving of this and he smiled as I said, "All over this country, there are lawyers and judges who listen to you as they drive to and from the courthouse."

Why then, has Irving Younger's *Ten Commandments of Cross-Examina-*

tion caused such discussion among great trial lawyers? Perhaps John Romano put it best when he said, "They should really be accepted as guidelines, not commandments."

Let's look at these "guidelines":

1. Be brief! Who can argue with this? Sometimes you MUST cover more than the limit of three areas. Two is better than three, and one is better than two, IF briefness does not give way to waiving an opportunity to give the jurors answers they want to hear.
2. Use short questions with plain words! True.
3. Ask only leading questions! Though good trial lawyers feel you cannot always follow this rule, Don Bekind agrees, "When in doubt, lead."
4. Never ask a question to which you don't know the answer! Even Irving Younger modified this commandment where, (a) you are prepared to deal with whatever is the answer, or (b) where the answer really doesn't matter. Russ Hermann said, "This is sound practice," and many great trial lawyers agree. John Romano has suggested this is easier in the classroom than the courtroom, and Stanley Preiser has modified the commandment to read, "Never ask a question unless you are prepared to handle the answer." Good trial lawyers are better prepared to handle answers than inexperienced lawyers.
5. Listen to the answer! Of course, yet lawyers still make this mistake, so this one should be a "commandment." Irving Younger loved to tell of the hypothetical questioning by Senator Gurney during the Watergate hearing. "When did you last see President Nixon?" "I walked into the oval office and the President was standing on his desk, naked as a bluejay." "Did you notice anything unusual about this visit?"
6. Do not quarrel with the witness! To this should be added, "Not unless the jury wants you to, and the judge will let you get by with it." Also, during depositions you may catch a witness off guard through argument, and you may bend this commandment more than you would in the courtroom.
7. Do not permit the witness to explain! You do control the witness better with "yes" and "no" answers, but if a deposition tells you his explanation will sink the witness, you may want to let it do just that.

8. Do not ask the witness to repeat the testimony given on direct! True, you should not let the jury hear bad news twice, and you should not give a witness a chance to clear up any mistake he or she has made. However, one of Irving Younger's favorite cross-examinations was the one in the shirt factory case, where Max Steuer asked the witness to repeat a statement many times, and in doing so, convinced the jury the statement had to have been rehearsed.
9. Avoid one question too many! This part of legal folklore is full of examples of why you should stop when you have accomplished your purpose. In the courtroom, it is not always easy to know when that is, but following the other commandments will help. Also, it will help to know your purpose before you begin, because your purpose in cross-examination should be a very limited one.
10. Save the explanation for summation! Following the other commandments (guidelines) will help you accomplish this. Everything you do during trial is preparing you for those precious moments when you argue your case to the jury. Especially, cross-examination!

[4.07] End Cross-Examination With A Bang! There is simply no excuse for letting a good cross-examination end without all the glamour it deserves. The jury expects it. Your client expects it. Your cross-examination depends upon it.

Letting the witness get in the last word weakens the control you have had up to that moment. Ending with something unimportant can turn a good cross-examination into a mediocre one. Leave the jury with the picture of your waltzing across the goal line scoring a touchdown.

TV's Matlock and other fictional lawyers often end a cross-examination by withdrawing the question. Opposing counsel is screaming an objection, the judge is hammering his gavel, and the jury is shocked by the horrible implication of the question.

You do not have to end with that much drama, but you do have to end with drama. If a witness answers your final question with an "I think so," come back with an attack, "What do you mean you THINK so, Doctor? Are you telling this jury you don't KNOW?" This may be a good time to withdraw the question and sit down. The jury has gotten the point, and you have not let the cross-examination end with the witness wiggling out of a definite commitment.

Save some of your best material for last. If you have a letter written by the witness that contradicts everything he has said on the witness stand, SAVE IT! Cover other points, lay the foundation, close all doors, THEN:

> "Mr. Jones, did you write my client a letter on the first of March?"
>
> "Yes."
>
> "Was that letter written with sincerity, and in an attempt to tell exactly what you witnessed?"
>
> "Yes."
>
> "Did it accurately tell what happend?"
>
> "Yes."
>
> "That was written before you went to work for the company my client is suing, wasn't it?"
>
> "Yes, but . . ."
>
> "That's all right, Mr. Jones, just tell the jury the truth, DID you smell alcohol on my client's breath?"
>
> "Yes."
>
> "And, did you smell alcohol on Mrs. Jackson's breath?"
>
> "No, I did not."
>
> "Mr. Jones, I hand you what has been marked Plaintiff's exhibit number eleven, is this the letter you referred to a few minutes ago?"
>
> "Yes, it is."
>
> "Will you please read to the jury the last paragraph of your letter?"
>
> "Sure . . . It was obvious to me that this lady was drunk and you had nothing to drink. The accident was clearly her fault."
>
> "No further questions, your Honor."

[4.08] Give An Image Of Fairness. Being totally fair may be the most important thing a lawyer can do on cross-examination. Jurors are waiting to catch a lawyer being unfair to a lay witness, or even to an expert who has testified in court many times.

Bob Gibbins put it well when he said, "Fairness in this context means that you were not unnecessarily hostile, angry, or argumentative and did not unnecessarily attack the witness as distinguished from the harmful testimony. The bottom line on fairness in the ideal cross-examination is having enhanced your credibility and weakened the opposition's."

He gave a good example of this: Asking an expert, "You didn't perform all available tests, did you?" is not as well received by the jury as, "Did you perform all available tests?" If he wants to lie about this, you can then follow up with questions that pin him down, but you were fair in giving him a chance to tell the truth.

[4.09] Attack the Witness's Memory. Testimony is no better than the memory of the witness testifying. The beauty of attacking memory is that you are attacking a natural condition, and not the witness. Jurors know of that natural condition. In your cross-examination you can remind them. This can often be done by way of example, jogging the witness's memory, but at the same time calling attention to a common experience of the jurors.

EXAMPLES:

"Mr. Jones, I don't remember what I had for breakfast on the fourth of December, last year, do you?"

"No. Of course not."

"If you had asked me an hour after I had eaten that breakfast I could have told you, and I am sure you could have done that, couldn't you?"

"Sure."

"If I had asked you, right after the accident, exactly what my client said, you could have told me, couldn't you?"

"I can tell you right now what he said."

"Exactly?"

"Yes."

"Did you write it down?"

"No, I didn't have to."

"Do you ever write something down so you won't forget it?"

"Yes."

"Did you do anything else that would keep you from forgetting exactly what was said?"

"No. I didn't have to."

"Do you remember what you told me at the deposition?"

"No."

"Do you remember what you told the officer who took your statement?"

"No."

"Do you remember what you told my investigator?"

"No."

STOP: The jury has the idea and you can argue memory during final argument.

[4.10] Attack the Witness's Perception. Studies have been made, seminars held, and books written about the untrustworthiness of eye witness testimony and about the tricks perception plays upon people. Start every cross-examination with the realization that the witness may not have really seen or heard what appears from the testimony.

Here are a few factors to consider:

1. Where was the witness?
2. What could a normal person see or hear from that position?
3. Can this witness see and hear as well as a normal person?
4. Were there any unusual conditions existing at the time that made it hard to see or hear?
5. Is there some reason the witness WANTED to see or hear the event a certain way?

Until you have asked yourself these questions, you are not ready to use perception as a basis for cross-examination.

[4.11] Attack the Witness's Prejudice. The jury expects a witness to tell the truth, which means being fair to both parties. One of the easiest ways to attack testimony is to show that the witness giving it is not impartial.

Irving Younger said that if he were called upon to cross-examine a mother who had testified in behalf of her son, he would ask one question and sit down: "You're his mother aren't you?"

The relationship is not always that close and the prejudice is not always that obvious. Jurors do not assume a passenger in a car will lie about how the accident happened to protect the driver of the car in which he was riding. Jurors do not assume a witness will lie to protect a person of the same race, religion, or economic class.

In each case you must show the relationship and then show that the relationship DID in fact influence the witness's testimony.

EXAMPLE:

"You and the Defendant attend the same church, don't you?"

"When my investigator called at your home a week after the accident, didn't you tell him you really didn't see what happened and didn't want to talk about it?"

"I guess I did say something like that."

"Then some of the people at church talked to you about one of the brothers at church being sued, is that right?"

"Some of them did talk to me."

"Then you suddenly remembered what happened and decided you DID want to get involved, isn't that right?"

"I decided I would tell the truth."

"And, the truth is you would not be here today testifying, but to help a fellow member of your church. Isn't that right, Mrs. Smith?"

NOTE: The answer makes no difference. By now the testimony has been discredited in the eyes of the jury.

[4.12] Use Depositions Effectively. One of the principal uses of a deposition, or other discovery, is the impeachment of a witness on cross-examination. You must prepare for trial with this in mind and must use the technique effectively once you reach the courtroom.

A good cross-examination begins at deposition, and you will not possess those priceless jewels that can sink a witness in the courtroom if you have not asked your questions properly at deposition.

Start the deposition with some kind of assurance from the witness that he will not later say he did not understand the question. The usual approach is, "Mr. Jones, I am going to ask you several questions about the accident. Now if you don't understand a question, you will let me know so I can rephrase it, is that fair enough?"

When you reach the questioning on a point that may give rise to impeachment at trial, follow all the rules of cross-examination, just as though you were at trial. You want to appear to be fair, you want to close all doors, you want to ask about documents used in refreshing memory, and you want to test memory, perception, and prejudice.

During trial, you begin with reminding the witness of the date, place, and circumstances of the deposition. Ask if there is anything about the deposition concerning which he wants to change his testimony. If he says, "Yes", inquire, but if he says "No," you have laid the foundation for a cross-examination.

When the witness testifies contrary to the deposition, you then proceed to impeach him:

> "Mr. Smith, you have just testified that you saw the Defendant driving the Buick at the time of the accident, is that right?"
>
> "Yes."
>
> "You were under oath at the time of the deposition we referred to a few minutes ago, were you not?"
>
> "Yes."
>
> "And you testified a few minutes ago there was nothing in that deposition you wished to change, is that not right?"
>
> "Yes."
>
> "And that deposition was taken within a month after the accident, which was about two years ago this month, is that not right?"
>
> "Yes."
>
> "Mr. Smith, I would like to read to you from page 42, line 15 of your deposition: I could not see who was driving the car." (Without waiting for an answer, approach the witness) "Mr. Smith, let me show you that part of the deposition." (Show him that page of the deposition) "Have I stated your testimony correctly, Mr. Smith?"

[4.13] Ask Hardball Questions. *The National Law Journal* asked Cornelius Pitts why his client went free while the other defendants went to prison. The Detroit lawyer replied, "The objective is to prevent the prosecution from winning, and to do that you have to attack the complainant's witnesses to the extent their testimony is no longer credible to the jury."

He does this by asking "hardball questions." His style is to "start off slowly," but to "end up in an attack." He not only attacks the witness, but also any physical evidence the prosecution has introduced. In one case he proved the video did not even show his client was present.

In trying to show the complaining witness was really after money, not justice, his cross-examination went like this:

"Did you sue the City for $1?"

"No."

"Did you sue the City for $50?"

"No."

"Did you sue the City for $6 million?"

"Yes."

Cornelius Pitts has said, "Generally, I don't put on witnesses. My job is to attack." He knows that in criminal cases you usually cannot or should not put your client on the witness stand, so you must win your case on cross examination.

[4.14] How To Handle Difficult Witnesses. Every witness has the potential of being difficult, so every witness must be approached with one "must." You must, during cross-examination, be in complete control.

When a witness tries to take control, the jury may be on his or her side. Laypersons may enjoy watching a lay person give an attorney his comeuppance. This means it is easier to keep control than it is to try to regain control once it is lost.

Susan E. Loggans of Chicago is one of America's best personal injury lawyers, and she warns against the "unfocused" cross-examination that lets the witness "reiterate his or her direct testimony." She gives an example of the wrong and then the right way to control the witness:

The wrong way:

Q. Ms. Jones, you said on direct that you were looking to your left before the collision?

A. Yes.

Q. And then what happened?

A. I just looked to my left for a second, just like you do when you drive down the street and you're checking everything out around you.

Q. Excuse me, Ms. Jones, but all I asked you is what happened next?

A. Well, like I said, I was going along at a normal speed and all of a sudden the car in front of me slammed on its brakes for no reason, and no one could have stopped in that time.

Q. But Ms. Jones, you have admitted that had you been looking in front of you, you would have had time to stop.

A. No, and besides that if I had to drive with my eyes plastered in front of me, someone would be suing me saying I should have seen something coming at me from the side or behind.

The right way:

Q. Ms. Jones, you realize as a driver, don't you, that vehicles have reasons to slow down or stop from time to time, don't they?

A. Yes.

Q. And one reason we don't ride right up on the rear of the car ahead of us is because if they do have to stop for some reason, it's going to take us time to react to that. In other words, we have to see the car in front of us slow or stop and then safely slow or stop our car to avoid striking the person in front of us.

A. Yes. I guess so.

Q. And if we're going to take our eyes off the road ahead of us, even to look at some of our high school friends alongside us, we may have to put more space between us and the car in front of us so we have time to react. Correct?

A. Yeah, I guess. (*Trial Diplomacy Journal*, Vol. 15, No. 4, p. 181.)

Through these examples we see what happens when counsel controls the cross-examination. Letting the witness "run with it" is extremely dangerous. That is particularly true with the difficult witness. If you CONTROL that witness, he or she will not be difficult.

[4.15] Remember The Legal Limitations Of Cross-Examination. There is a body of law relative to cross-examination that the trial lawyer must have mastered before entering the courtroom. Local citations should be a part of the trial notebook.

Bob Gibbins can immediately give the court authority for questions he may ask an expert witness on cross-examination:

1. Witness's financial stake in outcome. *General Motors v. Simmons*, 558 SW2d 855 (Tex. 1977).
2. Evidence of pending criminal charges. *Randall v. State*, 565 SW2d 927 (Tex. Cr App 1983).
3. Familial affiliation. *Hanner v. State*, 572 SW2d 702 (Tex. Cr App 1978).
4. Personal relation. *Smith v. State*, 490 SW2d 902 (Tex. Cr App 1972).
5. Employment relationship. *Shell Oil Co. v. Waxler*, 652 SW2d 459 (Tex. Cr App 1975).
6. Past business associations. *Longview v. Boucher*, 523 SW2d 274 (Tex. Cr App 1975).
7. Previous conflicts. *Rudd v. Gulf Gas. Co.*, 275 SW2d 809 (Tex. Cr App 1953).
8. Witness's own prior biased conduct. *Jackson v. State*, 482 SW2d 864 (Tex. Cr App 1972).

Commit to memory the Federal Rules of Evidence (nearly the same in every state court) relating to cross-examination:

Rule 611. Mode And Order of Interrogation And Presentation

(b) Scope of Cross-Examination. Cross-examination should be limited to the subject matter of the direct examination and matters affecting credibility of the witness. The Court may, in the exercise of discretion, permit inquiry into additional matters as if on direct examination.

(c) . . . Ordinarily leading questions should be permitted on cross-examination. When a party calls a hostile witness, an adverse party, or a witness identified with an adverse party, interrogation may be by leading questions.

Cross-examination may be used to contradict, modify, or explain the direct evidence. *U.S. vs. Dickens*, 417 F.2d 958 (8th Cir. 1969). If a party on direct "opens the door," then opposing party can explore otherwise inadmissible evidence on cross-examination. *U.S. vs. Lutt*, 466 Supp. 328 (Del.DC 1979).

On redirect a witness can be rehabilitated if his credibility has been attacked on cross-examination. *U.S. vs. Smith*, 778 F2d 925 (2d Cir. 1985). On re-cross counsel cannot go into a witness's credibility if it had not been a subject of testimony on redirect. *U.S. v. Sorrentino*, 726 F2d 876 (1st Cir. 1984).

[4.16] How And When To Attack The Expert Witness. To cross-examine an expert is to challenge the witness in his or her own backyard. In a world in which lawsuits are won by expert testimony, however, counsel must enter the witness's turf.

Roxanne Conlin suggests that long before you reach the courtroom, you must use discovery to obtain answers to the following questions:

1. Where were they educated?
2. What have they published?
3. Do they sit on any boards/commissions?
4. Are the experts on the editorial boards of any peer review journals?
5. Do they contribute to such journals? Which ones?
6. What are the areas of research interest?
7. When, where, for whom have they previously testified?
8. What organizations do they belong to and why?
   (a) Can you get an officer of the organization as your expert?
   (b) What about members of the organization's "journal"?
9. What exactly are their areas of expertise? Are they outside of these areas—even slightly?

Once you are ready for the courtroom, you must ask yourself how much the expert has hurt you, and how much you can lessen any negative impact. Then you decide whether or not to cross-examine.

There is an increasing need to cross-examine, because the role of the expert is becoming increasingly important. When you cross-examine an expert, remember:

1 His education and background may not be as great as he has professed.
2 His conduct may have been questioned by a hospital, professional association, the press, an unhappy former patient or client, or other source.
3 He may not have as much expertise in his "specialty" as he would have the jury believe.
4 He may agree that even experts really don't have the answer to the main issue in this case.
5 He may agree with your experts on important points.
6 He may not have conducted tests necessary to form the opinions he has given.
7 He may spend more time in court than in the field of his expertise.
8 He may be inclined to lean toward the point of view given by the other party.
9 He may be inclined to lean toward the other party for any one of a number of reasons.
10 He may have relied upon the wrong people for the basis of his opinion.

PART FIVE

WIN WITH FINAL ARGUMENT

[5.01] Remind Court Of Purpose Of Final Argument. The courts have defined final argument in many ways and if counsel followed the law in the strictest sense, he would do little good for his client. He must know the limits of the law and how to persuade within the law.

It is important to know what factors the court considers in deciding that an attorney went too far. One federal court set forth some important criteria in deciding prosecutorial misconduct, much of which will apply to all final arguments:

1. Degree to which remarks will mislead or prejudice;
2. Whether the remarks were isolated or extensive;
3. Whether they were accidental or intentional;
4. Amount of competent proof that lessens importance of improper remarks (in criminal case remarks should be considered unprejudicial only if evidence is overwhelming); and
5. The total effect of the improper argument, *Whiteside v. Kentucky*, 435 FedSupp 68 (D.C. Ky. 1977).

Counsel must be given wide range in arguing his case and may draw inferences. The fact that his inferences are faulty does not mean they are improper. *People v. Lewis,* 786 P. 2d 92 (Cal. App 1990). Opposing counsel must argue the faultiness of the argument to the jury, not to the appellate court.

One court held that final argument was either entirely warranted by the evidence or not prejudicial enough to require action, though it included remarks concerning (1) defendant's pleasure in killing, (2) what defendant must have been thinking prior to killing the victim, and (3) comparison of defendant and animals. *State v. Pinch,* 292 SE2d 203 (N.C. 1982). Look at the evidence to see how far you can go in argument.

You can remind the court of the purpose of final argument by showing that final argument is:

1. not an inflamatory plea to jury's passion, *Saginaw v. Staulis,* 242 NW2d 769 (Mich. App 1976);
2. not an appeal to self-interest, *Brokopp v. Ford Motor Co.,* 93 ALR3rd 537 (Cal. App 1977);
3. not a means of counsel giving his opinion, *State v. Locklear,* 241 SE2d 65 (N.C. 1977);
4. not an opportunity for counsel to testify, *Currituck Grain, Inc. v. Powell,* 246 SE2d 853 (N.C. App 1978).
5. not a time to vouch for witnesses, *U.S. v. Murphy,* 768 F2d 1518 (7th Cir. 1985).

Courts have held that the purpose of final argument is to convince the jury of the truth. *O'Barr v. U.S.,* 105 p. 938 (Ok. 1910). The courts should give counsel wide discretion as to how he wants to convince during final argument. *Bandoni v. Walston,* 179 P2d 365 (Cal. App 1947).

[5.02] How To Organize "Both Halves" Of Final Argument. If you have the burden of proof, then in most jurisdictions you will have the right to close, which means you must divide your argument into two sections. Though you are usually required by local rule or custom or trial strategy to use more time during the first part, we usually talk of the first and second "halves" of the argument.

If your argument is not divided, you must make reference to that fact, just as opposing counsel must do. You must let the jury know whether or not you will address it again.

EXAMPLES:

(a) If your argument is divided you may say, "After Mr. Smith is finished, I will have an opportunity to visit with you for a few minutes."

(b) If your argument is not divided, you may say, "I will not have an opportunity to talk with you again or to answer anything Mr. Smith might say. He argued his case fully when he addressed you earlier and I think all of the issues have been fully argued."

CAVEAT: Remember, if you do not mention an issue during the first half of your final argument and opposing counsel does not mention it, then you cannot discuss it during the second half of your argument.

EXAMPLES:

(1) You do not mention how much the verdict should be during the first half of your argument and opposing counsel does not mention it. During your second half of argument you say, "This woman is entitled to a million dollars. . . ." Objection. Sustained.

(2) You do not mention how much the verdict should be, but opposing counsel does. During the second half of your argument you say, "This woman is entitled to a million dollars. . . ." Objection. Overruled. Since opposing counsel discussed it, he or she cannot claim unfairness in not having had an opportunity to discuss it.

Once you meet the requirement of mentioning the subject in the opening half of the argument, consider how much attention should be given to damages and liability.

Factors that affect the liability–damages ratio and sequence:

1. If liability is not a real issue, do not spend much time on it–but do not ignore it.
2. If damages are pretty much agreed upon, do not spend much time on it–but do not ignore it.
3. If you have a real strength in liability or damages, dramatize that issue.
4. If you have a weakness in either damages or liability, go right to the jury with it and meet the issue with frankness and fairness.
5. All other factors equal, prepare the jury for damages by disposing of the liability question first.

6. If you are going to argue punitive damages, prepare the jurors for this by covering fully that which will cause them to perceive defendant as a person who should be punished.
7. Not only the sequence, but also the amount of time allotted to liability and damages is important. The defendant may spend more time on liability, but in most cases the plaintiff will spend more time on damages. Both must consider what the jury wants to know and what can best be dramatized in his or her client's favor.
8. How complicated each issue is should affect the priority given to either damages or liability.
9. The THEME of your case may involve either liability or damages, and that theme will automatically allot time to either factor.

Use more time during the first half of the argument:

1. Law or local custom or local rule may require it.
2. The fact that you must have mentioned it in the first half automatically makes the first half very important.
3. "Saving" till it is too late for opposing counsel to respond may appear to jurors as being unfair.
4. Telling your story, and the full story, FIRST during the first part of your argument is the best way of telling it.

Build toward the "second half": The second half of your argument is more than rebuttal; it is a continuation of the first half of your argument. In preparing the first half, keep the second half in mind. Use the second half to highlight or dramatize the first half.

EXAMPLES:

(a) During the first half, mention the sum you are going to ask for. Refer to evidence that supports this sum. Use demonstrative evidence to dramatize the amount. THEN, during the second half, HUMANIZE those figures. Show why he will need someone to help him get dressed in the morning.

(b) Show how inconsistent the other side's evidence was. Show how the key witness told a different story than he had on deposition. THEN, during the second half dramatize the fact that in America we don't send people off to prison on the basis of such perjured testimony.

When you sit down, you must remember that opposing counsel has the right to waive his argument. He will not do it, but it is wise to ask yourself what would happen if he did. That first half of final argument must be able to stand on its own and win your case.

[5.03] How To Avoid The "First Mentioned In Rebuttal" Objection. Fairness is the name of the game, and counsel who thinks he is going to take unfair advantage of his opponent will usually have the trial judge to contend with. The most basic of all fairness requirements is that which simply states that you cannot lay back and fail to mention something until opposing counsel cannot reply.

The most common scenario is the plaintiff's lawyer not mentioning anything about damages, or not mentioning a specific amount, in the first half of his argument. Then, after defense counsel gives his argument, plaintiff's lawyer covers the subject for the first time. The court will not let counsel talk about damages, or a specific amount, because he or she has not given opposing counsel an opportunity to discuss the subject.

If plaintiff does not mention a specific amount and defendant does, then plaintiff can, of course, discuss it. This is not an exception to the rule, it is simply not a "first mentioned" situation. The rule does not preclude one lawyer from getting "last crack" at a subject. It merely means that you cannot introduce a new argument in the second half of your final argument, unless opposing counsel has introduced the subject in his argument.

[5.04] When Is Conduct Of Counsel Error. Conduct of counsel is a two-edged sword that cannot be ignored by the trial lawyer. A trial lawyer's own conduct can hurt his case, and failure to hold opposing counsel to proper conduct is relinquishing an edge and that can be costly.

The law on this important subject is found in every section of Part V. Every lawyer who walks into a courtroom must know what he can and cannot do during final argument. He must go as far as the law allows if that will help him win, but he must be sure he does not cross any line that will:

1. cause a mistrial;
2. cause error that will prejudice his case on appeal;

3. cause the judge to take an action in front of the jury that will hurt his credibility; or
4. cause the jury, without any action from the judge, to question him as an attorney.

The appellate courts have given the trial judge considerable latitude in controlling the conduct of counsel. The judge will normally exercise that control outside the hearing of the jury, but DON'T DEPEND UPON IT! An attorney who is guilty of misconduct can hardly complain as to the method used by the trial judge in controlling the trial over which the judge is presiding.

Avoid misconduct on your part by:

1. Knowing the law, so you do not unknowingly enter forbidden territory;
2. Following the law, once you know it;
3. Knowing what the trial judge permits;
4. Letting the judge know if you are going to try something new and learn his or her feelings; and
5. Keeping fairness in mind at all times! It is the jury you are trying to persuade, and jurors simply do not appreciate unfairness. To them any kind of unfairness is a form of misconduct.

Misconduct is error if:

1. The judge thinks it is wrong; or
2. The jury thinks it is wrong.

The judge and the jury, however, may not realize that what opposing counsel is doing is wrong unless you object. When opposing counsel is doing something wrong during final argument, you must:

1. Object, to protect your record, and
2. Object in a way that will impress the jury.

One attorney suggested to me that the Matlock we see on television could never get away in real life with the way he talks to the jury. I disagreed, saying that good criminal lawyers get by with it all the time. It depends on HOW you "talk to the jury." For example, Charles Shaw did not rise and say, "I object, your Honor." This would cause the jury to feel he was hiding something. He jumped up and shouted, "Judge, you told him he couldn't say that!" This shifted suspicion to the prosecution.

Where an attorney broke down emotionally in front of the jury several times, the court viewed the conduct as "not spontaneous" and found it was a "shrewdly calculated attempt to solicit a sympathetic response from the jury." *Russell, Inc. v. Trento*, 445 So. 2d 390 (3rd DCA Fla. 1984). The court was even critical of such statements as counsel had "lived with the case" and had "carried the burden."

If a trial lawyer became paranoid about the limitations courts have placed on his conduct during final argument, he would be like the "stoic philosopher" John Adams talked about in *Commonwealth v. Preston*, "devoid of any human emotion." Such a lawyer would be, in my opinion, guilty of legal malpractice. It is the trial lawyer's challenge to work within the guidelines and still to present his final argument with all the vigor and imagination that his client deserves.

[5.05] Discussing The Evidence. Discussing the evidence is very much a part of final argument, and no trial judge will prevent this discussion. Misquoting the evidence will, however, bring not only an objection, but also a ruling from the court and a reaction from the jury.

Too many lawyers feel misquoting the evidence merely brings a standard response such as, "The jurors have heard the evidence and will be guided by what they remember the evidence to be." MUCH MORE CAN HAPPEN! The jury may well remember the evidence, and your misquoting it may injure your credibility tremendously.

Also, what you think is going to bring this standard response may bring error from the trial judge or the appellate court. This is especially true if the other party could be prejudiced by the misquoting:

EXAMPLE:

> During final argument counsel tells the jury, "You now know from the evidence that this man was convicted of this same crime. . . ." OBJECTION! At the side-bar counsel is reminded that the court excluded that evidence. An "Oh, I forgot" or whatever will not cure the misquoting.

The use of exact words and phrases demonstrates to the judge and the jury that you are quoting accurately. It may help to glance down at a pad and actually to read what you have written. This may be one time when using notes can be helpful, even for trial lawyers who hate referring to notes.

In some jurisdictions it is possible to have a transcript available prior to closing argument, or counsel has arranged for his or her own transcribing. This helps counsel in quoting accurately, and quotes must be accurate. If an entire transcript is not available, you may be able to obtain the exact words through one source or other for a crucial bit of testimony.

One simple way to assure an accurate quote for final argument is to use the transcript from a deposition. "Mr. Smith, I want to read you one paragraph from your deposition," and then read it. "Is that still your testimony?" You now have the significant paragraph in transcript form. You can then stand before the jury during final argument and read from the deposition as though reading from a transcript of the trial, because that, in effect, is what that paragraph is.

Some courts now permit jurors to take notes. If this is done, your job increases during trial and during final argument. During trial, notice which jurors are taking notes and remember whether during voir dire you felt those jurors were favorable or unfavorable. During trial let the good points set in! Give the note-takers time to write down that which is good and do NOT emphasize that which is bad.

When you begin final argument, if note-taking was permitted, remember who took notes and which testimony was "jotted down." The other jurors will turn to the note-taker during deliberation. The age-old problem of "who is foreman" may become "who will be a note-taker" and the role of the note-taker in the jury room must be reckoned with. Lawyers who have been loose with their quotes in the past had better be more careful when arguing to a note-taking jury.

[5.06] When To Appeal To Passion. Passion is more than prejudice. It moves a jury to act upon emotion and not upon evidence. It bases a verdict upon that which has nothing to do with the real issues of the case. An argument must have some relationship to the evidence and it must also be free from inflammatory remarks. *Louisiana and Arkansas Ry. Co. v. Capps*, 766 SW 2d 291 (Tex. App 1989).

The trial court will try to determine if your remarks are aimed at inflaming the jury! You can best avoid the wrath of the trial judge by tying your remarks to the evidence and by showing that it is the evidence itself that creates the passion.

EXAMPLE:

> Courts have generally held that you cannot talk about how many children a plaintiff has. *Golian v. Stanley,* 334 SW 2d 88 (Mo. 1960). The fact that plaintiff and his three children were in the automobile at the time of the accident and that all of them were injured is, however, certainly a part of the lawsuit. Use it!

The courts have permitted evidence of catastrophic injuries and have rejected the argument that such is prejudicial. Rule 403 of the Federal Rules of Evidence guards against "unfair" prejudice. One case contains a beautiful discussion of why he who creates a catastrophic injury cannot complain about it being catastrophic and cannot therefore claim prejudice. Read it! *Auerbach v. Philadelphia Transportation Co.,* 221 A2d 172 (Pa. 1966).

[5.07] When Can A Mathematical Formula Be Used To Determine Damages? The rule against using a mathematical formula in determining damages is based upon the fear that jurors will be sympathetic and that they may "exaggerate" damages. The attack upon this rule has at least brought about modifications or interpretations that have limited the rule's application.

When I began trying lawsuits in Missouri in 1950, I was told not to use a mathematical formula. For many years it was error to do so, and then the courts began to relax the rule. Let's look at how this problem was handled by two leading trial lawyers in the federal court in the Eastern District of Missouri:

> MR. ROSECAN: For the two years in the hospital, you can figure that. I took an arbitrary figure. You may think I am high. You may think I am low. I thought to spend two years in a hospital, I thought a thousand dollars a month. . . .
> MR. BUCKLEY: I am going to object to that, Your Honor. That per unit

argument is improper and prejudicial. There is nothing in the evidence to warrant such an argument, per unit cost for any particular thing, and I object to it. There is nothing to warrant a per unit assessment.
MR. ROSECAN: This is not a per unit assessment. We have some basis. . . . If you think I am high you may argue to the jury.
MR. BUCKLEY: I am objecting to the court.
JUDGE MEREDITH: Overruled. Proceed. (*Burger Chef Systems v. Govro*, 407 F.2d 921 (8th Cir. 1969).)

Terms used by the courts in discussing mathematical formulas vary. "Per diem" is the least acceptable, since it would pay a plaintiff a certain sum for each day of pain and suffering. It has been criticized as not based upon evidence and for asking the jurors to determine what they would feel entitled to for each day. The biggest objection is that verdicts would be much higher if jurors could "make the person whole," as in ascertaining other damages, by paying what it is really worth (more than a few dollars) to suffer a whole day. You don't read much about this objection.

The term "per unit" is more acceptable and attempts to place dollar signs on certain periods and for certain factors. For example, John was in the hospital for two months and it is certainly worth $10,000 for that experience. John has been confined to his home for two years since then and it would certainly be reasonable to pay him $50,000 for that experience.

Some courts have held a cold appeal to the jury to calculate the value of pain and suffering is not objectionable, since it is not an appeal to sympathy or passion. *Boop v. Baltimore & OL R. Co.*, 193 NE 2d 714 (Ohio App 1963). Even where the "unit of time" argument was held improper, it could be cured with an instruction. *Streeter v. Sears, Roebuck & Co.*, 533 So. 2d 54 (La. App 1988).

Some courts have held it improper to refuse the per diem argument. *Newberry v. Vogel*, 379 P. 2d 811 (Colo. 1963). That is not the majority rule, however. *Young v. Price*, 395 P.2d 365 (Hawaii 1964); *Caley v. Manicke*, 182 N.E.2d 206 (Ill. 1962).

Study closely the law of your state and know how far the trial judge in your case will let you go. Plaintiff's lawyer has a duty to carry this argument as far as it can be carried, without running afoul of the rule. Defense counsel has a corresponding duty to limit this argument, because it CAN increase the size of the verdict.

[5.08] Know The "Golden Rule" Limitations. Courts generally prohibit the "golden rule" argument in which jurors are asked to assess damages by placing themselves in the injured person's place and by basing the verdict upon what they would wish to receive. *Shaffer v. Ward,* 510 So2d 602 (5th Fla. DCA 1987). However, it was NOT improper to ask jurors to judge a party in light of what they, as reasonable people, would have done. *Cummins Alabama, Inc. v. Allbritten,* 548 So2d 258 (1st Fla. App 1989).

It is not improper to ask jurors to use their own experiences in everyday life to decide such issues, as when a sprain begins to hurt. *Smith v. Pettit,* 778 SW2d 616 (Ark. 1989). If there is an objection, cure the defect to avoid a mistrial.

The reverse argument of the golden rule (telling the jury that it would be wrong to put themselves in plaintiff's shoes) is also improper. *Woods vs. Burlington N. R. Co.,* 786 F2d 1287 (11th Cir. 1985). How prejudicial the argument was may well depend upon the size of the verdict (It is only when fishing that they make you throw back the small ones). *Thorpe v. Zwonechek,* 129 NW2d 483 (Neb 1964).

It has been held that the golden rule is:

1. APPROPRIATE, when asking jurors to assess reasonableness by relying upon their own common sense and life experiences, but
2. NEVER APPROPRIATE, when used to influence the damage award.

Lopez v. Langer, 761 P2d 1225 (Idaho 1988).

At an ATLA conference, mock jurors were asked the golden rule question in the abstract, using "you" in a general sense that might be acceptable in most states. They were impressed by the argument, but indicated they would have been more impressed if counsel could have come right out and asked them to put themselves in the position of the plaintiff and to decide how much they felt they would be entitled to for similar injuries.

The truth is that the golden rule argument IS effective. We are taught from age two that we should treat others as we would want to be treated. We are then taught in law school, or in the courtroom, that "golden rule" is a dirty phrase. Jurors do not feel that way. They are willing to give another what they would expect for themselves. Courts tell us the golden rule is wrong during final argument because it is based on sympathy, but the truth might well be that it is only wrong because it treats a plaintiff the way a plaintiff should be treated.

We must argue to the trial court and to the appellate court the need to arrive at a proper value for an injury and that in doing so we must use every approach that is fair and reasonable. To say that a verdict is adequate because the injury happened to someone else and not to you is a narrow and selfish approach. You will find ways around the golden rule prohibition easier if you really believe the jury has a right to consider what they would expect if they were the plaintiff.

What you can argue in most jurisdictions:

1. Use your common sense.
2. What do YOU think is fair?
3. What do YOU think the loss of an arm is worth?
4. What would YOU expect a fair verdict in this kind of case to be?
5. Call upon every experience you have ever had and from that experience tell us in your verdict what you feel is a fair verdict for a person who can no longer see.

[5.09] Bind Prosecutors To Their Special Rules. Prosecutors have a very special duty throughout the trial, and this extends into the final argument. It is necessary for the prosecutor to comply with this special requirement and it is the duty of the defense counsel to ensure that he does.

The prosecutor's duty is based upon fairness and upon the constitutional requirement that the accused be given due process. The Supreme Court has held this to mean that the prosecutor must reveal all that he has in his file that would help acquit the defendant. *Brady v. Maryland*, 373 U.S. 83 (1963).

It has been held that *Brady* applies to municipal court cases. *State v Tull*, 560 A2d 1331 (N.J. Super 1989). This is because no person can be confined by any court without having been given due process.

It has also been held that *Brady* applies to the prosecutor's withholding evidence that would have impeached his own witness's credibility. *Barkauskas v. Lane*, 876 F2d 1031 (7th Cir. 1989). The language of the cases that interpret *Brady* indicate a trend toward placing a duty upon the prosecutor to make a full disclosure of all that, in fairness, should be made known to opposing counsel and to the jury.

The prosecutor's duty to disclose is a positive one that requires him to take certain action. This implies a duty not to make statements that would mislead the jury.

EXAMPLE:

> No evidence was admitted relative to the defendant's failure to do a certain thing. Prosecutor knows it would have been impossible for defendant to do this. His making the statement, knowing it was impossible to do, was improper argument.

It is up to defense counsel to object to such improper argument and to do it with the jury in mind. All that happens in front of the jury will probably be noticed and remembered by the jury. This means that for anything which may adversely affect your client, you must:

1. try to have the entire matter handled outside the hearing of the jury, and
2. if that is not possible, be sure the jury knows that opposing counsel is doing something unfair, and that if the statement were proper and it was right for them to consider it, then the judge would not have decided to exclude the statement.

[5.10] Avoid Comment On Failure Of Accused To Testify. The "Griffin Rule" forbids "either comment by the prosecution on the accused's silence or instructions by the court that such silence is evidence of guilt." *Griffin v. California*, 380 US 609 (U.S. 1965). The Supreme Court held that such would violate the Self-Incrimination Clause of the Fifth Amendment, as made applicable to the states by the Fourteenth Amendment.

It has been generally held that violation of the "Griffin Rule" is reversable error, unless it was found "harmless beyond a reasonable doubt." *Chapman v. California*, 386 US 18 (U.S. 1967). Some courts have held such comment to be "automatic reversal." *Cape Girardeau v. Jones*, 725 SW2d 904 (Mo. App 1987).

Where comments were found "inflammatory" there was a reversal. *Anderson v. Nelson*, 390 US 523 (U.S. 1968). But, where the comment was of an "insignificant nature," there was no reversal. *Domberg v. State*, 518 So2d 1360 (Fla. App 1988).

Some states have adopted statutes prohibiting a prosecutor from commenting on failure of accused to testify. A federal statue (18 USC section 3481) provides that in a federal trial, failure to testify does not create a presumtion against defendant.

It has been held that the "Griffin Rule" does not prohibit comment on failure to put on a successful defense. *Jimpson v. State*, 532 So2d 985 (Miss. 1988). Neither does the rule prohibit comment that the prosecution's case was "uncontradicted." *Jordan v. U.S.*, 324 F.2d 178, (5th Cir. 1963). Some courts have held that the use of "uncontradicted" argument is permitted, even though only contradiction could come from testimony of accused. *People v. Norman*, 190 NE2d 819 (Ill. 1963). See, however, *Desmond v. Lane*, 345 F2d 225 (1st Cir. 1965).

Reference to failure to give handwriting samples is not improper. *Tindel v. State*, 748 SW2d 593 (Tex. App 1988). Nor is failure to take blood-alcohol test. *South Dakota v. Neville*, 459 U.S. 553 (U.S. 1983). Also, the "Griffin Rule" is not violated where defendant "invited" or "provoked" the comment. *Babb v. United States*, 351 F.2d 863 (8th Cir. 1965).

Prosecutor should: (a) avoid such comment, (b) move for instruction that would cure error if such comment is made.
Defense counsel should: OBJECT! If objection is overruled, APPEAL!

[5.11] Telling Stories. Story telling is an art that has been enjoyed for centuries. Good trial lawyers use it to maintain interest and to make a point. Jurors enjoy stories and are persuaded by them.

When I started part of an argument with, "Back in Missouri . . . ," the jurors knew I was going to tell something about my old home state and they seemed to be interested. Then I continued, "We had an open-range law, which meant if a train ran over a cow the owner could sue the railroad."

"We lawyers used to joke about the fact that the most ordinary cow in the world suddenly became a thoroughbred the moment it was hit by a train." The jury laughed a little and they could picture the old farmer talking about the thoroughbred.

Then I looked down at the list of items the other side was claiming damages for and said, "I sure see a lot of thoroughbred cows on this list that lawyer has given us." This tied the story in and they laughed again and this time they saw the point of my story.

I use this as an example because it took only a few lines to tell the story. It is a simple story of how people sometimes exaggerate. Every time I mentioned "another thoroughbred cow" the jury knew what I meant and smiled again.

When you talk with people you hear stories. Put them in a few sentences and see how they may fit into an opening statement or final argument. When you tell stories you are talking the language of the jury.

Let us look at how a little statement or incident can be used by the trial lawyer:

Excuses: Joseph Stalin murdered 20 million of his own people, but when my wife and I visited his home province of Georgia we were told, "But, we ate well under Stalin." What must a man do before people quit making excuses for him? That man sitting over there next to his lawyer killed three children in cold blood, yet people came into this courtroom and said, "But, he was a nice neighbor," or "He was a good worker at the plant." Yes, we ate well under Stalin.

[5.12] How To Use Exhibits Or Demonstrations. Using exhibits and demonstrations during trial is important. Using them during final argument can be equally important. However, deciding when and how to use them can determine whether or not you will win your lawsuit.

In structuring exhibits and demonstrations during final argument, remember:

1. Make notes DURING TRIAL as to what exhibits and demonstrations can be used during final argument.
2. Decide whether these should be used during the first or second half of the argument.
3. Decide WHY you are going to use them:
   (a) to enforce an argument;
   (b) to introduce a new argument;
   (c) to maintain interest in an argument.
4. Decide whether to use them for the first time during final argument.

A great example of using demonstrative evidence during a recent trial is Thomas J. Flaherty's use of the golf ball in *U.S. v. Lewis,* as discussed in *BNA Criminal Practice Manual,* Vol. 5, No. 14, p. 223. Prosecution told jury that defendant had a "golf ball size" rock of cocaine.

Counsel had to decide how to use most effectively as possible this jewel that was dropped into his lap. (Jewels don't actually drop in the lap, they are the result of blood, tears, and imagination.) Lawyering enabled counsel to learn that a golf ball would not fit into the container that held the "golf ball size" cocaine.

Counsel took advantage of this jewel in cross-examination and final argument. Saving it for final would have presented a few problems: (1) Effective cross-examination can begin the persuasion in such a way that you often cannot pass it up; (2) Use of the demonstrative evidence during final is sometimes dependent upon its already being used during the trial; and (3) Using the demonstration during cross fits into the structuring of your entire trial.

Notice how effectively Flaherty used the golf ball as an analogy during final argument:

> I indicated that the film canister was the bounds of the truth and that any testimony uttered by this person must fit into the canister if it were to be true. I then asked the jury to consider the golf ball as his testimony. When the two were put together, only a slight dimple would fit within the film canister. I offered to the jury my suggestion that the only statement the witness made that was true, that would fit within the canister, was his statement that he would lie to stay out of prison. The jury took two minutes to find the Defendant not guilty.

REMEMBER, using demonstrations during trial and during final argument gives you the advantage of repetition. The more often a juror hears something presented in a persuasive manner, the more likely the juror is to believe it.

Using the demonstration or exhibit during the last half of the argument is more effective because of recency. However, you must be sure to avoid a "first mentioned" problem.

EXAMPLE:

Plaintiff mentions figures during the first half of the final, or opposing counsel mentions figures during rebuttal. THEN, plaintiff can use a graph showing these figures during the second half of the final argument. (Had opposisng counsel known a graph was going to be used, he may have used one in his argument, but this should not keep plaintiff from using it, since the "first mentioned" rule is aimed at the matter discussed, not the manner of discussing it.)

[5.13] Prevent Appeals To Prejudice. The public might assume from what they see of jury trials as portrayed in the movies and on television that the purpose of final argument is to appeal to prejudices of the jury. Too often beginning lawyers feel that this is their role and they find themselves in trouble with the court and with the jury.

Rule 403 may be the most important rule of evidence, and it should guide the trial lawyer through every part of the trial. It provides that, although relevant, evidence may be excluded if its probative value is substantially outweighed by: unfair prejudice, confusion of issues, or misleading the jury.

This forms the foundation of all objections as to prejudice, appeals to passion, and all that is inflammatory. If argument violates any of these factors, the trial lawyer will find that the judge will call upon his background in evidence to rule upon the propriety of the final argument.

The mere mispronouncing of a party's name can be prejudicial and should be admonished by the judge. Once this has been done, however, there is no error in that the party has not really been prejudiced. *Mulkey v. Morris*, 313 P.2d 494 (Okl. 1957).

Even more serious forms of prejudice can be cured. Where reference to black witness that "due to the breed of the race, we were afraid she would change her testimony which she did," court held such was improper but cured. *Donald v. Macheny*, 158 So2d 909 (Ala. 1963). Stating witness was Puerto Rican, like plaintiff, and was trying to help him was fair comment and not appeal to prejudice. *Reyes v. Arthur Tickle*, Eng. Works, Inc., 152 N.Y.S.2d 698 (N.Y. App. 1956).

A few factors to consider:

1. Who is on the jury?
   The fact there was a black on the jury made reference to plaintiff as "colored" or a "colored boy" not an appeal to racial prejudice.

Greeson v. Texas & Pac. Ry. Co., 310 SW2d 615 (Tex. Civ. App 1958).

2. Who mentioned it first?
Where Plaintiff's counsel mentioned during voir dire his client's former affiliation with a certain organization, it was improper for opposing counsel to call Plaintiff a Nazi, but not a basis for mistrial. *Andritsch v. Henschel*, 134 N.W.2d 426 (Wisc. 1965).
3. What did court instruct the jury?
Where damages were stipulated and counsel tried to argue Plaintiff claimed more than market value, upon objection counsel did not pursue the argument and Court instructed jury damages had been stipulated, no error. *Szuch v. Grayce Farm Dairy, Inc.*, 61 Lack. Jur. 225 (Pa. Com. Pl. 1912).
4. Did the judge rebuke counsel?
The judge not only gave instruction but rebuked the attorney in front of the jury for making improper remarks and this rendered the remarks harmless. *Yellow Cab Co. v. McCullers*, 106 S.E.2d 535 (Ga. App 1958).
5. Did opposing counsel object?
Failing to object to improper argument can result in a waiver of the right to object.
State v. Warren, 190 N.2d 575 (Ill. App 1963).

CONCLUSION: Avoid prejudicial argument because it may harm your credibility with the jury, bring the wrath of the trial judge, or cause an appellate court to take a verdict from you. If opposing counsel uses prejudicial argument, STOP HIM OR HER! Protect your client, and in doing so, let the jury know what opposing counsel was attempting to do and why it was unfair.

[5.14] When To Comment On Failure To Present Witness Or Evidence. Nothing can bring a mistrial or a reversal on appeal quicker than violating a defendant's constitutional rights. The most basic of those rights is the right against self-incrimination, which includes, of course, the right to refuse to testify.

In a civil case the failure of a party to testify can be commented on if:

1. The party's testimony is unnecessary;
2. Party has no personal knowledge of facts;
3. Facts were otherwise fully established;
4. Party is unavoidably absent;
5. Party's mind is impaired; or
6. Party is incompetent as a witness.

Hinton & Sons v. Strahan, 96 So2d 426 (Ala. 1923).

The courts generally hold that if a party comes into court with a civil case and makes a prima facie case, he gives up the right not to have his failure to testify pointed out to the jury, though such would have been forbidden in a criminal proceeding. *Connolly v. Nicollet Hotel*, 104 NW 2d 723 (Minn. 1960). In such cases, counsel can suggest that the party did not testify because his testimony would have been damaging. *Kelsey v. Kelsey*, 329 SW 2d 273 (Mo. App 1959).

It has been held that counsel can comment on failure of defendant's partner to testify. *King Consrt. Co. v. Flores*, 359. SW 2d 919 (Tex. Civ. App 1962). It has also been held that counsel can comment on failure of party to be present at trial. *Craig v. Borough of Ebensburg*, 137 A2d 886 (Pa. Super. 1958). Where insurance carrier sent employee to a doctor in a worker's compensation case, claimaint's counsel could comment on carrier's failure to call the doctor as a witness. *Western Fire & Indem. Co. v. Evans*, 368 SW 2d 114 (Tex. Civ. App 1963).

In a civil case counsel can comment on failure to testify, even if refusal to testify was based on reasons of self-incrimination *Tice v. Mandel*, 76 NW 2d 124 (N.D. 1956). The right to comment is often based on the fact opposing party has the witness "under its control," such as an employee; *Miller v. DeWitt*, 208 NE 2d 244 (Ill. App 1965), or a police officer under its subpoena. *Johnston v. Key System Transit Lines*, 334 P2d 243 (Cal. App 1962). However, it was improper to comment on failure to bring in tavern owner who could have been produced by either party. *Ryan v. Monson*, 179 NE 2d 449 (Ill. App 1961).

It has been held proper to comment on failure to use right to require a physical examination, *Bradford v. Parrish*, 141 SE 2d 125 (Ga. App. 1965);

fact "no witnesses" brought in to show where deceased was, *Jensen v. McEldowney*, 270 NE 2d 472 (Mass. 1971); or failure to produce certain "evidence in his power" that may prove a relevant fact, *Connolly v. Nicollet Hotel*, 104 NW 2d 721 (Minn. 1960). Failure to present any evidence that could have resolved vital issue is subject to fair comment, since it must be assumed failure to produce the evidence was because the evidence would not have been favorable. *Williams v. Ricklemann*, 292 SW 2d 276 (Mo. 1956).

[5.15] How To Divide Opening And Rebuttal. If you represent the plaintiff in a civil action or the prosecution in a criminal case, you must decide how much time to devote and what parts of the argument should be handled during the opening and during the rebuttal portion of final argument.

First, you must cover what will be lost if not covered during the first portion of your final argument. If you want to ask for a certain amount, give that part of your argument during the opening portion, for the court will not let you argue it during the rebuttal, unless opposing counsel has mentioned it.

Second, be sure that most of your argument occurs during the first portion of final. At least two-thirds of your final argument should occur before opposing counsel argues.

Third, be sure that you do not have to rush the two important aspects of rebuttal. You must REBUT all that opposing counsel has said that needs rebutting. Then you must have plenty of time for the "FINAL FIVE," that closing moment in which you say in a few words, what your lawsuit is really all about, and why the jury should return a verdict in your favor.

[5.16] How Long Final Can And Should Be. When I ponder the question of how long final argument should be, two personal experiences flash to mind: (1) My first jury trial was under the old Magistrate Court system in Missouri, and the judge asked, "How do you want to divide your three minutes?" (2) In a murder trial, the judge turned to the prosecutor and me and said, "I assume neither of you are dumb enough to want more than thirty minutes to argue this case."

I did get a full five minutes to argue the Magistrate Court case, and I was satisfied with thirty minutes in the murder trial. The facts were simple in both cases, and trial lawyers must face the facts that uncomplicated factual cases do not require lengthy arguments.

Trial counsel must also realize that the trial judge has wide discretion in deciding how long argument should be. If counsel needs more time than allotted, he should argue vigorously for it. He should first consider, however, what best stands the test of trial advocacy. Opposing counsel will have as much time as you, and you should be able to persuade without putting to sleep.

The attention span of jurors is limited. Good drama can be sustained for a limited period of time. Judges and jurors appreciate brevity. These three factors should never be ignored in planning the length of final argument.

[5.17] When Can You "Send Out The Message"? It has been held by many courts that a prosecutor can ask a jury to "send a message" by convicting the accused. *Commonwealth v. Lawrence*, 536 NE2d 571 (Mass. 1989). In doing so, the prosecutor can suggest that the jurors are acting as the "conscience of the community."

There have been cases to the contrary, but where counsel usually gets into trouble is by asking to "send a message" in a civil case, in which the measure of damages does not include a punitive penalty.

One of the most effective uses of this technique is sending a message where the defendant is guilty of misconduct. See Section 5.68 for an excellent argument by Howard Nations.

[5.18] Know The Limits Of The Court's Discretion. The appellate courts constantly talk about the "sound discretion of the trial court." This is based on the fact that the trial judge can see and hear witnesses, and can sense situations that do not come through as clearly from reading a cold transcript.

It does not mean the appellate courts feel the trial judge can do no wrong. In fact, if the printed page can tell the whole story and the appellate judges can sense something wrong has occurred at the trial level, the trial judge will be taken to task.

The trial court's discretion is most often questioned if a constitutional right is involved. Where the prosecutor said that "he could not stand up under cross-examination," the trial court held such comments were mere references to defendant's "condition." The appellate court held the comments violated the defendant's right against self-incrimination. *Smith v. Fairman*, 862 F2d 630 (7th Cir. 1988).

The trial court was permitted to alter the order of argument, but only if it did not result in "jury confusion." *McCloud v. State*, 564 A2d 72 (Md. 1989). It was held that a trial court abused its discretion when it set a 30-minute limit on final argument in a murder case. *Stockton v. State*, 544 So2d 1006 (Fla. 1989).

It has been held that trial court did NOT abuse its discretion when it prohibited counsel from arguing two conflicting theories of the case, since the defenses were "too much in conflict with each other" to be argued (argued (1) that defendant was coerced into a conspiracy and (2) that there was no conspiracy). *U.S. v. Smith*, 757 F2d 1161 (11th Cir. 1985).

In looking for ways the discretion of the trial judge may be curbed, consider:

1. Situations where the appellate court can determine from the written transcript that what the trial judge did was unfair; and
2. Situations where the constitutional rights of your client are involved.

[5.19] When To Attack Parties And Witnesses. Good trial advocacy will often dictate that you do not attack a party or a witness in final argument. There are times, however, when trial advocacy not only permits such argument, but demands it of counsel.

It is for this reason that counsel must understand how far the court will permit him or her to go, when this area of argument is entered. Where counsel argued certain records were "sitting in an ashtray somewhere," he went beyond bounds of permissible argument, because he was suggesting that the other party had destroyed the records and there was no such evidence. *U.S. v. DeGeratto*, 876 F2d 576 (7th Cir. 1989).

That is an excellent place to start. In commenting on evidence, or in commenting on parties and witnesses, tie the argument to evidence or omit it. Where prosecutor said that defendant's case was "composed of lies and misrepresentations and innuendos," the court found such was improper argument. *People v. Emerson,* 455 NE 2d 41 (Ill. 1983).

Where counsel told jury certain evidence was of "questionable authenticity" and that the jury was a victim of fraud, such argument was objectionable, but did not constitute plain error. *U.S. v. Gaspard,* 744 F2d 438 (5th Cir. 1984). Defendant has a right not to testify, and it has been held that such right includes immunity from the prosecutor to argue about his "non-testimonial behavior in court" (prosecutor told jury defendant appeared to be explaining photo taken at bank to attorney, so he must have been at the bank). *U.S. v. Carroll,* 678 F2d 1208 (4th Cir. 1982).

Once a defendant testifies, he is fair game. One prosecutor was permitted to tell the jury that a person charged with driving while intoxicated had taken a second breath test, and to comment:

> "We don't know in this case what happened with the second sample. You can wonder to yourself what did happen, if it was to his benefit. A reasonable inference would be that he would have brought the evidence to you, but he didn't in this case." *State ex rel McDougal v. Corcoran,* 735 P2d 767 (Ariz. 1987).

This approach can be used in many instances if a party or witness has failed to bring in certain evidence. I once used it effectively in a questioned document case:

> "Why did this man go all the way to California and take a deposition to try to find out who signed this piece of paper? He could have walked right across the street from this courthouse and had George Swett, one of the best handwriting experts in the world, look at this signature and tell you who signed it. Why didn't he take this paper to a handwriting expert . . . or did he? If he did and he was told my client didn't sign it, you don't think he would bring that expert into this courtroom, do you?"

It would seem the prosecutor's calling the defendants "animals" would be improper, but one court held the reference to be "legitimate" and "supported by the evidence." In the use of such personal attacks, counsel should review that vast area of law surrounding Rule 403 of the Federal Rules of Evidence. This body of law gives us a feel as to when a judge may decide you have gone too far and that you are being "unfair" and your conduct is "prejudicial."

A part of this body of law reminds counsel that "fairness" is as important a factor as "prejudice." This is why counsel must decide how much of the prejudice springs from the party's conduct, and not from counsel's description of that conduct. In one case the court ruled "gruesome" evidence should be admitted because defendant had caused the "tragic misfortune" that created this kind of evidence. *Auerbach v. Philadelphia Transportation Co.*, 221 A2d 172 (Pa. 1966).

[5.20] How To Correct An Error. Error is constantly committed during trial, but this seldom stops the trial, is seldom the basis for mistrial, and is seldom the basis for a new trial. That is because the law favors "correcting" mistakes and "living" with the fact that error does occur.

The first duty of the trial judge is to decide whether the error is significant enough to specifically do something about it as soon as possible, or if it can be covered in a general instruction later in the trial.

EXAMPLE:

> Where the prosecutor said that in his opinion the defendant was lying, the trial judge thought it adequate to merely tell the jury at some time that the argument of counsel was not evidence. On appeal, however, it was held that the assertion by the prosecutor was serious enough to require a special corrective instruction. *State v. Smith*, 456 A2d 16 (Me. 1983).

In a similar situation, counsel prevented error by the way he handled the matter. Though the prosecutor said that in his opinion defendants were "guilty as sin," he also told the jury that his opinion was immaterial, his opinion was based on the evidence, and asked the jury to examine the evidence. Court held that there was no material prejudice. *U.S. v. McCaghren*, 666 F2d 1227 (8th Cir. 1981).

Counsel must give the trial judge an opportunity to correct any error. Though in one case, the court held objecting anytime before jury retired gives the judge time to give a corrective instruction, *U.S. v. Mandelbaum*, 803 F2d 42 (1st Cir. 1986), good trial advocacy and the probability of receiving a less-lenient ruling should cause counsel to object immediately.

Objecting may not be enough. One court ruled a failure to move for mistrial or admonishment failed to preserve error. *Dresser v. State*, 454 NE 2d 406 (Ind. 1983). If you object, *tell the judge what you want him to do*!

One thing you must always do: REQUEST CURATIVE INSTRUCTION! Courts have held that this will avoid possible misunderstanding. If you do not request it, you cannot later complain. *U. S. v. Glantz*, 810 F2d 316 (1st Cir. 1987).

Some comments cannot be cured and should not be excused. Where a prosecutor said that he was not quoting the defendant "exactly," this did not cure the prejudicial effect of his misquoting. *U.S. v. Brainard*, 690 F2d 1117 (4th Cir. 1982).

Courts have held that two wrongs do not make a right. If one attorney makes an improper argument, this does not entitle opposing counsel to make an improper argument. It can, however, negate the prejudical effect of the argument. *U.S. v. Mazzone*, 782 F2d 757 (7th Cir. 1986).

[5.21] Use Matters Of Common Knowledge. Too often counsel objects to argument on the basis that the matter being argued is not in evidence. It would simply be impossible to argue a case if you were limited to the evidence of the case.

It has been held that counsel may argue matters not in evidence that are "common knowledge," or "illustrations drawn from common experience, history or literature." *People v. London*, 254 Cal. Retr 59 (Cal. 6th 1988). The Court held, however, that counsel may not confuse the jury with "irrelevant facts" about "unrelated, specific crimes."

In *London*, supra, the appellate court held that whether a certain magazine article could be read to the jury is in the sound discretion of the trial court. Much of what is argued based on common knowledge is up to the discretion of the trial judge.

What the court can accept as judicial notice will usually be permitted as subject of argument. *Bone v. General Motors Corp.*, 322 SW 2d 916 (Mo. 1959.) It has been held proper to discuss the change in purchasing power of money, *Halloren v. New England Tel. & Tel. Co*, 115 A 1143 (Vt. 1921) or facts from the press, *People v. Woodson*, 41 Cal. Retr 487 (Cal. 1964).

[5.22] Keep Out Defendant's Record. The prosecutor must avoid making statements that even suggest a criminal record or more of a record than is in evidence. Insinuating that the defendant is trying to hide his criminal record is reversible error. *Powell v. U.S.*, 445 A2d 405 (D.C. App 1982).

The prosecutor may lose a conviction, but defense counsel has an even more serious problem in letting such remarks enter the minds of the jury. Often, improper argument is not *reversible* improper argument. If the jury feels there is a previous conviction, it will hold this against the defendant, and it may be hard to convince the appellate court that a conviction should be overturned, because of the "other substantial evidence."

[5.23] How To Argue Damages. There are several sections of this book that deal with specific errors counsel must avoid in arguing damages. In addition, counsel must develop a plan for arguing damages that will give full effect to this important part of the lawsuit.

First, remember the trial court will insist that you be fair. You cannot mention damages in your rebuttal if you have not mentioned damages in the first half of your argument. Your argument must be based on the record. Your damage argument must be based upon the law of damages and not upon sympathy or upon the mere fact the plaintiff was injured.

You cannot collect damages simply because the defendant is insured and, conversely, you cannot argue that damages should be less because the defendant is NOT insured. *Collinss v. Nelson*, 410 SW 2d 576 (Mo. App 1965). At least one court held it improper to argue how much ball players are paid in order to demonstrate that what he is asking for plaintiff is not all that much. *Faught v. Walsham*, 329 SW 2d 588 (Mo. 1960).

Pain is something that should be described to the jury, and courts have given counsel considerable opportunity to discuss pain, as long as (1) there is a basis in the evidence, and (2) it is not too emotional an appeal. One court permitted statements such as, "When you hear someone died, you say you hope they didn't have much pain," or "Pain is such a terrible thing that society invents ways to execute people so they don't have pain." *Arnold v. Edelman*, 375 SW 2d 167 (Mo. 1964).

[5.24] Avoid Mistrial Traps. A goo final argument can help win a case, but improper final argument can help you lose it. Every section on the law of final argument suggests situations where counsel can make a mistake by not knowing the law or not following the law which can bring about a mistrial and a halt to your march to judgment.

In the penalty phase of a capital punishment case it is important to remember the *Caldwell* Rule, which prohibits prosecutor from causing the jury to lessen its sense of its role in the sentencing process. *Caldwell v. Mississippi,* 472 U.S. 320 (1985). In determining whether this rule was violated, the court must first find if the remarks were the kind covered by the rule, and then find the effect of such statement on the jury. (Telling the jury it should not feel "responsible" in deciding to impose the death penalty was not a violation.) *Parks v. Brown,* 860 F2d 1545 (10th Cir. 1988).

To avoid mistrial, avoid improper argument (it just isn't worth it), and if opposing counsel objects, cure it yourself or ask the judge to cure it. This means that you explain to the jury fairly what you mean, withdraw the statement, or even apologize to the jury and the offended person. If this does not satisfy the situation, call upon the court to give a curative instruction and be ready to suggest to the court what should be in that instruction.

CAVEAT: Remember, some mistakes made in final argument simply cannot be cured and survive to haunt you even if opposing counsel does not object. They are plain error. Avoid them at all cost!

[5.25] Prepare For Law And Order Appeal. Polls show that the number one concern of those who serve on a jury is crime. "Law and order" is so popular that Presidents Reagan and Bush promised to appoint to the Supreme Court people who would "do something about it."

The prosecution will appeal to this fear, and defense counsel must be ready to object if argument becomes improper. Appeals for jurors to act as the "conscience of the community" have been permitted. *U.S. v. Alonzo,* 740 F2d 862 (11th Cir. 1984). One court held that the argument narcotics were "poisoning our community" and "our kids die because of this" did not go far enough to warrant a reversal. *U.S. v. Machor,* 879 F2d 945 (1st Cir. 1989).

In a capital case, prosecution was required to show that its improper argument was not prejudical. *State v. Smith,* 554 So2d 676 (La. 1989). In another death case, the prosecutor said that if he could decide to ask for death, the jurors could give the death penalty. The court reversed the conviction because the prosecutor had injected his personal opinion. *State v. Koon*, 298 SE 2d 769 (S.C. 1982).

One court permitted the prosecutor to tell the jury that the death penalty was needed so the defendant could not kill again, since there was evidence that supported this inference. *Haberstroth v. State*, 782 P2d 1343 (Nev. 1989). However, where prosecutor told jury to give death sentence so that he could not be paroled in 25 years to kill again, conviction was reversed due to this "prosecutorial overkill," and the "needless and inflammatory" remarks. *Teffeteller v. State*, 439 So2d 840 (Fla. 1983).

Where jury was told that defendant would be eligible for parole, death sentence reversed. *People v. Walker*, 440 NE2d 83 (Ill. 1982). At a penalty hearing in death case, prosecutor said that community was not a "moral community" unless it gave the death penalty, talked of possible escape from jail, and ended with, "I would not ask you to sentence him to death unless I could do that myself." Reversed. *Collier v. State*, 705 P2d 1126 (Nev. 1985).

It was held that prosecutor should not refer to defendant as "greedy, corrupt, dishonest and sleazy," *U.S. v. Prantil*, 764 F2d 548 (9th Cir. 1985); nor say that "all defense attorneys try to dirty up the victim," *People v. Emerson*, 455 N.E.2d 41 (Ill. 1983). But where a prosecutor called the defendant a "nine-headed, hydra-headed monster," the court held that prosecutor's use of metaphors did not violate due process. *U.S. v. Rewald*, 889 F2d 836 (9th Cir. 1989).

One court held that the prosecutor saying, "We don't put liars on the stand" was based on facts not on evidence. *U.S. v. DiLoreto*, 888 F2d 996 (3rd Cir. 1989). Where prosecutor said that jury could believe officers because he "read his report," reversed because no evidence introduced that he had read his report. *State v. Lake*, 485 A2d 1048 (N.H. 1984). Prosecutor's referring to needle holes on defendant's arm improper, since there was no evidence of needle holes and jury could not have seen needle holes on his arm. *Jordan v. State*, 646 SW 2d 946 (Tex. Crim. App 1983).

When prosecutor told jury during penalty phase of death case to consider fact defendant pleaded not guilty as proof of no remorse, reversed. *State v. Sloan*, 298 SE 2d 92 (S.C. 1982). Where prosecutor stabbed photo of victim who had been stabbed, interrupted, and ridiculed defendant's objections, told jury defendant would commit similar crimes if acquitted, and during sentencing stage said that homicide rate had increased 28% and that even though juries imposed the death penalty no one had been executed since 1966, reversed! *Brewer v. State*, 650 P2d 54 (Okl. Crim. App 1982).

Much of the law and order appeal is aimed at the defense counsel. In one case the court held it improper foı prosecutor to tell the jury "all criminal defense lawyers are paid to lie." *Bruno v. Ruschen*, 721 F2d 1193 (9th Cir. 1983). It was held that the statement, "as long as lawyers are for hire, justice is for sale" was so improper no instruction could have cured the prejudice and there must be reversal though no contemporaneous objection was made. *Borgen v. State*, 657 SW 2d 15 (Tex. Ct. App 1983).

[5.26] Communicate During Final Argument. The trial lawyer must "communicate" during final argument. This means he must call upon all available expertise in the field of communication and must learn from those who communicate effectively.

James Michener is a literary giant who knows how to tell a story. When he was interviewed by Rex Davis on KMOX radio in St. Louis, the interview went something like this:

> DAVIS: Tell us, Mr. Michener, what do you think it takes to be a good writer?
> MICHENER: First, a writer must master words, because they are the tools of the writer's trade. Second, he must master form. If a writer had the time and money he should go to architectural school, because an architect must know form.

When James Michener talks about "form" he means structuring, organizing, the telling of the story in an order that maintains interest and lets the reader or listener know each part of the story at the proper time.

Let us turn our attention to the other half of Michener's story-telling requirement: WORDS! Words are, indeed, the tools of a trial lawyer's trade. There are many ways words can be used effectively.

Oscar Hammerstein II was a genius in the use of words, for nearly fifty years supplying our best composers with words we love to sing. One of his favorite techniques was the use of "similar-sounding" words or phrases.

EXAMPLE:

> When Hammerstein saw Mary Martin on Broadway in "One Touch of Venus," he told a friend as he left the theatre, "Someday I am going to write a song in which Mary Martin comes out on stage singing, "I'm in love with a wonderful guy."
>
> It was about ten years later when the great lyricist did exactly that in "South Pacific." He had a choice of words in his opening line. First, he wrote, "I am as corny as Iowa in August," since Iowa was the state best known for corn.
>
> This did not sound right so he changed it to "I am as corny as Texas in August," since he was writing the song for Mary Martin, who was from Texas. This did not sound right so he changed it to "I am as corny as Arkansas in August," since the heroine of the musical was from Arkansas.
>
> Finally, he got it right and ever since we have been singing, "I am as corny as Kansas in August." The "K" sounds of "corny" and "Kansas" were exactly what he was looking for and helped make the song a popular one.

What does this have to do with preparing your final argument? EVERYTHING! Similar-sounding words and phrases can be just as effective in a final argument as in a song written for Broadway.

EXAMPLE:

> "We live in a world of wonderful women. We know what our mother means to us; without her we would not be here. We men joke about our wives but we know what they really mean to us. However many sons we have, our daughters are very special to us. Yes, we do live in a world of wonderful women.
>
> "John, sitting there at the counsel table had a wonderful woman who was very special to him. Opposing counsel told you during voir dire that she was "just a housewife," and I'll talk about that later, but right now I want to talk about the wonderful woman who meant so much to John Jenkins."

There is nothing that requires a lawyer to give the jury that similar-sounding dialogue, just as there was nothing that required Hammerstein to keep at it until he found a similar-sounding couple of "K" sounds for the beginning of his song. The last words must rhyme in a song; what Hammerstein gave the listener was a bonus, and that is what made him very special.

The lawyer who starts with "world of wonderful women" and continues with "wonderful women" gives his listener a little bonus. It is that extra effort in using words effectively that makes a trial lawyer special. What words to use and how to use them is the secret of communicating. This is how the lawyer uses the tools of his trade.

[5.27] Argue Briefly: Slip And Fall. When a lawyer asked if $28,000 was an adequate settlement for a slip and fall case, I replied, "In every slip and fall case, you must consider the possibility of losing." Slip and fall cases can be lost and THEY CAN BE WON!

Where the outcome on the question of liability is uncertain, the final argument is increasingly important. This kind of case demands the best effort of attorneys for plaintiff and defendant.

Suggested approach of defendant:

A million people walked over that little crack in the walk and did not fall. This man who is suing the city DID fall, and he tells us he fell because of that little crack. He tells us the fact he had a couple of beers is why he fell. Let us imagine for a moment that he had only two beers. Dr. Smith testified that these two beers probably did have some effect upon the way he was walking and the fact he fell. I suggest to you that the fact this man HAD been drinking is why he fell."

Suggested approach of plaintiff:

During voir dire, we talked about the importance of a jury following the court's instructions as to the law. We all agreed that our American judicial system just wouldn't work if everyone went off on a different direction and ignored the law. In this case you can make our system work and cause justice to prevail by doing exactly what is suggested in Judge Peterson's instructions.

"Those instructions give you the law as it applies to this lawsuit. It provides simply that if there is a dangerous condition existing on certain property and the owner of that property is on notice as to the condition and does nothing about it, then he is responsible in damages to anyone injured as a result of the dangerous condition.

"Let's look at the evidence. They ADMIT there was a crack in the sidewalk. They ADMIT they knew or should have known about the condition. They ADMIT John fell when he walked across the crack. They ADMIT he sustained serious injuries as a result of the fall.

"John didn't walk any differently than he ever walked before. They brought in this expert to help you decide the case for you. You heard the evidence. You know what happened out there and you don't need some doctor to come in here and tell you what happened.

"John fell because these people didn't care enough about people to fix it. John is sixty years old. Maybe he wouldn't have fallen if he were a young and agile athlete, but the law protects all of us. It protects you and me and, yes, a sixty year-old man who is walking down that sidewalk to earn a few extra dollars at a part-time job.

Follow the law of our State. Do your duty as a jury and bring back a verdict that is based upon the law and the evidence. Bring back a verdict of $100,000 in favor of John Watkins, the plaintiff in this lawsuit

[5.28] Argue Briefly: Pain. Every personal injury case and nearly every wrongful death case involves pain. Placing a dollar value on pain is so subjective that counsel may gain more from persuasiveness in arguing pain than in arguing any other kind of damages.

Remember that every juror has experienced pain, and this can either help you or return to haunt you. A man complaining about a little pain may not persuade a woman who has just gone through labor in a difficult pregnancy. A person who suffers from excruciating headaches knows that headaches can be excruciating.

One problem always present in arguing pain is in showing jurors the difference between pain caused by trauma and pain from which there can be no relief. Counsel must show the jury that there is certain pain that no one causes and no one can be held responsible for, but this cannot keep the jury from following the law and doing what is just and awarding for traumatic pain what the law and justice say must be awarded.

EXAMPLE:

We all feel a little pain when we get up in the morning and that pain grows a little as we grow older. There is no way we can be paid for that pain because no one caused it. But I'll tell you this: if this pain could be cured we would certainly cure it, and if pain were caused by some drunken driver, we would surely want him to pay for it.

You simply cannot discuss a personal injury case or a wrongful death case without discussing pain. You cannot discuss pain without appealing to sympathy. In the court's endless effort to balance the need for evidence or argument against the harm that might come to the other party, a realistic approach has generally been adopted. You CAN talk about the pain inflicted by the party whose counsel is objecting.

In arguing the value of pain, counsel was permitted to say:

> "When you hear someone died, you always say you hope they were fortunate enough that they didn't have much pain, or that they died quickly."
>
> AND
>
> "Pain is such a terrible thing that society invents ways to execute people so they don't have pain."
>
> *Arnold v. Edelman*, 375 SW 2d 167 (Mo. 1964).

Arguing that death is the only relief from pain was held to be legitimate argument. *Lanning v. Brown*, 377 SW 2d 590 (Ky. 1964). The basic test is whether verdict is based on an "unimpassioned evaluation of relevant, material evidence, uninfluenced by appeals of counsel to prejudice and passion." *Seabord Air Line R. Co. v. Ford*, 92 So2d 160 (Fla. 1957).

[5.29] Argue Briefly: The Finality Of Death. For centuries the law placed little value on the life of a human being. First, there was no recovery and later there were statutory limitations. But today there is a great recognition in the law of the loss a family suffers upon the death of a loved one.

There are many factors the jury will consider in a wrongful death case: (a) the difficulty in placing a dollar sign on a human life; (b) recognition of the fact there is no other way to render judgment in such cases; (c) death is an emotional issue with most people; (d) there can be no limit to damages in such cases if no limitation is set by law or jury reluctance; and (e) the fact that there is a finality present in this kind of case that is not present in any other kind of case.

These issues require in-depth consideration during voir dire. You must know what the jurors think about these issues in order to prepare your argument to them. Then, during trial, you must lay the foundation for talking about them during final.

EXAMPLES:

> If your son is arrested and makes the foolish mistake of being disrespectful to the officer, you may expect him to pay a higher fine or even to be beaten by the officer, but you don't expect to get a call that he is dead.
>
> OR
>
> Joan was a freshman in high school. She had never attended a high school football game, and she never will. She had never been asked to a dance, and she never will. She had never fallen in love or become a mother or travelled or done any of what makes life so much fun. She never will.
>
> OR
>
> Mary Smith and John Smith were husband and wife. They lived together, travelled together, ate together, talked to each other, watched television together, and shared their lives with each other for forty years. When that drunken driver ran over and killed Mary, he created a void in John's life that none of us can fill. Nothing can ever fill that void. All we can do here, today, is what the law provides for us to do. We have to try in some way to compensate John for this horrible loss. Let's talk for a few minutes about some of the factors we are supposed to consider . . .
>
> OR
>
> When you break a bone, that bone will probably heal. When you cut a human body, it will probably heal. When a body is infected the doctor will give you a shot that will probably kill the infection. There is nothing any of us can do for John Anderson. He died because this company did not provide him a safe place in which to work and there is nothing any doctor in the world can do for him.

[5.30] Argue Briefly: Talk About Prison. Life in prison is so foreign to us that we cannot imagine what it would be like. Giving up the next several years of your life is also hard to understand. Putting your life on hold for education or military service simply is not the same.

In an armed robbery case where the prosecution had asked for a ten-year sentence (in Missouri where the jury sets the sentence), I responded:

> The prosecutor tells you to send this young man to prison for ten years. What does that mean, being in prison for ten years? I'll tell you what it means, it means giving up ten years of your life.
>
> Ten years is a long time, and a lot happens in the next ten years if you are twenty-one years old. It is during that ten years that a young man

finishes his education. It is during that ten years that he tries to find the job, or at least the kind of job that will give him pride and security.

It is during that ten years that he will probably get married. It is during that ten years that the most exciting thing that can ever happen to a young man will probably happen to him. He will probably become a father for the first time.

When you send a young man to prison, you are not sending him to college. You are sending him to a place where they manufacture criminals, where few people survive as good, decent human beings, a place where men rape men and brutality is as brutal as you will find it anywhere in the world.

Some people would never take the life of a fellow human being, yet they seem anxious to take part of a human being's life by sending him to prison. That is what we do when we send someone to prison. If we send John to prison we will be taking from him the best ten years of his life.

[5.31] Argue Briefly: The Voir Dire Commitment. Though the law frowns upon counsel obtaining commitments during voir dire, a good trial lawyer will get as many commitments as possible. It is only on ultimate issues that counsel will be prevented from obtaining any commitment.

During voir dire PLAN for final argument. KNOW that you will eventually talk to the jury about certain commitments. AVOID conflict with the judge by knowing exactly when the judge will permit you to obtain a commitment.

Suggestions for reminding jury of commitment:

During voir dire we talked about basing the verdict upon the evidence and not upon some preconceived ideas about this lawsuit. We all agreed that it would be unfair to both parties to do anything but follow the law of our state that requires the verdict to be based upon nothing else but the evidence.

We now know how wise that law is. One member of the panel said that he would more likely believe a police officer than my client, and he was properly excused from serving. The rest of you agreed such would not be fair and we now know why it is not fair. We now know that the police officer was lying through his teeth and that John told you the truth about what happened.

During voir dire we talked about the fact this is a civil case, and we do not have to prove our case beyond a reasonable doubt as the prosecution

> does in a criminal case. We talked about the fact John made a stupid mistake in college and was convicted of using marijuana. I looked each of you right in the eye and said that you should give that fact as much consideration as you think it deserves, but I then asked if you could listen to what John said and if you believed his story you would decide in his favor and you each said you would do that.
>
> I suggest to you that you now believe what John said because it was his word against the police officer's word and we now know that this officer's word isn't worth a wooden nickel. We know that what John told you was backed up by two other witnesses. We now know that if you decide the police officer was wrong and John should recover from him for that wrong your verdict will be based on the law and the evidence.

IMPORTANT: Be sure it is WE who decided certain issues during voir dire and not YOU. Be on the same side as the jurors. Don't challenge the jurors and make them feel you are holding them to their word, even if you are. ASSUME they are going to keep their promise and they will.

[5.32] Argue Briefly: The Right To Depend On Others. There are those who feel the American spirit requires all of us to be totally independent and "make it on our own." We must prepare for this thinking in a world that chews up and spits out human beings with traumatic events over which we have absolutely no control.

A drunken driver can come out of nowhere and put you in a wheelchair for the rest of your life. A drug addict can jump out of darkness and stab you with a knife and cause an injury that will cost you several years of savings. You may sign a contract in which you depend upon the integrity of the other party.

Opposing counsel will always talk to the jury about what your client did or did not do to avoid the event that is being litigated. You must often talk to the jury about the right to depend upon others.

In a lawsuit over a mistake in a termite report that my client relied upon, the other attorney based his defense on my client's failure to fully investigate the condition of the house after learning of some termite history. This defense had to be handled:

> "I have been trying lawsuits for forty years, and I can promise you that if you get mugged some night, by the time you get to the courthouse to testify, there will be some lawyer there ready to tell the jury how it was

all your fault. That is exactly what has happened to my client in this lawsuit. This company gave him this piece of paper and he depended upon this company and he depended upon this piece of paper.

"We are taught as children to depend upon others: first our mother, then our teacher and then our friends. If we were raised in a Christian or Judaic home we remember those beautiful words from the Book of Psalms: "If I take the wings of the morning, and dwell in the uttermost part of the sea, even there, shall thy hand lead me."

"From the beginning of the Industrial Revolution we have been taught to depend upon those who get money from a commercial transaction. If we go to Disney World and ride Space Mountain, we depend upon the engineer who designed that ride to keep us from flying out into space. If we are hauled into the operating room of a hospital, we depend upon everyone in that room to do all they can to keep us from dying. If you finally save enough money to buy your dream house, you depend upon that termite company to tell you whether or not that house is rotten with termites."

[5.33] Argue Briefly: Burden Of Proof. During voir dire, it is extremely important in a civil case to talk about burden of proof, especially with jurors who have served on a criminal case. When you reach final argument it is imperative that you talk again about burden of proof.

I like to compare the burden in a civil case with that of throwing a runner out at first. If it is a tie, the runner is safe. If the ball gets there a fraction of a second before his foot touches the base, he is out.

I then tie that in with the burden of proof and tell the jury that if our proof is one ounce better than their defense, then we win. That is all it takes for us to prove our case and win their verdict. The jury understands such an approach.

In a criminal case the defendant must spend more time on the subject of reasonable doubt. See Section 5.65 for an excellent example of how Roy Black argued reasonable doubt in the William Kennedy Smith rape trial.

[5.34] Argue Briefly: Witness Credibility. Credibility is what a lawsuit is all about; not only your credibility, but also the credibility of every witness you put on the stand and of every witness opposing counsel puts on the stand. Use a small part of your final argument on this issue, but if it is an issue in your favor, USE IT!

CAVEAT: At the end of the trial, try to determine how the jury perceives each witness. Grade each witness, not on the basis of what YOU think of the witness, but what you feel the JURY thinks of the witness. When you have done this, you are ready to talk about witness credibility.

The old system of going down a list of witnesses and repeating what each witness testified can be boring and it violates every rule of courtroom drama. Remember, CONFLICT IS THE ESSENCE OF DRAMA, and it is your job to win each conflict. Note where there is conflict in testimony and talk about it because that is what the jury will be thinking.

Suggestions in arguing witness credibility:

> None of us will ever know for sure what happened out there on that cold Saturday night. We must decide on the basis of the testimony of the three witnesses who were there. We cannot judge any of that testimony, however, without first judging the person who gave the testimony.
>
> George Smith was standing on the corner, waiting for a bus. He did not know either party and had no reason to want to help either party. The other two witnesses were riding in the defendant's car and were both good friends of the defendant. We have every reason in the world to feel they would give the defendant every benefit of the doubt.
>
> Let's look at the testimony of these two friends. One thing I look for when I am judging testimony is to see how perfect the testimony was. And, if there are two witnesses telling the same story, then how EXACTLY THE SAME was the testimony? I am sure you noticed what I noticed about the testimony of these two witnesses.
>
> First, the testimony of both was too perfect, too good to be true. The other witness said that he wasn't sure how close my client was standing to the curb, he thought it was probably somewhere between three and five feet. The first friend said that it was exactly eighteen inches. How could this witness be so positive it was EXACTLY eighteen inches?
>
> What did the other witness say? You remember what she said. She said that it was exactly eighteen inches. In fact, everything the first witness said, the second witness repeated—word for word. What kind of testimony is that? All the second witness was telling us is that she wanted to help her friend as much as possible. Frankly, I don't think she helped her at all.

CAVEAT: Remember, your perception may differ greatly from the jury's perception and it is the latter that counts. You may be positive a witness is lying, but if you have not shown that the witness lied to the satisfaction of the jury, you have not earned the right to treat him or her like a liar during final argument.

[5.35] Argue Briefly: Show Malice Through Conduct. Malice is often important in (a) satisfying a legal requirement when establishing liability or proving damages and (b) appealing to the jury. Accusing the other party of malice will not suffice, however. In argument, as in evidence, what the party DID will be persuasive with the jury.

Study the law of punitive damages. Consider the difference between "legal malice" and "actual malice." Study the jury instructions and know what the judge will tell the jury about malice. In most states you do not have to prove malice was in a person's mind, you need only prove conduct from which the jury may conclude the person was malicious.

Suggested argument re malice:

> Judge Smith has instructed you that we need only show legal malice to entitle my client to punitive damages, and to prove legal malice we need only show what the defendant DID, not whether he intended to be malicious.
>
> Let me remind you of another part of his Honor's instruction. He said that if conduct is "wrongful, intentional and unlawful" it is presumed to be malicious. In our case the defendant admitted that he intended to hit my client and that he knew it was wrong. We have introduced into evidence the city ordinance that makes such conduct unlawful.
>
> OR
>
> Opposing counsel argues there is no law against what his client did. What his client did was intentional and wrongful, and under our law that is the kind of conduct that should be punished as malicious conduct. It was wrong, he knew it was wrong, and he INTENDED to do it. I suggest he should be punished far beyond the ordinary or actual damages.

[5.36] Argue Briefly: Financial Status. Financial status can greatly affect the outcome of a lawsuit or the size of a verdict. This means counsel must use the issue effectively during final argument.

In preparing to use this issue during final argument, remember the following: (a) reference to financial status may be considered improper prejudicial argument in some jurisdictions, (b) the makeup of the jury may cause a favorable or unfavorable reaction to such argument, and (c) you must JUSTIFY the use of the issue or the jury may suspect your motive.

Justify in your own mind the use of the issue and you will present it to the jury more persuasively. Financial status IS important in many lawsuits. The fact defendant borrowed money from a widow who has financial problems, the fact the huge medical bills caused by a huge corporation must be paid by someone, the fact the defendant is wealthier because of the activity which caused the loss, the fact the plaintiff is poor and can never raise money to pay for damages, all suggest a legitimacy of financial status as an issue. The law of most jurisdictions specifically recognizes the fact that it will take a larger punitive award to dissuade defendant from the complained-of conduct.

Suggested use of financial status:

> I don't like to discuss another person's finances because I think that is a person's own business. There is one exception, and the law wisely recognizes this exception. You will remember Judge Colson permitted me to introduce evidence of Mr. Brown's income and net worth. That is because the law recognizes it will take a larger judgment of punitive damages to keep this man, and others like him, from doing this horrible thing again. Under the law I have a DUTY to introduce such evidence and you have a right to know about such evidence because without such information you cannot reach a fair and just verdict under the laws of our state.
>
> OR
>
> The defendant in this case is John Broad, the president of the largest bank in town. He was driving his new Cadillac down Main Street last year on the way to play golf at the country club. Mary was standing on the curb of Main Street near Page, waiting for a bus so she could go to the doctor. Mary was run over.

[5.37] Argue Briefly: Punitive Damages. Before you talk to the jury about financial status or any other aspect of punitive damages, you must prepare the jury for this very special kind of case. The law is founded on "making the plaintiff whole," that is, giving a verdict for the actual damages sustained.

In a punitive damage case, you have a special task from voir dire through final argument. You must move the jury to accept the need for this special kind of damages. You must convince the jury as to the justice of a form of damages that has been criticized in the press.

CAVEAT: Jurors will lean toward punitive damages when they feel that (a) the law favors such damages, (b) the defendant should be punished, and (c) your client should benefit from this kind of damages. It will help if you believe in the position you are going to take.

Attorneys representing defendants honestly feel punitive damages are a "rip off" and if any punishment is to be dealt the defendant, there is no reason for the plaintiff to reap this reward. Believing this will help counsel argue it.

The plaintiff's attorney will find much to support his belief. A federal government study showed that punitive damage awards were not excessive and most of them were modified anyway. When a defendant's conduct is horrible enough to justify punitive damages, counsel should have little trouble getting emotionally involved in an argument for punitive damages.

Suggested argument for punitive damages:

The law allows for the fact there are times when the conduct of the defendant is so awful that it gives the jury the opportunity to punish him with an additional form of damages, which we call punitive damages. In such a case, the judge instructs the jury that it can award such damages.

In this case, Judge Smith will give you such an instruction. He will tell you that if you find from the evidence that the defendant's conduct was intentional and wrongful or unlawful, then in addition to all other damages, you may award my client punitive damages.

The court will further instruct you that such additional damages may be in such sum as you feel will discourage this defendant and other people from such conduct. The court will then instruct you that in doing so you can consider the defendant's income and net worth in deciding the amount of damages.

We now know why this is the kind of case in which punitive damages should be awarded. This man knew when he sent this letter to people that he would destroy Pam in the business she was starting. He knew that what he was saying was a lie and he knew that these people would believe these lies.

These lies destroyed more than Pam's business. They destroyed Pam's life for two years. They would have destroyed this woman forever, but she fought back because she was determined this man would not ruin her life.

What will it take to keep this man and people like him from doing this? This man is a wealthy person. You have heard the evidence. He clips about sixty thousand dollars a year in coupons. He has a net worth of more than a million dollars.

I suggest to you that if you return a verdict of $10,000 in punitive damages he can laugh at my client, laugh at me, and laugh at the entire judicial system. He can go right back and do the same thing all over again.

I suggest to you that you should bring back a verdict that will really get his attention. That would have to be a huge amount of money, at least a hundred thousand dollars, but if that is what it takes, then I feel it is your duty to bring back such an award.

We decided during voir dire that there are many laws we might want to change if we were in the state legislature, but that during this trial we would follow the laws now on the books. The law of our state provides that if you are fined for speeding the fine goes to the government; but when a person is punished with punitive damages the penalty paid by the defendant goes to the victim of his conduct. I see nothing wrong with this. I think victims SHOULD be compensated.

I think through your verdict you should send out the word that we are not going to tolerate this kind of conduct in our county. You should tell this defendant, and everyone else who even considers treating a fellow human being the way he treated Pam, that he is not going to get away with it.

We all get upset about the horrible things we read about in the papers and watch on television, but there is nothing you can do about it. Today, you CAN do something about it. You can bring back a verdict that can do something about it. You can bring back a verdict you will be proud of for the rest of your lives.

[5.38] Argue Briefly: Injury Is For The "Rest of Life." Most injuries that are worth filing suit over are permanent injuries. This means the negligence or intentional act of the defendant has caused an injury that will affect your client for the rest of his or her life. It is your duty to impress this fact upon the members of the jury.

States that prohibit the "golden rule" argument do so because such argument results in large verdicts. When you represent the plaintiff, it is your job to obtain a large verdict. The fact that a person who receives what a juror would expect if he were plaintiff is considered too much tells us that jury verdicts in personal injury cases should be substantial if permanency is involved.

States which prohibit the "per diem" rule do so because paying a person what he or she would be entitled to for every day of suffering from an injury would result in a substantial verdict. Every state permits you to talk about how permanent permanency is and about why a fair and reasonable verdict will be substantial.

In discussing permanency, you should (a) convince the jury that it is, indeed, a permanent injury, (b) show what your client cannot do now that he or she could do before, (c) show any suffering of your client, and (d) show that this will last forever.

Suggestions in arguing permanency:

> Before this accident, Mary got the kids ready for school and then went to work at the plant. She did not go to work because she wanted to, but because she had to. She, her husband, and three children could not afford to live on the small salary her husband receives. Mary had worked for ten years and she will never be able to work again.
>
> Mary cannot clean her house, she cannot play with her children, and she will never again be able to do anything around the house or to play with her children. She used to bowl in the league with the other women at the plant, but she can never do that again. She used to go camping with her family, but she can never do that again.
>
> This is not because Mary does not want to do these things. She tried to work and ended up in the hospital and her foreman testified in this trial that she tried, but she simply cannot do the work anymore. Her husband testified she played with the children at one family picnic and was in bed for a week because of it.
>
> Experts have testified Mary would work another thirty-four years and she would lose about $680,000 in wages during that time when she would have worked, but could not work because of this man sitting here who drove his automobile into her. Experts have testified that she would have lived at least fifteen years beyond her retirement from work, and the doctors have explained to you that every day from the date of the accident until the date of her death she will suffer from these injuries.
>
> Mary will suffer for the rest of her life. She will not be able to work, she will not be able to be a mother, she will not be able to be a wife, and that is for the rest of her life. That is a long time. That is why I have suggested to you that to do justice to Mary you must return a verdict that will take care of her . . . for the rest of her life.

[5.39] Get Jurors "Rooting" For Your Client. When you turn on the television and a football game is in progress and you know neither team, you will soon want to root for one team or the other. When jurors sit in the jury box they want to find out who is the "good guy," and when they find out who it is then they want to "root" for him or her.

Ask any friend who has served on a jury and you will find that even though the friend started jury service with an open mind, by the end of the trial he or she had good reason for casting the vote the way it was cast. It is your job to get the juror to find a reason to support your client's position.

This begins, of course, during voir dire, but all you do during the trial prepares you to help the jury root for your client during final argument. This can be done by (a) helping jurors identify with your client, (b) appealing to the best in each juror, and (c) presenting your client in a way that captures the reason and emotion of jurors.

Each juror has had experiences similar to those of your client and this must be brought out so the juror can identify. If your client has been unable to pay medical bills through no fault of his own, let the jury know how embarrassing this has been. Most people on the jury will have had a similar experience.

Most jurors feel people should try to overcome adversity and should not ask for pity because of it. Show how much your client has tried, and even show progress. If your client has kept at it and can now walk a few steps and testifies that he is going to keep at it until he can someday walk a mile, the jury may give him more credit for that than some doctor's testimony that he cannot walk at all.

Jurors root for people they like. They like people who appeal to their reason and emotions. They know how costly it is to pay medical bills for the rest of one's life, and they can reason that you are entitled to a huge verdict for that purpose. They can "feel" for a mother who cannot play with her children. There must be a factual basis for the emotion, but once it is there, counsel should build on it.

Suggested argument to get jurors "rooting" for your client:

> We all have some dream in our life and we all work toward that dream. Bill dreamed of being a big league ball player, but he knows and we all know that many try, but few are chosen. When you dream of playing in the big leagues you start with a high school team and then you just go as far as your dreams will take you.
>
> Bill will never know how far his dreams will take him. He has been told he will never play baseball again, but he refuses to believe that. He

has been told he may never walk again without the use of a cane, but he has refused to believe that.

He has not come before you in this trial as a cripple, because he refuses to think of himself as a cripple. Maybe he would be entitled to more money as a cripple, but walking means more to him than money. Running means more to him than money.

Under the laws of our state he is entitled to a certain amount of money in damages, and it is my duty as Bill's lawyer and your duty as a juror to see that he gets that amount of money. That is because we cannot give Bill what he really wants, the ability to walk, the ability to run, and the ability to play ball again.

Only Bill can give himself that. He has explained to you what he has to do to accomplish this. He must go through a few years of painful therapy. He must work hard every day and pray hard every night. Bill will never make it to the big leagues. To be honest, Bill will never make the high school team, but Bill WILL make it. We all know Bill well enough by now to know, he WILL make it.

[5.40] How To Use Instructions. How you use instructions during final argument can be very influential. In every jurisdiction, however, you should use them, because they ARE the law and the law is what tells the jury why it should decide in your favor.

In Missouri, the judge gives instructions BEFORE you give final argument. I much prefer this procedure, since you can hold a copy of the instruction that the jury has already heard and read from it or otherwise refer to it.

In Florida, and many other states, the judge gives the instructions AFTER argument, which has a decided disadvantage for the trial lawyer. He must talk to the jury about instructions the judge is going to give, and it has less impact, and a few mechanical requirements, not present under the Missouri procedure.

The jury wants to know which side the law is on, so that is why you must tell them. The only law jurors can know about is the law given in the instructions, so it is important to explain how those instructions fit into your evidence.

Suggested argument using instructions given before argument:

His Honor has instructed you as to the law, and I would like to talk to you for a minute about instruction number seven. It reads, "If you find from the evidence that the defendant did not know a crime was being committed . . . then you must find him not guilty." There is absolutely no evidence that my client knew anything about a crime being committed. His Honor has instructed you that, without such proof, you have no choice. He did not say that you MAY find the defendant not guilty. He said, "Under such circumstances, you SHALL find the defendant not guilty."

[5.41] Explaining The Counterclaim. The jury too often assumes that the plaintiff is suing and the defendant is defending. The fact that a counterclaim has been filed does not always get the jury's attention unless counsel properly explains this legal procedure.

Suggested argument explaining the counterclaim:

> This is a lawsuit in which both parties are suing each other, and as I explained during voir dire, the plaintiff is the person who just happened to reach the courthouse first. You agreed during voir dire that you would give my client's claim the same consideration it would deserve if he were the plaintiff.
>
> We now know why the law gives the counterclaim that same status as the original petition. In this case there has been no evidence to support the petition, but all the evidence from both sides tells us why my client should recover under the counterclaim.

This should suffice to put the counterclaim in proper perspective, but without it, jurors may fail to give it the same importance it gives the original petition. This brief introduction should be the springboard into the evidence that has been offered in support of the counterclaim.

[5.42] Make Your Experts Better Than Theirs. Hope that your experts are better than theirs, because in a battle of experts, your lawsuit may depend upon it. Having good experts is not enough; you must convince the jury as to their expertise.

In arguing the importance of your expert testimony, convince the jury that (a) your experts have the best expertise, (b) your expert testimony makes sense, (c) your expert testimony is crucial to the jury's determination of the lawsuit, and (d) your expert reached the conclusion that proved your case.

Suggested argument relative to expert testimony:

The only real issue in this lawsuit is whether or not the will was a forgery. We have brought into this courtroom the best expert we could find. He was with army intelligence for twenty years and has examined thousands of questioned documents. He not only attended school for years, he also taught school for years and is recognized as an authority because of articles he has written on the subject.

Mr. Wilson testified that there is no question the document is forged, and that makes a lot of sense. Why would this lady want to leave her entire estate to a woman she hardly knew? Every witness who testified in this case told us why this lady would want to leave everything to her children and nothing to the woman who is responsible for the forged will.

Our expert explained to you how he arrived at the conclusion that the will was a forgery. He obtained written instruments that had the signature of the deceased on them. He compared those signatures with the signature on the will and they were not at all similar. The "W" was so different that all of us could see that it could not have been written by the same person who signed the will.

What did opposing counsel do when confronted with the truth? Did he bring in an expert of his own? No, he tried to discredit Mr. Wilson by reading to him from a textbook on questioned documents. I suggest to you that if there were an expert anywhere in the world who would take this witness stand and testify that this was NOT a forgery, you would have seen that expert in this courtroom.

There is nearly a million dollars at stake here. Cost is no object in getting an expert into this courtroom if you can find one that will testify as to your position. We have but one expert. He is the best that can be found and he has testified under oath that it is a forgery and has explained to us why it is a forgery.

[5.43] How To Use Charts, Blackboard, And Exhibits. Demonstrative evidence does not end when the evidence is in. What has been used during trial can be used during final argument and additional information can be given graphically that has not been introduced.

If there is any question as to whether a chart, blackboard, or exhibit can be used during final argument, clear it with the judge. In most instances this will not be necessary, but do not take any chance that your presentation will be interrupted.

Exhibits have been used during final argument for centuries, so there is no problem. They should be used, and used effectively. This does not mean that you should bore the jury with exhibits that were introduced merely because they were necessary to "make your case."

Choose your exhibits with persuasiveness in mind. If you needed ten photographs to tell your story initially, you may need to use only one of them in final argument to remind the jury of how conclusive the photos were. If you are certain the judge will permit it, tell the jurors to ask for exhibit 13, or for all exhibits, and to take a close look at exhibit 13.

For many years counsel feared the temporary nature of a blackboard and the inability to preserve it for appeal. Taking a photo of it preserves it, and the fact that it can be erased has not kept it from being a popular courtroom tool. The spontaneity of writing on a blackboard as you talk to the jury or of having a witness use a blackboard while testifying can be effective. When jurors see and hear at the same time they retain more than through one communication technique.

Charts from the trial and charts to summarize are being used more than in the past. Counsel must be sure that anything appearing in the chart is based upon evidence or is proper argument, and the law and practice of your jurisdiction must be considered.

Suggested argument using demonstrative evidence:

> This man who ran into my client claims he was on the right side of the road, but how could he have been? Look at this diagram of the scene of the accident. The officer who investigated the accident found debris from both automobiles right here [pointing] and there is no way the point of impact could have been anywhere but on the south side of the road.
>
> Look at this photo of the debris. This photo was taken two minutes after the accident, and looking at this photo you can only conclude that the defendant was on the wrong side of the road. Look at this photo marked exhibit 18, it shows that the headlight of the defendant's car was broken and that glass was found five feet on the wrong side of the road.

CAVEAT: Remember, the jury wants to SEE as well as hear. It wants to have each part of your case shown to it with all the impact that demonstrative evidence and demonstrative argument brings to a lawsuit. Don't disappoint it!

[5.44] Differentiate Between Sympathy And Concern. Sympathy is a bad thing in the law, and it is an opportunity for opposing counsel to complain to the jury that your client is asking for something that is wrong. Long before final argument and then during final argument, counsel must deal effectively with this problem.

Sympathy is a human feeling that expresses a warm feeling for a fellow human being. On stage or screen or in a novel, such a feeling is considered admirable. But in a courtroom, it has been portrayed as a "cheap" appeal and is discouraged in the law and in the response of jurors. This simply means counsel must adjust to the peculiar requirements of courtroom strategy.

One effective way to do this is to use a more acceptable concept—that of "concern." People often reject sympathy because it suggests the need for one to depend upon another. Those same people may, however, feel others should be concerned about what has happened and should accept concern as a duty to "feel" something about the condition or occurrence without offering sympathy, which some think of as a form of charity.

Suggested argument using "concern" effectively:

Joan Jenkins does not want sympathy. I told you that during voir dire and I now tell you that again during final argument. Joan has NEVER wanted sympathy. In school she never missed a day, though she often felt bad and would have liked to stay home. After this accident she went back to work as soon as she could, even before she should have according to one doctor. She did not want to stay home and get sympathy; she wanted to get on with her life, and that is what she wants here today.

Though Joan does not want sympathy, she does appreciate the concern you have had for what happened to her in this case. I watched your faces as Dr. Johnson testified and I could see the concern on your faces. This is a genuine concern that one human being should have for another human being who has suffered from such a tragedy.

There is nothing wrong with being concerned. In fact, it would take a pretty cold person not to be concerned about what happened to Joan in this case. We all wish we could do something to ease the pain and all we can do is to be sure she receives the money she is entitled to under the laws of our state.

THAT we must do, and we can do that by following his Honor's instructions as to the law and by applying that law to the evidence you have heard in this case. Opposing counsel suggests that my client receive nothing. It is obvious his only concern is for the big corporation he represents.

That corporation showed no concern for Joan or for anyone else when it hired this man who had two drunken driving convictions. I suggest that if it had been as concerned about safety as it has been about defending this lawsuit, we wouldn't be here today. If it thought for one minute about protecting people like Joan from accidents, it wouldn't need to hire this law firm to defend it and to pay for these big experts to come in here and testify.

[5.45] Emphasize That Money Is The Only Remedy. From the time an insurance adjuster is assigned to a case, the defendant's position will be that some greedy person is after "money." Since that is the only remedy the law provides, it should come as no surprise to anyone that the plaintiff is suing for money, but this "only remedy" factor must be made known to the jury.

Though you have covered it in voir dire, you must bring it home even more forcefully during final argument. Some cases require more attention to this factor than others. That is why you often must cover it during the first part of your final, since if opposing counsel does not mention it, you cannot bring it up for the first time during the second half of the argument.

Suggested argument to show money as only remedy:

If there were some way we could give Jimmy his arm back we would not be here. That is all in this world Jimmy wants, but he cannot have it. That is what I would give him and that is what you would give him. That is certainly what his mother and father would give him. If his Honor could give you an instruction that would erase this tragedy from Jimmy's life we know he would do that, but he cannot.

The only remedy for Jimmy, under the laws of our state, is an award for that sum of money he is entitled to under our law. That law gives an inherently inadequate award. There is nothing anyone can do about that. What we CAN do, however, is make sure Jimmy does get what he is entitled to under the law. That has been my job during this trial, and I hope I have served my client the way he is entitled to be served.

I hope I have presented the evidence to you clearly. I hope I have helped the doctors tell of these injuries as thoroughly and accurately as possible. I hope I have argued this case to you in a way that you really appreciate the loss that my client has sustained.

My job is now over. I have carried this burden for two years, since the day Jimmy and his parents walked into my office. I must now turn this burden over to you. His future is now in your hands. I know you will do all within your power to right this wrong. That is why we are here. That is why our American legal system works. Because you will bring back a verdict that does for Jimmy all that anyone can do for him.

[5.46] Lay Foundation For Medical Expense Argument. Medical expenses are an important part of a personal injury trial. In the courtroom the word foundation means, "what you must do first." You must first present evidence of medical expenses before you can talk about them.

Proof of medical expenses must include: (a) that the money was spent, (b) that the expense was necessary to the injury, and (c) the expense was reasonable. Once you do this, you are ready to argue medical expense.

Suggested argument re medical expenses.

We all know that jury verdicts are higher now than they used to be, and the biggest reason for that is the dramatic increase in medical expenses. When I was in the hospital twenty-five years ago I paid $20 a day for a private room, and the doctor's bill for delivering our first baby was one hundred dollars.

You have heard our evidence relative to what Jim Davis had to spend for medicals in his injury. You heard Dr. Watkins tell us about these medical bills and why they were necessary. Opposing counsel complains about the amount of these bills, but I can only say that none of these bills would be necessary if his client had driven on the right side of the road.

Let's divide these medical bills into two groups. First, the bills that have already been paid [writing on the blackboard]. They come to $32,134.56. There can be no argument about this. This money has been paid and the doctor testifies that the amount is reasonable and absolutely necessary to proper treatment.

Now, let's look at future medical expenses. The doctors agree that there will be a need for medical care in the future. They also agree that this care will cost about $25,000. We can't wait and come back five years from now and find out, exactly to the penny, how much this medical care will cost. Under the laws of our state, we must decide today. And under the laws of our state, the only way we can do that exactly as we have done, by presenting to you the best evidence that is available at this moment.

[5.47] Quoting: How, When, And Why. Quoting adds another depth, another authority, and another style. It tells the jury, "Listen, this is important." It tells the jury, "Listen, this is what someone else admits is true."

We quote every day, without realizing it. We quote Shakespeare when we say such phrases as, "sink or swim," "having nothing, nothing can he lose," "winter of discontent," "I'll not budge an inch," "rotten apples," "spotless reputation," "what fools these mortals be," "the better part of valor is discretion," and "There is nothing either good or bad, but thinking makes it so."

We often quote the Bible without realizing it: "scapegoat," "apple of his eye," "a wise and understanding heart," "sold his birthright," "fat of the land," "milk and honey," "greater than I can bear," "a man after my own heart," "chariots of fire," "set thine house in order," "the shadow of death."

"The skin of my teeth," "one among a thousand," "the mouth of babes," "mindful of him," "the wings of the wind," "sweeter than honey," "his heart's desire," "cast lots," "all the days of my life," "clean hands," "smoother than butter," "everyman according to his work."

"Riotous living," "gave up the ghost," "the living among the dead," "brotherly love," "love one another," "eye hath not seen, nor ear heard," "in the twinkling of an eye," "the same yesterday, and today, and forever," More quotes from the Bible? "God forbid!"

Why so many biblical quotations? (1) To help us realize that we DO quote without realizing it, (2) to show quoting is no "big deal," and we should feel comfortable doing it, and (3) to show how much quotations are a part of our daily language and why it is an important part of effective communication. What we learn about quoting the Bible applies to every other kind of quotation.

How to make quoting easy: The quoter must feel comfortable quoting, and the quote must be applicable. Law Professor Elmer Hilpert enjoyed telling of his son's saying, "Hurry up, Dad, you know haste makes waste." There are many ways to use a quote and each manner may depend upon:

1. The Nature of the Quote. You may just use a line in passing, or you may use the quote as the basis of a major element of your argument.

EXAMPLES:

(a) Longfellow said, "time is fleeting," and I know Judge Jones agrees with this poet, so I am not going to spend much time on this, but. . . ."

(b) John Greenleaf Whittier once wrote:

"of all the words of tongue or pen,
the saddest words are these,
it might have been."

That is what this lawsuit is all about—what might have been for little Joey Brown.

2. The Length of the Quote. The length of the quote is important. The nature of the case will decide HOW you quote. The short quote can be emphasized with the same effectiveness as a long quote.

EXAMPLE:

For centuries we have known "a man's home is his castle." Out in the marketplace there is competition. In dealing with people there may be conflict. But, in your home you can do what you darned well want to do and no one can do anything about it. It is your escape from all in the world you do not like.

3. Makeup of the Jury. Remember your jury. Fundamentalists want you to quote the Bible, atheists may not. The educated may want you to quote Shakespeare, the uneducated may think you are "talking down" to them.

EXAMPLES:

(a) To a jury of Baptists, you may begin with "Christ said. . . ." With another jury, you may begin with, "We all gain strength from our own religion and one thought that has carried me through some rough times, is the old question, "Am I my brother's keeper?" The more concern I have for my fellow man, the better I feel about life. I know you are concerned about. . . ."

(b) To a jury of college graduates, you may begin with, "Shakespeare put it well when he said. . . ." To a jury of uneducated people you may begin with, "We have all heard that 'out of the mouth of babes . . ."

4. The Style of the Attorney. A city lawyer trying a case in a rural courthouse spends time showing the jury he is just "one of the boys." He would hardly begin with, "According to Shakespeare. . . ."

A serious attorney trying a serious lawsuit may find no place in the trial to inject humor. A prosecutor who depends upon a firm reaction may not use poetry that suggests a sense of freedom to a conviction.

EXAMPLE:

> The prosecutor can quote "an eye for an eye," or can talk about, "Whoso sheddeth man's blood, by man shall his blood be shed." He should not, however, attempt to come close to the beautiful Sermon On The Mount, nor to Tolstoy or others who wrote about man's love for man.

5. The Person Being Quoted. It is not only the Bible and Shakespeare that must be quoted with discretion. The person quoted will often determine whether you should quote and how you should quote.

EXAMPLE:

> To a jury of Democrats, or Missourians who may put their only President above partisanship, you may begin with, "When old Harry Truman was in the White House he said, "The buck stops here." To a Republican jury, even in Missouri, you might begin with, "The other day the President reminded us of that old Truman quote, 'the buck stops here.' "

CAVEAT: Remember, (1) Quoting CAN be an effective way to communicate; (2) The quote must, however, SERVE the message being communicated; and (3) Quoting is an art that must be developed and used only as the trial lawyer feels comfortable doing it.

[5.48] Quoting The Bible. Juries have heard quotes from the Bible as long as there have been juries. The thought that this is a dying art is itself dead. Quoting the Bible adds credibility, and credibility is what a lawsuit is all about.

In one jury trial, I began the first part of my final argument as follows:

> "Toward the end of the Sermon On The Mount we find those beautiful words, 'The rain descended and the floods came, and the wind blew, and beat against that house, and it fell not, for it was founded upon a rock.' Our lawsuit is founded upon a rock, the truth, and that truth can stand up against all the lies that these people can bring into this courtroom."

CAVEAT: Remember, the Bible has been such a part of our society that atheists quote it every day. So much of our music and writing have a religious history that we simply cannot separate from our communicating that which has religious significance. Extricating religious background from our lives would deny us the beauty of some of the greatest composers who ever lived.

It is the trial lawyer's role in communicating to: (1) have his or her argument IDENTIFY with what the jurors believe, (2) use any source the jurors look upon as being authoritative, (3) bring a style to his or her argument which puts it one level above that of opposing counsel.

Remember the importance of the "one-level above" syndrome. A lawyer should dress "one level above" others in the courtroom. He should talk "one level above" others in the courtroom. Being "one level above" others gains respect without establishing a distance between lawyer and juror. Most jurors expect the attorney to know more about many things than they do, and if counsel handles this advantage properly then it will remain an advantage.

This and all other rules of quoting and all rules of trial advocacy are especially important in quoting the Bible or other religious writings. A person's religion is personal, and when you enter this domain you must do so with the greatest of care and respect.

The best way to develop the art of quoting the Bible is to practice it. Practice it in daily conversation and then practice it in the courtroom.

Examples of quoting the Bible during argument:

1. The Earth. According to the Bible, it was intended that man have

> "Dominion over the fish of the sea, and over the fowl of the air, and over every living thing that moveth upon the earth."

I suggest to you that Man has done a poor job in exercising this responsibility and if we continue with programs such as the one being attempted by the defendant, Man won't have much left to have dominion over.

2. Man Alone. John Jones was a faithful husband for thirty years and if this drunken driver had not run down his wife and killed her, John would still have that woman he loved so much and would, indeed, be faithful to her. But, none of us can change that. For two years John was

destroyed and finally met a woman who is a good woman and is trying to help John put his life together again. I beg of you, don't second-guess John in his decision to remarry.

We all meet death differently. We all face loneliness differently. Some cannot stand it after a life that was so full of love. The Bible said, "it is not good that man should be alone." It may well be that John and people like him are whom the Bible had in mind.

3. Birthright. The Bible says that Esau sold his birthright. Isn't that exactly what the defendant did in this case?

4. Fat of the Land. The Bible talks about people living off the fat of the land. Some of the young people today want to live off the fat of the land, but they do not want to accept any responsibility. I suggest that you can teach the defendant a lesson he must learn, and I suggest you can do this by bringing back a verdict of guilty on all counts.

5. Stranger. The Bible talks about a "stranger in a strange land." I want to thank everyone for making me feel at home in this beautiful county. I have never tried a case here before, and if I have failed to follow a local procedure, I know you will not hold that against my client.

6. Understanding. The Bible suggests that we have a "wise and understanding heart." I know of no more important qualities for a juror to possess when judging a fellow man.

7. Life. The Bible says, "Our days on earth are as shadow." It is true that we do not know how long we will be on this earth, but that decision is not to be made by some drunken driver. We must love every minute and not let anyone take this life without paying a severe penalty.

8. Age. I think one of the saddest passages in the Bible is, "my days are past." Some of us who are growing a little older make sure our days are not past as long as there is one more wonderful day to live. That's how old Barney looked at it, right up to the day he was killed.

9. Wordy. The Bible talks about a man who "multiplieth words without knowledge." That reminds me a little of my opposing counsel's final argument.

10. Meekness. The Bible says, "The meek shall inherit the earth," and I guess old Jess believed that, because he was just that kind of guy.

11. Work. The Bible says, "Thou renderest to every man according to his work." Many people today just don't believe that, they are looking for something for nothing.

12. Weeping. The Bible says, "Weeping may endure for a night,

but joy cometh in the morning." There have been many long nights for Mary Smith since her daughter was killed.

13. Depending. We have a right to depend upon each other and we have a right to depend upon a higher authority. In the Bible it is written:

> "If I take the wings of the morning,
> And dwell in the outermost parts of the sea,
> Even there shall thy hand lead me."

14. Wife. The Bible says, "A virtuous woman is a crown to her husband, far above rubies." Jack Tracy knows that this crown can never be replaced.

15. Wealth. The Bible says, "Wealth maketh many friends." From the number of people who have rushed into this courtroom to testify for old man Johnson, I guess the Bible is right.

16. Self-Praise. The Bible says, "Let another man praise thee and not thine own mouth." I guess the defendant must have skipped that part of the Bible.

17. Man And Woman. The Bible says there are four wonderful things:

> "The way of an eagle in the air; the way of a serpent upon a rock; the way of a ship in the midst of the sea; and the way of a man with a maid."

Yes, folks, that IS a part of the Bible, just as it IS a part of life, and it IS a part of this lawsuit.

18. Mourning. The Bible says, there is "a time to weep and a time to laugh; a time to mourn and a time to dance." There has been little time for laughter or dancing in the Murphy home since the day little Billy was killed.

19. See And Hear. The Bible talks of people "which have eyes and see not, which have ears and hear not." God gave us eyes and ears and a mind with which to understand what we see and hear. It would, indeed, be a pity if we did not use them. Let me remind you of what you have seen and what you have heard in this trial.

20. Two Masters. The Bible says, "No man can serve two masters."

His Honor's instruction will tell you the same thing. That is why this man is liable in damages to my client.

21. Temptation. Even the Bible acknowledges that the flesh is weak. John knows he should not have been tempted, but we are not here to judge that. We are here to decide whether or not he has committed the crime with which he is charged.

22. Laborer's Worth. The Bible says, "The laborer is worthy of his hire." That is all my client wants, that is all he is asking for.

23. Admissions. In the Bible it is written, "Out of thine own mouth will I judge thee." Let's look at the evidence as it came from the defendant's own mouth.

24. Intentional Wrong. The Bible says, "Father, forgive them, for they know not what they do." Jack Smith knew what he did and now you know what he did.

25. Casting Stones. The Bible says, "He that is without sin among you, let him first cast a stone at her." The prosecutor told you he represents our state and I tell you it is common in this state for people to do every day exactly what my client did."

26. Childishness. In the Bible you will find,

> "When I was a child, I spake as a child, I understood as a child, I thought as a child, but when I became a man I put away childish things."

What we must realize and what we must make the defendant realize is that he is no longer a child.

27. Now. The Bible says, "Now is the accepted time." This company has been talking for many years about a safer product, but has done nothing about it. I agree with the Bible and I am sure you do, too. Tell this company with your verdict that we cannot wait any longer.

28. Think About It. In the Bible we find these beautiful words:

> ". . . brethren, whatsoever things are true, whatsoever things are honest, whatsoever things are just, whatsoever things are pure, whatsoever things are lovely, whatsoever things are of good report; if there be any virtue, and if there be any praise, think on these things."

I hope that, during your deliberations, you will think about what is TRUE, what is HONEST, what is JUST, what is PURE, what is LOVELY, and what is GOOD. Let us first talk about what is true. We now know that the truth is. . . .

29. Whose Ox? When President Thomas Jefferson purchased the Louisiana Territory for a few cents an acre, people protested vigorously, which prompted the President to ask, "Whose ox have I stolen?" I am sure that as my client sat here during this trial, listening to these ridiculous charges placed against him for doing what any good citizen would have done under the circumstances, I am sure he has asked himself, "Whose ox have I stolen?"

30. Prosperity And Pleasure. As children we were taught that according to the Bible, if we obeyed God, we would spend our "days in prosperity," and our "years in pleasure." I don't know who obeyed God more than Mary Clemons, teaching handicapped children all week and teaching children in her Sunday School every Sunday. Now, only you can give her those "days of prosperity" and "years of pleasure."

Quote other religious writings:

1. Defamation. According to the Hebrew scriptures,

> "Many have fallen by the edge of the sword; but not so many as by the tongue."

This man did not strike Mary with his fist or cut her with a sword, he destroyed her with words.

2. Her Job. It is a religious belief in China that "if a man finds a job he loves he will never have to work." John Morris found such a job. He had started such a career, but he can never work at that job again.

3. Truth. According to the Hebrew scriptures, "Great is truth and mighty above all things." That is the kind of dedication to truth a juror undertakes when he raises his or her hand and gives an oath. That is the kind of truth demanded from all of us if justice is to prevail.

4. What You Become. Whatever our religious belief may be, I think we all appreciate these words,

> "What you are, is God's gift to you,
> What you become, is your gift to God."

Ben Mackey was well on his way to making his gift to God. He had graduated from medical school and he had spent a summer helping people in South America.

QUOTE ACCURATELY! If you do not know what you are quoting, don't quote! The excerpt reprinted below from *Hall v. Brookshire,* 285 SW2d 60 (1955) is a perfect example of how NOT to quote the Bible.

> The last remaining point raised relates to the argument of plaintiff's counsel. It is contended that the argument was inflammatory, prejudicial, unethical, and untrue. The transcript contains only extracts from Mr. Orr's argument which the defendant claims were prejudicial. After argument of the case here the defendant moved to amend the transcript by filing an additional transcript of the full argument. This additional transcript that he sought to file shows that near the outset of the oratory of which the defendant complains learned counsel for the plaintiff stated:
>
> > "You may remember when Christ was preaching the gospel, in the Holy Roman Empire that Julius Caesar was Emperor of Rome. As Christ was making his way toward Rome, the Mennonites and the Philistines stopped him in the road and they sought to entrap him. They asked Christ: 'Shall we continue to pay tribute unto Caesar?' And you will remember, in the Book of St. Matthew it is written that Christ said: 'Render ye unto Caesar the things that are Caesar's and unto God the things that are God's."
>
> The Holy Roman Empire did not come into existence until about 800 years after Christ. Julius Caesar, who was never Emperor of Rome, was dead before Christ was born. Christ was never on His way to Rome and the Philistines had disappeared from Palestine before the birth of Christ. The Mennonites are a devout Protestant sect that arose in the Sixteenth Century A. D. This phrase is noteworthy only because of the ease with which the speaker crowded into one short paragraph such an abundance of misinformation.

[5.49] Quoting Shakespeare. Shakespeare spoke through so many characters, and so beautifully, that he is a great source of quotes. During argument, the trial lawyer must, however, follow a few basic rules in quoting Shakespeare:

1. Be Sure the Quote Is Applicable. If the jury thinks you are quoting just to be quoting, you will lose more than you will gain. Credibility depends upon applicability

2. Perceive Your Jurors' Attitudes Toward Such Quotes. Most jurors will appreciate your quoting Shakespeare, but some may think you are just "showing off." Understand your jury! With some juries you may begin with, "Shakespeare wrote," and with others you may begin with, "A poet once said. . . ."

3. Feel Comfortable Quoting or Don't Quote. If you do not feel comfortable quoting Shakespeare, the jury will know it and wonder why in the world you are doing it. Adjust, by first using a quote, or using it in a way, that you will feel comfortable.

4. Choose Your Quote and Method of Quoting Wisely. Study the examples given in this section. Some of these quotes will come easily to you, and some will not. Find a way of using the quote that will fit smoothly into your style.

Examples of quoting Shakespeare during argument:

1. Death. Shakespeare said, "The worst is death" and how well Mary Smith knows the truth of that. I have heard lawyers say that it is cheaper to kill than to injure, but your verdict must show the cold and brutal falsity of this. Yes, the worst is death.

2. Mercy. The prosecution would show no mercy, but I remind you of those beautiful words from Shakespeare:

> "The quality of mercy is not strained,
> It droppeth as the gentle rain from heaven,
> Upon the place beneath: it is twice blessed.
> It blessed him that gives and him that takes."

John is not asking for mercy, he is asking for justice. If your verdict considers all that this young man has suffered during his short life, you will be proud of that verdict and justice will be done.

3. Blindness. Shakespeare said, "Oh, how bitter a thing it is to look into happiness through another's eyes." Johnny Johnson will always look through another man's eyes, yet the beauty of Johnny Johnson is that he is not bitter. He is determined to see happiness and he deserves all the happiness we can give him.

4. Ingratitude. Shakespeare once wrote:

> "I hate ingratitude more in a man,
> Than lying, vainess, babbling, drunkenness,

Or any taint of vice whose strong corruption
Inhabits our frail blood."

When I first heard of this lawsuit I could not believe Ned was suing Fred, after all that Fred had done for him. After hearing all of the evidence, I still cannot believe it.

5. Tears. Shakespeare wrote, "If you have tears, prepare to shed them now." That day when the police officer knocked on Mary Smith's door and told her that her son was dead, she was not prepared to shed tears but she did and she has shed tears every day since then. Some wounds never heal.

6. Lending Money. Shakespeare once wrote:

"Neither a borrower,
nor a lender be.
For loan oft loses
both itself and friend."

Bill and John were good friends until Bill made the mistake of lending him money. I suggest that every excuse John has given you is based upon his refusal to face up to his financial problem, and not upon friendship, law, or justice.

7. Protests Too Much. The defendant told you he didn't hide the box. No one said he did. As Shakespeare said, "I think the lady doth protest too much."

8. Reputation. Shakespeare said, "I have lost my reputation, I have lost the immortal part of myself." When Mary's reputation was destroyed, much of her life was destroyed. She had, indeed, lost herself.

9. Patience. This lawsuit is all about patience. Shakespeare said:

"How poor are they that
have not patience!
What wound did ever heal
But by degrees."

This wound would have healed if the defendant had let it heal, and that is why we are here today.

10. Loquaciousness. You have heard the prosecutor speak for half an hour, but you have really not heard him say one thing about this case. Shakespeare said, "I want that glib and oily act, to speak and purpose not." I suspect that the only purpose of the prosecutor's argument was to tell you what kind of a man John used to be. I want to talk about John as he is today, and I want to talk about what happened on January thirteenth, because that is what this case is all about.

11. Thankless Child. Shakespeare once wrote, "How sharper than a serpent's tooth it is, to have a thankless child." John Smith had a thankless child and suffered every day because of it. Now that John can no longer suffer, this child wants his father's money and has come here to set aside the will.

12. Worthless Person. I look at you, John Anderson, and I tell you that you have raped and you have murdered. I tell you, as Shakespeare put it, "You are not worth the dust which the rude wind blows in your face."

13. Future of a Youth. For more than forty years I have walked in and out of courtrooms trying to help young people who have made a mistake. Some of these young men have become perfect people and some have not. Shakespeare once wrote, "If you can look into the seeds of time and say which grain will grow and which will not, speak!"

I cannot tell you what kind of a man Bill is going to grow into, but I think he is going to do just fine. I am sure you agree with me. I am sure that at least he should have the same opportunity as other young people to explore, even to make mistakes, but to try with all their hearts to make their parents proud.

I could give more examples, but time and space do not permit. "Ah, there's the rub."

[5.50] Quoting Poets And Writers. Poetry gives prose the change in style that keeps an argument from boring the jury. It emphasizes a point effectively. It lets the jury know the trial lawyer has mastered his or her art.

Clarence Darrow ended his plea for mercy in the *Loeb-Leopold* case with four full lines from a poem. If the argument some consider the best in legal history can include poetry, you should not hesitate to use this form of quoting.

Being comfortable is foremost, so if quoting poetry does not come easily, go slowly at first.

EXAMPLE:

A poet once wrote, "into each life some rain must fall." Well, in this case. . . . See how easy it is? Once you have accomplished this you will want to move on to quoting more than just a part of a sentence.

Examples of quoting poetry:

1. Today. Dryden wrote those beautiful words:

"Happy the man, and happy he alone,
He who can call today his own,
He who, secure within, can say,
Tommorow do your worst, for I have lived today."

As we grow older, we learn the importance of living for today. That is what Jim Ryan was learning.

2. Blindness. Only the poet Milton really understood his blindness as he wrote:

"When I consider how my light is spent,
Ere half my days, in this dark world and wide."

The dark world of Milton is very well known to Amy. She had eyes, but now cannot see.

3. The Mind. Milton once wrote:

"The mind is its own place,
and in itself,
Can make a heaven of hell,
A hell of heaven."

In this lawsuit my client has had to make her own heaven in a hell that was left her by this accident.

4. Lonely as a Cloud. I think one of my favorite poems as a child was that beautiful one by Wordsworth:

"I wandered lonely as a cloud,
That floats on high over vales and hills,
When all at once I saw a crowd,
A host of golden daffodils."

I have thought of that poem during this trial as I thought of young Judy, lonely as a cloud, floating over vales and hills.

5. Told You So. Byron wrote those beautiful words:

"Of all the horrid, hideous words of woe,
Sadder than owl songs, or the midnight blast,
Is that portentous phrase, 'I told you so.' "

Isn't that what opposing counsel has been saying, "I told you so"?

6. Honest Sweat. Let me tell you about the world I lived in as a boy, and I'm sure some of you lived in that same world. As a boy I loved Longfellow, and loved his words:

"His brow was wet,
With honest sweat,
And earns what'ere he can,
And looks the whole world in the face,
For he owes not any man."

This lawsuit is about the difference between honest sweat and getting something for nothing.

7. Our Hope. And, as the poet wrote:

"Our hearts, our hopes,
Our prayers, our tears,
Our faithful triumphant o'er our fears,
Are all with thee, are all with thee."

8. Duty. The duty of the military was set forth more than a century ago in Tennyson's "Charge of The Light Brigade":

"Theirs is not to make reply,
Theirs is not to reason why,
Theirs is but to do or die."

That is the code my client lived under and that is the code he was willing to die under. How can we now convict him for doing what he was trained to do?

9. Fate. Whatever happened to Tennyson's words, "For man is man, and master of his fate"? We live in a country where you CAN decide your future and for a man like this to refuse to do what he can is a horrible waste.

10. Success. Emerson could have been talking about my client as he wrote:

> "Born for success he seemed,
> With grace to win, with heart to hold,
> With shining gifts, that took all eyes."

11. Forgiveness. John Greanleaf Whittier, the famous American poet once wrote:

> "Dear Lord and Father, of us all,
> Forgive our foolish ways."

I am sure we have all, at one time or other, asked God for forgiveness, just as John stands before us today, asking our forgiveness. I am also sure that we have all done foolish things, maybe as foolish as what John did on that certain night last October.

QUOTE FAMOUS WRITERS! Famous writers knew how to use words and good trial lawyers "steal" those words effectively. Jurors understand words that tell a story or paint a picture, and they understand them best when told best.

The following are a few examples of quoting famous writers in a final argument:

1. Law. Samuel Johnson once wrote, "The law is the last resort of human wisdom acting upon human experience, for the benefit of the public." The law IS based upon human wisdom, and as we study his Honor's instruction we find that the law wisely protects people like little Mary Smith.

2. Don't Know. Mark Twain wrote, "I was gratified to be able to answer promptly, and I did. I said, 'I don't know.' " We need more Mark

Twain's on this witness stand. Did you listen to their expert? He knows everything about everything.

3. Truth. Emerson once wrote, "The highest compact we can make with our fellow man is, 'Let there be truth between us for ever more.' " That is the compact I want to make with you. Our evidence will be based upon the truth and I know your verdict will be based upon the truth.

4. Emerson said that a weed is "a plant whose virtues have not yet been discovered." We too often see virtue only in what others think have virtue. We do not see a child through the eyes of that child's mother. We have seen this young man described by the prosecutor as a man without virtue but I do not believe that, and I know you do not believe that.

5. Capable Of. Carlyle wrote, "The great law of culture is, 'Let each become all that he was capable of being.' " We will never know what Johnny might have become. He wanted to be a ball player, but the doctor says that he will never walk again.

6. Freedom. Ibsen wrote, "Never wear your good trousers when you go out to fight for freedom." I have been fighting for freedom in courtrooms for more than 40 years, and I have never torn my trousers. We work in nice air-conditioned courtrooms, but the fight here is just as important as anywhere in the world. If we let someone go to prison who is not guilty we have lost that fight. We have lost a little of what we believe in here in America.

7. Change. Thomas Wolfe wrote a book entitled "You Can't Go Home Again." That is the saddest title I have ever heard and the sad thing about it is that it is true. Have you ever tried to go home again? It just isn't the same, is it? The world changes every day and as hard as we try we cannot keep it from changing.

8. Circumstantial Evidence. Thoreau once wrote, "Some circumstantial evidence is very strong, as when you find a trout in the milk." In this case, I suggest to you that the circumstantial evidence was, indeed, very weak.

9. Relatives. Oscar Wilde wrote, "Relations are simply a tedious pack of people, who haven't got the remotest knowledge of how to live, nor the smallest instinct about when to die." I think some of the relatives in court here today must be students of Oscar Wilde.

10. Tilling a Field. Booker T. Washington wrote, "No race can prosper until it learns that there is as much dignity in tilling a field as in

writing a poem." This great man may have been talking to his own race when he wrote this, but people of all races would do well today, if they would listen to what he had to say.

11. Enemies. Oscar Wilde once wrote, "A man cannot be too careful in the choice of his enemies." Frankly, I think that is the only mistake my client made. I think he would have had many people testifying for him in this lawsuit, but he didn't go out of his way to please the boss and the boss has obviously influenced these witnesses.

[5.51] Model Final Argument: Civil. Two lawyers and one layman heard the case as arbiters and gave my client a judgment of $350. In that same case, the jury came back with a verdict of $72,500. One reason for the jury verdict was the following final argument:

"Toward the end of the Sermon on the Mount we find those beautiful words, "The rain descended and the floods came and the winds blew and beat against that house but it fell not, for it was founded upon a rock." Well our lawsuit is founded upon a rock—the truth, and that truth can stand up against all the lies that anyone can ever bring into this courtroom.

"I have thought of those words very much this week as I sat here, especially Monday afternoon when a fellow lawyer took the witness stand, testified under oath, and put on quite a show. He has spent most of his lifetime in a courtroom—he knew what to say and how to say it.

"He knew what gestures to make and when to look at the jury, and as we went home for supper that night I was a little concerned because I knew that if the jury believed this man, a great injustice would be done to my client. And I wondered as I drove home what was going on in the minds of each of you who is serving on the jury.

"But Tuesday morning I had an opportunity to cross-examine that witness. Cross-examination is a great privilege here in America. No witness was ever cross-examined in all of Europe until the Nuremburg trial, but that is a precious right we've always enjoyed here in America, and I think this week you've found out how important that is because this man who took the witness stand and talked about being such a great lawyer, a great father and a great man—then had to be cross-examined."

COMMENT:

Quoting the Bible can be effective if it fits. Also keep an eye on the makeup of the jury and be sure it is done naturally. When an opponent has made a good impression at one point, there is no harm in mentioning it if you can follow up with good argument that shows that has changed. Don't hesitate to point out false reasons for being impressed. Cross-examination is the truth seeker Dean Wigmore talked about, so talk about it to the jury.

"I started with the prenuptial agreement. He said that several copies were sent over the two months prior to the date of the planned wedding. Then he testified under cross-examination that no one even talked about the wedding until one month before that planned date. None of those several copies was introduced as evidence. One would have been, I'm sure, if it existed and that was the one in which my client wrote vulgarities all over it and sent it back to him.

"But you didn't see that copy introduced in the evidence either, but remember, remember the part of the cross-examination where I presented to him a letter that he had evidently forgotten about. I had him read that paragraph—I'm going to read it to you again:

"The afternoon of the wedding Dawn came by in my office and I presented her with a prenuptial agreement which she refused to sign and I refused to marry her without her signing it. That was presented a few hours before the wedding. This man who is so concerned about his children, who wants a family that's together—what he really wanted was a financial arrangement.

"When he didn't get it he refused to sign it. I ask Why? Why would he refuse to get this family unit back together the way he'd explained on his direct testimony? He said, 'Because this contract gave her more than she'd get under the law. If he's telling the truth, why didn't he take that piece of paper and tear it up? The caring father who didn't support his children, who wouldn't take his own son to the hospital when asked to do so."

COMMENTS:

Do not attack a party or witness in the courtroom until you have established in the minds of the jury that you are justified in doing so. When you are justified, document it carefully for the jury, to remind it of the evidence. Reading evidence to the jury can be an effective part of this documentation.

When they draw a picture of their client, pick it apart, piece by piece, but with something substantial.

"The attorney. What kind of attorney? You heard him testify that the Florida bar has publicly reprimanded him for dishonesty, deceit, and misrepresentation. Oh, he didn't remember those words, they were in the newspaper article that I confronted him with—he didn't remember what he was charged with.

"I suggest to you that if Judge O'Brien put a man out on the streets on probation who was charged with assault and battery, and the man didn't even remember what he was charged with and he just said, "Oh, it was nothing, I did nothing wrong," I suggest to you Judge O'Brien would bring that man back in and remind him—maybe that's what the Florida bar should have done.

"Remember, I had him explain to you that he knew, he told you the four levels of unethical conduct, first it didn't amount to anything, it was an honest mistake. No action taken. The second, a private reprimand, the third a public reprimand in which you tell the world that this man is guilty of dishonesty, deceit, and misrepresentation. That is what was involved here—one step from suspension."

COMMENT:

A personal attack should be avoided unless you have real ammunition. If you do have it, you must use it. Failing to is not fair to your client or the jury.

"There was another part of the cross-examination relative to his role as a lawyer I think we should discuss for just a minute. There's a lot of objecting during this trial (pointing to opposing counsel). That man has a right to object, sometimes a duty to object, but he did not object about one statement. I asked my client, "Why does this man enjoy being a lawyer?" She said, "He told me he enjoys being a lawyer because he likes to manipulate people."

"What does that mean—manipulate judges, manipulate juries, manipulate witnesses you're going to put on the stand to testify? There's no objection, there's no rebuttal. Did he take the stand and rebut this? He took that stand to tell you that he would not buy wine that cost less than $50 a bottle to drink in this great Waterford crystal that he had, but he didn't bother when he was on that witness stand denying that he manipulates people."

COMMENT:

When they don't deny what they should deny, USE IT AGAINST THEM.

"Next, on cross-examination we found that this man, who made such a great impression Monday afternoon, is a man who beat my client in front of his children that he's so concerned about. That neighbor who took the witness stand was, I think, the best witness of the trial. She saw him. Now, opposing counsel says that she only saw him once when he doubled up his fist and struck this woman while he was on top of her, only once.

"I suggest to you that once is enough, and that witness told you, he started to explain, 'He says, but there's a reason,' and she looked him right in the eyes as she did this jury when she took the witness stand and she said, 'No, ____, there is never an excuse for this,' and I suggest that in this day of violence that may sound like a cry out of the past, and a very welcome one. No excuses. No, ____, there is never an excuse for this."

COMMENT:

Watch the jurors during trial and if they are impressed by one of your witnesses, give them credit for being so perceptive. Have a good ear! When I interviewed this woman during recess I was thinking of a million things, but when I heard her say, "There is never an excuse for this" bells rang and red lights were flashing. You don't send millions of people to the gas chamber because they are Jewish, you don't shoot down unarmed Chinese students in Tienamin Square, and you don't beat a woman as her children stand by screaming. "There is never an excuse for this" are words you must have the witness repeat on the witness stand, and then you must repeat them during final argument.

"They talked about these items that were taken. I want to talk about them for a few minutes. Back in Missouri we had what we call an "Open Range" law which provided that if a train hit a cow the owner of the cow could sue the railroad. The lawyers used to joke about the fact that the most ordinary cow in the world, once it was hit by a train, suddenly was the most valuable thoroughbred you ever heard of.

"Well, I suggest to you that when I go through this list I see a lot of thoroughbred cows. Look at the old furniture that was left over from one of his previous marriages that the kids were using and he agrees that the kids should use—that old furniture you couldn't get $50 for—they give it to the Goodwill. He tells you it's worth $2,000. Here's a thoroughbred cow.

"Remember that little pot that they bought at the flea market for $5, by the time that old pot gets to the courtroom it's worth $75. The little trunk alongside the kid's bed, that little trunk, suddenly $250. The television set, remember there were three television sets. The big ones were left there, these small ones—$2500 for the three, $833 apiece.

"Let me remind you that my client brought one of these television sets into the courtroom. I placed it right in front of him and I asked him, "Do you want this television set?" and he said, "No, it has a little sand on it." So, suddenly, this $833 thoroughbred cow has a little sand on it so is worth nothing. My client told you it didn't work in the first place, so I suggest to you it was worth nothing the day she took it."

COMMENT:

My client left ten years of "live in" with nothing but two children and a lawsuit. Actually the lawsuit was against her and she recovered only on her counter-claim. The court, following Florida law, directed a verdict against my client for all items she took with her when she "split." Arbitration ordered her to pay $21,000, but before the jury we got that reduced to $6,000. An interesting cross-examination set the stage and a little Missouri heritage gave me the theme for accomplishing this.

"Adultery? You can't commit adultery if you don't marry the woman. I suggest to you that we should take a moment and look at the conduct of this man who introduced this woman as his wife. Bragged about going to houses of ill fame. Told you about Lisa who rented a room, an apartment in one of his big buildings, drove his truck. He bought a special waterbed for her and I suggest to you that maybe he helped her use it. Rita—he came home and one of his clients, Rita, was pregnant. She didn't know, but he was a little concerned about who the father may be, etc., etc., etc. That's this model person who testified on Monday afternoon."

COMMENT:

When opposing counsel pictures his client as a model person you have a duty to make a few observations.

"And the photo of the wedding. He admitted that he got this brooch back on the pretense that he needed it as a family heirloom—he had to use it at the wedding, the second wedding. He got a court order—he told the judge he needed it.

"So when I started the cross-examination, I asked him. "Did you use the brooch at the wedding the way you told the judge?" "Of course. Of course she wore that." Where did she wear it? "Right up here." Of course. What he didn't know when he testified under oath was that I would bring in a wedding photo, a wedding photo with no brooch on it.

"He thought fast. He saw things turning around, this attorney who's been in court all his life—he could have just told you he made a mistake but that's not enough, not for this witness—he wants to come up with an excuse, so what excuse did he come up with? "Oh, she spilled champagne on that dress.

"What does that mean? It was the same dress. If she spilled champagne on the dress and she had to change to another dress, we could see why the brooch was not there. Did he mean that there was champagne on the dress? Of course, there's no champagne on the dress. He said that they had to go in for awhile and that's why it was spilled.

"Look at the photo. The sun is shining, there's no sign of rain. What did he mean? The brooch was not there because champagne was spilled? Did he mean at 3:00 on a Saturday afternoon he sent the dress out and had it dry cleaned so that it was back by 3:15 for the wedding pictures?"

COMMENT:

Practicing law just isn't as much fun as it used to be. Discovery and pretrial orders keep you from surprising witnesses with devastating exhibits, but once you get one in, you had sure better talk about it during final argument.

"I suggest to you that that evidence alone proves to us that this man was lying through his teeth but he wasn't their only witness. They brought in two of the secretaries from their law office to testify that this lawyer tells you that you have to believe because they worked in the law office of this man?

"There's something unusual about the first secretary's testimony. The door was open when my client went in. It was still open. She could not see in because her desk was over a little too far—if she moved or she got up, she could see what was happening—but she sat there, listening, for ten or fifteen minutes.

"During that time my client was doing everything wrong—beating up on this man, using the worst of vulgar language. And during this ten or fifteen minutes he did nothing wrong, used no vulgar language, used no force, no violence whatsoever. During the ten or fifteen minutes she did nothing to get help or call the police or do anything.

"Now, that is not good evidence. But tie that in with something we lawyers notice every time in court and sometimes jurors miss this, so I want to point it out. The other witness testified exactly the same, exactly, word for word. Everything that happened on that date, 7 years ago, was recalled precisely the same and this is what makes us a little suspicious when evidence testimony is too good, too perfect. I suggest to you that this evidence was just too good to be true.

"But there is evidence that my client was at fault at that time. Where does the evidence come from? These little children that I tell you and you think that maybe that was hearsay and I shouldn't have objected—I can't. The rules of hearsay have exceptions and this is what the courts call a "present sense impression," or an "excited utterance." There's no way to keep this out—they know it.

"The only way we can rebut that testimony is to bring the children into court. Could I do that? Could I convince my client that she may get more money from this lawsuit if she puts the children through that traumatic experience? Forget it. There's no way this woman is going to do that and I respect her for it."

COMMENT:

Always look for testimony that is "too good." Especially if two witnesses say the same thing. This is easy to explain to the jury. Jurors have heard of the hearsay rule and wonder about a lot of things you may not realize they are thinking about. You never harm your cause by talking intelligently with a jury.

"But let's go to the next witness, the second secretary who testified. She proved to us beyond a reasonable doubt that she was lying through her teeth. She went along with all the testimony of the first witness, but something was missing.

"Jurors like an eye witness. Witnesses know that, attorneys know that, legal assistants know that, and so, toward the end of her testimony, we had an eye witness: she saw what was happening in the law library. How did she do that? Let me show you here on the blackboard.

"She says, 'This is the wall. The door was about twenty inches away, then there was a door jamb, and then the door opened from the other end' (showing on blackboard). She was pushing that door open—she with her 240 lbs. was trying to push aside my 165 lb. client. She finally got the door six inches open, so I said, 'Could you see straight ahead?' 'Oh, no, no.' Of course, she'd see nothing looking through the opening in the door where she has pushed it open. Did she look around? Of course she couldn't look around. It was only open 6 inches and a 240 lb. woman couldn't get around to see from that angle. There's only one other way she could have seen to become an eye witness.

"She said, 'I saw through the crack of the door.' I said, 'Down where the hinges are?' She said, 'Yes'. Now let me show you, let me go to the back of the courtroom and open this door (went to rear of courtroom and opened door). I'm opening the door, it is opened six inches wide, I am leaning against it, I look down the door—I can't even see the hinges. I can't possibly see. Now if I pull way back here three or four feet, I can barely see through that crack in the door, but how can I be doing that if I am pushing the door open? I think for the rest of my life every time I walk through a door I'm going to look back at the door that is six inches open and smile as I remember this lawsuit because there is no way her testimony could be true."

COMMENT:

> I spent part of the final argument in front of the jury box, part of it at the blackboard, and part of it in the doorway at the back of the courtroom. That's not bad in a state that ties you to a podium. Coming from Missouri, where you can lean into the jury box and chat with your neighbors, it was hard getting used to a podium, but I find Florida judges not to be as strict as I thought. They don't really "tie" you to the podium and often you can find good reason to move far from it. Showing while telling, whether at a blackboard or back door of the courtroom, can help the jury visualize.

"Let's get to the real meat of this issue: the question of whether or not this man was telling the truth when he told people that my client had given him a venereal disease. He had a venereal disease. No question, he's testified he went to the doctor. He was examined, but he doesn't know whether it came from Rita or Lisa or the prostitutes out in Nevada.

"He'd had relations with my client once in the six months prior to that exam, but he told my client and she went to Dr. Sam Siegal who had examined him, called him on the phone and said, 'What can I do? I understand Larry has this, if he has it he might have given it to me.'

"What does Dr. Sam Siegal say? He said, 'Well, just as a precaution, I'm calling the drugstore. You could pick up this prescription and then you'll be sure. So she did that. She went to the drugstore, got these pills, took them home and that night she stood in front of the mirror, looked in that mirror and looked herself straight in the eye and said, 'What am I doing? Why am I taking these when I don't even know whether or not I have this horrible disease?'

"So she called Dr. Wallace who knew her since she was eight years old and said, 'Jim, I'd like to come in to be examined,' told him why, and she mentioned that she had her period at that time. It was Wednesday, and Dr. Jim Wallace said, 'Why don't you come in Monday morning,' and she did. She was examined.

"You heard the testimony through deposition of Dr. Jim Wallace. No sign of any venereal disease whatsoever. This man told everybody he could, and those he told probably told others, that my client had given him a venereal disease. I suggest to you that he did that entirely out of vindictiveness."

COMMENT:

> "Let's get to the real meat of the issue" again tells the jury: Listen! This is important! Tell your story. Use direct quotes from the testimony as you tell your story. Remind the jury of any admissions made by the other party.

"Opposing counsel has promised you that I will tell you how much the damages should be in this case. Well let me say this, I have been trying lawsuits for 39 years and I do suggest figures to jurors. It's not that I'm bound by it. Like an old baseball umpire said, "The runner isn't out until I call him out," and you people on the jury decide these cases, and no verdict is a verdict until you say this is what we think should be a fair and just verdict.

"But, I suggest to you that the actual damages, what this woman went through, totally destroyed for 4 years, I suggest to you that that is worth $50,000. But I suggest to you that the punitive damages, His Honor will instruct you if you want to arrive at a figure for punitive damages, that you may use the net worth, the wealth of this person, what will it take to stop this person and others from doing this kind of thing.

"We know from the evidence, without getting into all these tax write-offs, apartment buildings and all that, we know he has a $200,000 house clear, we know he has a Porsche worth $50,000 clear, a couple of boats, and so forth. We know we cannot get his attention, we cannot punish him, we cannot deter him from this kind of conduct, unless we bring back a punitive damage award of $100,000."

COMMENT:

Talk about damages. Remind the jurors of their important role. Talk about punitive damages. Don't fall into the trap of talking about tax write-offs and negative income. Jurors understand a $200,000 home that is paid for, a $50,000 Porsche and boats.

"An old poet once wrote, 'For each one kills the one he loves, by this let all be heard; the lover does it with a sword, the lawyer with a word.' This lawyer's word was gonorrhea and he chose his word well because words are the tools of his trade. He knew that if he used this word, the way he used this word, he would utterly destroy this woman. And he did.

"She was a basket case—she was destroyed for four years. We're not asking any future damages. She is now a Girl Scout leader, she's raising her children, she's starting a new career in insurance, she's about to be married and she doesn't want one dime for the future, but for those four years she lost she should be compensated."

COMMENT:

It isn't easy to quote the Bible and Oscar Wilde in the same argument, but it can be done. Use such words as "utterly destroy," "destroyed for four years," and "basket case," but don't hesitate to follow up with positive words such as "Girl Scout leader," "raising her children," "starting a new career," "about to be married," and "doesn't want one dime for the future." IMPORTANT! After the trial a woman on the jury ran up to my client and threw her arm around her and said, "You'll make it, Honey." By giving up future damages you may not get anyway, you may get jurors who are "rooting" for your client. Jurors do not like cry babies, they do not like those who complain or exaggerate, but they sure like those who believe in the old American spirit of fighting to overcome adversity.

"What he did to her was an injustice—it wasn't fair. We see a lot of that nowadays. We see a lot of injustice. We see a lot of things that just aren't right, that just aren't fair.

"We see a little child playing in a school yard shot down by some idiot. We see a young lady attending our state university kidnapped off the campus, probably never to return. We see millionaires who don't pay one penny in taxes. We see homeless who don't even have a place to live and that's not fair, that's not right, that is an injustice.

"But, you and I can't do much about that. But today, today is the one day in your life when you can do something about it. You can stand up and be counted. You can shout out, 'Enough is enough.' You can send out the word to the whole world—that we are not going to let one human being treat another human being like this. You can do that with a huge verdict. That is the kind of verdict Dawn Lute deserves. That is the kind of verdict I am sure you will return. That is the kind of verdict that you will be proud of for the rest of your life. I thank you."

COMMENT:

Jurors can relate to injustice as something that just isn't fair, even if it is just someone getting in line ahead of them at a grocery store. Bring it home with what they experienced or how they felt when they watched the evening news on television. Take them from the helpless feeling of not being able to do anything about it to the present opportunity of being able to do something about it. MAKE THEM PROUD OF THE VERDICT THEY ARE ABOUT TO RETURN.

[5.52] Model Final Argument: Criminal. Judge Karl Grube announced in open court after the jury had retired, "That is one of the finest final arguments I have ever heard." When you do something right you should remember what you did, because you may want to do something right again. Let's look at this final argument:

"About a year ago my wife and I had one of our fourteen grandchildren down to spend a week with us. At the end of that week, Willie, about this high, and I were going down in the elevator of our condominium. I said, 'Willie, did you have a lot of fun with Grandma this week?' and he looked up and said, 'No.' I said, 'Well, Grandma's going to cry when I tell her that.' Then he looked at me and said, 'That was a joke, Grandpa.' "

COMMENT:

I talked about family, saying "Willie" and "Grandma" twice and "Grandpa" and "grandchildren" once. Telling a story creates interest, but you must do it in a few sentences.

"Well, when I read this policeman's report and I talked with my client about what actually happened out there that night, I was mad. I was outraged to think that this sort of thing could happen right here in the United States of America, and then I realized: 'This is a joke, Grandpa.' Some police officer is playing an April Fool's joke on you and you're too old to realize it."

COMMENT:

Notice school teachers become "angry," but out in the real world people get "mad." "What actually happened" tells the jury our story is the real story. "Outraged" is a powerful word, and "United States of America" is a popular phrase. Twice the state's case is described as a "joke," the second time as an "April Fool's joke."

"Yesterday I walked into this courtroom and I found out that they're not joking—they're serious—they're going to prosecute Joan for what happened out on this night. They want to send her to jail. You heard the prosecutor stand up before you and say, "We're going to prove beyond a reasonable doubt that this woman touched this police officer.

"What is this case all about? Let's talk first about their side of the story. I don't think we need really talk much about what my client said. I think that what she told you is the truth and I think that you understand it and certainly she didn't commit a crime under her story. But let's look at the story given to you by the State of Florida, through this police officer, and I'm sure when you analyze it that you'll find also there is no way that my client could be guilty of any crime."

COMMENT:

"Joan" not "Defendant." "Prosecute" which nearly rhymes with "persecute." "Beyond a reasonable doubt," always a good defendant's phrase. "I think," "I don't think," and "I'm sure" did not draw personal opinion objection. "What is this case all about?" tells the jury: Listen! This is important!

"What happened was that on that night the police department received a call from my client's daughter whom she had not seen for 2 years, and according to the officer, this daughter said that her mother was possibly suicidal. I'm not sure what that means, but I guess just about everybody in America is possibly suicidal.

"But these officers went out to this lady's house at midnight. According to their records, they arrived at midnight. The woman came to the door and talked to them through the screen door. She assured them everything was all right. They insisted—they demanded—that she come outdoors. They requested six or eight times according to their testimony that she come out of her home onto the front yard.

"Then finally she did, she came outside, she was there for about thirty seconds according to that officer's testimony. She explained again that everything was all right and she tried to go back into her own home and at that time both officers according to their own testimony slammed the door shut.

"The door had never opened more than six inches, remember that's their testimony. They slammed the door shut and they held it shut and she was trying to get in, turned, and touched one of the officers. According to one of the officer's testimony she shoved. He didn't fall down, he wasn't injured, but he was touched by my client. As a result of this she has been charged with the commission of a crime."

COMMENT:

> "Possibly suicidal" is repeated. "About everybody in America" includes my client with others. Twice "touched" is used. "According to the officer," "according to their testimony," "according to that officer's testimony," and "according to one officer's testimony" tells the jury they admit what I am saying.

"His honor will instruct you as to the law of Florida and under that law, if a person is on their own premises or in their own home or trying to get back into their own home they can use reasonable force. I suggest to you that in this case the touching of the officer was reasonable force.

"Oh, there was all sorts of testimony as to the fact there was a dog there, the fact that she had been drinking, there was testimony from the officer who testified yesterday afternoon that he was frightened by the dog. Remember, on cross-examination he said that once he saw that dog—that was before the woman ever came out of the house, from that moment on, he was worried about old Number One—he didn't care about this woman. He was worrying about himself.

"After my client explained her side of the story, opposing counsel had an opportunity then to bring back the officer and have him rebut anything my client had said. I thought it was interesting when they did this, the only thing they really talked about was intoxication and I want this prosecutor to explain to you when he gets up here in a minute what difference it really makes whether my client was intoxicated or not in her own home on this night. I suggest to you it makes no difference whatsoever."

COMMENT:

"His Honor will instruct you" tells the jury the judge and the law are on your side. "Their own premises" is used once and "their own home" is used twice. "Reasonable force" is permitted and is used twice. When opposing counsel does not answer an obvious question the jury wants answered, TELL THE JURY ABOUT IT!

"That is all, everything else my client said has to be accepted because they did not rebut it. I thought they would bring some evidence in on one very little thing—something I noticed and I wonder if you noticed. Sort of like when you're watching "Matlock" or "Murder She Wrote," when the program is over—Ah, there's one little thing we didn't notice—and that was what was most important."

COMMENT:

Jurors are constantly wondering about things, playing detective, placing their own importance on inferences. I see nothing wrong with discussing this with them, and even encouraging them to make deductions in your favor.

"What I think is the most important thing in my client's testimony that they did not rebut is the fact that when this officer put my client in the police car and drove her off to jail and the other officer went with him to jail, they went around the corner, they went down about a block and they stopped.

"They left my client handcuffed, sitting in the car while the officer in that car got out and went back and sat and talked for about five minutes with the officer in the back of that car. Why? They didn't explain that but I think you could probably figure out what happened.

"I know what happened. Why didn't they wait until they got to the county jail and then talk? Because when they get to the county jail there are people there, filling out forms, people are asking questions, asking, "Why . . . why did you insist this woman come out of her home? Why didn't you let her go back into her home?" You have to get your story straight, but they can't. Ah, the dog . . . remember, the dog is a vicious dog. The testimony of the owner is the dog can hardly walk but this is a vicious dog. And, she was intoxicated. They didn't know at that time that my client suffers from an ulcer and cannot drink more than just a little alcohol at a time. Sure, she's intoxicated. Another thing—she touched you, remember you can say that "she touched you"—that's what our case is all about. You write the report. You can because you were touched. That is why they were sitting there for five or ten minutes. But, I suggest to you that under the laws of the State of Florida, under their story or under our story, there is absolutely no way that my client could have committed a crime."

COMMENT:

"The most important thing" again tells the jury: Listen! This is important! Explain what happened and why it happened, with logic. "They didn't explain" challenges opposing counsel. Raise questions!

"Last summer, the Clearwater Bombers softball team, still the most famous team in the world, was invited by our State Department to travel to Cuba. As president of this ball club, I travelled with the team, and while there I took a picture of a woman I met, a college professor. I took a picture of her standing in front of her home where she now lives, it's a little home with just a few rooms and she and her husband, who is also a professor at the university, and their twelve-year-old son, and her elderly mother, all live in this little home and I took a picture of her standing in front of that home.

"Then I took a picture of the home where she lived when she was ten years old, the day that Castro took office. That was a beautiful home and that was taken from her; the police came in and said, 'This now belongs to the Communist Party.' That cannot happen in the United States of America. You cannot take someone's home from them. But what some people don't realize—you cannot take a person's home for one minute."

COMMENT:

A person's "home" is what our defense is all about and I notice that I used the word "home" eight times in these two paragraphs. Compare a home as treated by the Communist Party, and then how we value a home in the United States of America. Remind the jury that in America we don't have to give up our home for ONE MINUTE.

"Let me tell you what happened just a few days ago on New Year's Day. Six o'clock in the evening my wife and I are at home and she's fixing our New Year's dinner and the phone rings, and it's a man down at the guardhouse of the condominium, and the man wants to talk to me for a few minutes.

"I know my wife is about to make phone calls to children around the country and if we're sitting in the dining room or the breakfast room or living room near the telephone then she cannot comfortably talk personal business with these children so I said, 'I'll be right down.'

"This man and I talked in the living room of the condominium and there was no problem, there was no one else there yet I felt bad about that, I felt impolite, maybe a little rude that I did not invite this man into my home, and yet I didn't apologize for this because my wife and I, like most American people, feel strongly we have the right to the privacy of our own home, 24 hours a day—we don't have to open it up to anybody.

"That's what this lawsuit is all about. That's what America is all about. The fact you live in your home and nobody can take it from you—permanently, like they did to this woman down in Cuba or for one minute like these officers tried to on February eighth of last year.

Today is probably the only day in your life in which you will cast a vote on something important like this on this very issue that I've been talking about. And I know that you will cast your vote in favor of these things that we believe in here in America, and you can do that by bringing back a verdict of not guilty. I thank you."

COMMENT:

Bring the argument into your own home when your own wife is about to call your children. Admit a possible rudeness, but justify it with the value we place on our home in America. ALWAYS END WITH A REMINDER AND APPRECIATION OF THE IMPORTANCE OF THE JURY'S VERDICT.

[5.53] Model Final Argument: The "Final Five." Whether it is the final five, two or ten minutes, it is the last thing you will tell the jury before they retire. Only once in forty years of trying jury cases did I learn how a jury reacted to those closing moments of a final argument.

A client had refused to pay a $50,000 fee that had been agreed to in a divorce matter, and at pretrial the judge reminded me that I was suing my own client, and added that no jury would return a verdict for $50,000 and suggested that I take the $15,000 that had been offered. A week after the trial, a lawyer called and said that his aunt had served on the jury and thought I may be interested in knowing what transpired during jury deliberations.

Once a verdict was reached, the jurors discussed how and when they had arrived at the figure used in the verdict. They all agreed that before those last few moments they had pretty much agreed to award me $25,000, but after those closing moments they decided on their verdict: $56,000.

I did try my own lawsuit and I did not have a fool for a client, and I did receive an extra $31,000 for following two minutes of my final argument:

"Whatever your verdict is, it will make no difference to this woman. She will still have her condominium and she will still have her Jaguar in which to drive to and from the country club. She will still be able to travel around the world and she will still have that half a million dollars in the bank that I got for her.

"Whatever your verdict is will make no difference to her, but it will make all the difference in the world to me, because, if you bring back a verdict for one dime less than $50,000 principal and $6,000 interest, you will be telling me, my family, my profession, and the whole world that I took advantage of this woman, this woman who told me I couldn't get her one dime of that money because the stock was in her husband's name, and I got her one half of a million dollars.

"I know that your verdict will be in the sum of $56,000 because this is the verdict I am entitled to under the law and under the evidence, and this is the verdict you will be proud of for the rest of your life."

COMMENT:

Never tell jurors they must return a certain verdict, "or else." Such a challenge is often met with a verdict that is disappointing to the challenger.

However, you have a duty to share problems with jurors. This they will understand and appreciate. Jurors want their verdict to mean something. Show them what it means to you and your client. Notice, though the interest came to slightly more than $6,000, I reduced it to a figure the jury could remember.

Someday verdicts may be obtained by feeding facts into a computer, but as long as judges and juries try the facts, trial lawyers must begin with an opening statement and end with a final argument. Ending that final argument with what your case is all about and why you should win is what the jurors have been waiing for. DON'T DISAPPOINT THEM!

[5.54] Great Trial Lawyers: Pat Maloney–Two Multi-Million Dollar Verdicts In Two Weeks. Trial lawyers may find some satisfaction in knowing that Pat Maloney, who spearheaded million-dollar verdicts, is still getting such verdicts. In fact, he obtained two multi-million dollar verdicts in two weeks.

Let us examine the role of the final argument in these verdicts. Let us see how this part of the trial can result in a total of $66 million in verdicts in two weeks. Let us begin at the beginning:

"We began this case with the recognition that you, too, are officers of the court—just as we are. As such, you are now judges of the facts. In such capacity, you are more powerful than the governor of this state or the President of the United States. You can do what they or anybody else can't—fairly find the facts in this case. So we address you with real awe and recognize that you will treat your power and wisdom with great care and respect. It's important that your power not be abused and that you follow your oath that your decision be based only on the evidence admitted by Judge Baskin and the law that he has now given you in this charge. In only this way, do we continue to be a nation of laws—not of people. Force and wealth do not make right, and in my judgment, your verdict will shortly decide this basic, but vital premise. We know the intrusion on your lives by imposition of jury service is severe. But the price of freedom requires it, and you have heroically responded. As citizens, your proud community acknowledges you are the foot soldiers in defense of freedom.

"In accepting jury service—next to actually bearing arms for your country—there is no higher honor. It is up to you to safeguard the process for the future litigant and insure that it remains strong—free—and protective. It is in this capacity you have our sincere thanks and appreciation.

COMMENT:

Counsel begins with the importance of the jury. Interesting point: The transcript furnished me by Pat Maloney includes his "topical headings," such as "Jurors True, Officers of the Court," "Next To Actually Bearing Arms," "My Clients Can't Thank You," and "Big Guy Against the Little Guy." This helps "structuring" and "grouping thoughts."

"The implication of this kind of scenario happens all too often—'we are right because we are bigger—or richer—or more powerful.' You have the opportunity at this time to see that it doesn't happen. Not this time. It takes courage, tenacity and strong belief in the system to take on a billion dollar corporation which apparently has millions for defense and nothing for fulfillment of contracts. We submit, only belief in fair jury resolution and the knowledge that your cause is just—and a very good friend by the name of Gary Howard—will see you through such hazardous seas. Let me say this of Mr. Howard—he has been the principal participant in lawyering at its finest. It should always be the case that a just cause can find an able lawyer—and I applaud him for responding. He deserves much credit and respect from our honored profession that has been quick to defend against the wicked and wretched corporate abuse found in this cause.

"If you are busted as these guys are—but their cause is just as it is—then they ought to have a lawyer and I'm pleased we had the opportunity to respond. For four decades, Stanley Krist rightly characterized my professional attitude that a just cause should always find an able lawyer who will withstand the slings and arrows of an unrighteous opponent. That's why I applaud the cause of Mid Plains in withstanding the giant, and we are proud to assist in such a noble effort. Believe me, nobody ever said David with his solitary slingshot has an easy road but his aim was true and his heart was pure, and so is that of Mid Plains."

COMMENT:

Counsel moves right into his "big guy versus little guy" theme.

"When you get to my age you don't sugar coat things. Life has been so rich to me in all of the respects that really count. Last month I was married 40 years to a girl I married as soon as we both got out of law school. We have five children—they all practice law with me."

COMMENT:

> Counsel becomes personally involved with his lawsuit and begins to sell himself. He builds on this throughout his argument with comments like, "I'm president of the slow learners club," or "Let's reduce this case to its basics and not be diverted by all of the rabbit trails."

"Hopefully, you know all you need to know about these three citizens of your community, my clients, to judge their credibility.

"You know what they have done for a living all their lives. You know what they have contributed to your community; who their families are and what their children have done. How long they have been married. None of them is a stranger to your community because they have all lived here all of their adult lives. Their lives are an open book and the defendants, with all of their vast resources, have done nothing to tarnish their useful and proud accomplishments or tell you otherwise.

"We brought you all this because you need to determine are they worthy of belief. Under oath did they tell you the truth? If they did, then the answers flow like this chart before you, designating proper responses. If they did not, and you find your fellow citizens lacking in the crucible of truth and you don't believe them, then school's out, because we brought you all we had—everything we know, you know. I can't be straighter with you than that, can I? I give you—your fellow citizens—if they are telling the truth—stand tall with them—they have really been treated shabbily. They have travelled a lonely, tough trail and deserve your support. If not, if you don't believe them—you should reject them out of hand."

COMMENT:

> Now counsel introduces the other characters of his courtroom drama. He makes it clear they are the "good guys" and refers to them as "fellow citizens" who are not "strangers to the community."

"They pay this guy Ernest $225 an hour—and I really didn't think he was all that earnest—to tell you what the letter says and why you couldn't believe what you read—and I thought to myself—hold it, hold it. They are trying to sell a fairy tale with no substance. They want you to desert the written word, but refuse to bring you a single Farmland executive who was a party to that written word."

COMMENT:

Counsel attacks their expert.

"Not a single Farmland executive told you what Farmland says the June 17 agreement means though they agreed to the written contract. Lauderdale isn't. Would they not support the Farmland contention that the written agreement is not to be believed? Did they refuse to come here and take the oath and subject themselves to cross-examination as did Charlie, Dick, and Dave?

"Why didn't Farmland come clean? What are they trying to pull in this temple of truth and justice? Didn't Farmland think you need to know what the Farmland executives to the written agreement say?

"They all signed on to a written agreement they now want to welsh on. But none of them—not a single Farmland executive appeared to swear contrary to the written agreement they signed. They either couldn't or wouldn't swear that wasn't the deal. Sounds phoney to me. How about you, or you or you? Or all of you?"

COMMENT:

Then counsel attacks lack of testimony of executives of defendant.

"These may seem like just little misstatements, but they add up in the big picture of deciding who's telling the truth—Charlie—Dick—Dave and the writing or Lauderdale? If you'll tell little stories, you might spring for the big one—like—here's what Charlie told me it meant. In effect he's saying Charlie defrauded Farmland. And I'm saying Charlie didn't but Farmland did, because he, Lauderdale, is simply not telling the truth about what Charlie said.

"You can't have it both ways. One side is not telling the truth, and Farmland on the only crucial issue in the lawsuit left all their troops in Tulsa or Kansas. Apparently the better part of wisdom dictated they couldn't stand the light of truth and cross-examination."

COMMENT:

"Conflict is the essence of drama," and counsel is resolving that conflict in his client's favor.

"All I got from Sadler's testimony was Farmland was caught double dribbling and had to cut the best deal they could under the circumstances and decided to throw Mid Plains in the grease. Here's what I got. Farmland was cheating—Lauderdale inadvertently spilled the beans on them—the 15 mcf was a slam dunk until then—but when Lone Star called a technical on Farmland, the two biggest chips Farmland had (eight million owed in back pay by Lone Star and a 40 million dollar Mid Plains profit over five years) had to be thrown into the pot so Farmland wouldn't lose the whole Lone Star contract.

"This was so because it would forfeit a 16 million dollar profit for the sale of the Farmland assets to Enerfin. Before we cut and run and leave Mid Plains hanging high with that Texaco contract let's take our 16 million dollar profit and split.

"After all Lone Star did catch Farmland cheating and cheaters don't have much choice. Farmland felt they needed to sacrifice Mid Plains even if it mean welshing on the deal and even if Mid Plains had to be the innocent victim to Farmland's wrongdoing. That's the whole sordid tale and that's how when Farmland did cut and run, they took 7.9 million dollars with them that belonged to Mid Plains."

COMMENT:

Counsel tells his story with a typical Pat Maloney "hominess," using basketball terms the jury understands.

"Now let's talk about damages. It's not like we are asking them for money out of their pocket. Along with their 16 million profit in the sale to Enerfin, Farmland really took 7.9 million dollars belonging to Mid Plains and they've wrongfully kept it for almost three years.

"Mid Plains wants it back and Farmland—not Mid Plains—should pay the attorneys fees because they are the cheaters—Farmland defrauded Mid Plains just like they did Lone Star and now they have been caught. They took a calculated risk and it didn't pay off.

"They took a gamble and lost when they settled with Lone Star. They figured we'll hire a high-powered law firm from Austin and try to wiggle out of the Mid Plains contract. And I think you will agree, that when we call this the wiggle out case it's just that, WIGGLE OUT.

"The old 'wiggle out' theory is as old as when man first made money. If you have enough money, you will be able to wiggle out by getting many lawyers—slowing down the process of trial and driving the lesser opponent to the wall with delay, illusion and trumped defenses and bogus issues. It's a shameful game of smoke and mirrors. Only you can turn the rascals out!

COMMENT:

Counsel is now ready to talk about damages. The jury is prepared to make the defendant pay, and counsel wants to help the jury decide how much.

"Do you have to spend so much money if you're right? Why not just put it down in writing like Mid Plains did and then live up to your word? Doesn't Farmland know in West Texas you're expected to live up to your word? Don't they understand in Midland you've got little time for welshers?"

COMMENT:

An appeal to local pride!

"Ernest says don't believe the written word of June 17—I'll tell you what it really means. And he did so without benefit of a single Farmland executive who wouldn't or couldn't show up to tell you why the written word doesn't mean what it says. The point is, of course, you were entitled to 'eye ball' the executives, hear them, and decide for yourselves who is telling the truth.

That's the way Charlie and Dick and Dave feel about it. That's why they did show up. I can't tell you why the Farmland executives failed to make their appearance. Only they have the answer and they're not talking. It's called credibility, and Farmland doesn't have any."

COMMENT:

Counsel hits again at the failure of executives to testify.

"We now come to the end of our efforts, yours is now beginning. We conclude with Paul's marvelous admonition and teaching from Biblical days (uses chart):

When two people agree on a matter and sign an agreement, no one can break it or add anything to it. *Galatians 3:15*

"Let it be so with your verdict today and so in this temple of truth and justice, you will have affirmed what we knew. In Midland, your word is your bond—especially if it's in writing, and it gets around pretty fast if you try to welsh on a deal. That's the way we do business in West Texas—that's the way the cookie crumbles for welshers.

"God speed!"

COMMENT:

Counsel's conclusion is simple, but effective. Another multi-million dollar verdict.

Trial lawyers who depend upon auto accident litigation may be pleased to find that the $66 million in two weeks of verdicts did not involve this kind of lawsuit.

Let's look at the second case.

"When we began our remarks more than a week ago in the voir dire examination, we told you that we were collectively beginning a process which was the crown jewel of our democratic system—trial by a jury—unique among the civilized countries of the world. More importantly, we told you that as jurors you become the administrators of justice. No one else!

"Sylvia Uriegas, you were told, is a symbol for all the widows and fatherless children who probably have gone before her victimization, and perhaps even more importantly, for all of those who will again unless you strongly address this duplicity and injustice. You are the messengers and the verdict, you were told, is the message.

"The substance of that message is yours, and we said that it is spelled out in this chart of exemplary damages which we again bring to you, and all of the elements constituting this grievously overreaching and duplicitous act—which we say can only be rebuked by exemplary damages."

COMMENT:

Again, counsel begins his final with a message to jurors as to their importance. Notice how he reaches the same goal with a slightly different approach. Notice also the use of a chart at the very beginning of his final.

"The amount of your verdict in exemplary damages, in my judgment, will determine the quality of the justice we have under these circumstances, not only in this community, but in this country. The insurance world is awaiting your answer as to whether you regard seriously this type of conduct. I believe from your conduct that Woodmen are going to be shocked, and the world of widows and fatherless children very agreeably surprised. The real determination is whether Woodmen of the World can dupe you as they did the Uriegas family."

COMMENT:

Counsel moves right into the punitive damage argument, the crux of his damages.

"The only testimony as to what happened when the Woodmen agents prayed with Sylvia and less than two hours later, fraternally took her check of $69,000, representing more than seventy percent of her entire assets, was Sylvia's. She was here throughout the trial and testified several times so that you could judge her credibility. The Woodmen participants, Arty Mullis, Hurtado, Jr. and Sr., elected not to appear."

COMMENT:

Again, counsel takes after those who chose "not to appear."

"They say they have no plans or need for this accumulated $212,000,000. I say that you tell this multi-billion dollar corporation you do. Say to them, we're going to take that nest egg and give it to Sylvia. You took hers. We'll take yours."

COMMENT:

Discovery pays off! The fact counsel knew about a $212 million "nest egg" gave him a good argument on damages.

"Of course, the principal actor and culprit—Arty Mullis—elected not to appear, even though he could expect we would call him a two-bit hoodlum whose position is defended only by Woodmen hiring him a lawyer to be present at all of the discovery processes of this litigation, plus attendance at the trial, plus paying for an expert witness to appear in his behalf. Despite this, Mullis' attorney gave as one of the reasons for his absence was that Mullis didn't have money for air fare from Florida to San Antonio."

COMMENT:

Counsel closes the door as to the reason Mullis did not testify.

"Where are the Hurtados? Surely they knew we were going to say that when they prayed with Sylvia they were praying that she would give them a very large check, praying they wouldn't get caught, praying that there would be no witnesses around, praying that Woodmen would support them in their deceit and duplicity.

"Presumably, they have answers to none of these charges or they would have been here. By their silence, you shall know them. And they are still on Woodmen's payroll, because Woodmen say they did nothing wrong. If they are representative of Woodmen agents, then it's time for a major housecleaning. Let it start with this case."

COMMENT:

Failure of Hurtados to testify gave counsel an opportunity to talk about his praying with the victim, then taking advantage of a widow.

"This sham for the need of insurance devised in their perverse minds was to get at her money, which they did, for \$69,000—\$110,000—\$41,900—on three separate occasions. Woodmen knew Mullis shouldn't be giving advice as to estate tax, nor should they, but they did and they both profited. She paid.

"Now they must pay and in proportion to the vile misrepresentation that she paid. Even yet, Woodmen would try to defend this wicked hoax, knowing all the while, it was a scheme only to bilk the widow and her family. Woodmen basically feels you won't see through their facade of respectability and find grasping hands of manipulation.

"Truly this is the classical passion play of good against evil—a defenseless, innocent widow who was done wrong by Pilate, exclaiming 'her blood is not on our innocent hands.' They are Judas and Sylvia is their victim—only more than thirty pieces of silver was exchanged.

COMMENT:

Counsel tells his story, and with drama!

"With a tax exempt status, because of their fraternalism, one could well ask how much of this fraternalism the future widows and surviving families of this world can stand? And they intend to keep on with their kind fraternalism—unless you stop them. Realize even yet they have never apologized, never said we are wrong, never suggested that Sylvia has been fraudulently overreached.

"Their reply: she signed her name and got the product! We have heard a lot about widows and children, but none that they have befriended, only these four victims. Surely when you are exempted from paying any income taxes notwithstanding thirteen billion in premium income, a modicum of charitable and benevolent works should be forthcoming. Folks, we haven't been introduced to any. Don't you find such silence sinister?

"Yet every Woodmen executive and manager, including the chief counsel, say there's nothing wrong with these transactions, nor do they have any criticism. Unless you find their conduct reprehensible by reason of exemplary damages, they obviously intend to keep on doing it. If they can't see anything wrong, you simply must show it to them by taking their nest egg of $212,000,000 which, by their admission, is doing nothing and make it do something.

"The home office says it's inadvisable for any person to spend more than 20 percent of their income on insurance. Yet they approved an application showing Sylvia was a Karnes City teacher's aide spending 80 percent of her assets, 30 percent of this on life insurance for her children, which she didn't need nor could she afford without ever once investigating these applications. Her policies called for her to spend $57,000 annually even though she was making $13,000 a year as a teacher's aide for retarded children."

COMMENT:

Counsel builds his case for punitive damages, EFFECTIVELY!

"Treat them in the same fraternal manner as they treated Sylvia. They took 70 percent of her death benefits. What's wrong with taking $212,000,000 that's doing nothing? It's the only kind of message that will stop their brazen, cynical, and perverse fraud and duplicity for which they have yet to repent, recant, or relent, or to say we were wrong or to apologize. Only you can right this wrong. We have tried; George can't do it! You are George!

"We know the kind of prayer Woodmen had when they joined hands with the Uriegas family. Now let us pray:

"Seek justice,
Encourage the oppressed.
Defend the cause of the fatherless.
Plead the case of the widow."

"We wish you God speed—stand tall!"

"Thanks for letting me serve with you in the cause of the Uriegas family—Tony, Sylvia, Paul, Bryan, Mark."

COMMENT:

Counsel covered the evidence thoroughly and dramatically, and then concluded with a plea for the widow and her children. Pat Maloney's final argument is full of quotes, hominess, and drama. This is part of what has made him one of America's leading trial lawyers.

[5.55] Great Trial Lawyers: Philip Corboy—Placing Dollars Signs on Human Life. We often hear it said, "You just can't place a dollar sign on human life." Well, you can, and often must, if you represent plaintiffs, because wrongful death and personal injury take part or all of a human life and your job is to recover money for those damages.

No trial lawyer does a better job of talking to the jury about damages than Philip Corboy of Chicago. Let's take a look at exactly how he does it:

"I read in the paper the other day that a Picasso painting was sold for some $53 million. Now, if that painting were the subject matter of this suit, it got burned or maybe it was on that truck that squashed my client and instead of his leg, that was a Picasso painting.

"It was completely ruined or maybe just half ruined like his body, you would say to yourself we have to assess damages here and the damages were that the Picasso painting was worth $53 million, but it's now useless or maybe it's only half useless, maybe it has a little bit of use because it's a tarnished Picasso and it may still have some value. And the testimony would be, however, it's still a $53 million painting.

"I think you can appreciate how completely unfair it would be if you were to say $53 million for a fellow who came from Spain who has never been in the United States except to visit us, $53 million for a painting that we don't even know what it looks like. I'm not going to grant anybody $53 million, that's too much money, let's give him half of that amount.

"Well, you can appreciate how unfair that would be. Just as you can appreciate when His Honor asked you last week or a week ago, two weeks ago on Monday and Tuesday if you find that Mr. Ziarki is entitled to recover in this lawsuit, will you have any hesitancy in finding a verdict in millions of dollars? Each and every one of you when inquired or questioned put your hand on your heart and you signed your oath and you said you would have no hesitancy in signing millions of dollars if this man were entitled to it.

"So all the—I'm not going to suggest that my client, although he certainly should be entitled to the same evaluation as a Picasso, I'm suggesting that the fact that a Picasso is worth $53 million doesn't scare people today any more than rich horses, expensive horses, or baseball contracts, or basketball contracts, or football contracts.

"The term millions of dollars today means millions of dollars. It doesn't mean we will assess it in terms of what we will earn, it doesn't mean we will assess it in we can work the rest of our lives and never get it. That's not the issue.

"The issue is of the law. The law that you have sworn to uphold will allow you to reach such a verdict.

"And in this case, ladies and gentlemen, I know that you have said that you will reach a conclusion that consists with the law and is consistent with the evidence."

COMMENT:

Counsel covered liability before reaching this part of his final. He then talked about big dollars in terms of paintings, racehorses, and baseball players. Then he reminds them of their promise to follow the law.

"Now, we know that life is a succession of activities. We know as we go through each and every day we are able to do things, we are able to get up in the morning, we are able to make coffee, we are able to carry that coffee into the john. If we want we can watch television if we have time. We can get on a bus and come to work and we go to work and do all of the things one after another without even thinking of what is or is not within the purview of what our bodies can do for us.

"The human body is our servant. The human body allows us and makes us able to do things. If that body has been interfered with and we are disabled, the court—the law says you are entitled to recover damages in those amounts not as we who are healthy would imagine to be, but what the evidence is. And in this case it's uncontradicted what the evidence is.

"Now, ladies and gentlemen, in this case as Dr. McCray said, this man was incredible. Those are not Corboy's, those words are Dr. McCray's words. This man is incredible. This is the fellow, for a lack of a better word, who was macho. He was very, very athletic. He was very proud of his body. He bowled, he played baseball, he skied, he did all of those things which a person who is proud of his body was able to do. And he did it for 29 years.

"You know that he played baseball as often as he could. He has a very, very good fortune in playing baseball, he met his wife. So baseball was good to him and he was good to baseball. And he had a lot of fun doing it.

"The absence of that fun is a disability. The absence of opportunities to go out and slide into third base, even if most of us don't want to do it, is a disability. And this disability is something that is a function that we have to analyze in terms of what is this good and decent man now doing, that he tries to do—I should say, that he cannot do because of this loss of a leg."

COMMENT:

Counsel talks of the human body, of the wonderful things it can do, then the wonderful things it CANNOT do following an injury.

"And, ladies and gentlemen, I think probably he assessed it better than anybody else when he said to you in answer to one of my—the last question I put to him, what do you notice about yourself the most that you are not compared to the way you were before? And he didn't give an elaborate answer, he gave a very simple direct statement; I just don't feel competitive.

"Meaning he can't compete with those of us who have a full body. He can't do the things that those of us can do with the body that our God gave us, whether we have developed it into a better body than other people is not important."

COMMENT:

Not having a "full body" is a big part of the damages in this case.

"I respectfully suggest that with reference to this question of disability assessing it on a lump basis, keep in mind he is going to live approximately 36 years. I respectfully suggest that the figure $3,600,000 would be fair and reasonable for the disability that this man has incurred and will incur for the rest of his life for three and a half decades, plus the six or seven years since he got hurt on May 26, 1982."

COMMENT:

Now, counsel is ready to talk about dollars.

"We know that this man below his waist is a half man. It's just that simple. Unless you want to call his three or four inch stub more than half, more than a quarter. He is a half man below his waist. He will always be the guy who walks real funny.

"Ron, I hope you understand I have to say these things.

"He is always going to be the guy who doesn't have a limp, he has a throw. He throws his leg. He is always going to be the guy who has a cane in his hand or a guy who has crutches in his hands. And when he gets on a bus, if he is fortunate, he is the guy that people make way for."

COMMENT:

Counsel pictures a man who is a "half man" below the waist, he does it dramatically, and thoughtfully apologizes to his client for having to do this, saying, "Ron, I hope you understand."

"Now, the word pain—we will talk about suffering in a moment. But the word pain is so easy to say. The word pain, p-a-i-n. Most people do what they can to forget about pain whether that pain is as a result of the death of a loved one or whether that pain is the result of a loss of a limb or whether that pain is a result of the loss of an identity or self-image or whether that pain is something that is alien to all of us except that person who has it. All of us try to forget about it.

"Every day of his life as he puts his stump up on that sink as he is shaving he is going to remember the pain and suffering that has been with him since May 26, 1982."

COMMENT:

Counsel talks about pain.

"And don't forget he has been—he has had nine hours and 20 minutes of surgery. He has had six specific operations. One in which they whittled away until they got a ham bone out of it. The next one there was an infection. The next one when there was another infection, they had to get the pus out of it. The next one when there was an infection in his left leg. And then finally in August of 1984—1984 his last of six operations where they had to remodel the stump.

"And as the prosthetist told you, it was like starting all over again. He has an actual new amputation two years after this occurrence. Twenty-six months later, they started all over. And the pain and the suffering is continuing until today. Today."

COMMENT:

Counsel talks about surgery.

"He has told you and other people have told you that he is embarrassed. He is embarrassed. He is embarrassed because he doesn't have a leg. The most indolent, the most cautious, the most inactive person would miss a leg.

"But when you're an active physical human being—remember he cried in the hospital when his truck driver pal came in to see him because he was embarrassed. Just like he is going to be embarrassed when that new person comes into his family and that new person, when he or she grows up is going to see that daddy goes through constant pain and is aware that he is different. Cognizant of difference."

COMMENT:

Counsel shows dramatically what it means to have a missing leg.

"The costs of legs go up seven percent every year. And they are going to be up seven percent every year for the five years. So that the next time he has a limb to buy, it's not going to cost him $10,000, but five years from now it's going to cost $14,000, and that's uncontradicted. And ten years from now it's going to cost $19,000. And in 15 years it's going to be $27,000. And in 20 it's going to be 38. And in 25 it's 54. And in 30 it's 76. And 35 years from now, 35 years from now it's going to cost $106,000.

"Now, you may say, boy, that's almost unreal. Well, all we have to do is go back to those figures. And since that happened from 1909 to 1989 and see that average wages went from $500 a year, a dollar and a quarter a day, $3,500 a year, up to $20,000—$21,000 a year for 1988. So you can see the jumps that have happened.

"And I respectfully suggest that you do not have to ignore that testimony that was supplied to you by the witness that was brought in by the Railroad from Loyola University, a reputable institution in our community and reputable man who came in and told you what he thought would be the truth.

"If you add up all those costs, add up all those costs for the limbs, then it's uncontradicted that he is going to be required to pay $337,148 for it. You can say well, that's an awful lot of money for a fake leg.

"If you think it is, then you just ignore the testimony of the man that they brought in who used his calculator. And if he had made any mistake or the calculation was off, you would have heard an examination of him which would have changed his figures."

"Now, I do not suggest that those limbs entitle him to $338,000. Why? Because $338,000 has to be reduced to present cash value, and that's your job. That's why that man was brought in to assist you. And I respectfully suggest he did assist you and you bring this in. That simply means how much money will it take today to equal $347,000 which into the future, specifically, 36 years from now when he gets his seventh new limb."

COMMENT:

> This is a tedious part of the argument, but notice how effectively it can be done. IT MUST BE DONE! This is a big part of the damages and big damages in one part of the trial adds credibility to big damages in other parts of the trial. Counsel continued this part of his argument in greater detail, then talked about loss of income and earning capacity.

"He would only be making $40,000 a year today. And we know that $40,000 stretched out for the next 30 years—first, I wanted to supply the Figure 29 to their witness, but then I remembered that the Exhibit, the Exhibit that has the lost earnings on it only goes up to the year 1988.

"So it actually is one more year. It's this year because the 29 years that he works, no man works, no woman works, no person works throughout his or her lifetime in today's life in this country. Most people quit work at 65.

"And I think he is entitled to having his future damages assessed in the area of where he would work until 65.

"Now, at $40,000 a year with the increments that were reasonable according to the expert that was supplied to you by the Railroad and Mr. Dobbelaere, who, by the way, is very familiar with unions, uncontradicted. He is familiar with the labor movements, uncontradicted. He is familiar with how wages have gone up since 1909, uncontradicted.

"And I asked him to compare and give the same type of raises in the future that Mr. Ziarki got in the past and if you remember, he said that $14,000 a year, $14,000, excuse me, $40,000 a year would be a total, total dollars lost of $3 million. That's with the increments. That's with the increments. That's with the increments of earning seven percent or six percent or five percent or whatever the figure was. It was $3 million that he could have earned in the future for the rest of his working life expectancy.

"However, he has to reduce that to present cash value as I have to, and he gave an answer to it. I think you can accept his figure. His figure was reducing that figure to $988,429—$998,429.

"Now, that's the figure that he would have lost if he had lost $40,000 a year. But he is not going to lose $40,000 a year. He is back at work. So we certainly can't claim that he is going to lose $998,000, that would not only insult your intelligence, but certainly would invite a criticism to which I am not looking.

"So this $998,000 has to be reduced by whatever amount of dollars you think he will earn in the future. He is not making $26,000 or 27 with his bonus, $27,500 I guess it is, so that's about 65 percent of the $40,000 using that same formula if you were to assume that he is going to remain working. You would take about 65 percent off of this $998,000 because he is making 26 over 40 which is about the percentage. Sixty-five percent."

COMMENT:

Counsel explains what his client would have received in income in a way jurors can understand and makes it clear he is being very fair.

"Your damages have to be fair and they have to be reasonable. Not having no justification, and that's what he is suggesting. Give a million dollars or $2 million, whatever he is suggesting. What he really wants, what he really wants, is for you to say, well, these fellows have asked a proper compensation of somewhere in the neighborhood of $8 or $9 million for Mr. Ziarko and I'm going to suggest $1 or $2 million and maybe they will come right in the middle, maybe they will come right in the middle and that will make me happy, me meaning my Railroad.

"I think that's the suggestion that's being given to you. I think that's the suggestion that you are being asked to bite. Well, you can bite or you can wait to bite or it's your responsibility to not bite.

"Either way you have to follow the law. If biting means following the law, then you have to do it. But I respectfully suggest that if you follow the law, that young man is entitled to several million dollars on a rational, logical, and reasonable basis. Not on the statement that I have no justification for it. And not on the statement that it sounds like a lot of money.

"Now, you have been very, very respectful to all of us. You have allowed us to intrude again on your lunch hour. You will be eating soon and I apologize for taking as long as I have. I hope I haven't repeated things. I hope I haven't bored you. I have done my best to represent my client. And I want you to know that at this stage of this proceeding, I feel very honored to represent the Ziarkos. I think they are very honorable people. Keep that in mind.

"It was suggested here this morning, keep in mind it was suggested here this morning as to what he might have been doing not for 30 seconds, but for a minute and a half. What he might have been doing is something that he didn't say in court and they are making up that he said, they are dreaming up.

"If you believe that, then they are accusing Ron Ziarko of being a liar. It's just that simple. If that happened as they dreamed up, then that young man is a liar. And that's what they are calling him. In pleasant, courteous, quiet tones they are calling him a liar.

"Now, you have seen him. You saw him examined here. You saw how he admitted what he said and what he did and what he didn't do. He didn't beat around the bush when they asked was your truck on the tracks. He said I must have been—I got hit. Well, it wouldn't have happened if they followed that rule.

"Now, they said they are trying to find out what happened. That's why they are taking all those pictures. Well, here's what happened. They have told you what happened. And on Plaintiff's Exhibit Number 13 you have seen it. I won't get into it again. You have seen it, that's what happened.

"I respectfully suggest that they are saddled with what happened. And based upon that saddle, I think you will find that my client is entitled to several million dollars and not any of it cut just because a lawyer says I don't have any justification but cut it please so I can look good.

"Thank you, ladies and gentlemen."

COMMENT:

Counsel began the second half of his final argument rebutting opposing counsel's argument. Then he concludes with argument that covers liability and damages. Notice how he picked up something opposing counsel said about one or two million dollars and uses it as a bottom figure and pleads not to cut the two figures in half and end up with a compromise verdict.

These excerpts from a thorough final argument give the reader an excellent view of a great trial lawyer in action. Every trial lawyer has his own style, but the style of Philip Corboy is one that is so outstanding, and so basically sound, that it deserves close scrutiny by other trial lawyers.

[5.56] Great Trial Lawyers: Murray Sams—Half Justice Is No Justice. Justice is a term most often used in criminal cases, but those who fight for the injured know what justice means in a civil case. No lawyer knows this better than Murray Sams, for many years one of the nation's leading trial lawyers.

I have chosen a recent case in which Murray Sams talked about "half justice" being no justice. Notice how he begins:

"The lawyers always say to you, and I say to you, that this is a common-sense proposition. When you go back in that jury room, think of it as your living room and talk over all these things, and then you are going to come back in here with what you feel is a fair verdict."

COMMENT:

He pictures jurors sitting around their living room discussing the case, and this is how jurors will picture it.

"Any bodily injury—this is what you may make an award for—any bodily injury sustained by the plaintiff, Angela Cunningham, and any resulting pain and suffering, disability, disfigurement, mental anguish, and the loss of capacity for the enjoyment of life in the past and to be experienced in the future.

"There is no exact standard for measuring such damages. The amount should be fair and just and in light of the evidence.

"Now, this case, when you look at this child's leg, is, to me, beyond tragic. It is pitiful. It is pitiful that this girl who had so many things—now, remember, this is her life. She had the ability to do these things she loved and enjoyed, and now they are gone.

"As far as I am concerned, to have to go through life with that type of thing is a total destruction."

COMMENT:

Early in his argument, counsel stresses the seriousness of the injuries. He uses such phrases as "pitiful," "beyond tragic," and "total destruction."

"Robert is entitled to a loss of consortium. That means loss of enjoyment—the relationship of the marriage—from 1979–1982, a period of three years that he lost his wife. She was off being cared for by the family because that is what had to be, and they became divorced during that period of time. He is entitled to recover for whatever you feel is fair."

COMMENT:

Counsel covers the awkward question of consortium, not playing it up, yet not dismissing its importance.

"They talk about work, her having to go to work. Now, I want you to get this in perspective because what they are saying is that these losses she sustained because of the work before, she ought to be back now with this leg like it is and put in hours each day in order to reduce the amount of damages that they would have to pay. That is really what it amounts to. That is what it amounts to.

"This girl should not have to go back to work. She is embarrassed, humiliated, and in pain. She is frightened, and there is just no question in my mind that they can say to her, "We did this to you. We are the ones who did it. Go back to work."

"Not one soul testified to this jury, not one person, that she should go back to work, that it would be good to go back to work.

"She said she would like to go back to work, and she would like not to have this problem with the leg and the physical therapy.

"Not one soul has come in and said she should go back to work.

"All they say is that she can, that, physically, she could fight to do that certain limit. She cannot walk without these crutches. She does not know if that non-union will ever heal.

COMMENT:

This is how Murray Sams talks with the jury. Notice how effectively he makes it so clear that there is no way she should have gone back to work.

"I am always appalled at the low value that all of us place on human life.

"If there was a building that were destroyed, if there were a painting, if it were—say somebody had 20 million dollars' worth of insurance, and he came in here and said the insurance company would not pay, there is not a living soul on this jury that is going to say, 'What is he going to do with it?' We do not ask that.

"If I lend somebody a million dollars or ten million dollars or a bank does and gets a note in return, and I come in here for a debt owed, I say, 'Here is the note. They owe it.' The jury does not say, 'What are they going to do with this money?'

COMMENT:

Counsel makes it clear the defendant owes this money, and what to do with it is no one's business. He doesn't point a finger, but says "all of us" place too low a value on human life. I think the jury understands why we should be "appalled" at this.

"If you bought a Volvo today, it is 30,000 bucks. If you go forward 41 years, you are in the year 2030, and what is an automobile going to cost then? Run this back for 41 years and ask yourselves, in 1950, what that car cost.

"I mean, we were not born yesterday, folks. The cars cost—at that time, the same automobile was bought for five or six thousand dollars. The cost will be five times that. That is what we are talking about."

COMMENT:

Notice how effectively counsel uses the purchase of an automobile to show inflation. Every juror can understand this.

"You could make that happen. You never—you will never have another chance in your lifetime to do anything as good as you have a chance to do today for somebody who is deserving. She did nothing wrong."

COMMENT:

Bringing back an adequate verdict is described as a "chance of a lifetime." Talk with friends who have served on a jury. They will tell you they wanted most to do something right and something worthwhile.

"Do not settle this case for them. Do not come in here and make some compromise judgment because they come in with a lower figure. Do not say, 'Well, cut it in half' or 'give her less.' Half justice is no justice at all."

COMMENT:

"HALF JUSTICE IS NO JUSTICE AT ALL!" That is the theme of the lawsuit, and that has been driven home effectively by one of the nation's leading trial lawyers. That is the kind of argument that has enabled Murray Sams to obtain multimillion dollar verdicts.

[5.57] Great Trial Lawyers: Roxanne Conlin—Asking For A Million Dollars. When the *National Law Journal* named Roxanne Conlin one of the nation's ten best female trial lawyers, it recognized her as not just an outstanding woman lawyer, but also as one of the best of all trial lawyers. About the same time, the American Trial Lawyers Association slated her to become its 1992–93 President.

I have chosen as an example of Roxanne Conlin's argument to a jury a case in which she asked the jury for more than a million dollars. This case is a perfect example of a great trial lawyer obtaining credibility by communicating to the jury a sincere belief in her lawsuit.

She began by reminding the jury of the importance of its role in the lawsuit:

"You are performing a service of the highest order. Now, an opportunity like this doesn't come always to people, and you may not right at this moment, at ten after six on Thursday night, think this is just the greatest thing in the world that's ever happened to you, but, indeed, your service as jurors makes you an essential component of the system by which we live."

COMMENT:

> Notice phrases like "of the highest order," "an opportunity like this doesn't come always to people," and "an essential component of the system." It includes a word like "people" that every trial lawyer should use and a few other words that fit right into this lawyer's style.

"I've been trying to give you what I believe to be evidence on the explicit things that we must prove. No blue smoke and mirrors from this side of the table. I want you to understand what it is you need to find and nothing else.

"This matter of Clark's testimony, of course, I know this must be of some concern to you. Your decision to believe Clark does not condone what he did. He did not tell the truth, by his own admission, in a deposition with a bunch of us present.

"I don't condone that. Nobody condones that. That's not supposed to happen. But, ladies and gentlemen of the jury, before he sat before you on the witness stand, he retracted what he said. He said he told you the truth. He told you what be believed to be the facts.

"Clark is not on trial here. He is not. You don't need to determine anything about Ron Clark. I think he's believable because his testimony before you from this witness stand is corroborated by practically everybody.

"Who says he was drunk? He says he was drunk, Dougherty says he was drunk, Julie says he was drunk, Bill Christensen says he was drunk. I can hardly believe that they are seriously contending that he was not drunk."

COMMENT:

> Early in the argument, counsel accomplishes two things, the "telling of the story," and the facing up to any possible weakness in that story.

"Clark's own testimony was, with respect to whether or not he was intoxicated, that he always got in trouble. He quit drinking because he noticed that he always got in trouble when he was drinking.

"He was certainly in a lot of trouble that night. I simply cannot believe that there is a serious question as to whether or not Ron Clark was drunk at the time he purchased beer at the Western Convenience Store.

"I know of no evidence at all that he was drunk and then sobered up. This is a man who told you he was just drinking right along, right along, and he was drinking the beer he bought at Western.

"I have often thought in the course of this matter that I was trying a completely different case from that being tried by the Defense. I have wondered about the relevance of some of the material that was proved. I understand now that it is asserted that because Mr. Clark didn't—allegedly did not run any stoplights, that he wasn't drunk.

"I can't believe it. Keep in mind we have to prove to you he did buy beer. Yes, of course he did; of course he did. Was he drunk at the time? Yes. He was drunk at the time that he bought the beer. He kept on drinking the beer, and this awful accident happened."

COMMENT:

Counsel has now pinned down the factual situation.

"Now, why are you sitting in judgment on Western and not on Clark, not on 7-Eleven, when maybe he bought his last beer there? That is the concept of joint and several liability that I talked with you about earlier. I may not have made that very clear, however, so I want to try it again.

"In the lifeboat example, if the boat goes down, a person who loses—the estate of a person who loses the life in that may, of course, feel that the boat manufacturer, owner or line was negligent and sue that person and get compensation from that person, from the boat people. But if they get in the lifeboat and the lifeboat springs a leak, they might sue that person and get compensation from that person and not sue the boat people. Don't have to.

"And in fact, when the injuries are indivisible, if the boat goes down and the lifeboat springs a leak and the life jacket won't inflate, any one of those three things, those are all contributing causes. Any one of them could have been said to have caused—to have been the proximate cause of the injury alone. And that's the point here, alone, the Western's activities. Western's activities is what was the proximate cause of the injuries of Rick Gail and his family.

"One thing that I want to make sure that you understand is that this drawing of the squad car—Rick wants me to make sure you understand it. He drew his squad car into the roadway. He had the right-of-way, you know. The stop sign was for Clark, and he ran it.

COMMENT:

> Now that the factual situation has been established, counsel applies the law to that factual situation and does so effectively in a way the jury will understand it.

"Earning capacity, the ability to work in the work world, in the work force. There's no question about it. That's what the court will tell you. Now, that's one kind of thing. Please do not misunderstand me. The loss of Rick Gail's profession, his life dreams don't go as a part of the loss of earning capacity. It goes into the element of pain and mental anguish. That's where it goes. Loss of earning capacity is different.

"Now, I want to talk with you about the exhibit that Mr.—or, the material that Mr. Stefani had. According to his numbers, of course, it won't be 41 years as clergyman. It will only be 37. We know that because of the fact that he's got to do four years of college, at least four years of college, so we know that. But even using his numbers, there's a loss of over $300,000 using his numbers and his median.

COMMENT:

> Now counsel is ready to talk about damages, and begins with a strong part of her damage case, "earning capacity."

"Consortium, what is it? We're not contending that Rick and Janet Gail have lost their love for one another, that their relationship has been ruined. That is not the fact, but physically, he is not the same person. He's not. And she is entitled to compensation for that. He's been hurt. He can't mow the lawn. He can't shovel the snow. He can't make love.

"With respect to his children, it's quite the same thing with a father who can't take his kids sledding in the winter, can't wrestle with Neal, and they are entitled to compensation for those things. Hard work and industry and thrift, those are the things that we all think of, if you do that, that's the way to succeed, part of our American dream. If you work hard, if you're industrious, if you save your money, you'll make it. Rick Gail did all that. He did every single one of those things, and it's all gone in that grinding crash."

COMMENT:

Consortium has always been a problem for the trial lawyer. Here it is handled well, not making a "big deal" of it and explaining it so the jury will understand.

"Rick Gail has been, in his life, a hero to his friends, to his colleague, to the people whose lives and property he saved in the course of his career, to his family. But he's not a police officer anymore. He is, however, still a hero. He refuses to give up. He refuses to give in to these crippling injuries. He keeps trying. He's a fighter. He isn't going to quit. He's battled the odds, and he's going to keep on battling the odds. He wants to be all right. He wants to become a minister. He wants to make a contribution to society. He has a right to choose what he will do, not Marian Jacobs.

COMMENT:

The jury now knows the leading character of this courtroom drama and they know he "refuses to give up." He is not whining or complaining, he merely wants justice and is the kind of "guy" who deserves it.

"I asked you before and I ask you again to give Rick Gail 1.49 million dollars, $1,490,000, and I ask you to give his wife, Janet, $200,000 for their very substantial losses in this case. I ask you that without any embarrassment at all, and you should not be concerned about what others will say about your verdict, about whether they'll say it was a large verdict or a small verdict. That is not your concern. Your concern is only is it a just verdict, does it do justice to the Gails? That is your only concern.

"If you get back to that jury room and someone says, 'Boy, I just don't think we ought to do that; that is just too much,' please remind them and remember that that is not your consideration. It is only what is just.

COMMENT:

Now counsel has prepared the jury for the million dollar request. The jury is ready.

"When you reach your decision, you will go back to your jobs and your families and your lives, and you may not think of this case very often. I hope you'll think of it some, but you probably won't think of it every day. Rick and Janet Gail will think of it every day. They'll think of it when Rick can't do something that he wants to do. They'll think about it when he's not out sledding, if he's not out at all, because the weather's too bad. They'll think of it often. And when they think of it and when they think of you, I know that they will think that you were fair, because I know that you will be.

"Thank you."

COMMENT:

> This is the end of the first half of counsel's final argument. Too often a lawyer will end the first half of final with "I'll be back in a few minutes to continue." The beauty of this ending is that if opposing counsel, for some unknown reason, did not give a final, the jury would have been treated to the kind of closing that usually comes with the "final five." Getting "off stage" at half-way with drama IS important!

"Oliver Wendell Holmes was a great jurist, and he said this about strict liability: 'The safest way to assure care is to throw the risk upon the person who decides what precaution should be taken.'

"In this case it was Western. You decide what are working lungs worth. You decide what pain and suffering is worth. You decide what consortium is worth, but you must give full justice. If you give only—if you say, well, she asked for 1.49 million dollars and you say, well, shoot, that's really quite a bit. Let's just do half of that.

"If you believe and you think the evidence has shown and you think he's entitled to 1.49 million dollars and you only give him half of that, you've done 50 percent justice and 50 percent injustice. It has to be a full award, a total award, all of it. You have to do all of it. Nobody else—nobody else will ever get a chance to decide what these working lungs are worth.

"This award is through the good times and the bad times, through the ups and the downs of the economy. It's forever for Rick Gail. We never get to come again, not next week. We can't come back, you know, and say to another jury at another time, well, it wasn't enough; it turns out that the lung went bad faster than even the doctors thought, turns out that Rick Gail was in a wheelchair in five years, turns out that he couldn't work, he couldn't get through college. We can't come back and say that. We cannot.

"This is it. This is the only time, and you are the only people who make this decision. Not the Judge, not me, not Rick, not anybody else. Just eight people, who never saw this man before, are going to decide what kind of a future he has. You know that the magnitude of his losses are very, very great, and I trust that you will follow your oath and do him full justice.

"Thank you."

COMMENT:

Now, for the REAL "final five" and the million dollar verdict. When you ask for a multimillion dollar verdict, do it with the expertise of a great trial lawyer.

[5.58] Great Trial Lawyers: Tom Malone—Making The Medically Negligent Pay. Those of us who have been trying lawsuits for forty-plus years remember the REAL medical malpractice crisis. That was when a doctor or hospital was immune from being sued for damages because of restrictive laws and the absolute refusal of doctors to testify against doctors.

Much of this remains, but doctors and hospitals are being sued with much more success. No one can argue in favor of any lawsuit that is frivolous or for any reason not justified, but in medical negligence litigation there is a safeguard against this. Attorneys who would take all the $50,000 auto accident cases they can get, simply cannot afford to handle a $50,000 medical negligence case because of the cost of experts and other expenses.

It has been suggested that the present "crisis" began when doctors quit making house calls and started charging large fees in crowded waiting rooms. The same man who formerly asked the doctor to stay for dinner was late for dinner himself after waiting an hour after the time of his appointment and was ready to sue someone.

Sue a city doctor? Maybe. Sue a country doctor? Never. That was the feeling among lawyers who expected to win medical negligence cases, once medical negligence cases became winnable. Winning against country doctors and hospitals became possible through the efforts of such outstanding trial lawyers as Tom Malone, now of Atlanta.

In one lawsuit, Tom Malone sued the only anesthesiologist in a rural South Georgia community of less than 40,000 people. Once liability was established, the real problem was getting people on the jury to think in large figures. Let's look at the final argument in this case:

"You can just say you've got 77 years. Well, I know the number is large, but one way you might want to approach is the right to life. That's $770,000. Now, that's a lot of money.

"The Judge is going to charge you that you are to place, when you get to this point in your deliberations, a dollar amount that is equal to the full value, full value, of the life of this child had she lived without deductions for necessaries or other expenses, the full value of her life.

"It doesn't say award something you think everybody will be happy with. The law, the law you swore to follow, swore to uphold even if you might disagree with it, was to award the full value of her life and it's the full value of her life that we're considering.

"Now, if you want to just disregard what the Judge says, disregard the commitment you made to me as jurors, you can set up any kind of arbitrary standard you want. We can't go in that jury room and find out, but you took an oath before we even started talking to you that you would follow the law in this case. The law in this case is, if you award us a penny, you award us an amount equal to the full value of the life of Adrienne Nicole Kisner.

"Now, you know, so how do you decide, you know, what the full value of her life is? Well, it's the full value of her life, and the Judge is going to charge you this, it's the full value of her life to herself, not to her parents, but to herself. What is a life worth to a human being? I think anytime you deal with that figure, it's got to be enormous. Human life is valuable."

COMMENT:

Notice that counsel immediately talks about a "lot of money," but reminds jurors of their oath to follow the law.

"This is a wrongful death action and our legislature could have said, as some states do, that if you prove a case in a wrongful death action you get $100,000. They could have said you get $500,000 and half goes to the state. They could have said anything they wanted to, but they said, and it's in the law of our state, hasn't been any change at all in the way you measure compensation to be returned in a wrongful death case. It's the full value of the life as determined by the enlightened conscience of twelve impartial jurors without regard to the consequences of their verdict, but a truthful verdict."

COMMENT:

Counsel then pins down the question of the law.

"Now, this figure, the 235, you know, that's just with eight hours work at only $5,000, and that's just what you earn by the sweat of your brow, maybe eight hours a day, maybe that's part-time four hours a day; but, consider these things: her ability to earn, her right to earn.

"You know, that's just out-of-pocket stuff. It's just a small part of somebody's value. I would hate to think that my value is limited to only the money that I could make.

"Certainly the enjoyment that a person has getting up in the morning, certainly the enjoyment that Adrienne Nicole Kisner would have had loving her mama and loving her daddy and playing their screaming game and enjoying her first party dress, enjoying her first kiss, let's think about these things and they're the things that go into the value of a person.

"From their selfish standpoint, it's what they would have enjoyed, what they would have a right to do. You can say, if you want, it was just a kid, just a kid, you know. Everybody's got one. They tried to do something about that. So, they got another child.

"I'll tell you what I'd say is best to do. This little girl could have grown up loving her brother. She could have grown up enjoying every day playing kick-the-can and just things like that, the wonder of human life; but, when it's taken away carelessly, carelessly, our law says you must be compensated, and I think that what you have to do to honor your oath as jurors is decide what is the fair value of the life of this child for herself.

"You can say, well, maybe she'd have gotten run over. Well, that's not fair. You know, maybe she wouldn't have lived to be twelve and she might live to be a hundred. She might live to be fifty. This is about a reasonable way to determine how long she'd be expected to live, just what's reasonable as we sit here today and think what would have happened had she gotten good care before now.

COMMENT:

This is an excellent telling of the value of human life. Counsel does not let the jury use opposing counsel's criterion.

"Well, the figure should be large. Wrongful death actions are compensatory so far as the plaintiff is concerned, but punitive so far as the defendant is concerned. You must find your verdict in reaching a dollar amount equal to the full value of the life of this child, change the way some things are done, send the message out that you must make good charts, you must have a blood pressure. If you want to send the message out, keep on doing it just like you did in the Kisner case, just walk back there and don't waste any time and come back in here with a verdict for the defendant.

"If you approve of what has happened and think this is good anesthesia care, find for the defendant and encourage them to keep on doing what they're doing, encourage these respected members of the community to not know within fifty minutes or forty minutes whether or not an IV was established. The idea, the idea of people who occupy positions of trust being able to have a scenario with that much conflict.

"Please think about it. When life and death is in their hands, it's not a game. It's serious. It is time that the conscience of the community puts an end, speak to them, send a message."

COMMENT:

Notice how counsel talks about "full value of the life of this child," "send the message out," and "conscience of the community," ending with again, "send a message." This, of course, requires certain evidence and legal authority that depends upon the jurisdiction.

"If somebody on the streets were to say, and you have to worry about things like this, were you on that jury that awarded a million dollars for the life of that four-month-old baby? You know what your answer was, yeah, I was. Yes, I was. I got the case.

"I might not have liked dealing with those numbers. I might have personally thought that was just too much money in any case, but the Judge told us that we had to award an amount equal to the full value of the life of that human being without any deduction and it was the full value of her life to herself, and if you want to criticize me. . . . Somebody will ask you. Are you telling me that your life's not worth a million dollars or her life. . . . What was her life worth if it wasn't worth a million dollars?

"Get their attention by being fair."

COMMENT:

Fairness, regard for life and a duty to do what is right under the law forms an effective conclusion to this argument. The jury returned a verdict of $600,000 for the wrongful death of a four-month-old child in a rural community.

[5.59] Great Trial Lawyers: Bob Gibbins—Suing The Manufacturer. Bob Gibbins, a past president of ATLA, is one of the many great trial lawyers of Texas. One of his important cases was a $3.5 million verdict against McDonnell-Douglas in 1981.

He explained the problem so the jury could understand it:

"As a pilot I would say before I would assume the risk of an ejection I would have a right to know and expect what those risks are that I am assuming. If I eject in the envelope, within their advertisement, and do everything according to procedures just like I'm told to do and taught to do, first you control the aircraft and that is why he was still holding onto that control stick when he ejected.

"Every one of these pilots had to admit the first requirement is to control the aircraft. Then he ejected. But, if I am going to eject in their envelope and do everything I was trained to do under the circumstances, then I have a right to expect to survive, or I will stay with my aircraft and try to use my skills to survive a crash landing. Or, maybe unjam it.

In other words, ladies and gentlemen, these ejections, they can't be just random crap shoots. He did everything he was trained to do and then they have the audacity in front of this widow and this little boy to say that he assumed the risk and misused that airplane. I say to you, find against that, or all of our efforts will have been wasted.

COMMENT:

Now, counsel is ready to ask the jury to send a message. Notice how effectively he does it.

"Send a message! Not just a message to McDonnell-Douglas in Los Angeles or Republic Fairchild in New York, but to all these government contractors. When our servicemen are going out there putting their lives in that equipment sold to the cheapest bidder, make them take safety into consideration.

"Number one, this aircraft was defective because it was unreasonably dangerous due to the flight control jam in the white area, and you must answer that affirmatively and that was a producing cause of Captain Wahl's death.

"And, it necessitated him ejecting with a defective, unreasonably designed seat that was used as a temporary thing without even adequate testing."

COMMENT:

Then counsel turned to the important issue of damages.

"I know we are suing for a lot of money. I know it. It is a substantial amount, but the losses in this case are substantial.

"And the benefits, not just to Dianne Wahl and Billy Wahl, but to the whole United States Air Force and the United States Navy is at stake, too. Five hundred thousand dollars, he would love it. They won't get the message. They spend that much on advertising probably in a short period of time.

"Again, all I can do, it is in evidence, he isn't here to tell you how he did it right, and there wasn't one pilot from either side who could get up here and look at that man's record and say to you that it was pilot error.

"But, what do they do? They try to sneak in the back door and say, well, you know, you have got to equate pilot error with defect. I told you they were skilled. I told you they were crafty pleaders of defendant's causes. All I know is we are right. We are right!"

The jury decided the plaintiff was, indeed, right!

[5.60] Great Trial Lawyers: Gene Pavalon—The Loss Of Parents. When Gene Pavalon sued the telephone company, he represented children whose parents were killed by the negligence of the company. This outstanding trial lawyer told the jury what this meant:

"Parents were killed and three children at the most critical times of their life were orphaned instantly at the ages when they needed their parents most. The girls needed their mother particularly the most. Twelve years old, puberty, just beginning to enter adolescense; fourteen, early adolescence; and sixteen, middle adolescence.

"Suddenly within a matter of minutes the family unit is totally destroyed and their parents are taken from them.

"So as was stated, this isn't just placing a dollar value on each one separately. You must consider the impact in terms of awarding fair and reasonable damages for the death of each by considering the fact that Penny and Chris and Karen lost it all.

"Their whole family was destroyed. Their lives were changed irreparably and irreversibly because of the loss of the society and companionship which I believe the court will tell you means the warmth, affection, the love, and the protection that parents provide and offer to the children. It was all taken from them on October 11th, 1980, because of the conduct of General Telephone."

COMMENT:

Counsel is now ready to discuss dollars. He turned to the value of parents.

"And if you consider the services and think about what it would cost to go to the marketplace, to pay for people or a person who would do the cooking, who would do the housekeeping, who would do the gardening, who would do the nursing, if you will, when the children are sick, who would do all of these things, even the chauffeuring, all of those services are available; you can find people who will do them for money, that would add up to a considerable sum.

"But, there would be one thing missing the most important thing of all in the delivery of services, and that is when they are performed by a loving mother and parent they have unique value which you can never purchase, never purchase in the marketplace. When they are taken from you, they are taken from you forever."

COMMENT:

Counsel then was ready to discuss punitive damages.

"Last and certainly equally as important, when you receive the instructions from his Honor you will also be told, as Mr. Mirza indicated, that you are to consider whether or not the conduct of the telephone company was willful or wanton.

"Meaning you are to consider whether or not their conduct indicated an utter indifference for the safety of others. "And if you so find that it did, then you are to award an additional sum by way of punishment and to deter others from doing the same.

"You heard their net worth. I suggest to you it is your decision to award what is fair and reasonable so as to accomplish this for the public safety."

COMMENT:

> Counsel does not just ASK for punitive damages, he gives the jury reason to get excited about the conduct of the defendant.

"What I have heard in this courtroom concerns me and I am still concerned. You will recall in my opening to you I mentioned that by the testimony, the way this case was tried by the defendant, the telephone company, was what I perceived to be a perpetuation of their arrogance in the way they conducted their telephone system, out in the field, with regard to their total lack of concern for the public safety. And, what I heard in their closing argument was a continuation of that arrogance."

COMMENT:

> What the jury knows about the defendant's conduct out in the field it knows second hand, but what it knows of defendant's conduct during trial it has seen and heard. Counsel effectively brought home out-in-the-field arrogance through the arrogance defendant showed in the courtroom. He then proceeded to pin down this point with specifics.

"If you recall, you heard counsel for the telephone company saying, 'We don't have to inspect every day. We don't have to inspect every year. If that cable across the highway is still standing there, that's all we have to do. It becomes everybody else's responsibility to do our work and discharge our responsibilities.

"The responsibility is put on the phone company, not only under the law, to exercise ordinary care for all people, but placed on them by a state agency that has the responsibility to be certain that the utilities, including the phone company, maintain its telephone system, maintain its communications line, for the public good."

COMMENT:

The value of parents and the arrogance of the defendant were hammered home effectively, and the result was a $36 million verdict against the telephone company.

[5.61] Great Trial Lawyers: Clarence Darrow—A Plea For Mercy. Irving Stone's *Clarence Darrow For The Defense* was many trial lawyers' first introduction to the courtroom. Darrow's plea for mercy in the *Loeb-Leopold* trial is still the classic by which all final arguments must be judged.

Darrow talked about people and history and our feelings. He even talked of war:

"Now, your Honor, I have spoken of the war. I believed in it. I don't know whether I was crazy or not. Sometimes I think perhaps I was. I approved of it; I joined in the general cry of madness and despair. I urged men to fight.

"I was safe because I was too old to go. I was like the rest. What did they do? Right or wrong, justifiable or unjustifiable—which I need not discuss today—it changed the world.

"For four long years the civilized world was engaged in killing men. Christians against Christians, barbarians uniting with Christians to kill Christians; anything to kill.

"It was taught in every school, aye in Sunday Schools. The little children played at war. The toddling children on the street. Do you suppose the world has ever been the same since then?"

COMMENT:

You can see Darrow developing his theme. He opposed capital punishment because he felt government should not be in the business of killing. He hit head-on the thought that government is justified in killing during times of peace because we sanction killing during times of war. He then turned to the by-product of war:

"I know that growing out of the Napoleonic wars there was an era of crime such as Europe had never seen before. I know that Europe is going through the same experience today; I know it has followed every war; and I know it has influenced these boys so that life was not the same to them as it would have been if the world had not been made red with blood.

"Your Honor knows that in this very court crimes of violence have increased growing out of war. Not necessarily by those who fought but by those who learned that blood was cheap, and human life was cheap, and if the State could take it lightly why not the boy?

There are causes for this terrible crime. There are causes, as I have said, for everything that happens in the world. War is a part of it; education is a part of it; birth is a part of it; money is a part of it, all these conspired to compass the destruction of these two poor boys."

COMMENT:

Darrow has now brought his argument down to the two boys before the court. He then talks about the boys, and the effect of this terrible incident upon their lives.

"I do not know how much salvage there is in these two boys. I hate to say it in their presence, but what is there to look forward to? I do not know but what your Honor would be merciful if you tied a rope around their necks and let them die; merciful to them, but not merciful to civilization, and not merciful to those who would be left behind. To spend the balance of their days in prison is mighty little to look forward to, if anything. Is it anything? They may have the hope that as the years roll around they might be released. I do not know. I do not know."

COMMENT:

Then Darrow defends against what he knows is the chief objection to life as opposed to death. Will they ever be released?

"I know that these boys are not fit to be at large. I believe that they will not be until they pass through the next stage of life, at forty-five or fifty. Whether they will be then, I cannot tell.

"I would not tell this court that I do not hope that some time, when life and age has changed their bodies, as it does, and has changed their emotions, as it does, that they may once more return to life. I would be the last person on earth to close the door of hope to any human being that lives, and least of all to my clients. But what have they to look forward to? Nothing. And I think here of the stanzas of Housman:

> "Now hollow fires burn out to black,
> And lights are fluttering low:
> Square your shoulders, lift your pack
> And leave your friends and go.
> O never fear, lads, naught's to dread,
> Look not left nor right:
> In all the endless road you tread
> There's nothing but the night.

"I care not, your Honor, whether the march begins at the gallows or when the gates of Joliet close upon them, there is nothing but the night, and that is very little for any human being to expect.

"I have stood here for three months as one might stand at the ocean trying to sweep back the tide. I hope the seas are subsiding and the wind is falling, and I believe they are, but I wish to make no false pretense to this court.

"The easy thing and the popular thing to do is to hang my clients. I know it. Men and women who do not think will applaud. The cruel and the thoughtless will approve. It will be easy today; but in Chicago, and reaching over the length and breadth of the land, more and more fathers and mothers, the humane, the kind and the hopeful, who are gaining an understanding and asking questions not only about these poor boys, but about their own, these will join in no acclaim to the death of my clients.

"These would ask that the shedding of blood be stopped, and that the normal feelings of man resume their sway. And as the days and the months and the years go on, they will ask it more and more.

"I know your Honor stands between the future and the past. I know the future is with me, and what I stand for here; not merely for the lives of these two unfortunate lads, but for all boys and all girls; for all the young, and as far as possible for all of the old.

"I am pleading for life, understanding, charity, kindness, and the infinite mercy that considers all. I am pleading that we overcome cruelty with kindness and hatred with love.

"Your Honor stands between the past and the future. You may hang these boys; you may hang them by the neck until they are dead. But in doing it you will turn your face toward the past.

"I was reading last night of the aspiration of the old Persian poet, Omar Kyayyam. It appealed to me as the highest that I can vision. I wish it was in my heart, and I wish it was in the hearts of all.

> So I be written in the Book of Love,
> I do not care about the book above,
> Erase my name or write it as you will,
> So I be written in the Book of Love."

[5.62] Great Trial Lawyers: Vincent Fuller—Arguing Insanity. What do you do when your client shoots the President of the United States in broad daylight with television cameras rolling? Vincent Fuller had but one defense, that of insanity, and that was what the John Hinckley, Jr. trial was all about.

An insanity trial is one in which you throw all other defenses to the wind. This is one case in which you can talk about the "bad" part of your client, and often that is an important part of your defense. In one insanity trial, I suggested to the jury that the time has not come when we accept my client's conduct as being normal.

In the Hinckley trial, Vincent Fuller spent considerable time giving the history of his client's problem:

"This defendant is unique in this sense: He lived a solitary life. He was a prisoner of himself for at least seven years before this tragedy, and I will address myself in a few moments to what he did as a prisoner in those seven years, but to call him an ordinary boy, an ordinary man, an all-American boy, is silly.

"I don't believe I need to track Mr. Hinckley's very disconnected college career—it was a semester here, a semester out—but I do think it is important to focus on several points in that career. First is the spring of 1976 when John Hinckley impulsively goes out, abruptly sells his automobile, and goes to California to become a rock star or a song writer. Unrealistic, absolutely unrealistic. He had not had one moment of training in music.

"And he believed he would come on the front of Hollywood and be an instant success. Needless to say, he was a total failure and it resulted in his depression, despair, and disappointment.

"He made another aborted effort, I believe in 1978, where the doctors testified he went to Nashville again with great expectations of being a rock star. Once again his hopes were dashed, because, obviously, these were unrealistic goals."

COMMENT:

Notice counsel's reference to defendant being a "prisoner of himself." Also, notice the descriptive phrases, "disconnected college career," "absolutely unrealistic," "total failure," "hopes were dashed," and "again with great expectations."

"I say to you that at that point in time, in October of 1980, this defendant's mental condition had deteriorated to such a state that he was unable to communicate his innermost thoughts to anyone.

"The slight effort he made, he gave a signal. He gave a written signal to Dr. Hopper that he was obsessed "with the woman I referred to last week."

"Jodie Foster.

"And I think, through no fault of Dr. Hopper's, he thought that was simply a young man's fancy with a movie actress. I do not believe he had the slightest appreciation of the seriousness and the intensity of John Hinckley's involvement with Jodie Foster and John Hinckley's unreal expectation that he would one day have a relationship with Jodie Foster.

"I think the failure of the defendant to reveal his activities through the months of October, November, December, and January, to Dr. Hopper are a reflection of Mr. Hinckley's inability to communicate."

COMMENT:

Then counsel talks about Jodie Foster, the center of the fantasy, and defendant's failure to communicate.

"The defendant goes to New Haven and, as you can reasonably expect, there is no relationship. No real relationship to be established with Miss Foster. And in reaction to that, I don't think a realistic reaction, but in reaction to that the defendant is angry. He is distressed.

"Again, the identification with the film "Taxi Driver," he thinks of a way to remedy this. His remedy then becomes to stalk President Carter, which he does on several occasions in October of 1980.

"And, as you know, he changes his focus of that stalking to President Reagan following the election in November.

COMMENT:

Now counsel turns to specific things that were different. The fact he had stalked President Carter, showed that it was not just someone after President Reagan, and that the problem was not a recent one.

"A very significant piece of evidence is the New Year's monologue of 1981. This is Mr. Hinckley speaking to a tape recorder:

> 'John Lennon is dead. The world is over. Forget it. It's just gonna be insanity, if I even make it through the first few days. I still regret having to go on with 1981. I don't know why people wanna live.
>
> 'John Lennon is dead. I still think—I still think about Jodie all the time. That's all I think about really. That, and John Lennon's death. They were sorta binded together.
>
> 'I hate New Haven with a mortal passion. I've been up there many times, not stalking her really, but just looking after her.
>
> 'I was going to take her away for a while there, but I don't know. I am so sick I can't even do that. It'll be total suicide city. I mean, I couldn't care less. Jodie is the only thing that matters now. Anything I might do in 1981 would be solely for Jodie Foster's sake.
>
> 'My obsession is Jodie Foster. I've gotta, I've gotta find her and talk to her some way in person or something. That's all I want her to know, is that I love her. I don't want to hurt her. I think I'd rather just see her not, not on earth, than being with other guys. I wouldn't want to stay here on earth without her.'

"That is not exhaustive, but it is representative, I believe, of the thinking of the defendant at that time. I think it reflects a very disturbed state of mind, a state of mind which is totally detached from reality."

COMMENT:

Here counsel lets his client help him prove his defense. For the jury to hear this in the very words of John Hinckley must have been impressive.

"Once again the defendant departs. He goes to New Haven. And he leaves a series of communications with Jodie Foster. They are bizarre. 'I love you six trillion times. Wait for me. I will rescue you.'

"In fact, these notes were so disturbing to Jodie Foster—you saw a videotape of her—that she turned those notes over to her Dean. She was so concerned. These were bizarre thoughts that were being expressed to her."

COMMENT:

Back to Jodie Foster and again using words of the defendant, himself.

"I submit to you that it is not possible to reconstruct, as the government physicians have tried to do, the minute-by-minute progression of the defendant's thought processes from the moment he left the Hilton until the moment he shot the President and the three other innocent victims.

"For any of us to reflect back some moment in time and try to attempt to think what we were thinking is almost an impossible task. And I suggest to you that the efforts of the psychiatrists to build the moment-by-moment thoughts that Mr. Hinckley was entertaining in those moments, half-hour between the time he arrived at the Hilton and the time he actually did the shooting is impossible.

"I suggest to you that the entire time that Mr. Hinckley was at the Hilton, the moment he saw the President, when he arrived, he was in such a deluded state he knew if you asked him "Is it right to shoot the President?" Undoubtedly he would say "You don't shoot people."

"But in his delusion, he is not aware of the humanity of those victims. They play a very minor role in his delusional state. They are merely means to the end, to the end he wishes to accomplish: to win the love and affection and establish the relationship with Jodie Foster."

COMMENT:

Notice how counsel handles the opposing experts. He explains a complex psychiatric situation in terms the jury can understand. Counsel then explained the stress of this totally rejected human being and then concluded:

"Dr. Dietz agreed that under periods of extreme stress, transient psychotic symptoms may be present in the mental disorders which he admitted the defendant suffered from. And I submit to you that the stress, accepting the government's analysis of the mental disorder, the mental disease, I submit to you that the stresses that had built up in this man through the end of March of 1980 reached psychotic proportions.

"I submit to you that this evidence demonstrates the government has failed in its burden of proving that this defendant was mentally responsible, that this defendant had the capacity to appreciate the wrongfulness of his conduct on March 30, 1981, that this defendant was able to conform his conduct to the requirements of the law.

"I submit the government has failed to meet that burden."

COMMENT:

Let's let the prosecution comment. "We didn't go through six weeks of trial to have a lawyer stand up here and tell you to forget about what happened. We didn't go through six weeks of trial to have a lawyer stand up here for two and one half hours and not make one mention of the charges in this indictment, did we?" [From Adelman's rebuttal.] Of course, with an insanity defense, it is not what is in the indictment. It is what is in the jury's mind when considering the mental state of the defendant." Jurors are just ordinary people who do not want anyone to "get by" with something, especially in the horrible incident that formed the basis of the Hinckley trial. Fortunately for America, however, jurors take their duties seriously and will do all they can to render a fair and just verdict, even to one who shot the President and permanently disabled a very popular Presidential aide. This is why the jury accepted the insanity plea.

[5.63] Great Trial Lawyers: Paul Armstrong—Arguing The Right To Die. Paul Armstrong's argument had to be given to the Supreme Court in the *Karen Quinlan* case. That did not demand less of counsel, but demanded as much drama and reason as any argument ever delivered to a jury. Setting forth the facts was a good place to start:

"Accepting that their daughter and sister, Karen Ann, now lies in a gradually deteriorating chronic vegetative state in the intensive care unit of St. Clare's Hospital; that there is a hopeless prospect of her cure through the art of medicine; counseled by their shared belief and the teachings of the Roman Catholic faith and supported by the love, faith, and courage unique to a father and mother, sister and brother, the Quinlan family now turns for guidance to the law personified in this Honorable Court.

"Uncontroverted and expert medical testimony adduced during the course of this trial has revealed that Karen Ann Quinlan has sustained massive and irreparable brain damage, and that she now lies in a persistent or chronic vegetative state in the intensive care unit of St. Clare's Hospital where, through the use of a mechanical respirator, her deteriorating bodily functions are maintained.

"Let no one falsely state that the Quinlans' plea is based solely upon human compassion. Indeed, it is grounded under the most fundamental principles of common law and the United States Constitution."

COMMENT:

In three quick paragraphs counsel contends the law and facts are on his side.

"The testimony offered at this trial leads us to the conclusion that medicine must be the servant of man; and that technology must be the servant of medicine. The proper role of a physician is to promote the unified function of an organism.

"The testimony has also shown that both the treating physicians and the consulted medical experts know of no treatment which can offer any hope of improvement, or even arrest the deterioration of her body. Indeed, it has been testified that were she to have a sudden hemorrhage, or require major surgical procedures, no doctor would take such measures.

"From such testimony, the use of the terms "physical best interests" assumes a new meaning. In such cases, further treatment can provide no medical benefit to the patient, and thus commanding its continuance will in no way further Karen's physical best interests. Surely the Court, charged with determining the best interests of Karen, cannot advance that her maintenance in this chronic vegetative state in any way serves her interests, let alone her best interest.

"Next, in determining Karen's moral best interests we ask the Court to take into account that complex of values and attitudes which recognize and give meaning to the term, 'dignity of man.' At present, Karen lies in St. Clare's Hospital, no more than 60 or 70 pounds of flesh and bone; a poor and tragic creature whose life is no more than a patterned series of the most primitive nervous reflexes, while in this court room it is seriously proposed, in the face of the most compelling contrary medical testimony, that her now disunified and unperceiving body be constrained to function against all its natural impulses.

"Could anything be more degrading to a human being— a human being who has come on this earth full of love and promise, who has now peace and joy, who has been the daughter of Joseph and Julia Quinlan? Can anything be more degrading, than to be offered up as a living sacrifice to the materialistic and misguided belief that death can somehow be cheated, if only we find the right combination of wires and gauges, transistors and tubes?"

COMMENT:

Notice how counsel puts medical science and the dignity of man on his side, before getting into legal argument.

"In addition the Court, acting as guardian, cannot fail to consider the tenets of the faith to which Karen belongs. That faith, which holds that life is good but not an absolute good, and that death is an evil but not an absolute evil, wisely teaches that man need not make use of extraordinary means to preserve earthly life. And, lastly, the Court as guardian must realize expenditures and liabilities incurred on behalf of an incompetent should carry with them some reasonable hope of benefit.

"All the evidence indicates that Karen will receive no benefit from continuation of treatment and, therefore, neither she nor her estate nor indeed society should be charged with the burden that continued treatment would entail."

COMMENT:

Reminding jurors of the importance of their duty is done in arguments throughout this book. Doing the same for the judge is equally important.

"The evidence has shown that Karen has expressed a desire not to be subjected to extraordinary medical treatment, and that the family as a group has decided that her wishes should be honored. The right of individuals to be sovereign over their own person was enunciated by the United States Supreme Court as early as 1891 in the case of *Union Pacific Railway Co. v. Botsford* and was extended to include familial autonomy in *Meyer v. Nebraska* and *Pierce v. Society of Sisters* in the early 1920s. It received its fullest exposition in the case of *Griswold v. Connecticut* which found support for the right to privacy in all the specific guarantees enumerated in the Bill of Rights as well as in the Ninth Amendment protection granted to unenumerated rights.

"This right has grown to include individual and familiar life-influencing decision, and it cannot be denied that a family is legally competent to make the decisions implicit in the plaintiff's request.

"Further, the plaintiff sets forth that the free exercise clause of the First Amendment, as applied to the State's Fourteenth Amendment, protects the right of Karen Ann Quinlan and her family to discontinue the futile use of extraordinary medical measures. Plaintiff contends that this request is the product of a religiously based decision, made in accordance with the tenets of the religion to which he and his family belong.

"The evidence has shown that the Quinlan family, including Karen Ann Quinlan, are members and believe in the Roman Catholic faith which teaches that, as stated in the discourse of Pius XII admitted into evidence: 'Natural reason and Christian morals say that man, and whoever is entrusted with the task of taking care of his fellow man, has the right and the duty in case of serious illness to take the necessary treatment for the preservation of life and health.'

"This duty that one has toward himself, toward God, toward the human community, and in most cases toward certain determined persons, derives from well-ordered charity, from submission to the Creator, from social justice, and even from strict justice, as well as from devotion toward one's family. But normally one is held to use only ordinary means, according to circumstances of persons, places, times, and culture. That is to say, means that do not involve any grave burden for oneself or another.

"A more strict obligation would be too burdensome for most men and would render the attainment of the higher, more important good, too difficult. Life, health, and temporal activities are in fact subordinated to spiritual ends. On the other hand, one is not forbidden to take more than the strictly necessary steps to preserve life and health, as long as he does not fail in some more serious duty."

COMMENT:

Now, the Court is ready for law and reason.

"As Pope Pius XII stated: 'In ordinary cases one will grant that the anesthesiologist has the right to act in this manner, but he is not bound to do so unless this becomes the only way of fulfilling another certain moral duty. The rights and duties of doctor are correlative to those of the patient.'

"The doctor, in fact, has no separate or independent right where the patient is concerned. In general, he can take action only if the patient explicitly or implicitly, directly or indirectly, gives him permission."

COMMENT:

Counsel has now squared his case with the Pope and the doctor.

"Here the State, in its case, has demonstrated no compelling interest in overcoming either the Quinlan's right of privacy, or their right to the free exercise of their religion."

COMMENT:

Any balancing of state interest against private rights is not even necessary.

"Six long months of vigils over Karen's bed, six long months of loving conversation with Joe and Julia in their anguish, six long months of searching and of doubt, these will be counted nothing by us. Take counsel, once again among yourselves, far from crowded courtrooms. We have seen enough to know that your decision will be true.

"Take your sister Karen, and if in your heart of hearts, counseled by your brother physicians and unfettered by fears that uncomprehending law will stay your hand, you determine that further ministrations would be no more than useless punishment, return her with our blessing to that state where her own body can heed, if it will, the gentle call that beckons her to lasting peace."

COMMENT:

If you have what would be a dramatic argument before a jury, do you use it before the judge? OF COURSE! This is an excellent example of how effective argument can be before a judge. The factual situation may give you drama, but it does not reach the trier-of-fact until you do something about it.

[5.64] Great Trial Lawyers: F. Lee Bailey—Defending Patty Hearst. By the time Patty Hearst went to trial, most of America had seen her on television waving a gun at people in a bank, appearing to be a part of a rather unpopular gang of people. This posed a special challenge in the fascinating career of F. Lee Bailey.

Early in his final argument, F. Lee Bailey said:

"This is not a case about a bank robbery. The crime could have been any one of a number. It is a case about dying or surviving—that is all Patricia Campbell Hearst thought about. And the question is what is the right to live? How far can you go to survive?

"We all know that it is a human impulse, a generic, irresistible human impulse to survive. People eat each other in the Andes to survive. The big question is, and we don't have it in this case, thank God: Can you kill to survive?

"We do it in wartime, but that is a different set of rules. We allow ourselves all kinds of special privileges when we fight the enemy. G. Gordon Liddy would have been an international hero if it was only the Russians who caught him instead of the reporters and ultimately the Department of Justice.

"A novelist once wrote a most disturbing book—you may have heard about it. It was a bestseller and a movie. A man who was condemned to hang for killing his wife, killed his executioner to survive, and then it was determined that he had not killed his wife. And a judge had to decide whether or not he could be tried for that second killing.

"Does one have an obligation at some point to die? It was called *A Covenant With Death*, and we all have a covenant with death. We're all going to die and we know it. And we're all going to postpone that date as long as we can. And Patty Hearst did that, and that is why she is here and you are here.

COMMENT:

Counsel has now put the issue in focus. The jury is wondering, however, how all this applies to the robbing of a bank. Counsel tells them.

"The prosecution offered only the statement of Patricia Hearst, admitting that she robbed the bank—and she did rob the bank. You are not here to answer that question, we could answer that without you.

"The question you are here to answer is why? And, would you have done the same thing to survive? Or, was it her duty to die, to avoid committing a felony? That is all this case is about, and all muddling and stamping of exhibits and the little monkeys and everything else that has been thrown into morass don't answer that question."

COMMENT:

The battle of experts eventually had to come and it did. Not only in testimony, but in argument.

"I do not suggest that my friend Mr. Browning deliberately asked anyone to lie. I'm sure that he did not. I do not suggest that until it was exposed in open court he had any idea that he had caused an expert, a psychopath and an habitual liar purporting to know something about a subject he'd never studied and charging the government $12,500 to read 240 books, including *Alice In Wonderland*. But, nonetheless he called him."

"Now, all they came up with is a couple of people whose only claim to fame is they testify a lot. I plead guilty to bringing in academicians, each of whom is a full professor at distinguished universities, Yale, UPA, UCLA, and one of them the head of the department.

"I plead guilty to bringing you men who don't have much experience on the witness stand, and I tell you with sorrow that the lawyer's dilemma is, 'Shall I get a good doctor as a witness, or should I get a doctor who is a good witness?' "

COMMENT:

Counsel turned to the questions of each juror voting his or her convictions and of proof beyond a reasonable doubt.

"Everybody is all excited about this case. Some people may be concerned, 'Well, if I decide this way, am I going to be criticized, and what is the reaction going to be?'

"I hope your isolation and your thoughtful reflection, for which you have had more than ample time so far as to your personal views and the combination of those views, which you will tomorrow be authorized for the first time to exchange with one another, will address itself to this discipline."

"If there is any doubt, it is far better to let the Government lose than to risk that somebody who did not do anything to offend our laws and certainly who did not do it deliberately, be punished to spite the innocent mind.

"If you are in any way perplexed as to what the truth was, you can get it through Patricia, through the circumstances and the inferences you can draw, or you can face the fact that no one will ever get the truth, except as she recalls it. If any doubt remains, your duty is clear, you are to report, 'Not proven beyond a reasonable doubt.' "

COMMENT:

Counsel, a little later in his final argument, identified with the jury.

"I give you final admission, ladies and gentlemen, because I recall very well I was one of the community—I am really not a flaming liberal that some people like to think. I was one of the community that was offended by the fact that two anguished parents would give up all they would give up—a much larger segment of what they had to give than what the press seems to think—in the one hope they could get their daughter back, and have her come on the air, and insult them and call them pigs.

"The whole country was split up, we were all angry at her, and we had to sort you out pretty carefully to make sure that none of that feeling carried beyond the day when you said, 'I can be fair.' And, the fact that we believed you when you said that is the reason you are in the box and the other 70 people are not."

COMMENT:

Though the evidence was strong and the conviction inevitable, counsel concluded with his one hope of acquittal:

"There is not anything close to proof beyond a reasonable doubt that Patty Hearst wanted to be a bank robber. What you know, and you know in your hearts to be true is beyond dispute. There was talk of her dying, and she wanted to survive. Thank God so far she has."

[5.65] Great Trial Lawyers: Roy Black—Arguing Reasonable Doubt. Defending a person charged with rape is a difficult task, but when that person causes world-wide attention, special challenges must be met. In defending William Kennedy Smith, Roy Black had to minimize the Kennedy factor, while maximizing the reasonable doubt defense.

Notice how Roy Black met both of these problems head-on right from the very beginning of his final argument:

"The Court is going to instruct you on the law, and I agree, the law is the most important part of this case, because you need to understand that there are certain principles of law that have made this country great, there are certain principles that come right from our constitution that apply directly to this matter that you have to decide.

"There are certain constitutional provisions that Will is entitled to, regardless of who he may be, he's entitled to the protection of our constitution, just as anyone else who came into this courtroom. Regardless who you may be, you are entitled to those protections of this constitution.

"The first one is that every citizen when he is brought into this courtroom is presumed innocent. The Court will tell you being presumed innocent means the jurors are to BELIEVE you are innocent. This is not just some form, this is not just something we mouth, this is something we believe.

"We BELIEVE that a person is innocent when he comes into this courtroom. Because of that, the state, the prosecution, is the ONLY party that has the burden of proving evidence. No citizen has to prove his innocence. He does not have to put on any evidence. Will did not have to call a single witness. He did not have to testify. He did not have to introduce any evidence. There was no requirement to do this, because he does not have to prove his innocence.

"It is the STATE that has that great burden, of proving him guilty beyond a reasonable doubt. If there is a reasonable doubt, then that means he must be found not guilty. The Court will give you an instruction that reasonable doubt means to have an ABIDING, an ABIDING conviction of guilt.

"That word was not selected loosely. There is a reason for that. Abiding is an important word. It is like in an abiding faith. It is something you hold tightly. It is something you deeply believe in. It is something you believe in from the bottom of your heart. That's what abiding means.

"The law says, you have to have an abiding conviction before you can ever return a verdict of guilty. It has to be an abiding conviction of proof beyond a reasonable doubt. There is no higher standard of that in the law than you have in a criminal case.

"The State has to prove that burden to you. If you have something less than an abiding conviction, if there is something less than proof beyond a reasonable doubt, you must return a verdict of not guilty.

"And, this is the key part of the instructions, because those are provisions of our constitution every person has. If we dilute those provisions, then we dilute our entire system of justice, and emasculate our constitution. We throw away rights that we fought so hard and so long, and with such difficulty, to obtain and keep."

COMMENT:

Counsel has argued reasonable doubt as effectively as it can be argued. He now makes sure one juror is not persuaded by another juror.

"Proof beyond a reasonable doubt is the actual key to this case. There is not just one verdict here, ladies and gentlemen, there are six individual verdicts. Each one of you makes your own decision. Each one of you looks at this evidence, looks into your conscience, looks into your heart, and comes up with your determination, your verdict of proof beyond a reasonable doubt. Each one of you has that obligation to make an independent determination.

"You can't decide the matter just because someone else has made a decision. You can't put this decision on anyone else. You, individually, have to make that decision. And, you are the one who wants to make a decision you will be proud of, that you are going to consider for the rest of your life."

COMMENT:

Counsel has not used the word Kennedy, and twice he has referred to his client as Will. Now he turns to the subject, without names, but with great skill. Notice the appeal to fairness, and the plight of an individual, ANY individual, when up against the prosecution.

"There is no unequal justice in our country. No matter where you may be, whether you be down in the lowest possible job there is, or all the way to the President of the United States, there is no unequal justice. And, that also means, that you cannot be prosecuted on who you are, you cannot be treated differently from everyone else because of who you are or where you come from, or what your name is or who your family is.

"You take a look at what went on in this case, from helicopters to untold number of police officers all around the country, dragging all kinds of things. I don't know how many rolls of film, I don't know how many universities they go to, how many FBI agents, how many crime labs. They went after this man with everything they had. And, then they come in here and try to criticize us because we have the nerve to defend ourselves.

"We don't have a crime lab to work with. We don't have the same resources the State of Florida does. All we can do is go out and ask people, and retain them to come in and do some work and prove the facts of this case. And, yet, we get criticized for this.

"They would only be happy if you give up. We said right from the beginning that this charge was untrue. Will says that it is a damnable lie. The charge of rape is a damnable lie!"

COMMENT:

Roy Black then reviewed the evidence and showed how inconsistent the State's case was. The jury returned a verdict of not guilty.

[5.66] Great Trial Lawyers: Benjamin Marcus—Argue Your Case On Appeal. A lawyer must prepare a good appellate brief, but he must also ARGUE his case on appeal. Arguing a case before appellate judges differs from arguing before a jury, but only in that it requires a more "sophisticated" argument.

Even the written brief can include effective argument. Benjamin Marcus of Muskegon, Michigan, specializes in appellate work, and won a case with argument in his brief. He won the case on the basis of the following paragraph:

"IF BESSIE WERE A BEAST OF BURDEN.

"If only Bessie were a beast of burden her owner would long ago have enjoyed the monies awarded him by a judge or jury for the illegal oveloading of an animal by her bailee. What's more, the Humane Society would have sought and obtained a criminal conviction for cruelty to animals. But our defendants insist that since only a female human being is involved, not a horse or a mule, the law against overloading can be ignored with impunity and, of course, without compensation. Yes, if Bessie were a mule this case would not be before this high tribunal."

The appellate court decided that Bessier Underwood's disability was compensable, though it reached an opposite conclusion in a similar case on the same day. This could only have been because of the persuasiveness of the written argument.

Bob Gibbons of Austin, Texas, argued before an appellate court that a fellow lawyer should not be suspended from the practice of law. If you think his argument to judges would not include a "human appeal," you don't understand how Bob Gibbons tries a lawsuit.

An argument on appeal by Bob Gibbons: "Now, I ask Your Honor, where is the human heart that would not be satisfied with a reprimand in this case? I say that because this man, his family, his friends, his relatives, are all gathered around him in his hour of need. Undoubtedly they are as good and loyal and faithful as any man could have on earth but still he is unknown to you and his fate lies in your hands.

"There are other people to consider in this matter. What about his wife and his children, ages sixteen, fourteen, five, and three. More important, what about his clients? Do his past Bar activities stand for anything with his profession that they would now urge this court to suspend him from?

"That man would not intentionally violate the Canon of Ethics and I say, Judge, just to talk cold turkey, that if he did he ought to be disbarred. If he is that foolish over a couple of thousand dollars to intentionally undo everything that the man stood for for the better part of fifteen years as a practicing lawyer then he needs to go to an institution.

"If this man is suspended for thirty, sixty, ninety days, or whatever, six months to two years as they say, which I can never bring myself to imagine, what effect will that have, Judge? The *Bar Journal* will carry it, perhaps the newspaper, he will stop practicing law for a while, it will be carried into the homes of his loved ones, his friends, his clients, his colleagues, but will it make this man better or worse? I would like to put this to the intelligence of His Honor. I would like to appeal to your feelings as a human being."

COMMENT:

From these excerpts you can see why the attorney went "without punishment." A trial lawyer should believe in his cause, and if he believes in his cause he should argue it with passion.

[5.67] Great Trial Lawyers: Scott Baldwin—"Get The Hogs Out of The Creek." Scott Baldwin of Texas, is a past President of ATLA and one of the nation's leading trial lawyers. Down in his part of Texas, they have a saying, "The water won't clear until you get the hogs out of the creek!"

This great trial lawyer uses these words to remind himself that during final argument, you must:

1. Make things clear!
2. Talk so the jury will understand you!
3. You must get the jury's attention!
4. You must keep the jury's attention!
5. Move people with stories.
6 Develop a theme to your case.
7. Use that theme in your final argument!

At the conclusion of a complicated case he tried, he was thinking of the final argument as he was dropping off his eight-year-old son at school. Knowing he could not explain such a case to an eight year old, he merely replied, "Oh, it's a civil case, Jack."

This did not satisfy the son. "But, what's it about, Daddy?"

"Oh, it's just a civil case."

"I know, Daddy, but what's it about?"

Finally the great lawyer realized he wasn't going to get to the courthouse until he explained further.

"Well, Jack, it just involves two people that agreed they would do something, and then one of them changed his mind and backed out."

"Well, Daddy, which one do you represent?"

Scott replied, "Jack, I represent the man who wanted to continue with the deal." His son then said, "Daddy, I'm glad."

That became Scott Baldwin's theme of the case!

If your eight-year-old son can understand a complicated lawsuit, then the chances are the jury will also understand it, IF YOU GET THE HOGS OUT OF THE CREEK. Making the water clear is the farmer's problem, but making the lawsuit clear is the trial lawyer's problem.

Scott Baldwin is a great believer in repetition, and a great believer in stating a proposition, and then backing it up! He suggests John F. Kennedy's call for more help for the downtrodden was merely a proposition, but he persuaded when he backed it up with "twenty million people will go to bed tonight without supper."

In a complicated products liability case, Scott Baldwin explains he did not really get a handle on the case and did not really appreciate the case until he heard his expert explain, "The failure of that manufacturer to provide operator protection converted an otherwise trivial incident into a catastrophic event."

Whether the words come from an eight year old or from one of the leading experts in the world, the trial lawyer must LISTEN, because what he hears may help him understand the case, and may enable him to help the jury understand the case.

It was the simplicity of the son's theme, and it was the colorful explanation by the expert that, in each case, made the issue clear. In both instances, the case was explained in one sentence.

Don't dilute your argument with:

1. Long readings from depositions,
2. Use of too many exhibits.

Scott Baldwin warns against:

1. Apologizing or in any way letting the jury think you are not there for justice;
2. Criticizing opposing counsel; ("I act like he's not there.")
3. Saying whatever the jury does is all right; ("I let them know I'm going to be mad as hell if they decide against me.")

Let's take a look at Scott Baldwin in action. Here are a few examples of how he has argued in a few of his cases:

"The court will tell you what the law is and how it applies to the case. He will use a lot of whereases and wherefores, and other legal terms. But, in just plain cornbread language, it will be something to the effect that if you find that the punch press was defective because it did not have a safeguard and that defect made it unreasonably dangerous which was the cause of the plaintiff's injury, then your verdict must be for the plaintiff. It is just that simple."

COMMENT:

When the jury is deliberating, it may well remember this paragraph of counsel's final argument, rather than the instructions.

"This case, as do most, breaks into two parts. First, the question of liability, or who is at fault. Second, the question of damages, or how should the plaintiff be compensated. First, I shall discuss with you the question of liability and then the question of damages."

COMMENT:

Counsel has outlined his final argument, so it will be easy for the jury to follow it.

"The element of lost earnings in the future should not be difficult for you to evaluate. It simply is a matter of mathematics. I suggest to you that the plaintiff is 25 years of age, he was earning $30,000 per year and if he worked to the retirement age of 70 his earnings would have been $1,350,000. Now this is gone, and that figure is a conservative one. Why do I say it is a conservative one? Because it does not include a single solitary penny for bonuses. This figure, therefore, should give you no difficulty."

COMMENT:

Counsel deals with this in a matter-of-fact manner, as an EXACT amount.

"Now we come to the question of pain and suffering. This will not be easy to resolve. Your task to award adequate damages for this element will be more difficult than the matters we just discussed relating to loss of earnings. Nevertheless, this element of damages is real and it is just as important as any damage element in the case."

COMMENT:

Counsel prepares the jury for discussion of intangible damages, stresses its importance, and again makes it clear tangible damages are exact.

"Now, let's consider the damages in this case. The liability in this case is foreclosed. The life of Mrs. Potter is gone—needlessly destroyed. Destroyed by a man who didn't even know what he hit.

"So what is left? There is Jeffrey Potter, a young man at the very threshold of life; there is Mary, their daughter, almost 15 and going on 21; and there is little Tim, just 4, who really does not realize what has happened yet. Mrs. Potter is gone—she will never return. She can never make her contribution to her family she loved except through you.

"How, then, do you perform this duty under the law? You cannot return Mrs. Potter. I wish you could. I wish this was but a terrible nightmare and make Mrs. Potter appear in that empty chair that counsels, so unforgettably, referred to. If so, our jobs would be easy. But you cannot, you can only do what the law says you must and that is award only those damages the law provides. You must be careful to see that they are adequate."

COMMENT:

Counsel pins down liability, but with a brief, but forceful, statement that helps his damages. Note phrases such as "needlessly destroyed." He describes the loss dramatically, then gives them their duty under the law. When you tell a person to "be careful," that person is more cautious about bringing back an inadequate verdict.

"The question of children is not so easy to resolve. The court tells you in awarding money damages to them you must consider care, nurture, guidance, and counsel. How do you determine this? What is a mother? She is like a mother bird who feeds her young, teaches them to fly, and finally, gently kicks them from her nest. She is an oracle of virtue who is at once a maid who sews on buttons before they come off, a psychiatrist, a nurse, an eternal bank of knowledge. She is a tower of strength with delicate charm. She is a cool thinker with warm ways. What is more descriptive to say, than she is a mother."

COMMENT:

Dizzy Dean said, "It ain't braggin' if you can do it," and in a courtroom sentimentality is always justified where the facts make it appropriate. Here it is used with warmth and skill.

"It now becomes your duty to return a verdict and assess damages in this case. It is your opportunity to determine the type of future Mrs. Jones will have. When you return a verdict as we suggest, you can be proud to have played some small part in providing some pleasure to this man's future."

COMMENT:

"DUTY," "OPPORTUNITY," and "PROUD"! They are all power words and counsel worked all three of them into the final three sentences of his final argument.

How valuable are a few minutes of your final argument? Scott Baldwin answers with a story of years ago when he and his partner retained Joe Jamail as co-counsel in an important trial. Since the judge limited their final argument, Scott had to tell Joe he would not participate in final argument.

Joe Jamail sat at the counsel table and listened as the opposing lawyer said, "These people are asking for money. Anyone can ask for money. When I was a boy I would ask my father for a dollar, hoping he would give me a quarter so I could go to the show."

Joe Jamail could no longer just sit there. He handed Scott a note which read, "I'll give you $15,000 of my fee for five minutes of your final argument." Scott agreed and listened to his friend rip the defense up one side and down the other.

As his five minutes was about to end, Joe Jamail paused, then said, "And then they float this guy in from Dallas who admits right here in our courtroom in front of all of us that he even tried to cheat his own daddy."

Scott said he knew then Joe was going to amount to something, and he did. Joe's multibillion dollar verdict in *Penzoil v. Texaco* brought with it an estimated $450 million fee. That warms the heart, quickens the pulse and challenges the imagination of every trial lawyer, young and old.

That's what happened to one trial lawyer who knew, years ago, that every minute of your final argument is worth at least $3,000.

[5.68] Great Trial Lawyers: Howard Nations—Why We Ask For Money. Howard Nations is not only one of America's best trial lawyers, but one of its best public speakers. He has used his speaking talent to advantage during final argument.

Howard Nations is a student of persuasion. That is why his effectiveness does not come by accident. He talks of learning fundamentals with the same vigor of a basketball coach or the teacher that he is.

When he speaks of "repetition" he points out that in Martin Luther King's most famous speech, he said, "I have a dream," eight times. When advising that we talk in "threes," he reminds us of Winston Churchill's, "We will fight them on the sea, we will fight them in the streets, we will fight them in our homes. We will never, never, never surrender!"

Johnny Carson said that he had the easiest job in the world. He read the morning paper and his monologue jumped out at him. Howard Nations maintains the trial lawyer can do the same thing.

EXAMPLE:

> Howard Nations delivered a final argument the day after the Spinks-Tyson fight. He admitted a just award for his client would be an awful lot of money, but told the jurors that as they sit in the jury room deliberating the amount, two men will be dividing up 33 million dollars for 93 seconds of work. The jury was asked to compare that with fifty years imprisoned in a now worthless body.

One of Howard Nation's most outstanding arguments was his explanation to the jury of why we ask for money. The following is the beginning of that argument:

"Now we talk of money. We talk of money because there is no magic. Is anyone so callous as to believe that if you, as a jury, had the power to wave a magic wand and bring young David Taylor back through those courtroom doors, that there would be talk of money? NO! We would see only exultant joy as this young couple emerged from the depths of despair, into the heights of happiness.

"We would see the three happiest people on the face of the earth as they left this courtroom, smiling, together, as a happy family again.

"But, there is no magic. There is only despair. There is no magic. There is only reality. There is no magic. So ladies and gentlemen, we talk of money.

"Magic exists only in the world of children, such as young David Taylor. The magic of each new day in David's life, his new challenges, his dreams, his fantasies. The magic of new friends, the testing of David's God-given talents against his friends, his young cousins. Hitting the ball as far, running as fast, the magic of each day, his toys, his birthdays, Christmas, although there were only seven and there will be no more."

COMMENT:

Howard Nations has held the jury with his theme of "magic" and the world in which a child lives. Then he turned to his own boyhood and a saying his mother had on the wall.

"It's called, 'What Is A Boy?' And, I'd like to share just a small part of it with you. Between the innocence of babyhood and the dignity of manhood we find the incredible creature, we call a boy.

"Boys come in assorted sizes, but all boys have exactly the same creed. To live every second of every minute of every hour of every day until that final moment at night when Mom and Dad drag them off to bed, kicking and screaming and protesting with noise, their only weapon.

"Boys are found everywhere. On top of, underneath, inside of, climbing on, emerging from, running around and jumping, too. Mothers love them. Little girls hate them. Brothers and sisters tolerate them, and heaven protects them.

"A boy's a magical creature. You can lock him out of your workshop, but you can't lock him out of your heart. You can get him out of your study, but you can't get him out of your mind. You might as well give up, he's your captor, your jailer, your boss, a freckle-faced, pint-size, cat-chasing bundle of noise.

"But, when David, Sr., came home at night, with only the shattered remains of his day, little David could mend them all with those two magic words, 'Hi, Dad.' But, ladies and gentlemen, David, Sr., will never again hear those magic words, because the magic of young David's life ended on November 3rd, 1989, when the inevitable time bomb, manufactured by this defendant, exploded, and took with it, the life of this young man, and the hopes, and the dreams, and the aspirations of this young couple.

"So, since there is no magic in our justice system, we talk of money. But, never forget, as you contemplate this case, that we talk of money now, because they talked of money five years ago in their corporate board room, when they made that horrendous, profit-motivated decision not to recall this product. Why? Because a recall would have cost them four million dollars."

COMMENT:

Notice how this great trial lawyer persuaded the jury on the value of a human life before talking about the blame of defendant.

"So, they refused to recall, and the inevitable tragedy occurred. Ladies and gentlemen, is that the standard of safety we will tolerate in the state of Texas? Or, is that reprehensible corporate conduct, which must not be allowed to occur again? That, and the value to be placed on the life of this young man is your decision."

COMMENT:

Counsel soon turned to the subject of sympathy, and notice how effectively he handled this age-old problem.

"Ladies and gentlemen, the defendant warned you against sympathy for this family, and we agree. Don't look at this family with sympathy. Believe me, they have received plenty of sympathy.

"They received sympathy at the funeral, when they looked at the eyes of their friends and loved ones. They received sympathy when they returned to their church and looked into the eyes of their minister and fellow parishioners. They received sympathy when they returned to their workplace, and looked every day in the eyes of their co-workers.

"They have received enough sympathy to last them ten life times. We're not here about sympathy. We are here about justice. Now, in evaluating the damages in this case, don't look at the death of this young man, but look rather at the life that never will be."

COMMENT:

Counsel then took the jury through all of the moments in life that this boy and his parents would miss. It was then time to drive home blame and cause the jury to really want to do something about it.

"But, remember as you write the final chapter in his book of life, that there's another set of books which you must examine closely in this case. Because, as we speak here today, the life of young David Taylor is carried as a four million dollar profit item on the books of this corporation.

"This corporation which made the willful decision to gamble. They gamble their four million dollar profit against the safety of the public, they gambled on the judicial system, they gambled on the life of young David Taylor.

"We know that the Taylors lost that gamble, but the question is, 'Did this corporation win their horrendous gamble?' Ladies and gentlemen, that is your decision."

COMMENT:

Counsel is now ready to tell the jury to SEND OUT A MESSAGE! Note with what excellence he does it!

"You are serving as the conscience of our community. With your verdict, you have the opportunity and the responsibility to serve as the conscience of our community, to tell the Taylors what their family, and their young son, meant to this community, and the value that we in Houston place on the life of our children, and to tell this corporation if their horrendous gamble paid off, and if they should gamble this way in the future or not, with the lives of other children.

"Therefore, as you act in your role, and take your opportunity to speak as the conscience of this community, send a message to this corporation. When you walk through that jury room door, you have an opportunity on behalf of all parents, all citizens, and all consumers in this great country to talk directly to the board of directors of this corporation, because, believe me, they are watching this trial, and they are waiting for your reply.

"It is likely, in serving as a jury in this case, you will never again have an opportunity to do so much good, for so many of your fellow citizens by demanding safe products for our children, by demanding protection of the public from defective products, and by sending a clear message to corporations which ignore safety that such action will be punished in the courts of this state.

"If your verdict is large enough your verdict will be heard not only by this company, but by the entire industry that we, the citizens of Texas, value life infinitely more than we value the profits of corporations."

COMMENT:

Then counsel turned to the ultimate question of HOW MUCH?

"Opposing counsel says four million dollars is too much money, but ladies and gentlemen, we live in a society in which paint on canvas recently sold for 53 million dollars. Why? Because it was the work of a master, Van Gogh. If paint on canvas is worth 53 million dollars because it is the work of a master, then can four million dollars even begin to compensate for the destruction of the greatest creation of the greatest master of them all, God's creation of the human child? That, is your determination."

COMMENT:

What more can be said? Listen!

"When you go back to your families and they say, 'What did you do in court?,' you can look them straight in the eye, and say, 'We made this country a safer place to live. We told a young couple that their son was a very valued member of this community, and we rendered full and complete justice.' Thank you, very much."

COMMENT:

Yes. THAT is why we talk of money!

[5.69] Great Trial Lawyers: Gerry Spence—Tell Your Story In One Sentence. To say Gerry Spence is a man of few words would ignore his love to talk about those causes close to his heart. The full transcript of his opening statement in the case discussed in Section 2.23 was 110 pages, quite a few words for some judges to permit.

Gerry Spence will look you right in the eye, however, and tell you that if you can't tell the jury what your lawsuit is about in one sentence, you are not ready to try it. If you think that is mere talk, ask him for an example.

He may tell you about the case that was turned down by other lawyers because the clients did not have a written contract with the McDonald hamburger people. Gerry took the case because he believed in his clients' cause.

During final argument he walked right up to the jury, looked each of them right in the eye and said, "Let's put honor back in the handshake." The jury understood what Gerry was talking about and brought back a verdict of $53 million.

INDEX

A

Abuse of discretion, 75–76, 113
Accused not testifying, 78, 110, 263–64, 268–70
ACLU, 88
Acosta, Laura, 193–95
Adams, John, 257
Adams v. *Texas*, 116
Alternate jurors, 92
Amendments, to U.S. Constitution
  Fifth, 37, 263
  Fourteenth, 46
  Seventh, 38
  Sixth, 37, 96
Anderson v. *Nelson*, 264
Anderson v. *Universal Delta*, 162
Andritsch v. *Henschel*, 268
Appeal, 218–19
  model final argument, 387–88
Appearance
  client's, 6–7
  lawyer's, 2, 3, 137–38
Armstrong, Paul, 377–81
Arnold v. *Edelman*, 276
Art of Cross-Examination, The, 233–37
Atkinson, Linda Miller, 229–30
Atmosphere, creating, 1
  during opening statement, 183–85
Attitude(s)
  client's, 7–8
  juror's, revealing, 29, 65–67
    toward capital punishment, 114
    toward courts, lawyers, jury system, 83–84
    toward people who sue, 90–91
    toward certain professions, 99
    toward damages for death, 106
    toward illegal drug use, 120
    toward subjective injuries, 125–26
  lawyer's, toward jurors, 2, 4
  of men versus women, 96–98
Attorney-client factor, 76
Auerback v. *Philadelphia Transportation Co.*, 259, 274
Authoritarian personality type, 138–39

B

Babb v. *United States*, 264
Babcock v. *Northwest Memorial Hospital*, 99
Bailey, F. Lee, 381–84
Bailey v. *McCleod*, 76
Baldwin, Scott, 211, 388–93
Bandoni v. *Walston*, 252
Barkauskas v. *Lane*, 262
Basiak v. *Board of Ed. of City of Cleveland*, 164
Bateh, George, 47
Batson v. *Kentucky*, 47, 140–47
  annotations, 144–47
    federal, 144–45
    state, 145–47
  facts, 142
  held, 142–44
Bekind, Don, 238
Bell v. *State*, 65
Belli, Melvin, 155–56, 215
Bennett v. *Commonwealth*, 72
Berryhill v. *Zant*, 96
Bias, 41
  against crime rather than defendant, 118
Bible, quoting, 302–10
Bifurcated voir dire, 115
Black, Justice, 148
Black, Roy, 287, 384–87
Blackboards, and evidence, 225, 297–98
Block v. *State*, 76
Boop v. *Baltimore & OH R. Co.*, 260
Bone v. *General Motors Corp.*, 275
Border v. *Carrabine*, 76
Borgen v. *State*, 279
Bradford v. *Parrish*, 269
Brady v. *Maryland*, 262–63
Brewer v. *State*, 279
Brickey v. *U.S.*, 65
Brokopp v. *Ford Motor Co.*, 252
Bruno v. *Ruschen*, 279
Burden of proof
  discussing, 69–73
  final argument and, 287
Burger, Justice, 141
Burger Chef Systems v. *Govro*, 260
Burley v. *State*, 118
Business records, as evidence, 221–22

C

Caldwell Rule, 277
Caldwell v. *Mississippi*, 277
Caley v. *Manicke*, 260
Cape Girardeau v. *Jones*, 263
Capital cases, 113–16
  law and order appeal, preparing for, 277–79
  law review articles recommended, 115
  qualifying death penalty opponents, 147–54

Carter v. *State*, 45
Caylor v. *Casto*, 164
Challenges
juror's knowledge of case and, 53–54
juror's knowledge of party, attorney, or others, 55
made after voir dire, 46–47
poisoning the panel, 46–47
made before trial, 41–42
made during voir dire, 42–46
poisoning the panel, 43–44
preemptory, 140–47
Change of venue, 42
Chapman v. *California*, 263
Charts
and final argument, 297–98
and opening statement, 162–63
Chicago Seven, 39–41
Chicago Study, 182
Child abuse and molestation, 118
Civil case, model final argument, 318–28
Civil rights, 88, 100–101
Clarence Darrow For The Defense, 370
Client('s)
appearance, 6–7, 9
attitude, 7–8, 9
background, 6
conduct, 8–9
exposure, 8, 9, 10
Coates v. *State*, 46
Collier v. *State*, 278
Collins v. *Nelson*, 276
Commenting on the law, 165–66
Commitments, from jury, 13–14, 31
pining down, 25
reasonable doubt, 72
Commonwealth v. *Lane*, 113
Commonwealth v. *Lawrence*, 271
Commonwealth v. *McBee*, 45
Commonwealth v. *Preston*, 257
Commonwealth v. *Smith*, 113
Communication, verbal and nonverbal, 175–76
Comparative negligence, 108, 132
Compassion, 9
Computer print-outs, using properly, 23
Computers and "computer people," studying, 132–33
Computer simulations, as evidence, 220
Concern, 2, 127, 298–300
Conduct of counsel error, 255–57
Conlin, Roxanne, 158, 248, 356–62
Conner v. *United States*, 38
Connolly v. *Nicollet Hotel*, 269, 270
Conscientious scruples, against capital punishment, 114
Consideration, 4
Contempt power, balancing with voir dire rights, 39–41
Cook v. *Kansas City*, 53
Corboy, Phil, 134, 345–53
Core v. *Core's Admrs.*, 61, 662
Corens v. *State*, 45
Counterclaim, explaining, 296
Craig v. *Borough of Ebensburg*, 269
Credibility, 1, 52
establishing, during opening statement, 174–76
of witnesses, 113, 287–89
Criminal cases
criminal record of defendant, 275–76
general, 110–13
homicide, 113–16
juror personality types and, 138–40
model final argument, 328–33
other violent crimes, 116–17
sex and morality, 117–19
Cross-discussion, creating, 30
Cross-examination. *See* Witnesses, cross-examination of
Cummins Alabama, Inc. v. *Allbritten*, 261
Cunningham, Tony, 81–82
Curative instruction, 275
Currituck Grain, Inc., 252

D

Damages
determining with mathematical formula, 259–60
final argument and, 300–301, 393–98
medical expenses argument, 301
permanency of injuries, arguing, 292–93
punitive, 130–31, 290–92
for wrongful death, 104–7
arguing finality of death, 283–84
arguing pain, 282–83
model final argument, 345–53
Darbin v. *Nourse*, 39
Darrow, Clarence, 138, 183, 370–73
Davis, Rex, 279
Day-in-the-life videos, 220
Death penalty
law and order appeal, preparing for, 277–79
opponents, qualifying, 147–54
Defamation, 103–4

Demonstrative evidence
  in final argument, 297–98
  in jury selection, 33–35
    citing the law, 34
    court approval for, 34
    dramatic presentation of, 35
    proper preparation, 35
  video evidence, 219–20
DeMott v. *Smith*, 44
Depositions, 217–18
  cross-examination and, 243–44
  final arguments and, 258
Directed verdict, after opening statement, 163–65
Direct financial interest, of prospective juror, 44
Discrimination, 100
  See also Civil rights; Prejudice
  preemptory challenges and, 46, 140–47
  proving, 229
DNA, 224
Doe v. *Hafen*, 128
Domberg v. *State*, 264
Donald v. *Macheny*, 267
Doubt, and prospective juror, 45
Douglas, Justice, 147–48
Drama, opening statement and, 173–74, 180, 183–85, 190
Drawings, as evidence, 220
Dress, lawyer's, 3
Dresser v. *State*, 274

E

Economic interest, 74–77
Egomaniacs, as jurors, 139–40
Eichstadt v. *Underwood*, 34
Elderly persons, representing, 214
Ellis v. *Victor Elec. Products*, 164
Emotional distress, 125. *See also* Subjective injuries, seriousness of
Equal Protection Clause, 142, 143
Evidence
  blackboards, using, 225, 297–98
  business records, 221–22
  demonstrative, 18–19, 33–35
    citing the law, 34
    court approval for, 34
    dramatic presentation of, 35
    in final argument, 297–98
    proper preparation of, 35
    video, 219–20
  depositions, 217–18
  DNA, 224–25
  experts, direct examination of, 222–24
  final argument and, 257–58
  know what you're proving, 214
  leading question problem, avoiding, 212–13
  making notes for appeal, 218–19
  photographs, 225–26
  presentation of exhibits, 216–17
  presenting in proper order, 211–12
  problems in presenting, 229–30
  redirecting, 228
  refreshing recollection, 221
  trend away from live testimony, 214–15
  witnesses
    see also Expert witnesses
    before and after, how to use, 226–27
    speaking jury's language, 227–28
    as storyteller, 215–116
    talking to jury, 214
Exhibits
  opening statement and, 162–63
  presentation of, 216–17
Expert witnesses
  cross-examination, 235, 248–49
  direct examination of, 222–24
  establishing juror's relationship with, 61–62
  final arguments and, 296–97
  reconstructing events, 229

"Fair juror," 65
"Fair trial," 65
Fallacies of testimony, 236
Faught v. *Walsham*, 276
Featherston v. *U.S.*, 39
Federal court, and jury selection, 37–41
Federal Rules of Civil Procedure (Rule 47) 37
Federal Rules of Criminal Procedure (Rule 23), 37
Federal Rules of Evidence
  Rule 403, 259, 267, 273
  Rule 606(a), 53
  Rule 611(a), 215
  Rule 611(b), 247
  Rule 611(c), 248
Feeling toward a party, 44
Felder v. *State*, 113
Ferraro, Mark, 115
Final argument
  appealing to passion, 258–59
  appeals to prejudice, preventing, 267–68
  attacking parties and witnesses, 272–74

Final argument (*cont'd*)
avoiding "first mentioned in rebuttal" objection, 255
burden of proof, 287
communicating during, 279–81
conduct of counsel error, 255–57
counterclaim, explaining, 296
court's discretion, knowing limits of, 271–72
damages
arguing, 276, 300–301
determining with math formula, 259–60
defendant's record and, 275–76
demonstrative evidence in, 297–98
dividing opening and rebuttal, 270
error, correcting, 274–75
evidence, discussing, 257–58
exhibits and demonstrations during, 265–67
expert witnesses and, 296–97
failure of accused to testify, 263–64
failure to present witness or evidence, 268–70
finality of death, arguing, 283–84
financial status, arguing, 289–90
golden rule limitations, 261–62
great trial lawyers and
Armstrong, Paul, 377–81
Bailey, F. Lee, 381–84
Baldwin, Scott, 388–93
Black, Roy, 384–87
Conlin, Roxanne, 356–62
Corboy, Philip, 345–53
Darrow, Clarence, 370–73
Fuller, Vincent, 373–77
Gibbins, Bob, 366–67
Malone, Tom, 362–66
Maloney, Pat, 335–45
Marcus, Benjamin, 387–88
Nations, Howard, 393–98
Pavalon, Gene, 367–70
Sams, Murray, 353–56
Spence, Gerry, 398
injury's permanence, arguing, 292–93
instructions, using, 295–96
jurors' attitude toward client, 293–95
law and order appeal, preparing for, 277–79
length of, 270–71
matters of common knowledge, using, 275
medical expenses argument, 301
mistrial traps, avoiding, 276–77
model
see also Final argument, great trial lawyers and
civil case, 318–28
last minutes of, 334–35
opening statement and, 176–78
organizing both halves, 252–55
liability-damages ratio and sequence, 253–54
pain, arguing, 282–83
prison, arguing, 284–85
prosecutors' special rules, 262–63
punitive damages, 290–92
purpose of, 251–52
quoting during, 301–4
Bible, 302–10
poets and writers, 313–18
religious writings, other, 309–10
Shakespeare, 310–13
right to depend on others, 286–87
sending out message, 271
show malice through conduct, 289
slip and fall cases, 281–82
storytelling, 264–65
sympathy and concern, differentiating between, 298–300
voir dire commitment, 285–86
witness credibility, arguing, 287–89
Financial interest in case outcome
juror's, 74–77
witness's, 247
Firearms issue, 88
First impressions, 33
Fixed opinion, 44
Flaherty, Thomas J., 266
Fludd v. *Dykes*, 47
Follow-up questions, 136–37
Foreman, 14–15
educational background of, 48–49
Francis, Connie, 109
Frankness, 36–37
potential verdict size, discussing during voir dire, 128–30
Friendliness, 4, 9
Fuller, Vincent, 373–77

G

Garzilli v. *Howard Johnson's Motor Lodges*, 109
General Motors v. *Simmons*, 247
Genova v. *Kansas City*, 52
Gibbins, Bob, 241, 247, 366–67
Gilbert v. *Rothschild*, 164
Gladys Affett v. *Milwaukee & Suburban Transport Corp.*. 34
Goldberg, Justice, 141

Golden rule limitations, 261–62
Golian v. *Stanley*, 259
Graham v. *Cloar*, 162
Grammar, 3–4
Greeson v. *Texas & Pac. Ry. Co.*, 268
Griffin Rule, 263–64
Griffin v. *California*, 263–64

H

Haberstroth v. *State*, 278
Halloren v. *New England Tel. & Tel. Co.*, 275
Ham v. *South Carolina*, 44
Hammerstein, Oscar II, 279–80
Handicapped discrimination, 100. *See also* Civil rights; Prejudice
Handwriting samples, 264
Hanner v. *State*, 247
Hardy, David, 193–95
Harlan, Justice, 148
Harris v. *People*, 65
Harrisburg Bank v. *Forster*, 45
Harrison v. *Missouri*, 76
Haslam v. *U.S.*, 38
Hayes, Judge Hugh D., 115
Health problems, of jurors, 91–92
Hearst trial. *See U.S.* v. *Hearst*
Hermann, Russ, 238
Hernandez v. *Baucum*, 34
Hessler v. *Nellpowitz*, 164
Hilpert, Elmer, 302
Hilyard v. *State*, 162
Hinckley, John Jr., 373–77
Hinton & Sons v. *Strahan*, 269
Hobbies (juror's), exploring, 89–90
Hobbs v. *State*, 44
Home ownership (juror's), significance of, 86–88
Homicide cases, 113–16. *See also* Capital cases
Houston & T.C.R. Co. v. *Waller*, 92
Hovey v. *Superior Court of Alameda County*, 115
Hulverson, Jim, 63–64
Humor, 183

I

Impartiality
- of prospective juror, 44, 45
  - "inside information," 58
  - juror's familiarity with facts of case, 52–54
  - juror's knowledge of party, attorney, or others, 54–58
- of witness, 242–43

Individual inquiry, conducting, 30–33
- commitments, obtaining, 31
- controlling the inquiry, 32
- imposed limitations, knowing, 30–31
- open-ended questions and, 31
- questioning techniques, 32–33

Innocence. *See* Presumption of innocence
Insanity defense, 373–77
Inside information, 58
Insurance (casualty), 58–61, 276
Interview method, 137
Irvin v. *Dowd*, 113

J

Jackson v. *State*, 247
Jamail, Joe, 11, 36, 155, 156–58, 184
Jeans, James, 212–13
Jensen v. *McEldowney*, 270
Jimpson v. *State*, 264
Johnson v. *Charleston & W.C.R. Co.*, 34
Johnson v. *Larson*, 164
Johnston v. *Key System Transit Lines*, 269
Jordan v. *State*, 278
Jordan v. *U.S.*, 264
Judges, federal, 38–41
Jurisdiction, selecting, 135
Jury/jurors
- *see also* Jury selection; Mock juries
- alternate, 92
- basic data on individual members of, 23
- importance of role, 22
- leaders and followers in, 15–16
- opening statements and, 172–73
- profiles, 134
- witnesses and, 227–28

Jury selection
- *see also* Jury
- accused not testifying, preparing jury for, 78
- addressing entire panel, 22–27
  - avoiding repetition, 25–26
  - individual questioning, 26–27
  - pinning down commitments, 25
  - saving time, 23
  - skipping around panel with ease, 24
  - telling story smoothly, 26
- asking if there is any reason juror cannot serve, 92–94
- attitude toward courts/lawyers/jury system, discovering, 83– 84
- basic questions for, 78–79
- burden of proof, discussing, 69–73
- challenges before trial, 41–42

Jury selection (*cont'd*)
civil rights litigation, 100–101
commitments, obtaining, 13–14
final argument and, 285–86
comparative negligence, juror's understanding of, 132
computers and computer people, studying, 132–33
criminal cases
general, 110–13
homicide, 113–16
sequestering during voir dire, 114–15
narcotics, 119–20
sex and morality, 117–19
violent crimes (other than homicide), 116–17
white collar crime, 120–21
death penalty opponents, qualifying, 147–54
defamation and privacy invasion, 103–4
demonstrative evidence and, 33–35
citing the law, 34
court approval for, 34
dramatic presentation of, 35
proper presentation, 35
desire to serve on jury, 94–95
distinguishing sympathy and concern, 127–28
educational background, of juror, 48–49
embarrassment of prospective jurors, 26
establishing juror's relationship with experts and other witnesses, 61–62
experience in similar matters (juror's), 62–64
expertise
attorney's, development of, 136–40
juror's, on key issues, 64–65
explaining voir dire to prospective jurors, 19–22
familiarity with facts of case (juror's), 52–54
federal court, adapting to, 37–41
financial interest in case outcome (juror's), 74–77
foreperson, importance of, 14–15
health problems of jurors, 91–92
hobbies and special interests, exploring, 89–90
home ownership, significance of, 86–88, 109
homicide cases, 113–16
individual inquiry, conducting, 30–33
commitments, obtaining, 31
controlling the inquiry, 32
limitations, knowing, 30–31
open-ended questions and, 31
questioning techniques, 32–33
innovation, 155–56
insurance question, asking, 58–61
jury identification with client, 4–10, 112–13
appearance, 6–7
attitude, 7–8
background, 6
conduct, 8–9
exposure, of client, 8, 10
telling client's story, 5–6
knowledge of party, attorney, or others, 54–58
marital status of juror, 51–52
men versus women, 96–98
"military mind," spotting, 84–85
morality cases, 117–19
narcotics cases, 119–20
occupational history, of prospective juror, 49–51, 112
organization memberships, 88–89
participation, of jurors, 27–30
atmosphere, creating, 28–29
cross discussions, creating, 30
discarding outmoded approaches, 28
projecting informality, 27
purpose of, 28
questions requiring involvement, 29
personal injury case, 97–98, 159–60
personality types and, 138–40
"poisoning" of one juror by another, 14–16
potential size of verdict, discussing, 128–30
prejudice and preemptory challenges, 140–47
premises liability, 108–9
presumption of innocence, 77
pre-trial experts, using, 133–36
pre-trial investigation of prospective jurors, 135
pre-trial requirements, 16–19
insurance considerations, 16–17
persuading with demonstrative evidence, 18–19
"remarried widow," protecting, 17–18
separate settlement, setting stage for, 17
prior jury service of juror, 65–67
product liability case, 101–3
professional liability case, 98–100
publicity factor, investigating, 121–25
punitive damages and, 130–31
reading and television habits of prospective juror, 79–83
seatbelt use, 96

selling your cause, 10–12
selling yourself, 1–4
sex cases, 117–19
sex consideration, of juror, 96–98, 109
slip and fall cases, 107–8
social pressure, resisting, 101
subjective injuries, seriousness of, 125–27
telling story within voir dire limitations, 12–13
time elements, explaining, 73–74
travel and former residency of juror, evaluating, 85–86
trial lawyer and, 156–58
violent crimes, 116–17
weaknesses in case, preparing jury for, 35–37
criminal cases, general, 110
frankness, 36–37
willingness and ability to follow instructions (juror's), 67– 69
women versus men, 96–98
wrongful death case, 104–7

K

Kaufman, Judge Bruce E., 224, 225
Kelsey v. *Kelsey*, 269
Kiernan v. *Van Schaik*, 58, 59–60
Kimbell v. *Noel*, 34
King, Clifford, 186–92
King v. *County of Nassau*, 47
King v. *Kayak Manufacturing Company*, 186–92
King Consrt. Co. v. *Flores*, 269
Klink v. *State*, 76
K. & S. Realty Co. v. *Rosen*, 164
Ku Klux Klan membership, 88
Kunk v. *Howell*, 52

L

Lacy, Judge Frederick, 232
Lanning v. *Brown*, 283
Larence v. *Scully*, 44
Laverty v. *Gray*, 53
Law and order appeal, 277–79
"Lawsuit crisis," 99, 128
Leading questions, 212–13
Lewis v. *State*, 53
Liability-damages ratio and sequence, 253–54
Liberty Mutual Ins. Co. v. *Mercantile Home Bank*, 164
Lindsey v. *Tennessee*, 92
Little v. *State*, 72
Littrell v. *Smith*, 61
Live testimony, trend away from, 214–15
Lockett v. *Ohio*, 115
Loeb-Leopold trial, 370
Loggans, Susan E., 245–46
Longview v. *Boucher*, 247
Lopez v. *Langer*, 261
Louisiana and Arkansas Ry. Co. v. *Capps*, 258

M

McClain, Bill, 47
McCloud v. *State*, 272
McCorquodale v. *Balkcom*, 116
McCoy v. *Lynaugh*, 118
McKenzie v. *State*, 92
Malice, 289
Malone, Tom, 362–66
Maloney, Pat, 335–45
Marcus, Benjamin, 387–88
Marital status, of juror, 51–52
Marshall, Justice Thurgood, 141
Marshall Durbin, Inc. v. *Tew*, 45
Martin, Mary, 280
Medical expenses argument, 301
Medical negligence, 10, 230
model final argument, 362–66
Medical testimony, 223–24
Merrit v. *Ash Grove Lime & Portland Cement Co.*, 53
Michener, James, 279
"Military mind," spotting, 84–85
Miller v. *DeWitt*, 269
Miller v. *Loy*, 34
Minnesota Code of Rules, Rule 31, 61
Mistrial traps, avoiding, 276–77
Mize v. *State*, 88
Mock juries, 134–35, 261
Models, as evidence, 220
Molestation, child, 118
Morality cases, 117–19
Morrow v. *Flores*, 52
Motor vehicle case, and evidence, 229
Mulkey v. *Morris*, 267

N

Narcotics cases, 119–20
National Association of Manufacturers, 88
National Rifle Association, 88
Nations, Howard, 271, 393–98
Naylor v. *Metropolitan*, 45
Newberry v. *Vogel*, 260

Nonverbal communication, 175
North, Oliver, 68
Nuchols v. *Commonwealth of Kentucky*, 65
Nurses, 50

O

O'Barr v. *U.S.*, 252
Objections, avoiding during opening statement, 166–67
Obscenity, 118–19
Occupational history, of prospective juror, 49–51
Ogborn, Murray, 229
Oliver v. *State*, 44
One-step-above rule, 3
Opening Statement (book), 186
Opening statement
  appealing to fairness, 181–82
  arguing the case, avoiding, 161–62
  begin final argument during, 176–78
  brevity, 171–72
  charts and exhibits, using, 162–63
  commenting on the law, 165–66
  defending the defenseless, 200–209
  directed verdict after, 163–65
  drama of, 173–74, 183–85
  establishing credibility, 174–76
  importance of, to verdict, 182–83
  jurors, talking to each during, 172–73
  large verdicts and, 186–92
  maintaining interest during, 178–79
  messages sent during, 185–86
  objections, avoiding, 166–67
  organizing, 167–69
  orienting case and role of jurors, 170–71
  "our evidence will show" technique, 163
  primacy, recognizing importance of, 169–70
  weak points of case, handling, 180–81
  whiplash verdict, 192–200
Oregon v. *Jones*, 201–9
Organization memberships (juror's), 88–89
Orienting the case, 170–71
"Our evidence will show" technique, 163
Overhead projections, to present evidence, 220

P

Parental loss, model final argument, 367–70
Parks v. *Brown*, 277
Pavalon, Gene, 367–70
Penzoil v. *Texaco*, 156
People v. *Bettistea*, 92
People v. *Conte*, 76
People v. *Dry Land Marina, Inc.*, 92
People v. *Emerson*, 273, *278*
People v. *Kurth*, 92
People v. *Lewis*, 252
People v. *London*, 275
People v. *Norman*, 264
People v. *Walker*, 278
People v. *Woodson*, 275
Perfectionist personality types, 139
Perillo v. *State*, 113
Perjury, 232–33, 234–35
Perlman, Peter, 186–92
Personal Injury Valuation Handbook, 50
Personal injury cases, 97–98
  arguing permanence of, 292–93
  pain, arguing, 282–83
  slip and fall cases, 107, 281–82
  subjective injuries, seriousness of, 125–27
Personality types, 138–40
Personal objects, as evidence, 220
Petteway v. *State*, 113
Photographs, as evidence, 220, 225–26
Pitts, Cornelius, 244–45
Plaintiff profile, 102
Plea bargained testimony, 113
Poets, quoting, 302–3, 313–18. *See also* Shakespeare, quoting
Porter v. *State*, 213
Powell, Justice, 141
Powell v. *U.S.*, 276
Preemptory challenges, 140–47
  decided cases regarding, 144–47
Preiser, Stanley, 238
Prejudging, 14
Prejudice, 42, 44, 45, 154–55
  See also Civil rights; Impartiality
  preemptory challenges and, 140–47
  preventing appeals to, 267–68
Premises liability, 108–9
Presumption of innocence, 77, 110, 121
Pre-trial experts, using, 133–36
Pre-trial publicity, 42
Pre-trial requirements, 16–19
  insurance considerations, 16–17
  persuading with demonstrative evidence, 18–19
  "remarried widow," protecting, 17–18
  separate settlement, setting stage for, 17
Primacy, and opening statement, 169–70
Prior jury service, 65–67
Privacy invasion, 103–4

Product liability, 88, 101–3
  model final argument, 366–67
Professionalism, 2
Professional liability case, 98–100
Proof, preparation of, 136
Proper Affectum, 41–41
Proper Defectum, 41–42, 92
Proper De Lictum, 42
Proper Honoris Respectum, 42
Property rights, 109
Prosecutors, special rules of, 262–63
Publicity factor
  challenges and, 42
  guidelines, 123–24
  investigating fully, 121–25
Punitive damages
  arguing, 290–92
  jury selection and, 130–31

Q

Question(s)/questioning
  basic, for jury selection, 78–79
  burden of proof, 69–73
  closed-ended, during jury selection, 13–14
  discovering attitudes with, 84, 85
  explaining voir dire, 19–22
    avoiding resentment, 20–21
  Federal Court and, 38–41
  follow-up, 136–37
  if any reason juror cannot serve, 92–94
  to individual, important techniques of, 32–33
  home ownership, 87–88
  insurance, how to ask, 58–61
  leading, 212–13
  listening to answers, 31
  open-ended, in individual inquiry, 31
  organization membership, exploring, 88–89
  requiring involvement in voir dire, 29
  revealing philosophy with, 29
  short and to the point, 23
  "612", 232
  where publicity is factor, 124–25
Quinlan, Karen, 377–81
Quoting, during final argument, 301–4
  Bible, 302–10
  poets and writers, 313–18
  religious writings, 309–10
  Shakespeare, 310–13

R

Race, and jury selection, 46, 47
Racial prejudice, 100
  see also Civil rights; Prejudice
  preemptory challenges and, 140–47
Ramey, Mary Beth, 230
Randall v. *State*, 247
Ratner v. *Arrington*, 34
Reading habits, of prospective juror, 79–81
Reasonable doubt, 71, 110
  model final argument, 384–87
Rebuttal, 270
Recollection, refreshing, 221
Redirect, 228
Redwine v. *Fitzhugh*, 75
Rehnquist, Justice, 141
Religious discrimination, 100. *See also* Civil rights; Prejudice
Reyes v. *Arthur Tickle, Eng, Works, Inc.*, 267
Right of trial by jury, 38
Right to die, 377–81
Ristaino v. *Ross*, 47
Rodgers v. *Crum*, 165
Romano, John, 238
Romano, Rodney, 1, 159–60, 192
  opening statement, *Scala* v. *Acosta*, 193–200
Rudd v. *Gulf Cas. Co.*, 247
Russell, Inc. v. *Trento*, 257
Russell, Sir Charles, 236
Russo v. *Birrenkott*, 128
Ryan v. *Monson*, 269

S

Saginaw v. *Staulis*, 252
Sams, Murray, 353–56
Sannito, Thomas, 138
Scala, Karen, 193–200
Scala v. *Acosta*, 193–200
Scarborough v. *Arizona Light & Power*, 165
Scarlett, Sir James, 237
Schiles v. *Schaefer*, 63
Schmidt v. *New York Union Mut. F. Ins. Co.*, 53
Seaboard Air Line R. Co. v. *Ford*, 283
Seatbelts, 96
Self-incrimination, 78, 110, 263–64, 268–70
Sequestering jurors
  during voir dire in capital cases, 114–15
  in camera questioning of, 123
Settlements, and pre-trial experts, 135
Sex cases, criminal, 117–19
Sex discrimination, 100. *See also* Civil rights, Prejudice
Shaffer v. *Ward*, 261
Shakespeare, quoting, 310–13
Shaw, Charles, 257

Shell Oil Co. v. *Waxler*, 247
Shrager, David S., 214
Silverthorne v. *U.S.*, 123–24
"Similar experience/similar litigation," 66
Sincerity, 1, 3, 33
"612" question, 232
Slides, presenting evidence with, 220
Slip and fall cases, 107, 281–82
Smith, William Kennedy, 287, 384–87
Smith v. *Ames*, 53
Smith v. *Fairman*, 272
Smith v. *Pettit*, 261
Smith v. *State*, 247
Social pressure, and juror, 101
Sorseleipo v. *Red Lake Falls Mill Co.*, 76
"Sound discretion of the trial court," 271–72
South Dakota v. *Neville*, 264
Southern Railway Company v. *Miler*, 61
SPEAK THE TRUTH, 114
Spector, Howard A., 165–66
Spence, Gerry, 3, 36, 154–55, 184
  depositions and, 218
  model final argument, 398
  Oregon v. *Jones* opening statement, 201–9
Standard of care, 230
Stark, Sheldon, 229
State v. *Allen*, 115
State v. *Blair*, 116
State v. *Davis*, 92
State v. *Fleming*, 162
State v. *Gray*, 117
State v. *Guiidice*, 44
State v. *Holt*, 68, 115
State v. *James*, 118
State v. *Jones*, 115
State v. *Koon*, 278
State v. *Lake*, 278
State v. *Locklear*, 252
State v. *Lottmann*, 118
State v. *McGraw*, 76
State v. *Parsons*, 92
State v. *Pinch*, 252
State v. *Pratt*, 45
State v. *Rodgers*, 45
State v. *Sacoman*, 113
State v. *Schwer*, 113
State v. *Sloan*, 278
State v. *Smith* (La. 1989), 277
State v. *Smith* (Me. 1983), 274
State v. *Taylor*, 45, 46
State v. *Thompson*, 115
State v. *Tull*, 262
State v. *Walton*, 66
State v. *Weatherbee*, 118
State v. *White*, 88
State v. *Williams*, 115
State v. *Wilson*, 118
State ex rel McDougal v. *Corcoran*, 273
Statutory disqualification, 44
Stauder v. *West Virginia*, 46
Stehura v. *Short*, 60
Stereotyping jurors, avoiding, 157, 158–59
Steuer, Max, 231, 239
Steward v. *State*, 44
Stewart v. *Alvarez*, 128
Stone, Irving, 370
Storytelling, 178–180
  dramatizing certain details, 180
  final argument and, 264–65
  first person, 179
  flashbacks, 178–79
  third person, 179–80
  by witness, 215–16
Strauder v. *West Virginia*, 141
Streeter v. *Sears, Roebuck & Co.*, 260
Strickland v. *Tegler and Northland Obstetrics & Gynecology*, 63
Subjective injuries, seriousness of, 125–27
Summary, during voir dire, 12–13
Supreme Court (U.S.), and preemptory challenges, 140–47
Swain v. *Alabama*, 40, 47, 140–44, 156
Sympathetic indulgers, as jurors, 140
Sympathy, 106, 127–28, 157, 298–300
Szuch v. *Grayce Farm Dairy, Inc.*, 268

T

Taylor v. *Blake*, 164
Technical occupations and backgrounds, of jurors, 48, 49–50
Teffeteller v. *State*, 278
Television habits, of prospective juror, 81–83
Ten Commandments of Cross-Examination, 237–38
Testimony
  accused not testifying, 78, 110, 263–64, 268–70
  trend away from live, 214–15
Texaco, 11
Thermography, 126
Thomas v. *State*, 113
Thorpe v. *Zwonechek*, 261
Tice v. *Mandel*, 269

Tidmore v. *Mills*, 61
Time elements, explaining, 73–74
Tindel v. *State*, 264
Tollackson v. *Eagle Grove*, 92
Toxic tort cases, 229–30
Transcripts, final argument use of, 258
Trial publicity, 42
Turner v. *Murray*, 47
Tyler v. *Kansas City Public Service Co.*, 162

U

Underwood v. *State*, 113
United States Constitution, Amendments to, 37–38
U.S. v. *Alonzo*, 277
U.S. v. *Anderson*, 39
U.S. v. *Bamburger*, 39
U.S. v. *Booher*, 39
U.S. v. *Brainard*, 275
U.S. v. *Brown*, 39
U.S. v. *Carroll*, 273
U.S. v. *DeGeratto*, 272
U.S. v. *Dellinger*, 41
U.S. v. *Dickens*, 248
U.S. v. *DiLoreto*, 278
U.S. v. *Eubanks*, 39
U.S. v. *Gaspard*, 273
U.S. v. *Giese*, 39
U.S. v. *Gordon*, 46
U.S. v. *Hearst*, 72, 73, 77, 121–23
  final argument, 381–84
U.S. v. *Klaw*, 119
U.S. v. *Lee*, 224
U.S. v. *Leftwich*, 39
U.S. v. *Lewis*, 266
U.S. v. *Lutt*, 248
U.S. v. *McCaghren*, 274
U.S. v. *Machor*, 277
U.S. v. *Mandelbaum*, 274
U.S. v. *Mazzone*, 275
U.S. v. *Murphy*, 252
U.S. v. *Nell*, 39
U.S. v. *Prantil*, 278
U.S. v. *Rewald*, 278
U.S. v. *Ross*, 92
U.S. v. *Smith* (778 F2d 925), 248
U.S. v. *Smith* (757 F2d 1161), 272
U.S. v. *Sorrentino*, 248
U.S. v. *Two Bulls*, 224–25
U.S. v. *Washington*, 39
U.S. v. *Wooten*, 39

V

Verdict, discussing potential size of during voir dire, 128–30
Video evidence, 219–20
Violent crimes, 116–17. *See also* Homicide
Voir dire. *See* Jury selection

W

Wainscott v. *Young*, 164
Weaknesses in case
  opening statement and, 180–81
  preparing jury for, 35–37
Weghman v. *Hadley*, 162
Wellman, Francis L., 233–37
Western Fire & Indem. Co. v. *Evans*, 269
Whiplash verdict, 159–60, 192–200
White, Justice, 140, 148
White collar crime, 120–21
Widow, protecting remarried, 17–18
Wigmore, Dean John Henry, 231
Williams v. *Ricklemann*, 270
Witherspoon v. *Illinois*, 114, 115, 116, 147–54
  annotations of, 152–54
Witnesses
  before and after, how to use, 226–27
  credibility of, 113, 287–89
  cross-examination of, 231–49
    "commandments," of Irving Younger, 237–39
    depositions, effective use of, 243–44
    difficult witnesses, 245–47
    divide/limit "areas of questioning," 231
    expert, how and when to attack, 248–49
    fairness in, 240–41
    hardball questions, 244–45
    jurors' perception of witness, 232
    legal limits in, 247–48
    memory, attacking, 241–42
    perception, attacking, 242
    perjury, 232–33
    prejudice, attacking, 242–43
    "612" question, 232
    strong ending to, 239–40
  establishing juror's relationship with, 61–62
  evaluation of, 136
  expert, 61–62, 248–49
  leading, 212–13
Woods v. *Burlington N. R. Co.*, 261
Woodward v. *State*, 92
Writers, quoting, 310–18

Wrongful death case, 104–7
  arguing finality of death, 283–84
  arguing pain, 282–83
  model final argument, 345–53

X

X-rays, as evidence, 220

Y

Yellow Cab Co. v. *McCullers*, 268
Young v. *Price*, 260
Younger, Irving, 80, 242–43
  "commandments of," 237–39